Introduction to ABAP™ Programming for SAP®, Third Edition

Gareth de Bruyn, Robert Lyfareff, Mark Balleza, and Dhruv Kashyap

Cengage Learning PTR

CENGAGE
Learning®

Professional • Technical • Reference

Australia • Brazil • Japan • Korea • Mexico • Singapore • Spain • United Kingdom • United States

CENGAGE
Learning·
Professional · Technical · Reference

Introduction to ABAP™ Programming for SAP®, Third Edition
Gareth de Bruyn, Robert Lyfareff, Mark Balleza, and Dhruv Kashyap

Publisher and General Manager, Cengage Learning PTR: Stacy L. Hiquet

Associate Director of Marketing: Sarah Panella

Manager of Editorial Services: Heather Talbot

Senior Acquisitions Editor: Mitzi Koontz

Senior Marketing Manager: Mark Hughes

Project/Copy Editor: Kezia Endsley

Interior Layout: MPS Limited

Cover Designer: Luke Fletcher

Proofreader: Gene Redding

Indexer: Sharon Shock

For product information and technology assistance, contact us at **Cengage Learning Customer & Sales Support, 1-800-354-9706**.

For permission to use material from this text or product, submit all requests online at **cengage.com/permissions**.

Further permissions questions can be emailed to **permissionrequest@cengage.com**.

ABAP and SAP are the trademarks or registered trademarks of SAP AG in Germany and in several other countries.

All other trademarks are the property of their respective owners.

Library of Congress Control Number: 2014939195

ISBN-13: 978-1-305-26647-6

ISBN-10: 1-305-26647-1

Cengage Learning PTR

20 Channel Center Street

Boston, MA 02210

USA

Cengage Learning is a leading provider of customized learning solutions with office locations around the globe, including Singapore, the United Kingdom, Australia, Mexico, Brazil, and Japan. Locate your local office at: **international.cengage.com/region**.

Cengage Learning products are represented in Canada by Nelson Education, Ltd.

For your lifelong learning solutions, visit **cengageptr.com**.

Visit our corporate website at **cengage.com**.

Printed in the United States of America
1 2 3 4 5 6 7 16 15 14

To my wife Sophia and my son Jackson; you are my inspiration each and every day. —Gareth de Bruyn

For Robert, Jack, and Richie, who are an endless source of inspiration, and for Cathy, who makes all things possible. —Robert Lyfareff

To my wonderful wife Lori; without you I wouldn't be where I am today. Thank you for being the core and strength of our family and ensuring that the boys and I are always taken care of. To my sons, Mark Jr. and Tyson; I am very proud of both of you and enjoy seeing you both grow and work hard every day. Always keep reaching for your goals in sports and especially in life! —Mark Balleza

I would like to dedicate this book to my father, who has always encouraged me to welcome new opportunities. I hope to continue to contribute immensely in this field and increase my passion for writing. —Dhruv Kashyap

Acknowledgments

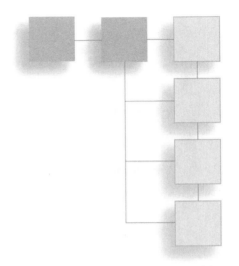

First and foremost, we would like to thank the publishing team at Cengage Learning PTR for their hard work and patience with us during this time. Specifically, thank you Stacy Hiquet for publishing our text. Thank you Mitzi Koontz for facilitating this book. Thank you Kezia Endsley for your calm management of the editing and deliverables. You are by far the best editor we have had the pleasure of working with. Thank you to the team at Cengage.

We want to thank our employers and families for their patience and support during this time. Coming home from a long day and then spending long hours finishing the book is not only hard on the authors, but the families as well.

We wish to thank SAP for their enterprise technology systems. We are very appreciative to be a part of the growing ecosystem at SAP.

About the Authors

Gareth de Bruyn is the Mobility Director at Accrete Solutions, LLC, and the CTO at two exciting new startups. Over the past five years, Gareth's passion has been building and integrating a simplified mobile experience with intricate backend enterprise systems and processes. He brings to the mobility space more than 19 years of SAP experience. He is a certified SAP R/3 Application Consultant and has written numerous books on the technical aspects of SAP. Gareth began his career as a software developer, but has held many different positions, including business analyst, architect, and IT director. His clients and employers are leaders in the oil and gas, healthcare, pharmaceutical, heavy equipment, defense, technology, and banking industries. Gareth received a Bachelor's of Science in Chemical Engineering from the University of California, Davis, and holds a Software Security Foundations Certificate from Stanford University.

Robert Lyfareff has been delivering enterprise class business solutions for more than 15 years. As a manager, architect, coder, and analyst, he has provided leadership and technical expertise in areas such as supply chain enablement, merger-related integration, and order-to-cash optimization. Currently he is a senior manager responsible for innovation and "The New Style of IT," where he works to identify and incubate great ideas that deliver rapid business growth.

Mark Balleza is an industry veteran, with more than 17 years of experience in enterprise architecture and development. He currently works as a senior technical manager, leading efforts in all technical aspects of an SAP deployment, which includes managing an offshore team of 60–100 developers and technical resources. He is the owner of his own consulting firm, MARBAL LLC., and has been working with SAP since graduating in 1997. His 17 years of experience in SAP includes ABAP programming, utilizing both past and present development platforms within the major SAP modules that include HR, BW, FICO, AM, and SD/MM/PP/QM/PM, just to name a few. His clients and employers include the oil and gas industry, insurance agencies, defense industry, as well as other government agencies. There are no limits to his career goals, and he is always looking to explore new fields in the enterprise and emerging technology space. Mark holds both a BS and an MA degree in Industrial Technology with an Information Systems concentration from Cal Poly, San Luis Obispo.

Dhruv Kashyap is a Senior SAP CRM consultant at Accrete Solutions LLC. During the past five years, Dhruv has implemented SAP solutions for a wide variety of industries, including high tech, heavy equipment, consumer retail, and safety equipment. In the last two years he developed mobility solutions and integrated those services into SAP. Dhruv received his Bachelor's degree in Electrical Engineering from the University of British Columbia. In his leisure time, he likes to travel and enjoys adventure activities.

CONTENTS

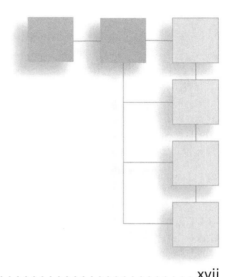

Chapter 9 — Working with External Files 183

Chapter 10 — Advanced Data Outputs 195

Chapter 11 — Adding Subroutines to Your Program 209

Introduction

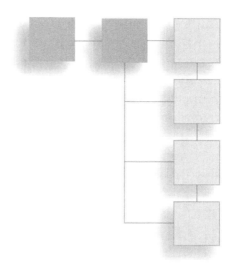

SAP is a German software company that produces the R/3 system. R/3 is an example of an ERP (Enterprise Resource Planning) system. ERP systems are used by corporations to track all information related to the business, such as financials, sales, and materials data.

ERP (Enterprise Resource Planning) Systems

R/3 is based on a client-server architecture and uses a relational database to track all information related to a corporation. The application layer is made up of thousands of small programs called *transactions*. A transaction is a program and set of screens that can be used to enter, change, or display data; monitor events within the R/3 system; and change functionality in the R/3 system. R/3 gathers related transactions into groups known as *modules*. A module is a set of transactions that deals with the same area of business functionality. There are modules for materials, financials, human resources, sales, and other common business functions.

Throughout this book, we refer to the R/3 system simply as *SAP* because that's how it's known in the industry. SAP runs on several operating systems, including UNIX, Windows, and AS/300, and can use several databases, including Oracle and SQL Server. Within the SAP application, the operating system and database layer are normally invisible to both users and programmers.

Introducing the SAP Software Program

In the past, other vendors have offered applications that manage a single area of business functionality—such as inventory control, general ledger accounting, or customer lists. Rather than package several such applications together into a single box, SAP has produced a suite of tightly integrated major business applications. One of the reasons for the immense success of SAP is this integration between its modules. Thus, when a vendor fulfills a purchase order by sending the requested materials, inventory levels are adjusted, invoices are verified, checks are issued, and so on. An event in one module, such as Materials, can initiate automatic responses in others, such as Sales or Plant Maintenance. All of this processing takes place within the normal SAP functionality—without any custom programming.

The Role of Configuration in Implementing SAP

What makes this integration work is the configuration of SAP to work with an individual corporation's business practices. In the context of SAP, the term *configuration* refers to the act of assigning values to thousands of possible settings within the modules. These settings give SAP users tremendous control over how SAP functions.

As you can imagine, corporations are much like individuals—they have very different personalities. SAP must be flexible enough to adapt to many different ways of doing business. For example, a purchase order may be configured to require that a person's name be entered as the requester of the purchase. In this setup, when a user creates a purchase order in the system, he or she must enter the name of the requester in order to save the information. On the other hand, if the purchase order form is set up without this requirement, the system allows a purchase order to be created without the name of the requester.

This configuration is done by analysts experienced in *Business Process Reengineering*, the art of identifying business processes and changing them to achieve greater efficiency. After SAP is installed, these configuration experts customize the modules to meet the corporation's needs or help the corporation change its business practices to achieve the most efficiency out of SAP. This configuration doesn't usually involve programmers but is instead done by business analysts. When the configuration process is nearing completion, the programmers are brought in to extend any part of SAP that can't be configured to meet the needs of the corporation.

Although business analysts are responsible for configuration, the impact of this customization process on programmers can't be overstated. A program can't be designed adequately until the configuration is stable. Unfortunately, because of time constraints, the configuration is seldom completely finished before the programmers must begin their design work. This is one of the unique challenges that face SAP programmers.

Programming ABAP

ABAP is the programming language used by SAP's developers to build the transactions that make up the R/3 application. It's also used by corporations to customize the R/3 application. In general, ABAP isn't used by customers of SAP to develop complex applications from scratch but is used instead to provide additional business functionality. For example, it's not necessary for a customer to write a program in ABAP to manage inventory levels because SAP has already written transactions to accomplish this objective.

The two most common uses for ABAP are producing custom reports and developing custom interfaces for SAP. In this context, a report is an ABAP program that reads specific data from SAP's database and then displays the data via a computer screen or a printed page. An *interface,* on the other hand, is an ABAP program that moves data into SAP or reads data from SAP and writes it out to a system file to be transferred to an external computer system, such as a legacy mainframe. Other uses for ABAP include conversion programs that change data into a format usable by SAP and custom transactions similar to the SAP transactions that make up the R/3 application, but are written by users to fulfill some business function not provided by SAP. This new version of the book covers programming in ABAP up to the ECC release of SAP R/4.

How ABAP and Data Interact in SAP

Almost all ABAP programs manipulate data from the SAP database to some extent. Data managed by SAP is often broken into two categories: *master data* and *transactional data* (called *documents* in SAP):

- Master data is information that usually corresponds to physical objects, such as materials, vendors, customers, or plants.

- A document is information that usually corresponds to an event such as a purchase order, an invoice, a change in inventory, or a sales order. Documents can be identified in the system by a document number, which can be externally assigned or assigned by SAP, depending on the configuration.

Master data is needed in order to create any document; for example, an invoice can't be created without a vendor to issue it. A change in inventory, referred to in SAP as a *material movement,* must refer to a material and a plant. Each SAP module has master data that it manages and documents that are created in the course of normal business operations. For example, the FI module, which manages finances and accounting, manages master data such as general ledger accounts and documents such as journal entries and check payments.

How to Use This Book

ABAP is a fourth-generation programming language with many of the features of other modern programming languages such as the familiar C, Visual Basic, and PowerBuilder. It allows variables and arrays to be defined, modulation of programs via subroutines and function calls, access to the database via SQL, and some event-oriented programming. Because this book covers all these major topics, you can use the information contained here to learn how to write ABAP programs that meet the most demanding business requirements.

SAP is an extremely complicated system; no one individual can understand all of it. This book focuses on ABAP programming but includes background information on the SAP environment, within which all ABAP programs run.

Each chapter discusses an area of ABAP programming such as displaying data, accessing the SAP database, and using conditional operators. The chapters build on each other, with examples taken from real-world business problems.

The first half of the book is a reference, detailing the specific ABAP commands to accomplish typical programming objectives. The second half of the book looks at specific business requirements such as writing reports, developing data interfaces, and performance tuning of SAP.

Part I—ABAP/4 Basics

The first seven chapters of this book introduce you to important basics of ABAP programming such as data types, conditional operators, and how to display or print data within SAP. These chapters assume that you have some familiarity with basic programming techniques, but you don't need to be an expert by any means. The chapters are broken into functional groups such as looping and using the Data Dictionary:

- **Chapter 1,** "Data Types and Definitions," is an introduction to ABAP syntax, variables, and data types.

- **Chapter 2,** "Displaying and Printing Data," shows you how to display text to the screen and printer. It includes detailed information on formatting text and variables for display.

- **Chapter 3,** "Manipulating Data," covers the commands for arithmetic calculations and manipulation of character strings.

- **Chapter 4,** "Using Conditional Operators," explains how to use commands to evaluate conditions and control the execution of a program.

- **Chapter 5,** "Using the Looping Commands," discusses the types of looping commands available in ABAP.

- **Chapter 6,** "Working with Internal Tables," introduces the ABAP concept of the *internal table*—a temporary database table used in programming.

- **Chapter 7,** "Working with the Data Dictionary," is an introduction to the SAP Data Dictionary. A *Data Dictionary* contains information about what's in a database (often called "metadata" because it's data about data). This chapter shows you how to get information about the SAP database.

Part II—Accessing the Database

The whole point of creating programs for SAP is to work with data. This part of the book provides detailed information on how to write programs that read, modify, delete, and use records from the database:

- **Chapter 8,** "Using SAP SQL to Access Database Tables," describes the ABAP implementation of SQL, which is a set of industry standard commands that you can use to read or change information in a database.

- **Chapter 9,** "Working with External Files," covers commands used to manipulate text files outside the SAP system. Text files are often used by SAP to exchange information with external information systems.

- **Chapter 10,** "Advanced Data Outputs," continues the discussion of displaying and printing the data that began in Chapter 2. The chapter gives details on how to do more advanced output work, including hiding information from specified users and using ABAP events to control output.

- **Chapter 11,** "Adding Subroutines to Your Program," explores how to use subroutines to break up a large program into small self-contained objects. This chapter presents a number of examples of using subroutines in SAP.

- **Chapter 12,** "Using Function Modules and BAPIs," describes how to manage *function calls*—subroutines that exist independently of any single ABAP program.

This chapter shows you how to make function calls in a program and how to write your own customized function calls.

■ **Chapter 13,** "Working with Logical Databases," explains how you can use logical databases to retrieve information from the SAP database.

Part III—Common ABAP Programs

There are a number of common problems that all SAP installations must solve. Part III of this book presents common business problems and ABAP programs that solve them. The examples are taken from several years' experience at several major installations:

■ **Chapter 14,** "Writing a Report," presents some common reports that produce information for users of SAP. Using ABAP to produce custom reports is the most common of all activities.

■ **Chapter 15,** "Web Dynpro," discusses the process of creating a Web Dynpro program from scratch.

■ **Chapter 16,** "Writing a Data Extract," discusses the process of developing programs to extract data from SAP and write it to an external file. Data extracts are a form of outbound interface—a program that sends information to a system external to SAP.

■ **Chapter 17,** "Writing a BDC Program," covers inbound interfaces. Inbound interfaces are usually implemented in the form of a BDC session in SAP. This chapter shows how to write a BDC session to load external data into SAP.

■ **Chapter 18,** "Working with SAP Security and Authorizations," covers how your programs are tied to SAP security. Adding security and authority checks are covered in this chapter.

Part IV—Advanced Technical Issues

The last six chapters cover advanced technical issues, including using the debugger, web services, BADIs and user exits, and object oriented ABAP:

■ **Chapter 19,** "ABAP Workbench (Debugger)," covers the ins and outs of using SAP's debugging tool. Techniques and technical guides are presented in this chapter.

■ **Chapter 20,** "Performance Analysis and Tuning," deals with the performance tools that come with SAP R/3. These tools give the programmer a powerful way to review the performance programs.

- **Chapter 21,** "Web Services," introduces the developer to web services with regard to SAP. It covers SOAP and REST web services, as well as how to create each of these in SAP.

- **Chapter 22,** "BADIs and User Exits," covers the various places that a developer can insert custom code in standard SAP objects without modifying SAP objects.

- **Chapter 23,** "Object Oriented ABAP," covers the new features of object oriented ABAP.

- **Chapter 24,** "One Order Model for CRM ABAP Programming," covers a different way to access data in SAP CRM. In SAP ERP, all the tables relate to one another. In CRM, the data model is different, so you must adjust your code acordingly.

Part V—ABAP Appendixes

- **Appendix A,** "Using the ABAP Editor," is a brief tutorial and review of how to use the Editor's interface to work with the programming commands. Read this appendix if you're not yet familiar with how to work with the Editor or if you need a refresher.

- **Appendix B,** "SAP System Fields," is a listing of important SAP system fields that contain information on the state of the system.

- **Appendix C,** "ABAP ERP and CRM Tables," is a listing of important ERP and CRM tables in ABAP.

AVAILABLE ON THE WEBSITE

All source code from the book's examples, as well as sample versions of the programs in the text and executable code for all types of SAP applications, is available at www.cengageptr.com/downloads. From there, you enter the book's title or ISBN to be directed to the downloads for this book.

CONVENTIONS USED IN THIS BOOK

This book uses a number of typographical conventions to make it easier for the reader to understand how to use the commands, syntax, menus, and so on:

- Commands, options, parameters, and so on are presented in a special monospaced computer typeface—for example, the `LOOP AT` command. Command syntax shows variables in *`italic monospace`*. Syntax lines and code lines are separated from the regular text with blank lines for readability. A typical syntax line, for example, might look like this:

```
EXTRACT field group.
```

In this example, you would substitute the appropriate field group name for *field group* when typing the command.

- Table names (`MSEG`), field names (`BKPF-GJAHR`), and other parts of the database are also printed in the computer typeface.

- Terms being defined or emphasized appear in *italics* within regular text.

- Text that the reader is instructed to type appears in `bold monospace`.

- Menu commands and options are indicated with an arrow to divide menu levels: Tools > Case > Development.

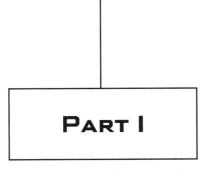

Part I

ABAP/4 Basics

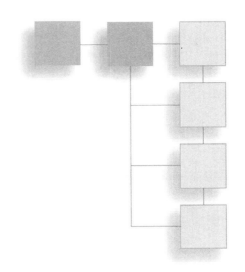

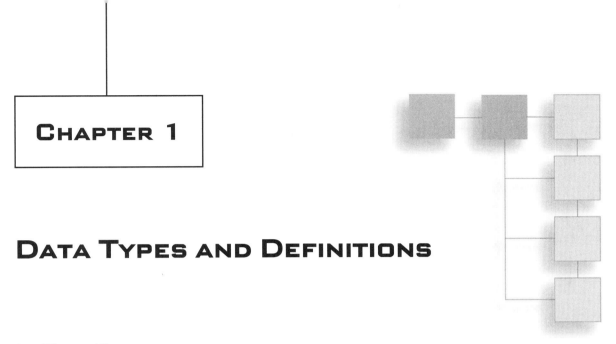

CHAPTER 1

DATA TYPES AND DEFINITIONS

IN THIS CHAPTER

- Building ABAP/4 Statements
- Using Variables
- Assigning Values to Variables

This chapter introduces some of the basics of ABAP/4 programming. ABAP/4 is an event-driven language that consists of *multiple statements*. The general rules for programming for ABAP/4 are much like those for other languages; this chapter describes some of the differences and also reviews some of the similarities. The chapter proceeds fairly rapidly through descriptions of features (statements, procedures, comments, and so on) that are common to programming languages, with the assumption that these parts of basic programming are already familiar to you, from C++, Visual Basic, and so on.

The second part of this chapter covers the data types supported by ABAP/4 and how to define variables for use in programs. The data types should be familiar to anyone with prior programming experience. ABAP/4 supports several types of variables that can be used by the programmer to accomplish many tasks.

This chapter doesn't cover how to write a complete program; instead, it draws contrasts between the requirements and syntax of ABAP/4 and the familiar strategies of languages that are commonly in use throughout the programming community. Specific areas where new ABAP/4 programmers trip up are discussed in detail; but in general, showing examples of correctly written code is more helpful in getting the point across than long descriptions.

BUILDING ABAP/4 STATEMENTS

In ABAP/4, statements consist of a command and any variables and options, ending with a period. Keep in mind the following points when considering how to write statements:

- The ABAP/4 editor converts all text to uppercase except text strings, which are surrounded by single quotation marks ('), and comments (described shortly). This doesn't mean that case is unimportant in ABAP/4. Data stored in the SAP database can be stored in mixed case, and both data and commands that interact with the operating system are affected by case.

- Unlike some older programming languages, ABAP/4 doesn't care where a statement begins on a line. You should take advantage of this fact to improve the readability of your programs by using indentation to indicate blocks of code.

- ABAP/4 has no restrictions on the layout of statements; multiple statements can be placed on a single line, or a single statement may stretch across multiple lines.

- Blank lines can be placed anywhere in a program and should be used to help separate blocks of related code from unrelated code.

The following example demonstrates the freedom ABAP/4 allows in the formatting of program statements:

```
WRITE 'Hello World'. WRITE 'You can use multiple statements on a line'.
WRITE 'Or a single command can
stretch across many
lines. It is all the same to SAP'
    WRITE 'Statements can begin anywhere on a line.'.
```

Commenting Your Code

Like most languages, ABAP/4 allows for the use of *comment statements* inside programs or inline. A comment is a statement that isn't processed by the system; it's used by a programmer to document the purpose of various statements in a program. The use of comments is critical in developing programs within SAP. Because of the extensive use of contractors, high turnover in ABAP/4 programmers, and rapidly changing business processes, comments can save time and money when code needs to be modified.

Programmers have a responsibility to leave behind well documented code. Most companies don't consider a programming job complete until it's fully documented both offline and online. The comments within a program can be used as a starting point for the offline documentation that many companies now demand.

Inline comments may be declared anywhere in a program by one of two methods:

- Full-line comments are indicated by placing an asterisk (*) in the first position of the line, in which case the entire line is considered by the system to be a comment. Comments don't need to be terminated by a period because they may not extend across more than one line:

```
*Echo the current user to the screen
WRITE W_USER
*Now prepare to compute balance
*This is a monthly balance only
```

- Partial-line comments are indicated by entering a double quote (") after a statement. All text following the double quote is considered by the system to be a comment. Partial-line comments also don't need to be terminated by a period because they may not extend across more than one line:

```
WRITE W_USER. "Echo the current user to the screen
```

Unlike ABAP/4 statements, commented code isn't capitalized by the ABAP/4 editor.

Improving Statement Readability with the Colon Notation

To reduce the amount of typing needed in a program, ABAP/4 allows a simple form of inline code expansion called *colon notation*. Inline code expansion is the ability of the system to fill in certain pieces of code for a programmer, saving repetitive typing. Consecutive statements can be chained together if the beginning of each statement is identical. This is done with the colon (:) operator and commas, which are used to terminate the individual statements, much as periods end normal statements. The final identical statement is terminated with a period, as a normal ABAP/4 statement would be.

Here's an example of a program that could save some keystroking:

```
WRITE 'Hello '.
WRITE 'World'.
WRITE W SYSTIME.
```

Using the colon notation, it could be rewritten this way:

```
WRITE: 'Hello',
    'World',
    W_SYSTIME.
```

Like any other ABAP/4 statement, the layout doesn't matter, here is an equally correct statement:

```
WRITE: 'Hello ', 'World ', W_SYSTIME.
```

Because the system simply duplicates all code found before the colon, even more complicated statements are possible.

For example, the following lines:

```
MOVE SY-SUBRC TO W_ONE.
MOVE SY-SUBRC TO W_TWO.
MOVE SY-SUBRC TO W_THREE.
```

Become this version:

```
MOVE SY-SUBRC TO: W_ONE,
                  W_TWO,
                  W_THREE.
```

And then this example:

```
PERFORM DEBIT_GL USING W_ACCOUNT1 W_AMOUNT1.
PERFORM DEBIT_GL USGIN W_ACCOUNT2 W_ AMOUNT2.
```

becomes this:

```
PERFORM DEBIT_GL USING: W_ACCOUNT1 W_AMOUNT1,
                        W_ACCOUNT2 W_AMOUNT2.
```

As you can see, there's no subtle logic behind the colon notation. The system duplicates the code found to the left of the colon. This feature can be a big help as you create longer programs. The colon notation reduces the amount of keystroking and increases the readability of the code.

Defining Programs (REPORT)

The first non-comment line in a program must be the REPORT statement. This command names the program and may affect the way in which output is formatted by the system. This is the syntax:

```
REPORT program name      [NO STANDARD PAGE HEADING]
    [LINE-SIZE number of columns]
    [LINE-COUNT number of line[(number of lines reserved for footer)]]
    [MESSAGE-ID message id].
```

The REPORT statement is automatically generated by SAP whenever a new program is created, although it has no options.

The following list describes these options:

- ■ [NO STANDARD PAGE HEADING] disables the default page header generated by SAP and allows the programmer to define a custom page header.

- ■ [LINE-SIZE *number of columns*] defines the number of columns appearing in the output of the program. The number may range up to 255. If the output of the program is to be printed, the number of the columns must not exceed the maximum for the paper size being used, which is normally 132 characters for North American printers. Because ABAP/4 supports very limited typesetting and no scalable fonts, all printing is done in monospaced fonts up to the column limit.

- ■ [LINE-COUNT *number of lines* [(*number of line reserved for footer*)]] defines the number of lines on each page of output. The second option reserves a specific number of lines for the page footer. SAP doesn't provide a default page footer; if you want a page footer, you must reserve the space with this option.
  If this output of the program is to be printed, the total number of lines must not exceed the maximum for the paper size being used, which is normally 65 lines for North American printers.

- ■ [MESSAGE-ID *message id*] determines which set of messages is used by the program when the MESSAGE command is used. This command is discussed in Chapter 2, "Displaying and Printing Data."

Some examples:

```
REPORT ZTEST1
    LINE-SIZE 132
    NO STANDARD PAGE HEADING
    LINE-COUNT 56(1).
```

```
REPORT ZGLOUT
   LINE-SIZE 80
   LINE-SIZE 65.
```

USING VARIABLES

One of the most basic operations of a programming language is providing temporary storage of data. Once upon a time, programmers had to track these storage locations manually. Modern programming languages allow for the assignment of *variables*, a symbolic reference to a memory location that stores information temporarily. These variables persist only during the execution of the program, and the data they contain is lost when the execution is complete, unless it's transferred to a database table or system file.

Variables must be declared in the program. This declaration process consists of telling the system what type of data (integer, character, and so on) will be stored in the temporary location associated with the variable.

Variable Data Types

All variables must be declared *before* they're used in the program. The following list describes some of the rules regarding use of variables in ABAP/4:

- Variables can be declared at any point in a program but, for the sake of consistency, should be defined at the beginning of a program or subroutine.

- Variables can be up to 30 characters in length and should be long enough to allow for easy reading of their functions.

- Begin each variable with a letter and then any mixture of letters and numbers. The hyphen or dash (-) is allowed but should never be used because it has a specialized function (described shortly). Instead, use the underscore character (_) to separate distinct words.

- No variable can have the same name as an ABAP/4 command.

- ABAP/4 follows traditional rules about the scope of variables. All variables defined at the program level are considered global and are visible to all subroutines. Variables defined within subroutines are visible only to that subroutine. Variable scope is discussed further in Chapter 11, "Adding Subroutines to Your Program."

Table 1.1 describes the data types used in ABAP/4.

Table 1.1 ABAP/4 Data Types

Type	Description	Example
C	Character	"Example Char"
D	Date	"20141101"
F	Floating-point number	5e7
I	Integer	600
N	Numeric text	00600
P	Packed decimal	100.50
T	Time	"223010"
X	Hexadecimal	23A

© 2014 Cengage Learning.

Defining Variables (DATA)

Variables are defined using the DATA statement, which has two possible forms:

```
DATA var[(length)]  [TYPE type]  [DECIMALS number]  [VALUE initial value]
DATA var LIKE table-field [VALUE initial value]
```

The following sections describe the two forms.

DATA Statements, Form One

Form one explicitly defines the type and length for the variable. This form is appropriate for variables that aren't dependent on values in the SAP database, such as counters or flags. If no length is specified, the variable uses the default for that data type. If no data type is specified, the variable defaults to character.

For example:

```
DATA  REP_PRICE(8)  TYPE P DECIMALS 2 VALUE '1.00'.
```

This statement creates a variable named rep_price, which is a packed decimal of length 8, with two of the spaces reserved for decimals, and a default value of 1.00.

Note

When working with decimals in ABAP/4, the number must be surrounded by single quotes (' and ') in much the same way a string is placed in quotes. Numbers without a decimal can be written without the single quotes. The decimal point doesn't figure into the length of the field.

The following statement creates a variable named `gl_flag`, which is a character string of length 1 and initially blank:

```
DATA GL_FLAG.
```

DATA Statement, Form Two

Form two allows the type and length of the field to be determined dynamically at runtime. This notation tells the system to look up the data type and length of the specified field and use that information to define the variable. Thus, if a data element such as a Company Code or Business Area changes, the program code won't need to be altered to reflect those changes. Any active field found in the SAP Data Dictionary can be used with `LIKE` in a `DATA` statement, as in this example:

```
DATA ERROR_FLAG LIKE SY-SUBRC.
```

This statement creates a variable that has the same data type and length as the field `SUBRC` found in the table `SY`. If a change is made in the Data Dictionary to `SY-SUBRC`, that change is used by the program with no recording.

The following example creates a variable that has the same data type and length as the field `werks` (used to store plant codes), found in the table `T001W`, with a default value of `PDR1` (on the following page):

```
DATA CO_CODE LIKE T001W-WERKS VALUE 'PDR1'.
```

Remember to surround character strings with single quotes.

When declaring multiple variables using the colon notation, the two forms can be mixed, as in this example:

```
DATA: REP_COUNT(8)   TYPE 1 VALUE 1,
    GL_FLAG,
    ERROR_FLAG LIKE SY-SUBRC,
    CO_CODE LIKE T001W-WERKS VALUE 'PDR1'.
```

Grouping Variables into Records

In addition to single-value variables, ABAP/4 allows the grouping of several variables into a single *record*. Records are used when you have a group of related data that needs to be kept together.

For example, a mechanical part could be described by a name, a part number, cost, and weight. It's possible to declare four separate variables to hold that information, but a variable called name could mean different things. Suppose you are writing a program to track parts used by engineers in the field. You would have a name for the engineer, a name for the part, and perhaps a name for the customer site. How do you keep all these name variables straight? What you could do is declare a record called part that consists of four fields: name, number, cost, and weight. Additional records could be declared for the engineer and customer.

Record Syntax

Records are referenced as *record name-field*. They are defined by using a group of DATA statements with the following syntax:

```
DATA BEGIN OF record name.
DATA field 1.
DATA field 2.
.
.
DATA field N.
DATA END OF record name.
```

The individual fields within the record may be defined using either of the DATA statement forms and any of the options, as in the following example:

```
DATA BEGIN OF MATERIAL_DUMP.
DATA MATNR LIKE MARAV-MATNR.
DATA MATL_PRICE (12) TYPE P DECIMALS 2.
DATA MATL_QTY(6) TYPE P DECIMALS 1.
DATA CHANGE_FLG VALUE 'N'.
DATA END OF MATERIAL_DUMP.
```

To access the matl_price field with this example, you would have to use the notation material_dump-matl_price. When defining records, the colon notation greatly improves the readability of the statement. This statement is functionally equivalent to the previous one, but much easier to read:

```
DATA: BEGIN OF MATERIAL_DUMP
    MATNR LIKE MARAV-MATNR,
    MATL_PRICE (12) TYPE P DECIMALS 2,
    MATL_QTY (6) TYPE P DECIMALS 1,
    CHANGE_FLG VALUE 'N',
END OF MATERIAL_DUMP.
```

Defining Records (INCLUDE STRUCTURE)

Much as you can use the LIKE command to dynamically assign a data type to a variable, you can use the INCLUDE STRUCTURE command to dynamically declare a record. For example, if you want to re-create the material_dump record from the preceding section, but instead of the custom record created in the last example, use the SAP materials table (MARAV) as the record layout, here's how you'd do it:

```
DATA BEGIN OF MATERIAL_DUMP.
    INCLUDE STRUCTURE MARAV.
DATA END OF MATERIAL_DUMP.
```

With this statement, if any changes are made to the SAP materials table, those changes are automatically made to the material_dump record—with no changes needed to the programming code. The structure included must be either an active table or a structure from the SAP Data Dictionary. It's also possible to combine the INCLUDE statement with explicit fields in one record.

```
DATA BEGIN OF MATERIAL_DUMP.
    INCLUDE STRUCTURE MARAV.
 DATA: CHANGE_FLG VALUE 'N',
    END OF MATERIAL_DUMPT.
```

In this case, the record contains all fields found in the MARAV table plus the change_flg field.

Defining New Data Types (TYPES)

In addition to the eight data types built into ABAP/4, it's possible to define new data types within a program. These new data types are often referred to as *user-defined types*. Typically, new data types are used to define variables that map to business concepts. For example, a financial program might make reference to a bank account number, so several variables might be needed to track different bank account numbers. They could be defined directly as:

```
DATA: CUST_ACCT(28)   TYPE C,
      MER_ACCT (28)   TYPE C,
      TMP_ACCT (28)   TYPE c.
```

In this case, three variables are created to hold account numbers. Instead of defining each variable in terms of the standard ABAP/4 character data type, you could declare your own new type called BANK_ACCT.

```
TYPES BANK_ACCT(28)   TYPE C.
DATA: CUST_ACCT   TYPE BANK_ACCT,
      MER_ACCT    TYPE BANK_ACCT,
      TMP_ACCT TYPE   BANK_ACCT.
```

This approach has a number of benefits. One, it allows you to define the exact data type only once in the TYPES statement and then use it multiple times in your program. If the length of a bank account changes from 28 to 35 at a later time, you can simply change the TYPES statements instead of having to change every variable throughout the program. Two, this approach is much easier to read and understand. Finally, it is immediately clear that all three of the variables in the example hold the same type of information.

New types are defined using the TYPES statement, which has three possible forms:

```
TYPES name [(length)] [type type] [DECIMALS number]
TYPES name LIKE table-field
TYPES BEGIN OF rectyp.
0
TYPES END OF rectyp.
```

TYPES Statement, Form One

The syntax of the TYPES statement is identical to the DATA statement. You must remember that TYPES does not actually create a variable; you must still define the variable with a DATA statement. The first form of the TYPES statement defines the data type explicitly. For example:

```
TYPES: PRICE_TYPE (8) TYPE P DECIMALS 2,
       NAME_TYPE (24),
       PART_TYPE (28),
       COUNT_TYPE TYPE1.
```

TYPES Statement, Form Two

Form two allows the type and length to be determined dynamically at runtime. This notation tells the system to look up the data type and length of the specified field and use that information to define the type. Any active field found in the SAP Data Dictionary can be used with LIKE in a TYPES statement, as in this example:

```
TYPES: FLAG_TYPE LIKE SY-SUBRC.
```

This form is not very common since the LIKE option and the TYPES command have similar functionality. Typically, only LIKE is used, for example, when defining a record as in the next section.

TYPES Statement, Form Three

The third form of the TYPES statement allows for the user-defined record types. Like variable records, a user-defined record type consists of grouping several types into a single-record type. The syntax is as follows:

```
TYPES BEING OF record name
TYPES field 1.
TYPES field 2.
.
.
TYPES field N.
TYPES END OF record name.
```

Using the colon notation can improve the readability of these statements, as seen in these examples:

```
TYPES: BEGIN OF PART_LIST,
       MATERIAL (18) TYPE C,
       DESC (36) TYPE C,
       PRICE TYPE P DECIMALS 2,
END OF PART_LIST.
DATA: NEW_PART TYPE PART_LIST,
      OLD_PART TYPE PART_LIST.
```

Defining Constant Data Elements (CONSTANTS)

In addition to variable data elements, it is valuable to have data elements that do not change their value. These elements are referred to as *constants*. A constant is declared like a variable, but it must be assigned an initial value, and this initial value never changes. If you try to change the value of a constant, a syntax error occurs. Using a constant can make your code clearer and easier to maintain. Often values must be coded directly into a program, such as the total number of manufacturing plants a company has. If you simply code the number 7 directly in the code, it may be difficult to update the code later when the number changes to 8.

Constants are defined using the CONSTANTS statement; the syntax is identical to that of the DATA statement, with the exception that the VALUE addition is always required and the OCCURS option is never allowed:

```
CONSTANTS var[(length)] [TYPE type] [DECIMALS number] VALUE initial value [IS INITIAL]
CONSTANTS var LIKE table-field VALUE initial value [IS INITIAL]
CONSTANTS: BEGIN OF rec,
    ...
    END OF rec.
```

Some examples:

```
CONSTANTS C_PANTS TYPES I VALUE 7.
CONSTANTS CHARX VALUE 'X'.
CONSTANTS C_CLIENT LIKE VBAK-MANDT VALUE '100'.
CONSTANTS: BEGIN OF C_PART,
    MATNR LIKE MARA-MATNR VALUE IS INITIAL,
    DESC(24) VALUE 'Default Part',
    CHGUM TYPE I VALUE 1,
END OF C_PART.
```

Using Runtime Parameters

Another type of variable is the *runtime parameter*. Parameters enable users to pass data to an ABAP/4 program at the time it's executed. For example, a report may be written to use a parameter to narrow the range of the report to a particular month or a range of products.

There are two types of parameters in ABAP/4: the first allows the user to enter a single value, and the second allows the user to enter multiple values. The following sections provide details on the two parameter types.

Using PARAMETERS to Define Variables

The first type of parameter is defined with the PARAMETERS statement, which has the following syntax:

```
PARAMETERS parm[(length)] [TYPE type] [LIKE field] [DEFAULT val]
    [LOWER CASE] [AS CHECKBOX] [RADIOBUTTON Group num ] [OBLIGATORY].
```

Much like using the DATA command, the data type of a parameter can be defined by using the LIKE option or the TYPE option (which explicitly defines the data type). Unlike variables, parameters must have a name made up of fewer than eight characters or numbers. Another difference is that parameters can't use the DECIMALS option. Also, parameters can't be part of a record.

The PARAMETER command has several options that you can use:

- DEFAULT *val* assigns a default value to a parameter, much like the VALUE option of the DATA command. This default value is seen by the user at runtime and can be overwritten by the user.
- LOWER CASE allows entry of lowercase data. By default, SAP converts all data entered to uppercase unless this option is specified.
- AS CHECKBOX is only used with a parameter one character in length. Instead of appearing as a text box, it creates a push button that the user can click to be on or off.

If the user sets the push button to on, the variable will contain an X. This can be used when the user is presented with a yes/no option.

■ RADIOBUTTON GROUP *num* is only used with a parameter one character in length. Like the CHECKBOX option, it creates a push button that the user can click on or off. The difference is that several push buttons can be grouped together, and the user may only select one of them. The others are deselected automatically when the user checks one.

■ OBLIGATORY forces the user to enter some value before the program will execute.

Following are some examples of how to use PARAMETERS.

This statement creates a parameter p_minqty of type integer, with a default value of 1; a value must be filled in before the program will execute:

```
PARAMETERS P_MINQTY TYPE I DEFAULT 1 OBLIGATORY.
```

In the following statement, a parameter of length 30, type character, is defined with a default value of matl_dump.txt. This parameter allows lowercase characters and must be filled in before the program will execute:

```
PARAMETERS P_FILENM(30) DEFAULT 'matl_dump.txt' OBLIGATORY LOWER CASE.
```

This example creates a list of three check boxes. The user can choose one or more of these check boxes:

```
PARAMETERS: P_SHOW1 AS CHECKBOX DEFAULT 'X',
            P_SHOW2 AS CHECKBOX,
            P_SALL AS CHECKBOX.
```

This example creates a list of three option buttons, from which the user can choose only one:

```
PARAMETERS: R_ALL RADIOBUTTON GROUP 001,
            R_NONE RADIOBUTTON GROUP 001 DEFAULT 'X',
            R_EVEN RADIOBUTTON GROUP 001.
```

Using SELECT-OPTIONS to Define Variables

The second type of parameter is defined with the SELECT-OPTIONS command. Unlike a parameter, a select-option allows the user to enter a set of multiple values and/or ranges of values. When the user enters one or more ranges of values, they are stored in an internal table that the system uses to evaluate comparisons against the select-option. The internal table has the same name as the select-option. See Chapter 6, "Working with Internal Tables," for an explanation of internal tables. Also, a select-option must be declared for a database field or a previously defined variable, but usually a database field is used.

The programmer doesn't have to anticipate when the user will enter multiple values or ranges. The processing is handled entirely by the system and requires no additional programming. This set of values can then be used in comparisons, such as IF, SELECT, and CHECK with the operator IN. For examples of the use of SELECT-OPTIONS, see Chapter 8, "Using SAP SQL to Access Database Tables," and Chapter 13, "Working with Logical Databases."

The syntax is as follows:

```
SELECT-OPTIONS var FOR field  [DEFAULT val]  [DEFAULT val option]
   [DEFAULT [NOT]  val TO val]  [MEMORY ID id]  [MATCHCODE OBJECT object]
   [LOWER CASE]  [NO INTERVALS]  [NO EXTENSION]  [OBLIGATORY].
```

Most of the options are identical to those of the PARAMETERS command. Some of the differences are the additional default options and the lack of a check box option:

- DEFAULT *val* sets the select-option equal to a single value.

- DEFAULT *val option* sets a default value and an optional operator such as equal, greater than, or not equal to. Table 1.2 describes the available operators.

- NO INTERVALS forces users to enter an exact value by not allowing them to enter ranges of values.

- NO EXTENSION forces users to enter a single value or range by not allowing them to enter multiple ranges and values.

- DEFAULT [NOT] *val* TO *val* sets a default range of values to be included by the select-option. Using the NOT option allows a range of values to be excluded.

Table 1.2 Option Operators

Operator	Description
EQ	Equal
NE	Not equal
CP	Contains part of a string
NP	Doesn't contain part of a string
GE	Greater than or equal to
LT	Less than
LE	Less than or equal to
GT	Greater than

© 2014 Cengage Learning.

The following statement creates a variable called `s_date` for the field `BLDAT` (Document Date) from the table `BKPF` (Financial Documents) with a default range from January 1, 2013, to December 31, 2014:

Note

Dates appear in quotes. See Chapter 3, "Manipulating Data," for more information on assigning values to date fields.

```
SELECT-OPTIONS S_DATE FOR BKPF-BLDAT DEFAULT '20130101' TO '20141231'.
```

This statement creates a variable called `s_doc#` for the field `BELNR` (Document Number) from the table `BKPF` (Financial Documents), with a default value greater than or equal to 0050000000:

```
SELECT-OPTIONS S_DOC# FOR BKPF-BELNR DEFAULT '0050000000' OPTION GE.
```

Using RANGES to Define Variables

The `RANGES` command creates a variable that behaves identical to one declared with the `SELECT-OPTIONS` command. Unlike a select-option, variables defined with the `RANGES` command do not appear to the user as runtime parameters. They must be filled using the default option or directly by the programmer. The syntax of the `RANGES` command is similar to `SELECT-OPTIONS`:

```
RANGES var FOR field [DEFAULT val] [DEFAULT val option]
[DEFAULT [NOT] val TO val].
```

Some examples:

```
RNAGES: R_PLANT FOR VBAP-WERKS,
R_DATE FOR BKPF-BLDAT DEFAULT '20130101' TO '20141231'.
```

Like variables declared with `SELECT-OPTIONS`, variables declared with `RANGES` are stored in an internal table. The structure of the table for both types of variables is the following:

```
DATA: BEGIN OF var OCCURS 10,
SIGN(1),
OPTION (2),
LOW LIKE f,
HIGH LIKE f,
END OF var
```

The OCCURS option is explained in Chapter 6, but for now it is only important to understand what values are placed in each field. The LOW field holds the low value of the range. The HIGH field holds the highest value in the range. The OPTION field holds the operator for this range (see Table 1.2 for valid operators). Finally, the SIGN field holds the value I or E. When this sign is I, it indicates the range is inclusive, meaning that comparisons with any value that falls inside of the range are true. When the sign is E, it indicates the range is exclusive, meaning that comparisons with any value that falls inside of the range are false.

For example, if you entered an inclusive range of 12/1/2013 to 1/1/2014 into the R_DATE range just declared, the values stored are shown in Table 1.3.

Table 1.3   Field Values

Field	Value
Sign	I
Option	BT
Low	12/1/2013
High	1/1/2014

© 2014 Cengage Learning.

In another example, if the range was all dates not greater than or equal to 1/1/2014, the field values would be as shown in Table 1.4.

Table 1.4   Field Values

Field	Value
Sign	E
Option	GE
Low	1/1/2014
High	

© 2014 Cengage Learning.

As you can see from this example, when you are using operators such as "not greater than" or "not equal," there is no high value to the range, only low. Ranges and select-options are used extensively in ABAP/4, and more examples of their usage are presented in later chapters. For now it's only important to know how they are declared.

Using Field Symbols

The final type of variable is a called a *field symbol.* A field symbol is different from all the previous types of variables discussed because it doesn't actually hold values. Instead, it maintains a reference to another variable that has been defined by a DATA or PARAMETERS statement. This is similar to the concept of a *pointer* in a language such as C. Instead of holding a value such as 5, a field symbol references a variable such as counter, which has previously been defined as an integer variable with the value 5. Thus, if the command COUNTER=COUNTER+1 is issued, the field symbol would automatically refer to the value 6 without any additional programming. This is because the field symbol doesn't hold a particular value but instead refers to another variable.

Field symbols have a particularly annoying syntax; the name of the field symbol must always be enclosed by angle brackets. So the field symbol POINTER1 would appear in the program as <POINTER1>. When referring to a generic field symbol, this book uses <fs> as a placeholder.

Here's the syntax:

```
FIELD-SYMBOLS <fs>.
```

Notice that there's no data type specified. Because field symbols don't hold any value—they simply point to the contents of other variables—the field doesn't care what type of variable it points to. In fact, that is what makes field symbols so powerful. A single field symbol may refer to numbers, dates, and character strings—all in the same program.

The ASSIGN command is used to assign a variable to a field symbol. This command is explained in detail in Chapter 3. For now, simply examine this example of how different variables can be assigned to a single field symbol.

```
DATA: STRONG(4) VALUE 'test',
      NYM TYPE P VALUE 100,
      TODAY TYPE D VALUE '20140124'.
FIELD-SYMBOLS <TEMP>.
ASSIGN STRONG TO <TEMP>.
WRITE <TEMP>.
ASSIGN NUM TO <TEMP>.
WRITE <TEMP>.
ASSIGN TODAY TO <TEMP>.
WRITE <TEMP>.
```

Here's the output:

```
TEST 100 20140124
```

ASSIGNING VALUES TO VARIABLES

An initial value may be assign to a variable by using the VALUE option of the DATA command. But variables are useless if they can't be changed within the execution of a program. ABAP/4 provides several ways to make changes to the value of a variable, as described in the following sections.

Using MOVE to Assign Variables

The most basic way to change the value of a variable is to use the MOVE command. The MOVE command has two forms, which are functionally equivalent.

```
MOVE value TO var.
```

```
var=value
```

The first version should be familiar to COBOL programmers, while the second is commonly found in languages such as C or Pascal. Either version is acceptable, but for the sake of consistency, you should choose one version and stick with it throughout a program.

When using the second form, multiple assignments are allowed, occurring right to left. For example, this code assigns the value 10 to QTY3, QTY2, and QTY1:

```
DATA: QTY1 TYPE I,
      QTY2 TYPE I,
      QTY3 TYPE I.
QTY1=QTY2=QTY3=10.
```

Following is an example of using the colon notation in conjunction with the MOVE command to do multiple assignments:

```
DATA: QTY1 TYPE I,
      QTY2 TYPE I,
      QTY3 TYPE I.
MOVE: 10 TO QTY1,
      QTY1 TO QTY2,
      50 TO QTY3.
```

In the next example, two records are declared and values are assigned to the doc# and doc_date fields of the finance_rec record. Then temp_rec is assigned the values of finance_rec:

```
DATA: BEGIN OF FINANCE_REC,
      DOC# LIKE BKPF-BELNR,
      DOC_DATE LIKE BKPF-BLDAT,
      END OF FINANCE_REC.
```

```
DATA: BEGIN OF TEMP_REC,
      INCLUDE STRUCTURE FINANCE_REC.
DATA END OF TEMP_REC
FINANCE_REC-DOC#='0004000000'.
FINANCE_REC-DOC_DATE='20130101'.
TEMP_REC=FINANCE_REC.
```

This type of assignment is possible because temp_rec and finance_rec have the same structure. If two records with dissimilar structures are assigned, the results are uncertain.

Data Type Conversion During Assignments

ABAP/4 allows an assignment to be made using variables of two different data types. When this occurs, ABAP/4 automatically converts the data from the source type to the target type. This type of conversion is usually referred to as an *implicit conversion* by the system. Normally the programmer doesn't need to worry about this type of conversion, as long as the values being converted make sense logically.

For example, assigning a character field containing the value -256 to a packed field is no problem. But if the character field holds the value DOG, an error results when ABAP/4 makes the conversion attempt.

Chapter 3 includes more information about implicit conversion.

SUMMARY

Here ends the discussion on the declaration and assignment variables. Of course, variables in and of themselves are of little use without commands to display and manipulate them. Those commands are the focus of the next two chapters.

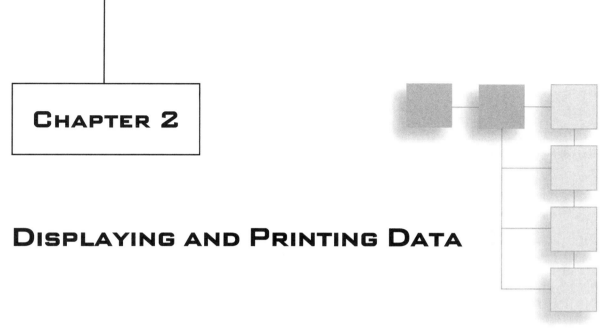

CHAPTER 2

DISPLAYING AND PRINTING DATA

IN THIS CHAPTER

- Setting Up the Page (REPORT)
- Learning the General Features of the WRITE Statement
- Formatting the Output
- Using Text Elements
- Learning the Advanced Features of the WRITE Statement
- Displaying Messages
- Using the FORMAT Command

One of the most basic tasks of the ABAP programmer is writing code to generate reports for end users. To code reports, you need the commands to retrieve the data, organize it, and then output the data and general text to the screen and printout. The beginning of this chapter covers how to output and format data and text to the screen. The rest of the chapter deals with data and page formatting. The commands discussed include WRITE, SKIP, ULINE, POSITION, MESSAGE, and FORMAT.

Figure 2.1 shows the difference between what a program would output as text (column headings) and data (the numbers under the column headings). This chapter discusses both text and data; the figure illustrates the difference between the two.

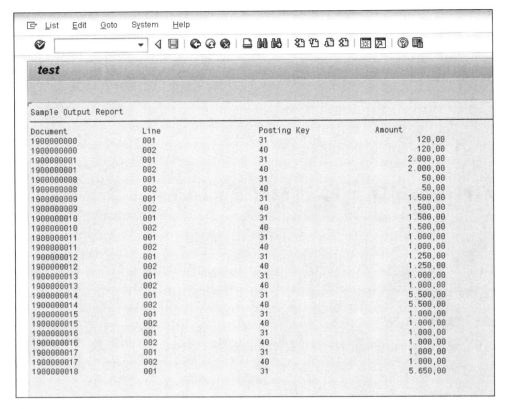

Figure 2.1
A report with differences shown between text and output data.

Note

One point to realize early on is that whatever is sent to the screen can very easily be sent to the printer to produce a hardcopy. Because we are working more and more in a paperless society, this chapter presents options other than printing the data, but sometimes hardcopies are essential. Alternatives to printing include instant download capability to the user's PC (covered in Chapter 12, "Using Function Modules and BAPIs"), PDF creation, and spool display (covered in Chapter 10, "Advanced Data Outputs").

SETTING UP THE PAGE (REPORT)

The first item you must consider is the page definition of your output. You must define in the REPORT statement on the first line of code how many lines you want per page and how many columns per page. *Columns* are the number of characters that can be printed on a single row of type across the page, from one side to the other; *lines* are the number of rows that can appear on a page from top to bottom.

For SAP, certain formats are defined for each type of printer (for instance, for the Hewlett-Packard LaserJet III). The system comes with default formats, but custom formats can be defined as well. Each format includes column and line spacing. The lines and columns of the report should match one of the print formats of the printer that is to be used for the output.

Note

The values of the lines and columns are fixed and can't be set by a data field to make the values variable.

The REPORT command was covered briefly in Chapter 1, "Data Types and Definitions," as you use it to start a program, but let's review the syntax:

```
REPORT program name     [NO STANDARD PAGE HEADING]
[LINE-SIZE number of columns]
[LINE-COUNT number of lines[(number of lines reserved for footer)]].
   MESSAGE-ID message id.
```

If the number of lines and number of columns values aren't specified, the default values are specified by the default print format defined by the user profile. Under the System menu, a user default can be defined to specify the default printer. If you don't use the LINE-COUNT and LINE-SIZE options, the syntax for REPORT is pretty simple:

```
REPORT program name.
```

With this version of the command, the system would use the user default printer. You can display the user defaults (system settings defined for each user) by navigating along the menu path illustrated in Figure 2.2 (System > User Profile > Own Data) and then specifying a printer at the resulting user default screen.

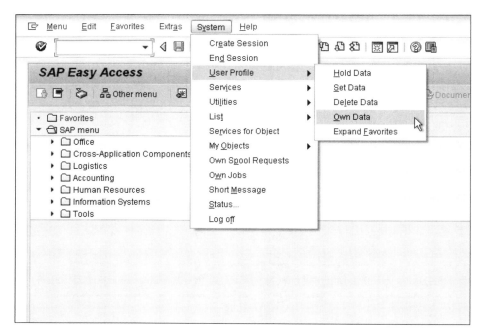

Figure 2.2
The menu path to the user default screen.

The MESSAGE-ID command is related to the MESSAGE command (explained later in this chapter in the section, "Formatting the Output"). The SAP system keeps a library of messages defined by a two-character definition. For each definition, the ABAP program can call 1,000 possible messages, numbered from 000 to 999. Often, programs in the same module (for example, SD, FI, MM, or PP) or with the same purpose (such as Report, Extract, or Interface) use similar messages. The MESSAGE-ID command defines which message ID library is used. Many different ABAP programs can then reference the same library of messages, rather than defining a unique library for each program. The message libraries keep the system messaging lean and efficient. (See the later section on the MESSAGE command, called "Displaying Messages (MESSAGE)," for a more detailed discussion.)

GENERAL FEATURES OF THE WRITE STATEMENT

The first and most basic command of ABAP is the WRITE statement. The general syntax is as follows:

```
WRITE data.
```

data can be pure text, a field name, or a previously defined variable.

Note

The important point to realize early on when working in ABAP/4 is that every line of code must end with a period. When you generate (SAP's terminology for compile) the program, if the periods are missing, the compiler won't be able to determine where one line ends and another begins. Make sure that every line of code ends with a period. If a period is forgotten, the code generally won't compile. When you first begin programming in ABAP/4, don't be discouraged if you forget periods. Having to find a missing period is a much better scenario than finding a large flaw in programming logic!

Outputting Plain Text

To output text to the screen or to a printer, enclose the text in single quotes (' '). The syntax to write text within the WRITE command is as follows:

```
WRITE 'text'.
```

Here's an example of a command with text:

```
WRITE 'This is TEXT output'.
```

The output from this line would be as follows:

```
This is TEXT output
```

Text can also be output using text elements. Text elements are discussed later, in the section called "Advanced Features of the WRITE Statement."

Outputting Field Names (Variables)

The syntax to output a field name or a variable is generally the same as for outputting plain text to the screen, except that the quotes are replaced by a variable name:

```
WRITE field name.
```

The field name can either be a field defined in the data declaration portion of the program or a field that's part of an internal or database table, also defined in the data declaration portion of the program. Here's an example:

```
*DATA DECLARATION PORTION OF PROGRAM
DATA:   W_FIELD(12)  TYPE C
"OUTPUT PORTION OF PROGRAM
MOVE   'ABAPER'   TO W_FIELD.
WRITE W FIELD.
```

In this example, the output field will be called W_FIELD, is a character field, and has a length of 12. In the data manipulation portion of the program, the word ABAPER is placed inside this field. The output from these lines of code would be as follows:

```
ABAPER
```

Outputting Groups of Text and Data Fields

To output multiple pieces of data, just separate them with commas and add a colon at the end of the WRITE statement:

```
WRITE:    'I am a soon to be', W_FIELD.
```

The output would be as follows:

```
I am a soon to be ABAPER.
```

Note

Notice that the value ABAPER falls directly one space after the text. W_FIELD is defined as a type c field, which by default makes it left aligned. Other data types might differ. Positioning the items horizontally on a line is covered in the following section.

FORMATTING THE OUTPUT

The general format for the WRITE statement is as follows:

```
WRITE /column position(length) data
```

The *column position* setting defines at what position the *data* is output. The slash (/) denotes a new line. The number inside the parentheses (*length*) defines the maximum number of characters output from that data. Look at this example:

```
WRITE:    /15(10)    'ABCDEFGHIJKLMNOP'
```

The output to the screen would be

```
ABCDEFGHIJ
```

The data is displayed after 15 spaces, and only 10 characters of the data are displayed.

Column Positioning

To place the data in the desired position in the output, you specify the number of the column on which the first letter of the data field or text must start:

```
WRITE 20 W_FIELD.
```

The output in this case would be the word ABAPER, printed 20 characters to the right of the left edge of the page or screen.

Dynamic Positioning and Output

Column positioning as well as output length can be determined dynamically. However, the syntax of the WRITE command changes to WRITE AT rather than just WRITE. The syntax is demonstrated as follows:

```
DATA: IMPOSITION TYPE I VALUE 10,
W LENGTH TYPE I VALUE 5.
DATA:
W_DATA(30)  VALUE   'ABCDEFGHIJ KLMNOPQRSTUVWXYZABCD'.
WRITE AT /W_POSITION(W_LENGTH)W_DATA.
```

The output is:

```
ABCDE
```

The output starts at the eleventh position and only displays five characters, as specified by the variables declared. The dynamic positioning can also be used with the ULINE command defined later in this chapter. As with the WRITE command, the new syntax is ULINE AT.

Breaking to a New Line (Inserting Carriage Returns)

When you want to break to a new line of data, add a slash (/), followed by the data that you want to include on the next line:

```
WRITE:/  'First Line',
/        'Second Line'.
```

Here's the output:

```
First Line
Second Line
```

If you leave out the second slash, like this:

```
WRITE:/ 'First Line',
'Second Line'.
```

the two texts will appear adjacent to each other:

```
First Line Second Line
```

Controlling the Output Length

It's possible to control output length of a field by using this general syntax:

```
WRITE (output length) field name.
```

The output length of the field displayed on the screen or page is determined by the number in the parentheses (output length). The field name can also be text enclosed in quotes. Here's a typical example:

```
DATA:  W_FIELD(10)  TYPE C.
MOVE:   '0123456789'  TO W_FIELD.
WRITE:/(5) W_FIELD.
```

The output from this code would be

```
01234
```

Because the output length is defined as 5 in this example, only five characters are displayed on the screen or page.

When you write a program, a functional analyst talks with the user and finds out from them what they want displayed on the report. The analyst then writes program specifications and passes on those specifications to the programmer (you). At times the amount of data that the user wants in a report exceeds the maximum column length of the report. Some functional analysts know from experience to check if what the user wants can actually be provided in a proper fashion.

Tip

Always begin your first WRITE statement with a slash following it, just in case a previous WRITE statement was overlooked. An example of when this might happen is when a different part of the program might be a subroutine or just a previous section code. If the forward slash is neglected, the data appears on the screen on the same line as the previous output.

Here's an example:

```
WRITE:/'FIRST SECTION OF CODE'.
Code between WRITE statements
WRITE 'SECOND SECTION OF CODE'
```

The desired output in this case would be achieved if the slash is placed on the second WRITE statement:

```
WRITE:/ 'FIRST SECTION OF CODE'
WRITE:/ 'SECOND SECTION OF CODE'.
```

The output would be

```
FIRST SECTION OF CODESECOND SECTION OF CODE
```

By providing that slash, a carriage return is guaranteed, and the output makes sense.

Controlling the output length on some unimportant fields may free some space for more information to be displayed on the report. An example of this situation might involve a report where the company name is displayed. If the company name is ABC CORPORATION OF THE GREATER MISSISSIPPI AREA, rather than display the entire name, ABC CORPORATION would generally suffice.

As a general rule, check some sample data to see what will be output and try to determine the minimum number of spaces that can be displayed in order to minimize output without confusing end users.

Default Data Alignment

The rule of thumb for the default alignment of data types is that character fields are left justified and numeric fields are right justified. Table 2.1 shows the default alignment for typical field types in SAP.

Table 2.1 Field Type Default Alignment

Type	Output	Justification
C	Character	Left
D	Date	Left
F	Floating-point number	Right
I	Integer	Right
N	Numeric text	Left
P	Packed decimal	Right
T	Time	Left
X	Hexadecimal	Left

© 2014 Cengage Learning.

USING TEXT ELEMENTS

Text elements are fields (maintained by the user) that hold text that's used throughout the program. For a report, for example, all the column headings might be defined as text elements.

Figures 2.3 and 2.4 illustrate where text elements would be used in data output. Figure 2.3 shows the output of the text elements as column headings in a report; Figure 2.4 shows where the text elements are defined.

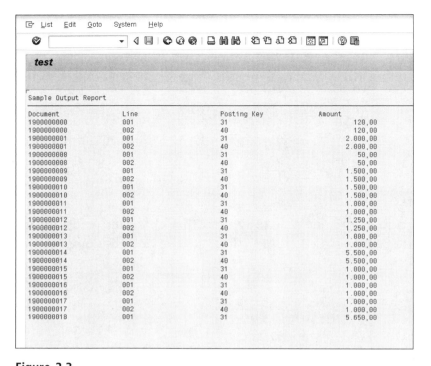

Figure 2.3
A report with column headings as text elements.

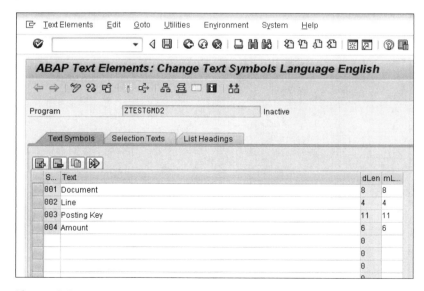

Figure 2.4
The Text Elements screen with column headings defined.

Text elements are defined with the menu path Goto > Text Elements in the ABAP/4 editor screen. You first choose Goto > Text Elements, as shown in Figure 2.5, and then select Text Symbols. You can also go to the text elements from the se38 editor screen (see Figure 2.6).

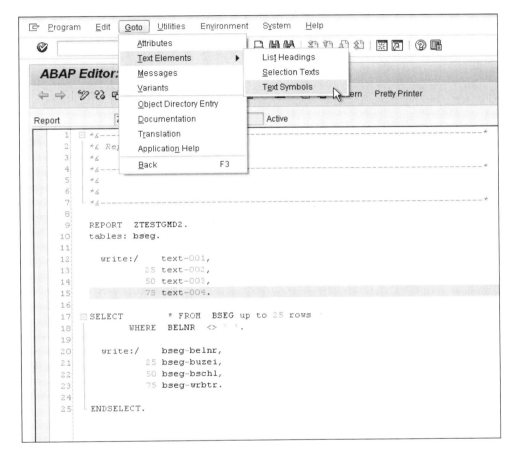

Figure 2.5
The menu path to the Text Elements maintenance screen.

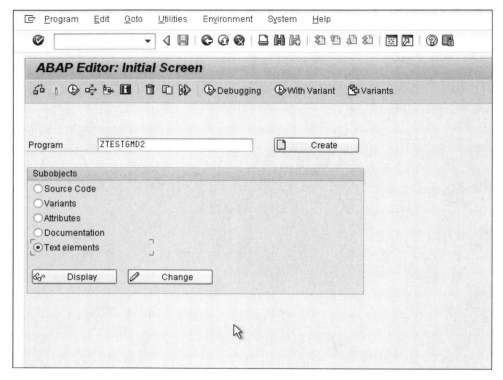

Figure 2.6
The Text Elements maintenance screen from the editor home screen.

A screen with several columns appears (see Figure 2.7). The column that holds only three characters is for the number associated with the text. The longer field holds the text associated with that number.

To enter or define a text element, follow the menu path Goto > Text Elements > Text Symbols; type a number into the column on the left and its associated text in the column adjacent to it. After entering the text, click the Save button on the menu bar to save your new entry.

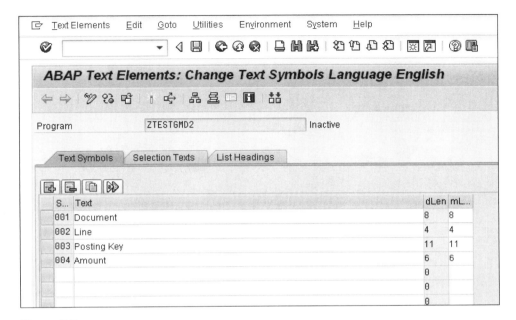

Figure 2.7
The Text Symbols maintenance screen.

Source: SAP AG or an SAP affiliate company. All rights reserved.

After the text is entered, a number associated with it, and the data saved, you can then return to the ABAP/4 editor. Click the green Back arrow button twice to return to the ABAP/4 editor screen.

To output this text, you use a WRITE command with this general syntax:

```
WRITE TEXT-text element number.
```

The text element number is the number you assigned to the text element (refer to the left-hand column of Figure 2.7). Here's an example of such a command:

```
WRITE    TEXT-001.
```

Text elements can be defined for numbers 1 to 999. They can also be defined as alphanumeric, meaning that the range also exists from A to ZZZ. (But the examples in this book, along with most code, use just numeric.) There are text elements defined for input parameters (selection texts) and for titles and headers (header texts). Selection texts are texts associated with PARAMETER or SELECT-OPTION fields defined in the data declaration portion of the program. To associate a text with a parameter or SELECT-OPTION, follow the same menu path as before (Goto > Text Elements). This time, click the Selection Texts button (see Figure 2.8). A list of parameters and SELECT-OPTIONS appears onscreen with a column adjacent to the fields for text entry.

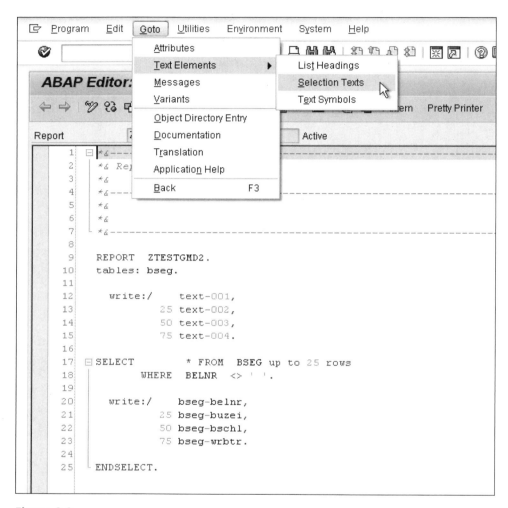

Figure 2.8
The Text Elements maintenance screen with the Selection Texts option selected.

If a parameter or SELECT-OPTIONS is defined in the data declarations portion of the program, it is listed in the left column of this screen. Type the text that you want to be associated with that field in the column adjacent to the field; the text you type appears onscreen on program startup.

For example, suppose that you had in mind the following code:

```
PARAMETERS: P_YEAR LIKE BSEG-GJAHR
```

This code defines a parameter to enter the fiscal year onscreen upon startup. If you follow the menu path Goto > Text Elements > Selection Texts and associate the text FISCAL YEAR with it, as shown in Figure 2.9, the initial startup screen of the program looks something like Figure 2.10.

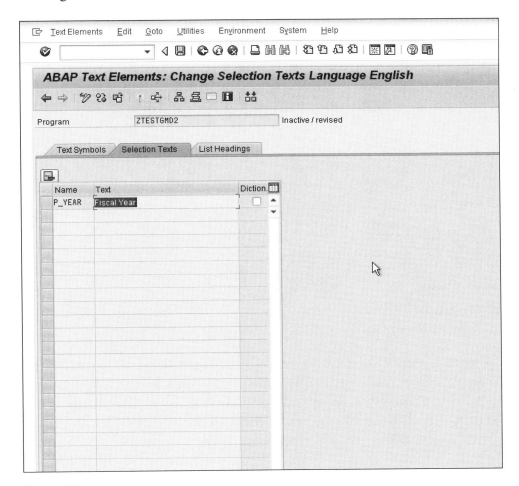

Figure 2.9
The Selection Texts maintenance screen.

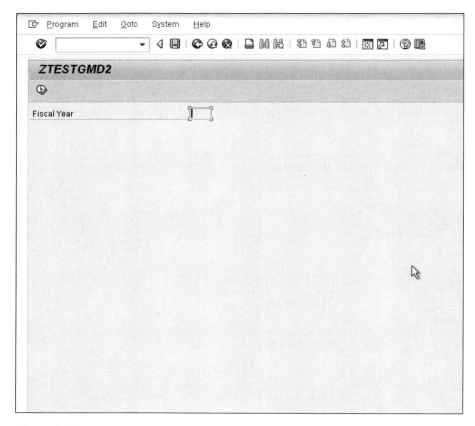

Figure 2.10
Sample output using selection texts.

To access the Titles and Headers Text Elements screen, follow the same menu path to the Text Elements screen (Goto > Text Elements), select the Titles and Headers option button, and then click the Display button or the Edit button to access the screen (refer back to Figure 2.8). The Title Header screen looks like Figure 2.11.

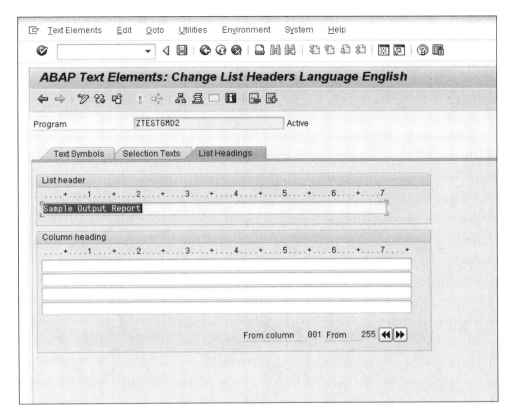

Figure 2.11
The Title Header maintenance screen.

ADVANCED FEATURES OF THE WRITE STATEMENT

The general syntax of the WRITE statement with the advanced options listed is as follows:

```
WRITE field   [USING EDIT MASK mask]   [USING NO EDIT MASK]
              [NO-ZERO]   [NO-SIGN]   [DD/MM/YY]
[MM/DD/YY]   [DD/MM/YYYY]
[MM/DD/YYYY]
 [CURRENCY currency]
\[UNDER field]
[NO-GAP]
[DECIMALS number of places behind decimal point].
  [LEFT-JUSTIFIED, CENTERED, RIGHT-JUSTIFIED]
```

Each variation of the command is explained in the following sections.

Masking the Output (USING EDIT MASK and USING NO EDIT MASK)

The USING EDIT MASK command places your data in a specified format of your choice. For example, in the following command:

```
DATA:    W_TIME(8) TYPE C.
MOVE '123456' TO W_TIME.
WRITE W_TIME USING EDIT MASK   :   :
```

The output would be as follows:

```
12:34:56
```

Each underscore represents one character in the data field. Anything other than an underscore (in this case, the colons) is output as regular text.

Sometimes you have data using a format defined by the Data Dictionary, but you would prefer to use a different format for the output of that data. To output the data using no format, you use the command USING NO EDIT MASK:

```
WRITE    SY-UZEIT USING NO EDIT MASK.
```

SY-UZEIT is the system field for the current time. At 5:34 a.m., the output would appear in the following format:

```
053400
```

USING NO EDIT MASK is generally used for date and time fields.

Suppressing Blanks (NO-ZERO)

The NO-ZERO command follows the DATA statement. It suppresses all leading zeros of a number field containing blanks. The output is usually easier for the users to read. Here's an example of a number field containing leading zeros that's pretty difficult to read:

```
DATA: W_NUMBER(10)   TYPE N.
     MOVE 23 TO W_NUMBER. WRITE W_NUMBER.
```

The output from this code would be:

```
0000000023
```

With the NO-ZERO command, the leading zeros are suppressed:

```
WRITE W_NUMBER NO-ZERO.
```

Here's the output:

```
23
```

Suppressing Number (+/-) Signs (NO-SIGN)

The NO-SIGN command suppresses signs with the integer (I) and packed field (P) data types. The NO-SIGN command is similar to the NO-ZERO command. It suppresses all signs in the output:

```
DATA:  W_INTEGER(10)  TYPE I.
MOVE 5 to W_INTEGER.
W_INTEGER = WJNTEGER *      -1.
WRITE W_INTEGER NO-SIGN.
```

Although the output should be -5, the NO-SIGN suppresses the negative sign. The output would be:

```
5
```

You would use this option when you want data in an absolute value format. Also, when sending data to other systems, the format for the data on the other system might have the negative sign formatted differently from SAP, so you would want to suppress the SAP negative sign.

Choosing a Date Format

Depending on user requirements, dates are output in a variety of ways. Date formats are an important item to focus on if you're working for an international company. In the United States, the date format is mm/dd/yyyy; in the European community, the format is dd/mm/yyyy. The formatting commands for dates are as follows:

- DD/MM/YY: Displays days, months, and then the last two digits of the current year.

- MM/DD/YY: The same format as DD/MM/YY except that the month and day positions are reversed.

- DD/MM/YYYY: The same format as DD/MM/YY except that all the digits of the year are displayed.

- MM/DD/YYYY: The same format as MM/DD/YY except that all the digits of the year are displayed.

The formats discussed previously are used in the following context:

```
WRITE SY-DATUM date format.
```

Suppose today is December 25, 1950. For the following command:

```
WRITE SY-DATUM DD/MM/YY.
```

the output would be:

25/12/50

With this version:

WRITE SY-DATUM MM/DD/YY.

you would get this:

12/25/50

Here's another version:

WRITE SY-DATUM DD/MM/YYYY.

Here's what you'd see:

25/12/1950

And, finally:

WRITE SY-DATUM MM/DD/YYYY.

would produce this:

12/25/1950.

Note

Tables are discussed in detail in Chapters 7, "Working with the Data Dictionary" and 8 "Using SAP SQL to Access Database Tables," but basically, to view the contents of a table, you use the general table display transaction code se16, or follow the menu path from the first screen after login (Tool > Application Development > Overview > Data Browser). Enter the table name **TCURX**, press Enter, mark off the field(s) you want to display, and click the Execute button. The different currency types are displayed in a report format on the screen.

Displaying Currency (CURRENCY)

Due to SAP's international presence, the need to display currency in the appropriate formats brings the CURRENCY command into play. The format for using this command is as follows:

WRITE data CURRENCY currency

data is a numeric data field that holds the currency value, and currency is the currency format defined in the SAP table TCURX. The currency formats are generally defined for all countries; however, some smaller or newer countries might need to be added. Examples of different currencies include pounds, dollars, deutschmarks, and rands.

Aligning Fields Vertically (UNDER)

The UNDER command enables you to position your text/field under a previous field. This convenient feature allows for easy maintenance of reports. Instead of changing all the position numbers of all the data, you only have to change the header data. All the subsequent data automatically falls directly under the specified header.

For example, in the following code lines, Field1 is displayed at column position 20. Field2 is displayed on the following line, also at column position 20, right under Field1 (see Figure 2.12). If for some reason a user decides that the report format must be changed (which happens frequently), you only have to change the position number of Field1, and Field2 automatically relocates itself to that new position:

```
WRITE:/20          field1.
WRITE:/field2 UNDER field1.
```

Figure 2.12 illustrates how the UNDER command works. The first text is written to a line and contains the word OVER. The second text is written under the first text and contains the word UNDER.

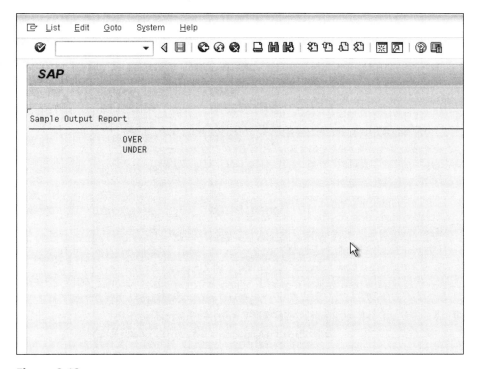

Figure 2.12
Output using the UNDER command.

The code for this example would be as follows:

```
DATA:  W_DATA1(20)  TYPE C,
W_DATA2(20)  TYPE C.
MOVE   'OVER'   TO W_DATA1.
MOVE   'UNDER'  TO W_DATA2.
 WRITE:/20 WDATA1.
 WRITE:          W DATA2 UNDER W_DATA1.
```

Closing Gaps Between Fields (NO-GAP)

To display several fields one right after another, with no gaps between, you have two choices:

- ■ Move all the fields into one long field and use the CONDENSE field NO-GAPS command (discussed in Chapter 3, "Manipulating Data").

- ■ Write out the individual fields and attach the NO-GAP command to the end of the code line.

Here's an example of the NO-GAP command:

```
DATA:   W_FIELD1(3) TYPE C,
W_FIELD2(3) TYPE C,
     W_FIELD3(3) TYPE C.
  MOVE: 'ABC' TO W_FIELD1,
  'DEF' TO W_FIELD2,

     'GHI' TO W_FIELD3
     WRITE: W_FIELD1   NO-GAP, W_FIELD2 NO-GAP,  W_FIELD3.
```

The data output is a concatenation of all three fields:

```
ABCDEFGHI
```

When might you want to concatenate fields? Suppose that the user has entered a file name and path separately. Because the entire path must include the file name, you would want to concatenate the two together. This is an example of how you might use the NO-GAP command.

Specifying Decimal Places (DECIMALS)

For packed fields, integers, and floating-point numeric fields, it's sometimes necessary to specify the number of places displayed after the decimal point. The DECIMALS command specifies the number of places:

```
DATA:   W_NUMBER(10) TYPE P DECIMALS 9.
W_NUMBER = '1.234567890'.
WRITE    W_NUMBER DECIMALS 2.
```

For this example, the output has two decimal places:

```
1.23
```

When prices are figured, many times the decimals are more than two places, but price is only two decimals long. The output must then be only two decimal places in length; the DECIMALS command allows for this situation.

Specifying Justification (LEFT-JUSTIFIED, CENTERED, RIGHT-JUSTIFIED)

For any field, the justification can now be set using the commands just listed. The syntax is as follows:

```
DATA: W_NAME(20)  TYPE C.
W_NAME =   'BARNES'.
WRITE:/ W_NAME RIGHT-JUSTIFIED.
```

The output is as follows:

```
BARNES
```

The alignment refers to the output field. When used with the WRITE TO command, the alignment refers to the target field.

Transferring Data with a Specified Format (WRITE... TO)

You will appreciate the advanced WRITE features when you need to convert data to a certain format for an interface from SAP to another computer system. You might think that to move data from one field to another, you would use the MOVE command. This assumption is correct when working solely inside the SAP environment. However, when data needs to be transferred from one field to another field and then sent to another system in the form of a file, it needs to have a certain format. The MOVE command doesn't modify the format of the data. The WRITE...TO command has the functionality you need to move the data in a specified format.

Here's the syntax:

```
WRITE field1 TO field2[+offset(length) [advanced options]].
```

This code transfers the contents of field1 to field2 in the format defined by the advanced options previously discussed in this chapter. The data in the first field can be placed anywhere in the second field, utilizing the offset and length features, which are numeric fields. offset represents the starting column in field2 where the data from field1 will be placed, and length defines how many characters of field1 will be placed in field2. It's also plausible to use offset and length with field1 to specify which characters are placed in field2.

Here's an example using the WRITE command in this fashion:

```
DATA:    W_DATE(8) TYPE C VALUE '122550',
W_DATE2(8) TYPE C.
WRITE W_DATE TO W_DATE2 DATE MM/DD/YYYY.
WRITE W_DATE2.
```

The output of W_DATE2 would be

```
12/25/1950
```

Essentially, the WRITE command, used in this fashion, is similar to the WRITE command with advanced features in combination with the MOVE command.

Inserting Horizontal Lines (ULINE)

The ULINE command automatically inserts a horizontal line across the output. It's also possible to control the position and length of the line. The syntax is pretty simple:

```
ULINE.
```

Here's an example:

```
WRITE    'THIS IS UNDERLINED'.
ULINE.
```

This command outputs a solid horizontal line across the page, as shown in Figure 2.13.

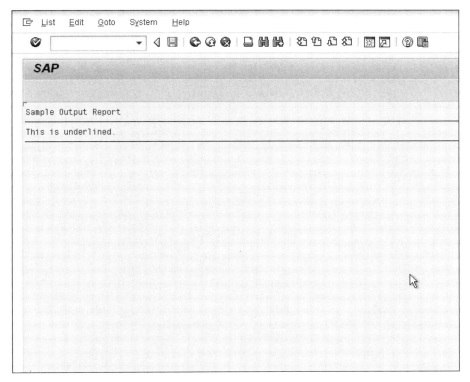

Figure 2.13
Underlined output.

If you want to be a bit more specific about how the underline should look, use this syntax:

```
ULINE /position(length)
```

Add the slash (/) if a new line (carriage return) is desired. position specifies the column number in which the line will start, and length indicates how many spaces the line should extend.

Look at this example:

```
WRITE:/   'THIS IS UNDERLINED'.
ULINE:/   (18).
```

The output is shown in Figure 2.14.

Just as with the WRITE command, position and length are fixed values and can't be defined by variables.

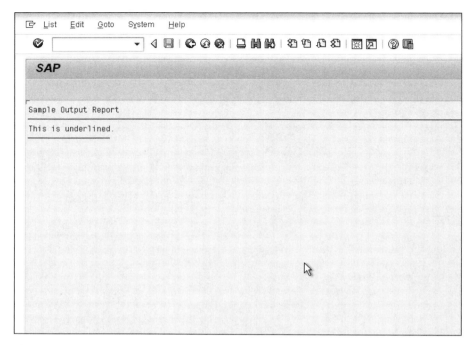

Figure 2.14
Underlined data with a specified length on the underline.

Inserting Blank Lines (SKIP)

The SKIP command inserts blank lines on the page or moves the cursor to a certain line on the page. This command skips one line:

```
SKIP.
```

Here's an example:

```
WRITE  'This is a line of a report'.
SKIP.
WRITE 'This is another line of a report'.
```

And here's how it looks:

```
This is a line of a report
This is another line of a report
```

It's possible to use the SKIP command to insert multiple blank lines onto the page:

```
SKIP number of lines.
```

The output from this context of the command would be several blank lines defined by number of lines. The SKIP command can also position the cursor on a desired line on the page:

```
SKIP TO LINE line number.
```

This command is used to dynamically move the cursor up and down the page. Usually, a WRITE statement occurs after this command to put output on that desired line. Keep in mind that the number of the line to which you want to skip can't exceed the number of lines defined by the page (the number defined by the LINE-COUNT statement in the REPORT statement at the beginning of your program). For example, if you define the page as having 60 vertical lines and your command says SKIP TO LINE 80, the command won't work, and the data won't appear on that page.

Controlling Horizontal Positioning (POSITION)

The POSITION command is like the SKIP TO LINE command except that it controls where the cursor is positioned horizontally:

```
POSITION N.
```

Tip

It's a good idea to maintain as few message IDs as possible. Try to group programs together and have all of them use the same message ID. For example, a group of different reports from the Finance module that focus on the general ledger might all share common error messages. If a group of programs all use only one message ID (or message library), space in the system is conserved, and the messages are easily maintained.

The N is defined as any number from zero to the number of columns defined in the LINE-SIZE command, along with the REPORT statement on the top of the page. Just as with the SKIP TO LINE command, the POSITION command can't specify a number greater than the number of columns defined horizontally across the page.

DISPLAYING MESSAGES (MESSAGE)

The MESSAGE command displays messages defined by a message ID specified in the REPORT statement at the beginning of the program. The syntax of the message ID is discussed earlier in this chapter. Essentially, the message ID is a two-character code that defines which set of 1,000 messages the program will access when the MESSAGE command is used. This ID can be already defined in SAP or a custom user ID that your company defines.

The messages are numbered from 000 to 999 and are maintained via the menu path Goto > Messages. Associated with each number is message text, up to a maximum of 80 characters in length. When message number is called, the corresponding text is displayed.

Here's the syntax of the MESSAGE command:

```
MESSAGE message type message number [WITH text].
```

message type is a single character that defines the type of message displayed and the events associated with that message, as described in Table 2.2.

Table 2.2 Characters for Use with the Message Command

Message	Type	Consequences
E	Error	The message appears, and the application halts at its current point. If the program is running in background mode, the job is canceled, and the message is recorded in the job log.
W	Warning	The message appears, and the user must press Enter for the application to continue. In background mode, the message is recorded in the job log.
I	Information	A pop-up window opens with the message text, and the user must press Enter to continue. In background mode, the message is recorded in the job log.
A	Abend	This message class cancels the transaction that the user is currently using. (Developing online transactions is an advanced ABAP/4 topic, utilizing Screen Painter and Menu Painter. You don't develop any transactions in this text.)
S	Success	This provides an informational message at the bottom of the screen. The information displayed is positive in nature and is just meant for user feedback. The message does not impede the program in any way.
X	Abort	This message aborts the program and generates an ABAP/4 short dump.

© 2014 Cengage Learning.

Usually error messages are used to stop users from doing things they aren't supposed to do (for example, running a large system-draining report online rather than in background mode, where the system handles it more efficiently). Warning messages are generally used to remind the user of the consequences of his/her actions. Information messages give the user useful information (for example, the purchase order they created was saved).

For example, if you created the message shown in Figure 2.15 for message ID AB, the MESSAGE command:

```
MESSAGE E011.
```

would give you this message:

EAB011 This report does not support sub-number summarization.

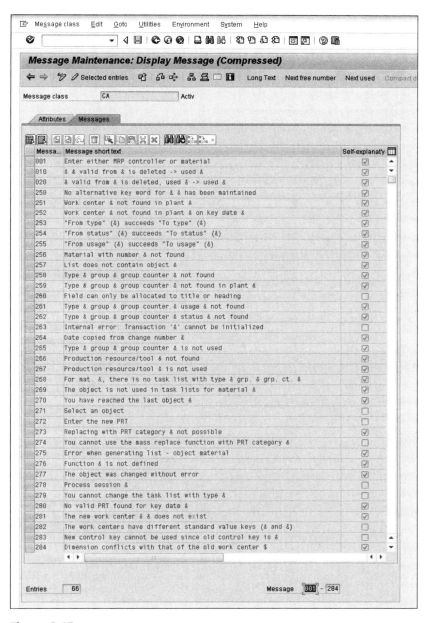

Figure 2.15
The message maintenance screen.

You can use the MESSAGE command with variables to make the messages dynamic. In the message text, an ampersand (&) is considered a string. Add a WITH statement to the MESSAGE command, along with the field name that will replace the ampersand (see Figure 2.16):

```
MESSAGE E999 WITH SY-UNAME.
```

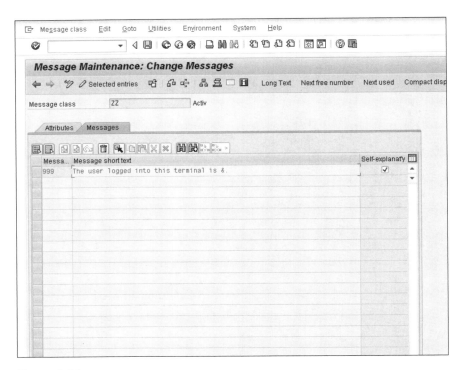

Figure 2.16
The new message for 999 in the message maintenance screen.

Tip

If your system administrator frowns on the maintenance of the message classes and IDs, a way to display a message of your choice is to use a blank message number and associate a TEXT element along with it:

```
Message E999 with TEXT-001
```

Assume that TEXT-001 contains the text SAMPLE TEXT. The output would display the following information:

```
EZZ999 SAMPLE TEXT
```

One negative aspect of this method is that the contents of TEXT-001 aren't incorporated into the job log if the program is run in background mode.

`SY-UNAME` is the system field that holds the user ID of the user currently logged on, or the user ID of the person who scheduled a background job. For a detailed list of all the system fields, see Appendix B. System fields are very useful in programs; you should become familiar with the system table.

Multiple ampersands can be used in the `MESSAGE` definition. It's up to you to define the text of the messages and the requirements of the message IDs.

The `WITH` text addition overrides the message number stored in the message ID library. Instead of writing the text associated with the message number, text is output, text can be a text element, or text enclosed in single quotes:

```
MESSAGE E999 WITH   'This system is slow.    Please be patient'.
```

The output would be

```
E999: This system is slow.    Please be patient
```

USING THE FORMAT COMMAND

The `FORMAT` command defines screen attributes and some printed attributes. This command controls the format in which the data is displayed. The general syntax for the command is as follows:

```
FORMAT   [INTENSIFIED]
[INTENSIFIED OFF]
[COLOR color]
[COLOR OFF]
[INVERSE]
[INVERSE OFF]
[RESET].
```

The `FORMAT` command by itself does nothing. Instead, four additions help define the format of the output:

- INTENSIFIED
- COLOR
- INVERSE
- RESET

These settings are described in the following sections.

Boldfacing (INTENSIFIED)

If you want the text to be **boldfaced**, use the INTENSIFIED addition:

```
FORMAT INTENSIFIED.
WRITE    'WORD'.
FORMAT INTENSIFIED OFF.
```

Note

Obviously, we can't show a color example in this printed text! However, a list of colors can be found if the words **HELP FORMAT** are typed in the command line in the ABAP/4 editors. While colors are nice, remember that some users are color blind. Keep all users in mind.

In this case, the word WORD appears in bold on the screen. Notice that after the WRITE statement another FORMAT command turns the INTENSIFIED addition off. Turning these formats on and off is helpful, as you want to be selective about what appears on your page.

Changing Colors (COLOR)

The possible colors from which you can choose are from 0 to 7. A little experimentation on the part of the programmer will show what these colors are set to on that user's system. Here's how the COLOR variation of the FORMAT command works:

```
FORMAT COLOR color.
WRITE    'WORD'.
FORMAT COLOR OFF.
```

Reversing the Text (INVERSE)

Another addition is INVERSE. The background color becomes the foreground color and vice versa:

```
DO 8 TIMES.
col = sy-index - 1.
FORMAT COLOR = col.
   WRITE: /   col                COLOR OFF,
              'INTENSIFIED ON'   INTENSIFIED ON,
              'INTENSIFIED OFF'  INTENSIFIED OFF,
              'INVERSE ON'       INVERSE ON.
ENDDO.
```

The output would show something like that shown in Figure 2.17.

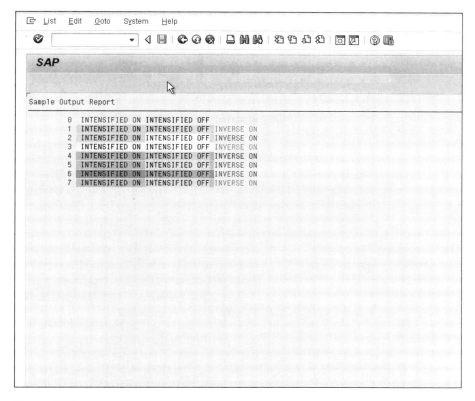

Figure 2.17
Inverse output.

Restoring the Default Settings (RESET)

The last addition to the FORMAT command is RESET. This addition resets all the formats to their original system defaults. The syntax for RESET is:

```
RESET.
```

SUMMARY

Data output is one of the simplest but most important features of ABAP/4. The format of a report helps the users get their jobs done and reflects back on the MIS team coordinating the SAP system.

The WRITE command outputs data or text to the page. It's possible to position that data where you want on the page and control how much of the data is visible by using column positioning and output length. The SKIP command inserts one or multiple blank lines on the screen. It also can position the cursor dynamically on any line on the page. The POSITION command also positions the cursor on a particular line on the screen. The ULINE command outputs a solid horizontal line across the page. This line can also be positioned and the output controlled in the same way the WRITE command controls its output. Text elements hold text that the report utilizes throughout the report. Message IDs hold text in the same manner, except that the messages can be used by a variety of programs, whereas text elements are local to that particular program. The FORMAT command simply defines the format of the output text onscreen.

CHAPTER 3

MANIPULATING DATA

IN THIS CHAPTER

- Working with Numeric Data
- Manipulating Character Data
- Working with Date Variables
- Using Time Variables
- Manipulating Field Symbols

So far you have seen how to declare a variable, assign a value to a variable, and output the value of a variable using ABAP/4. The next area of interest is manipulating the values of variables.

Variables can be broadly classified into numeric or character data. ABAP/4 has commands to manipulate both types of data. The most common type of manipulation of numeric data is arithmetic computation, such as addition or multiplication of data. For character data, the most common type of manipulation is string manipulation, such as concatenation of strings or taking substrings of character data. This chapter also explores a special form of character data—date and time variables. Finally, the use of field symbols (introduced in Chapter 1, "Data Types and Definitions") is discussed in detail.

All the techniques discussed in this chapter for character and numeric data have identical effects whether they're manipulating individual variables or fields within a larger record.

WORKING WITH NUMERIC DATA

The first type of data to be manipulated is *numeric*, which includes integer, packed, floating, and hexadecimal data types. Numeric data is altered using arithmetic functions, from addition to cosines.

Performing Math (COMPUTE)

The command to perform arithmetic operations on numeric data is COMPUTE. The COMPUTE command has the following syntax:

```
[COMPUTE] var = expression.
```

In this case expression may be any combination of arithmetic operators and ABAP/4 functions. ABAP/4 supports the arithmetic operators shown in Table 3.1.

Table 3.1 ABAP/4 Arithmetic Operators

Operator	Description
+	Addition
-	Subtraction
*	Multiplication
/	Division
EXP	Exponential
DIV	Integer quotient of division
MOD	Integer remainder of division

© 2014 Cengage Learning.

In addition to these operators, ABAP/4 also provides common functions that work with all number types, as described in Table 3.2.

Table 3.2 ABAP/4 Arithmetic Functions

Function	Description
SIGN()	Sign, returns 1, 0, -1
ABS()	Absolute value
TRUNC(X)	Truncate, returns integer portion of X

FRAC(X)	Fraction, returns decimal portion of X
CEIL(X)	Ceiling, smallest whole number value not less than X
FLOOR(X)	Floor, largest whole number value not greater than X
STRLEN()	Integer length of a character string, excluding trailing spaces

© 2014 Cengage Learning.

Finally, ABAP/4 also provides several functions, which return floating-point numbers, as described in Table 3.3.

Using these operators and functions, you can assemble expressions.

Expressions are evaluated from left to right; however, when multiple operators or functions are combined into a single expression, the order of evaluation is as follows:

1. ABAP/4 functions
2. **
3. * / j. , /
4. DIV, MOD
5. + , -

For operators with equal precedence, such as multiplication and division, the order is determined left to right. The exception is the exponential operator, which is evaluated right to left in the case of multiple usage such as 2**3**4. This order of operation can be altered by use of parentheses.

Table 3.3   ABAP/4 Floating-Point Functions

Function	Description
EXP( )	Exponential function
LOGO	Natural logarithm
LOG10( )	Base 10 logarithm
SIN( )	Sine
COS( )	Cosine
TAN( )	Tangent

(Continued)

Table 3.3 ABAP/4 Floating-Point Functions (*Continued*)

Function	Description
TANH( )	Hyperbola tangent
SINH( )	Hyperbola sin
COSH( )	Hyperbola cosine
ASIN( )	Arc sine
ACOS( )	Arc cosine
ATAN( )	Arc tangent
SQRTO	Square root

In the following case, the value of RESULT would be 51:

```
DATA: VAR1 TYPE I VALUE 10
VAR2 TYPE I VALUE 5,
RESULT TYPE I. COMPUTE
RESULT = 5 * VAR1 + VAR2 / 5.
```

In this case, the value of RESULT would be 15:

```
DATA:VAR1 TYPE I VALUE 10,
VAR2 TYPE I VALUE 5,
RESULT TYPE I. COMPUTE RESULT
= 5 * ( VAR1 + VAR2 ) / 5.
```

Notice the single space separating all operators, including the parentheses, in the COMPUTE statement. An arithmetic operator in ABAP/4 is considered a word and must be preceded and followed by blanks like any other word. The following code would generate a syntax error:

```
COMPUTE RESULT = 5*(VAR1+VAR2)/5.
```

The exception to this rule involves ABAP/4 functions for which the parentheses are considered part of the command:

```
DATA:VAR1 TYPE I VALUE 10,
VAR2 TYPE I VALUE 5,
RESULT TYPE F. COMPUTE RESULT = SIN( VAR1 + VAR2 ) /
5.
```

Notice that no space separates SIN and the opening parenthesis, but that spaces are included between the opening parenthesis and VAR1.

Controlling Precision in Expressions

When an expression involves decimals, ABAP/4 maintains any intermediate results to the maximum possible precision. Rounding, if necessary, occurs only during the final assignment.

In the following example, the value of RESULT is 0.67 because the system evaluated the expression as (.33333... + .33333...), which is .66666..., and rounded it to .67 because RESULT has only two decimal places:

```
DATA RESULT TYPE
 DECIMALS 2.
RESULT
=1/3+1/3.
```

Alternatives to COMPUTE (ADD, SUBTRACT, MULTIPLY, and DIVIDE)

In addition to the COMPUTE command, four commands for addition, subtraction, multiplication, and division can perform simple computations. They compute only a single operation and aren't widely used. The syntax for the commands is as follows:

```
ADD value TO van.
SUBTRACT value FROM van.
MULTIPLY value BY var.
DIVIDE value BY var.
```

The equivalent of each command, using COMPUTE, would be as follows:

```
ADD value TO var.          var = var + value.
SUBTRACT value FROM var.        var= var- value.
MULTIPLY value BY var.      var = var* value.
DIVIDE value BY var. var = var I value.
```

The following statements are identical:

```
ADD 1 TO W_COUNTER. W_COUNTER = W_COUNTER + 1.
```

Adding Sequential Fields (ADD)

Often a single record in SAP contains several numeric fields that need to be summed. For example, a record from the general ledger may contain 12 fields holding the debits or credits for each month of a year. In order to get a year-end balance, all 12 of the fields must be summed. The ADD command can sum fields in a record if they're sequential and identical in size. The syntax is as follows:

```
ADD field 1 THEN field 2 UNTIL field N [TO var] [GIVING var].
```

The TO option takes the sum of field 1 through field N and adds it to var. The GIVING option replaces the value in var with the sum.

In the following example, the output would be 15:

```
DATA: BEGIN OF REC,
F1 TYPE P VALUE 1,
F2 TYPE P VALUE 2,
F3 TYPE P VALUE 3,
F4 TYPE P VALUE 4,
F5 TYPE P VALUE 5,
END OF REC,
TOTAL TYPE P VALUE 10.

ADD REC-F1  THEN   REC-F2 UNTIL REC-F5 GIVING TOTAL. WRITE TOTAL.
```

In this case, SAP takes the values in REC-F1, REC-F2, REC-F3, REC-F4, and REC-F5 (1, 2, 3, 4, and 5, respectively) and adds them to get a result of 15. Then the program places 15 in the variable TOTAL, replacing the old value of 10.

In the next case, the output would be 25:

```
DATA: BEGIN OF REC,
F1 TYPE P VALUE 1,
F2 TYPE P VALUE 2,
F3 TYPE P VALUE 3,
F4 TYPE P VALUE 4,
F5 TYPE P VALUE 5,
END OF REC,
TOTAL TYPE P VALUE 10.

ADD REC-F1 THEN REC-F2 UNTIL REC-F5 TO TOTAL. WRITE TOTAL.
```

Again, the fields in REC are added to get 15; in this case, however, the GIVING option isn't used, so 15 is added to the value contained in TOTAL (10) to get 25.

Using the CORRESPONDING Commands

Another group of commands for dealing with arithmetic operations on records are the commands ADD-CORRESPONDING, SUBTRACT-CORRESPONDING, MULTIPLY-CORRESPONDING, and DIVIDE-CORRESPONDING, which perform operations on fields of the same name, much as the MOVE-CORRESPONDING command moves all fields of the same name from one record to another. The syntax for these commands is identical to the syntax of MOVE-CORRESPONDING. Also like MOVE-CORRESPONDING, these commands are very inefficient and shouldn't be used in most circumstances.

Here's an example:

```
DATA: BEGIN OF REC1,
REC1_KEY(5) TYPE C VALUE 'TEST11,
AMNT1 TYPE I VALUE 5,
AMNT2 TYPE I VALUE 10,
END OF REC1. DATA: BEGIN OF REC2,

REC2_KEY(5) TYPE C VALUE 'TEST2',
AMNT1 TYPE I VALUE 20,
AMNT2 TYPE I VALUE 5,
AMNT3 TYPE I VALUE 0,
AMNT4 TYPE I VALUE 0,
END OF REC2.

ADD-CORRESPONDING REC1 TO REC2.
WRITE: REC2-REC2_KEY, REC2-AMNT1, REC2-AMNT2, REC2-AMNT3, REC2-A
```

The output of this code would be:

```
TEST2 25  15   0
```

The ADD-CORRESPONDING command adds fields in two records with identical names, if they contain numeric variables, and places the result in the second record. In this case, REC1 and REC2 are added. The fields with common names between the two are AMNT1 and AMNT2, so those are added, and the result is placed in REC2. REC1-AMNT1 holds 5, and REC2-AMNT1 holds 20, so the result of 25 is placed in REC2-AMNT1 and displayed by the WRITE command. For the next field, REC1-AMNT2 holds 10, and REC2-AMNT2 holds 5, so the result of 15 is placed in REC2-AMNT2 and displayed by the WRITE command. The other fields in REC2 have no corresponding fields in REC1, so they're left unchanged by the command.

MANIPULATING CHARACTER DATA

ABAP/4 provides several commands to manipulate character data. Text processing is one of the most common functions in ABAP/4 programming. It's used in the conversion process, for example, when information formerly stored in legacy systems is moved to SAP, or to process information transmitted to SAP during ongoing interfaces. These commands allow a programmer to carry out common operations such as working with substrings, replace characters, or search strings. When working with character data, ABAP/4 provides a system variable called SPACE. As the name implies, this is the equivalent of ' ' and is of use in many operations.

Defining Substrings with Offsets

A *substring* is a portion of a full-character string. For example, the string DOG is a substring of THE SMALL DOG IS BROWN. No command exists to extract a substring from a variable; instead, ABAP/4 provides a notation, similar to the notation used in both the WRITE and MOVE commands, to deal with substrings. The notation is referred to as the *offset notation* and uses this syntax:

```
var+offset(length)
```

In this syntax offset is the number of positions from the leftmost character in the variable at which you want to start, and length is the total number of characters to extract. Assuming that TEMP contains the string abcdefghij, Table 3.4 shows some examples of possible substrings you could create from TEMP with the offset notation.

Table 3.4   Substrings Created with the Offset Notation

Field	Contents
TEMP+3	defghij
TEMP+1 (4)	bcde
TEMP+0(10)	abcdefghij

© 2014 Cengage Learning.

This notation can be used in a statement in which you would typically use a variable. Normally, when the MOVE command is used to assign a value to a variable, it replaces any prior value. But when you use the offset notation, only the individual characters specified by the notation are replaced:

```
DATA VAR1(10)   TYPE C VALUE   'abcdef'.
DATA VAR2(10)   TYPE C VALUE   '123456'.
MOVE   'X'   TO VAR1+2.
WRITE:   / VAR1.
```

The output would be abX; the offset of +2 moves the value X into the third position of VAR1 and clears the rest of the variable, because no explicit length is given.

```
MOVE   'Z' TO VAR2+3(2). WRITE:   /
VAR2.
```

The next output would be 123Z 6 because the offset of +3 moves the value Z into the fourth position, and the length of 2 tells the system to overwrite two characters of VAR2. Because Z has only one character, the second character is overwritten with a space.

```
MOVE VAR1+1(1) TO VAR2+1(1).
 WRITE: / VAR2.
WRITE: / VAR2+1(3).
```

The final output would be b3Z. In this case, both variables have offset and length. The MOVE command takes VAR1+1 (1), which is b, starts at the second character, and takes a length of 1. This value is placed in VAR2+1 (1), starting at the second character and taking a length of 1, so if VAR2 is 123Z 6 this would be the position occupied by 2. To make it more complicated, the WRITE command also specifies offset and length. So after the MOVE command, VAR2 holds 1 b3Z 6. The WRITE command specifies VAR2+1 (3); starting at the second position and taking three characters, this gives you b3Z.

Using Variable Offsets to Define Substrings

In addition to using constants for the offset and length values, you also can use integer variables to vary the substring being displayed. Variable offsets can be used only with the TO portion of the WRITE ... TO command. If you want to use a substring as a source, use the MOVE command instead. Variable offsets are especially handy when combined with the ABAP/4 looping commands, as discussed in Chapter 5, "Using the Looping Commands."

Here's an example of integer values used with WRITE ... TO to vary a substring:

```
DATA:   BEGIN OF REC,
VAR1(10)   TYPE C VALUE     'abcdef',
VAR2(10)   TYPE C VALUE     '1234',
END OF REC.
DATA:   OFF TYPE I VALUE 0,
LEN TYPE I VALUE 1.

WRITE     'X' TO REC-VAR1+OFF(LEN). WRITE:
  /, REC-VAR1.
ADD 1 TO OFF.

WRITE 'X' TO REC-VAR2+OFF(LEN). WRITE:
  /, REC-VAR2.
```

Output:

```
Xbcdef

1X34
```

In this example, REC-VAR1 is initialized to abcdef. The first WRITE ... TO command moves X to REC-VAR1+0(1). The offset of 0 means to start at the first character, and the length of 1 causes only one character to be replaced. This results in the output of Xbcdef. Then the next WRITE ... TO command moves X to REC-VAR2+1 (1). The offset of 1 means to start at the second character, and the length of 1 causes only one character to be erased. So REC-VAR2 starts as 1234 and after the WRITE... TO command becomes 1X34.

The ability to work with substrings is a powerful tool and forms the basis of all text processing in ABAP/4. It's used extensively in future chapters when programming reports and interfaces.

USING OTHER TEXT-PROCESSING COMMANDS

A number of ABAP/4 commands are designed to manipulate character variables. They are used in many ways:

- In reports, they are used to control the appearance of data.
- In interfaces, they are used to format incoming and outgoing data.
- In interactive transactions, they are used to process user requests.

Shifting Characters Right or Left (SHIFT)

The SHIFT command is another text-processing command. In its most basic form, it shifts the contents of a field one position to the left, erasing the leftmost character and placing a space in the rightmost position.

There are three versions of this command. This is the simplest:

```
SHIFT van  [CIRCULAR]   [RIGHT]   [LEFT].
```

The second version of SHIFT enables the programmer to specify the number of times to shift the contents of the variable:

```
SHIFT van BY N PLACES [CIRCULAR]   [RIGHT]   [LEFT].
```

The third version causes the command to continue to shift the contents of the variable until a specified character is reached.

```
SHIFT var UP TO character [CIRCULAR]   [RIGHT] [LEFT].
```

The following list describes the options you can use with SHIFT:

[CIRCULAR]	Causes the leftmost character to be moved to the rightmost position of the variable.
[RIGHT]	Causes the SHIFT to move the contents of the string from left to right.
[LEFT]	The default for SHIFT; moves the contents of the string from right to left.

Here's an example:

```
DATA: TEMP(5)VALUE    '12345',
MUM TYPE I VALUE 3.
SHIFT TEMP.
WRITE: /, TEMP.
SHIFT TEMP BY NUM PLACES CIRCULAR.
WRITE: /, TEMP.
SHIFT TEMP UP TO '5' RIGHT. WRITE: /, TEMP.
```

And the resulting output:

```
2345 5

234 5
```

The fourth version shifts the contents of the variable to the left only if it begins with the value specified in val and continues to shift left as long as the first character is the value specified in val. It will pad the end of the string with blanks.

```
SHIFT C LEFT DELETING LEADING val.
```

The final version is the opposite of the fourth one. It shifts the contents of the variable to the right only if it ends with the value specified in val and continues to shift right as long as the last character is the value specified in val. It will pad the beginning of the string with blanks.

```
SHIFT c RIGHT DELETING TRAILING val.
```

Here's an example (remember SPACE is the same as ' '):

```
DATA: TEMP(14) VALUE '    The Start',
TEMP2(10) VALUE 'The EndXXX'.
SHIFT TEMP LEFT DELETING LEADING SPACE.
```

```
SHIFT TEMP2 RIGHT DELETING TRAILING 'X'.
WRITE: /, TEMP. WRITE: /, TEMP2.
```

And the resulting output:

```
The Start
    The End
```

Changing the Capitalization (TRANSLATE)

The TRANSLATE command converts a character string to all uppercase or lowercase or replaces one character with another.

The first two versions of this command translate a string to uppercase and lowercase, respectively:

```
TRANSLATE var TO UPPER CASE.
TRANSLATE var TO LOWER CASE.
```

The third version replaces characters in var based on the pattern in the string submitted:

```
TRANSLATE var USING string.
```

string must consist of pairs of characters. The first character in the pair is the character to be replaced, and the second is the character to replace with. The pairs aren't separated by spaces, because spaces are valid characters that can be used as replacements.

Here are examples of the TRANSLATE command:

```
DATA: STRING(10) VALUE '  abcdefg', TEMP(6) VALUE 'a1A2 X'
TRANSLATE STRING TO UPPER CASE.
WRITE: /, STRING
TRANSLATE STRING USING TEMP.
WRITE: /, STRING.
```

Output:

```
        ABCDEFG
        XXX2BCDEFG
```

In the first case, the TRANSLATE command simply changes the variable to uppercase. In the second, TRANSLATE uses the variable TEMP to translate one character to another. It changes all V to T, then all 'A' to '2' and finally all ' ' to 'X', thus changing 'ABCDEFG' to 'XXX2BCDEFG'.

Replacing Individual Characters (OVERLAY)

Another command that replaces characters with other characters is OVERLAY. This command compares two strings and replaces any spaces in the first with the corresponding character from the second. If the first string is longer than the second, spaces in positions exceeding those of the second string remain unchanged.

This command isn't widely used but has some applications when working with text masks.

Here's the syntax:

```
OVERLAY var1 WITH var2 [ONLY var3].
```

The ONLY option enables you to provide a list of characters to be replaced in the first string, instead of just spaces. So if var3 is a period followed by an asterisk ('.*'), any occurrence of a period or asterisk in var1 is replaced with the corresponding character in var2.

Examples:

```
DATA: STRING(25) VALUE 'JONES **** FIELD ENGINEER',
MASK(25) VALUE '1234567890123456789012345'.
WRITE / STRING. OVERLAY STRING WITH MASK. WRITE / STRING.
OVERLAY STRING WITH MASK ONLY '*+-'.
WRITE / STRING.
```

Output:

```
JONES **** FIELD ENGINEER
JONES6****1FIELD7ENGINEER
JONES678901FIELD7ENGINEER
```

Replacing Multiple Characters (REPLACE)

Similar in function to the TRANSLATE command is REPLACE. Where TRANSLATE replaces individual characters, REPLACE replaces several characters:

```
REPLACE string1 WITH string2 INTO var [LENGTH len].
```

The command replaces the first occurrence of string1, from left to right, with the contents of the strings in the variable specified. These strings are case sensitive. The LENGTH option limits the search to the length specified, searching from left to right.

The return code is set to 0 if a string is replaced or greater than zero if no replacement is made.

Example:

```
DATA TEMP(33) VALUE 'Now was the time for all good men'.
REPLACE 'was' WITH 'is' INTO TEMP. WRITE TEMP.
```

Output:

```
Now is the time for all good men
```

Searching for Characters (SEARCH)

Another related command is SEARCH. In this case, a variable is searched for a word, and the return code informs the program if that word was found. A word is any group of characters delimited by any of the following characters:

```
(space) + !;/,?.   ( ) : =
```

The use of the asterisk (*) as a wildcard character is allowed. If the asterisk precedes the string to be searched, any word ending in the string is a match. If the asterisk follows the string, any word beginning with the string is a match. To search for words ending in *ing*, for example, the string would be ' *ing'. You can place a string to be searched between two periods to indicate it can be found in the middle of a variable. To look for the following string inside of a variable:

```
mid
```

the string would be

```
'.mid.'
```

The search is conducted from left to right. If any of the characters are found, the search is successful and the return code is set to 0; otherwise, it is set to 4.

Following is the syntax for the SEARCH command:

```
SEARCH van FOR string   [ABBREVIATED]      [STARTING AT number]
  [ENDING AT number]    [AND MARK].
```

The following list details the options available for the SEARCH command:

[ABBREVIATED]	This option allows other characters to be inserted between the characters of the string, as long as the first character of the string and the first character of the word in the variable match. So a variable containing Pipe, 2in. ceramic would produce a match with the string 'Pipe2ceramic'.
[STARTING AT *number*]	Starts the search at the specified position and continues from left to right. The first character in the variable is considered position one.
[ENDING AT *number*]	Stops the search at the specified position.
[AND MARK]	If the string is found, all the characters of the string and any characters occurring between them (if the ABBREVIATED option is used) are converted to uppercase in the variable.

Example:

```
DATA QUOTE(50) VALUE 'SMITH, JOHN ACCOUNTANT II 04/18/91'

SEARCH QUOTE FOR 'ACC*'.
WRITE / SY-SUBRC. "0 indicates success, 4 failure
SEARCH QUOTE FOR 'ACCOUNTANT' STARTING AT 15.
WRITE / SY-SUBRC.
SEARCH QUOTE FOR 'ACON' ABBREVIATED.
WRITE / SY-SUBRC.
```

The first search succeeds; the value of SY-SUBRC is set to 0. The second search fails because starting at the 15th position, there is no string ACCOUNTANT to be found. So SY-SUBRC is set to 4, indicating that the command failed. The third search succeeds because the ABBREVIATED option tells it to ignore the space in AC ON. So the output is as follows:

```
0
4
0
```

The SEARCH command can also be used to search an internal table for a string (see Chapter 6, "Working with Internal Tables," for a description of internal tables). The string can use any of the forms described in the previous section. Use the following syntax for searching an internal table:

```
SEARCH itab FOR string   [ABBREVIATED]    [STARTING AT line]
   [ENDING AT line]    [AND MARK],
```

The value of SY-SUBRC is set to 0 if the search string is found in the table. The value of SY-TAB IX will contain the index of the line, which contains the string. Finally, the SY-FDPOS field will hold the offset of the string within the line.

Dividing Strings (SPLIT)

The SPLIT command is used to break up a character string into smaller parts. It accepts a string, a delimiter, and a list of variables or an internal table. The delimiter is used to indicate when to end each part of the string. Each part of the string is placed into a separate variable or a separate row of the internal table.

Here is the syntax:

```
SPLIT str AT char INTO var1 ... varN.

SPLIT str AT char INTO TABLE itab.
```

For example, when translating an interface file into a data structure:

```
DATA:    BEGIN OF WSJIATL,
MATNR LIKE MARA-MATNR, WERKS LIKE MARC-WERKS, DESC(30), DIV(2),
    END OF WS_MATL.
DATA INPUT(100) VALUE   '    92345•A52,USA1,        Pipe 3 m. L,
                             Joint A1'.

SPLIT INPUT AT   ','   INTO WS_MATL-MATNR WS_MATL-WERKS
WS_MATL-DESC WS_MATL-DIV.

WRITE:    / WSJIATL-MATNR,
/ WS_MATL-WERKS, / WSJIATL-DESC, / WS_MATL-DIV.
```

In this case the output would be:

```
92345-A52
 USA1
Pipe 3 m. L
 Joint A1
```

Merging Strings (CONCATENATE)

One of the most important commands used to manipulate character variables is CONCATENATE. This command merges multiple character strings into a single string. Any trailing spaces are ignored by this command.

Here is the syntax:

```
CONCATENATE var1 var2 var3 INTO var4 [SEPARATED BY char].
```

Here is a pretty simple example:

```
DATA: C1(5) VALUE 'ONE',
C2(5) VALUE 'TWO',
C3(5) VALUE 'THREE',
LAST(30) VALUE 'AND SO ON'.
CONCATENATE C1 ',' C2 ',' C3 ',' LAST INTO LAST.

WRITE: / LAST.

CONCATENATE C1 ',' C2 ',' C3 INTO LAST SEPARATED BY SPACE.

WRITE: / LAST.
```

The output of this would be:

```
ONE,TWO,THREE,
AND SO ON ONE ,
TWO , THREE
```

Another important command when using CONCATENATE is RESPECTING BLANKS. It takes in the length of the variable in consideration and places ' ' according to the length of the string.

Here is the syntax:

```
CONCATENATE var1 var2 var3 INTO var4 [RESPECTING BLANKS].
```

Here is an example:

```
Data: var1(10) value 'abcde',
var2(10) value '12345',
var3(5) value 'uvwxy',
var4(25).

CONCATENATE var1 var2 var3 into var4 RESPECTING BLANKS.
```

The output will be:

```
abcde     12345     uvwxy
```

Since the length of var1 and var2 is 10 and there are only five characters present in each string, the output has ' ' for the remaining length.

This statement is very useful when passing logical keys to tables.

Removing Spaces (CONDENSE)

The final command used to manipulate character variables is CONDENSE. This command removes spaces from within a character string. It can be used to concatenate multiple strings into a single string. By default, it removes all but one space between words. If the NO-GAPS option is used, it removes all spaces from within a character string.

Here is the syntax:

```
CONDENSE van [NO-GAPS].
```

For example, when accessing an external system file, you need both a path and a file name. If these two pieces of information are received separately and need to be combined, you might find a piece of code like this:

```
PARAMETERS: F_PATH(40) LOWER CASE,
F_NAME(20) LOWER CASE.
F_PATH+20(20)   = F_NAME.
  CONDENSE F_PATH NO-GAPS.
```

If the user enters the following information for F_PATH:

```
/data/incoming/
```

and then adds this line for F_NAME:

```
test01.dat
```

the value of F_PATH after the assignment will be:

```
/data/incoming/   test01.dat
```

The CONDENSE command with NO-GAPS changes that to:

```
/data/incoming/test01.dat
```

Had the NO-GAPS option *not been* used, F_PATH would contain this:

```
/data/incoming/ test01.dat
```

WORKING WITH DATE VARIABLES

Date manipulation is one of the basics of data processing. Dates can be added or subtracted, and portions of the date can be extracted or altered. Date variables act much like eight-character fields; the data is stored in the format YYYYMMDD. You can control the appearance of the output of a date variable by using an output mask with the WRITE statement.

To extract portions of a date variable, use the substring notation explained earlier in the section, "Defining Substrings with Offsets." For example, to determine the month of a date variable named TODAY, you use TODAY+4(2). So if TODAY contains 20140401, TODAY+4(2) is 04 or the fourth month.

The COMPUTE command can also be used to add or subtract dates. For purposes of computation, dates are treated as packed fields containing the total number of days since January 1, 1900. A system field called SY-DATUM contains the current date, much like SY-SUBRC contains the current return code.

Here are some examples:

```
DATA TODAY TYPE D.
TODAY = SY-DATUM.
WRITE:   /, TODAY MM/DD/YY,
/,  TODAY+2(2),
/, TODAY+4(2), /,
TODAY+6(2).
```

Here is the output:

```
04/11/14
14
04
11
```

This code shows how the offset notation can be used to return part of a date field in order to extract the day, month, or year only.

Now suppose that you want to process invoices and need to know the difference between the ship date and the order date. The billing date will be incremented by that difference. Part of the code would look like this:

```
DATA: BEGIN OF INVOICE,
DOC#(10),
ORDER TYPE D,
SHIP TYPE D,
BILLING TYPE D,
END OF INVOICE.
DATA DIFF_DAYS TYPE P.

DIFF_DAYS = INVOICE-SHIP - INVOICE-ORDER.
WRITE: 'Shipping Delay', DIFF_DAYS, 'Days'.
WRITE: /, 'Current Billing Date', INVOICE-BILLING MM/DD/YY.

INVOICE-BILLING = INVOICE-BILLING + DIFF_DAYS.

WRITE: /, 'Revised Billing Date', INVOICE-BILLING MM/DD/YY.
```

Here is the output:

```
Shipping Delay 17 Days Current
Billing Date 04/01/14 Revised
Billing Date 04/18/14
```

In this example, adding the DIFF_DAYS to INVOICE-BILLING changes the date fields. When adding and subtracting date fields, the results are always in days.

USING TIME VARIABLES

Time variables act much like date variables. Like dates, time variables can be added or subtracted, and portions of the time can be extracted or altered. Time variables act like six-character fields; the data is stored in the format HHMMSS, where hours are in 24-hour notation.

To extract portions of a time variable, you use the substring notation explained earlier, in the section "Defining Substrings with Offsets." For example, to determine the minutes of a variable named NOW, use NOW+2(2).

You can also use the COMPUTE command to add or subtract times. For purposes of computation, time variables are treated as packed fields containing the total number of seconds since midnight. The system field called SY-UZEIT contains the current time, much like SY-SUBRC contains the current return code. ABAP/4 uses military notation; if you want to display time in the more common AM/PM notation, you'll have to do the formatting in your program.

Here's an example:

```
DATA NOW TYPE T.
DATA LATER TYPE T VALUE '171530'.
DATA DIFF TYPE P.

NOW = SY-UZEIT.  "Assume it 3:15:30 pm
WRITE: /, NOW USING EDIT MASK '_:_:_',
/, 'It is now', NOW(2), 'Hours and', NOW+2(2), 'Minutes'.
DIFF = LATER - NOW.
WRITE: / 'The difference in seconds between now and later is', DIFF.
```

Here is the output:

```
15:15:30
It is now 15 Hours and 15 Minutes
The difference in seconds between now and later is 7200
```

In this case, time fields are added and subtracted. ABAP/4 converts time fields into seconds for the sake of arithmetic.

MANIPULATING FIELD SYMBOLS

The final type of data manipulation to be discussed here is the use of field symbols. As noted in Chapter 1, field symbols don't actually contain data but instead serve as a pointer to other variables, which in turn contain specific values. Although not widely used, field symbols offer tremendous flexibility. The tradeoff for that flexibility is that it's almost impossible for the compiler to detect errors with field symbols because no type-checking can take place until runtime. So it's critical that you use the field symbols properly. See the example in the next section for possible errors for field symbols.

Assigning a Variable to a Field Symbol (ASSIGN)

The ASSIGN command is used to assign a variable to a field symbol. Once assigned, field symbols can be used anywhere that a normal variable can be used (so all previous discussions in this chapter apply to field symbols).

Following is the syntax for ASSIGN:

```
ASSIGN var TO <fs>. ASSIGN (var) TO
<fs>.
```

The variable var can be any variable or field symbol, regardless of data type. It's acceptable to use offset and length operators with variables or even with field symbols.

In fact, ASSIGN supports variable offsets and lengths just like the WRITE ... TO command. Here are some examples:

```
DATA STRING(10) VALUE 'ABCDEFGHIJ'. DATA NUM TYPE P VALUE 2.
    FIELD-SYMBOLS <FS>.

ASSIGN NUM TO <FS>.
WRITE <FS>. NUM = NUM
+ 2. WRITE <FS>.
ASSIGN STRING TO <FS>.
WRITE <FS>.
ASSIGN STRING+2(NUM) TO <FS>.
WRITE <FS>.
```

Here is the output:

```
2   4   ABCDEFGHIJ CDEF
```

In this example, <FS> is pointed at the field NUM, so when the first WRITE command is issued, 2 is output. Then 2 is added to NUM, so the next WRITE command outputs the new value of NUM (4). Then <FS> is pointed to the field STRING, so the third WRITE command outputs the value ABCDEFGHIJ. Finally, <FS> is pointed at part of the field STRING, showing how the offset notation can be used with field strings. In this case, STRING+2(4) is set to <FS>, so the output of the last WRITE is CDEF.

The following example would generate an error at runtime but not during the syntax check, because the system doesn't know what the data type of a field string will be until the program runs:

```
DATA STRING(10)  VALUE  'ABCDEFGHIJ'.
DATA NUM TYPE P VALUE 2. FIELD-
SYMBOLS <FS>.

ASSIGN STRING TO <FS>.
NUM = NUM + <FS>. "Adding a string to a number causes an error
                "But the system does not know until too late
```

In form two of the command, the parentheses surrounding the variable (which must be a character string) indicate that instead of referring to var, the field string should refer to the variable with the name contained in var:

```
DATA: FIELD(8) VALUE 'WS_BUKRS',
WS_BUKRS LIKE BSEG-BUKRS VALUE 'WRNR'.
 FIELD-SYMBOLS <FS>. ASSIGN (FIELD) TO
<FS>. WRITE <FS>.
```

Here is the output:

```
WRNR
```

The field symbol is set to the field named in the variable FIELD, WS_BUKRS, which has a value of WRNR. So when <FS> is written, the value WRNR is output.

Summary

The ability to work with and change different types of data is central to all programming. As shown in this chapter, ABAP/4 offers a wide variety of commands to manipulate data.

Now that basic data processing is out of the way, you can move on to the procedural elements of the ABAP/4 language. These commands include conditional and looping operators, which are used to take full advantage of the data-manipulation commands just discussed.

CHAPTER 4

USING CONDITIONAL OPERATORS

IN THIS CHAPTER

- Using the CASE Statement
- Using IF with Logical Operators
- Comparing Non-Numeric Values
- Using Equal/Not-Equal Operators
- Determining Whether Values Have Changed
- Determining Whether a Value Is Included in a Range
- Using the NOT Operator
- Comparing Character Fields
- Nesting Statements

Logical statements are the heart and soul of programming. These statements sort through all the data and put it into some order, from which you can generate reports and data extracts that are useful to your company.

ABAP has two pure conditional logic statements: the CASE statement and the traditional IF statement. (The looping commands incorporate logic into their statements as well. See Chapter 5, "Using the Looping Commands.")

Note

A third conditional statement, ON CHANGE OF, deals with the changing data in a field. Essentially, when the contents of a field change, the commands are executed. Single fields generally don't change, but values in the header field of an internal table change as different records of the table are viewed. Here's the syntax:

```
ON CHANGE OF field.
commands
ENDON.
```

This command is discussed in Chapter 6, "Working with Internal Tables," as an understanding of internal tables is applicable to this command.

USING THE CASE STATEMENT

The CASE statement is used to indicate conditions for data that fall into certain specific categories. For example, you might use the CASE statement with language. If the user logs on with the language set to German, all the output should be in German. If it's in English, the output should be English, and so on. (This is an extreme example, used only to show how the CASE statement works. A more practical example is discussed a bit later.)

The CASE statement can be divided into groups. These groups usually are unique data fields that classify the data in a category. An example of such a group is a country code, which defines where the company is located or does business. The CASE statement is used when you have data that falls into certain categories. The general format is as follows:

```
CASE field.
WHEN value1.
command lines.
\
WHEN value2.
command lines.
WHEN OTHERS.
command lines.
ENDCASE.
```

field is a data field or internal table field holding numeric or character data that defines the group. When those values/characters match one of the values assigned to the WHEN statements, the command lines under that WHEN statement are executed. If the field doesn't match any of the values with the WHEN statements, the WHEN OTHERS statement allows for an exception, and the command lines under it are executed.

The WHEN OTHERS statement isn't required; however, it's a good idea to include it so that other programmers who follow you can see that you chose to "do nothing" when none of the data matches:

```
WHEN OTHERS.
*DO NOTHING.
```

Another time to use the WHEN OTHERS statement is when dealing with the system field, SY-SUBRC. As you know, when something occurs that is not expected (usually an error), the value of SY-SUBRC is set to a value other than zero. You cannot code the statement WHEN <> 0 because it is syntactically incorrect. Instead you use the expression WHEN OTHERS.

```
SELECT SINGLE * FROM MARA
INTO LS_MARA      "(HERE LS_MARA IS A STRUCTURE)
WHERE MATNR = 'CDROM'. CASE SY-SUBRC.
WHEN 0.
WRITE: 'THERE IS A CDROM IN THE MATERIAL MASTER'.
WHEN OTHERS.
WRITE: 'THERE IS NO CDROM IN THE MATERIAL MASTER'.
ENDCASE.
```

To review the example in plain English, a SQL statement searches the material master table (MARA) for the material CDROM. If there is a CD-ROM, then the program responds in the affirmative. If there is not a CD-ROM, the program responds in the negative.

Here's another example of the CASE statement:

```
DATA:   W_YEAR(4) TYPE C.
W_YEAR =   '2012'.
CASE W_YEAR.
WHEN      '2011'.
WRITE     'The year is 2011!'.
WHEN      '2012'.
WRITE     'The year is 2012!'.
WHEN      '2013'.
WRITE     'The year is 2013!'.
WHEN OTHERS.
WRITE     'The year is undefined.'.
ENDCASE.
```

This piece of code is hardcoded to respond to year 2012. In a regular program, the year would be a parameter that the user enters or a field read from a table in the database. In this case, the output would be as follows:

```
The year is 2012!
```

If the year had been earlier than 2011, later than 2013, or anything other than the years mentioned in the WHEN statement, the WHEN OTHERS command line would have written The year is undefined.

Note that for character fields, the value associated with the WHEN statement must be in single quotes, but for numeric fields the value associated with the WHEN statement doesn't require quotes. With the WHEN statement, the value is defined. The equivalent statement in English would be, "When *field* is equal to *value*, do this." No greater than (>), less than (<), or any other logical operators can be used.

Tip

> To improve the performance of your program, place the most likely WHEN statement at the top, the next likely after that, and so on. The faster the program makes a logical choice, the fewer lines of code it processes and the faster it runs. In a large integrated system like SAP, performance counts. Obviously, the WHEN OTHERS command always has to be at the end.

The CASE statement is used when the contents of the field are known to exist in a certain set of values. CASE doesn't compare values, check for string contents, or anything complex. It's used simply for this purpose. The simplicity of the statement makes it an efficient tool when making logical decisions and a good command to organize your data if given the opportunity. However, if a more complex comparison is needed, the CASE statement can be replaced by the IF statement, as described in the following section.

Note

> CASE must end with an ENDCASE statement.

Using IF with Logical Operators

Like the CASE statement, the IF statement is a conditional command that executes command lines after logical expressions have been satisfied. Unlike the CASE statement, the IF statement offers the power and flexibility of logical comparisons between fields. The IF statement uses this general format:

```
IF logical expression #1.
command lines.
ELSEIF logical expression #2.
command lines.
ELSE.
command lines.
ENDIF.
```

The program checks to see whether logical expression #1 is true. (*Logical expression* and the operators are defined in the following section.) If logical expression #1 is true, the program executes the command lines under that statement. If not, the program checks the second logical expression. If that expression is true, the command lines under that statement are executed. If that expression is false as well, the program executes the lines under the ELSE statement.

Keep in mind the following points when using ELSE:

- The ELSE statement has an implied logic: If all the other logical expressions are false, the ELSE statement is true. It is comparable to the WHEN OTHERS command in the CASE statement.

- The command lines can consist of any code available in ABAP/4.

- IF must end with an ENDIF statement.

- The logical expressions offer great flexibility in their definition. For example, ELSEIF and ELSE are optional statements. The ELSEIF statement lets you specify additional logical expressions if the first logical expression is found to be false, and the ELSE statement specifies commands that are executed if all the logical expressions under IF and ELSEIF are found to be false.

Tip

You can have as many ELSEIF statements as you want; however, for the sake of performance, you should try to limit ELSEIF statements to a maximum of four. As with the CASE statement, put the statement that's "most likely to be true" first, for better performance. That way, most of the time the program will execute fewer lines of code.

USING COMPARISON OPERATORS

The logical expression can be defined in several ways. For example, the expression could contain two fields that are compared:

```
DATA:    W_YEAR1(4) TYPE N,
W_YEAR2(4) TYPE N.
W_YEAR1 = 2013.
W_YEAR2 = 2014.
IF W_YEAR1 > W_YEAR2.
WRITE 'Year 1 is greater than Year 2.'.
 ELSEIF W_YEAR1    < W_YEAR2.
```

```
WRITE 'Year 1 is less than Year 2.'.
ELSE.
WRITE 'Year 1 equals Year 2.'.
ENDIF.
```

In this case, the output would be Year 1 is less than Year 2. (2013 is not greater than 2014.)

In comparing fields, you can use several operators, with this syntax:

```
IF FIELD1 operator FIELD2.
command code.
ENDIF.
```

operator is used to compare FIELD1 and FIELD2. Table 4.1 describes the possible operators.

Table 4.1 Logical Operators

Operator	Meaning
>, GT	Greater than
<, LT	Less than
>=, => GE	Greater than or equal to
<=, =< LE	Less than or equal to
=, EQ	Equal to
<>,><,NE	Not equal to
BETWEEN *value 1* and *value 2*	Inclusively between the two values
IS INITIAL	The contents of the variable haven't changed
IS NOT INITIAL	The contents of the variable have changed
CO	Contains only
CA	Contains any
CS	Contains string
CP	Contains pattern

Tip

As with CASE and ELSEIF, put the most likely logical expression at the top of the IF statement to improve performance.

In both the WHEN and IF statements, several conditions/logical expressions can be grouped together with AND or OR.

The definition of inclusive for the BETWEEN operator means that the two outer range values are included as being part of the true value range. The last four operators in the table are strictly used for string comparison. The first nine comparison operators can be used for either character comparisons or value comparisons.

COMPARING NON-NUMERIC VALUES

For the greater than/less than operators, two fields are compared, and one is greater than/ equal to/less than the other. If the fields being compared are numeric values, it's relatively easy to determine the status (greater than/equal to/less than). For non-numeric values, the way a character is determined to be greater than or less than another character is based on position in the alphabet. A word beginning with Z would be "greater than" a word beginning with A. And of course two letters that are identical would be equal to each other.

USING EQUAL/NOT EQUAL OPERATORS

For the equal/not equal comparison operators, the one value is either equal to or not equal to the second value. The logical expression is true or false, depending on which operator is used. The logical expression for the following example is true, as 3 doesn't equal 5; if the not equal sign (< >) is replaced with an equal sign (=), on the other hand, the logical expression is false:

```
IF 3 <> 5.
WRITE '3 does not equal 5.'.
ENDIF.
```

DETERMINING WHETHER VALUES HAVE CHANGED (IS INITIAL)

For the IS INITIAL comparison, the program determines whether the contents of the current variable have changed since the beginning of the program. If the contents are the same, the logical expression is true. It checks whether the contents are equal to the initial value for that type of field, as shown in Table 4.2.

Table 4.2 IS INITIAL Values after Formatting

Data Type	Initial Value
C	...(blank line)
D	00000000
F	0.0
I	0
N	00....0
P	0
T	000000
X	X00

© 2014 Cengage Learning.

In the following code lines, the program checks whether the contents of a variable have changed. If they haven't, a WRITE statement executes:

```
DATA:     W_DATA(10) TYPE C.
IF SY-DATUM = '122596'.
W_DATA = 'CHRISTMAS'.
ENDIF.
IF W_DATA IS INITIAL.
WRITE.'Today is not Christmas'.
ELSE.
WRITE:     'Today is Christmas'.
ENDIF.
```

DETERMINING WHETHER A VALUE IS INCLUDED IN A RANGE (IS BETWEEN)

The IS BETWEEN comparison operator checks to see whether the mentioned field is equal to or between the two fields mentioned in the logical expression. Because it checks to see whether the field is equal to either of the two limits, this comparison is inclusive.

Here, because 3 is in the specified range (3 to 9), the logical expression is true, and the WRITE statement is executed:

```
IF 3 BETWEEN 3 AND 9.
 WRITE 'The value is in the number range.'.
ENDIF.
```

USING THE NOT OPERATOR

It's possible to set up a logical expression to see whether the logical expression is false by using the NOT command. The format of the NOT command looks like this:

```
IF NOT (logical expression).
command line.
ENDIF.
```

If the logical expression in the parentheses is true, the entire logical expression is false, and vice versa. It's a little confusing to understand at first, but the NOT statement makes whatever is true false and whatever is false true.

COMPARING CHARACTER FIELDS (CO, CA, CS, AND CP)

The last four comparison operators are used to compare character fields.

CO (Contains Only)

CO is essentially the same as EQ (=), but with a little bit of flexibility. If one field contains only the same data as the other field, the logical expression is true:

```
DATA:    W_FIELD1(4) TYPE C,
         W_FIELD2(4) TYPE C.
MOVE 'ABCD' TO W_FIELD1.
MOVE 'ABCD' TO W_FIELD2.
IF W_FIELD1 CO W_FIELD2.
WRITE 'The two fields are exactly the same'.
ENDIF.
```

CO is one of the strictest comparison operators. The comparison is case sensitive. However, if the first field contains only characters that are represented in the second field, the logical expression would evaluate as true.

```
DATA:    W_FIELD1(5),
W_FIELD2(5).
MOVE 'ABABAB1' TO W_FIELD1.
MOVE 'ABC' TO W_FIELD2.
IF W_FIELD1 CO W_FIELD2.
WRITE 'True'.
ENDIF.
```

The system field SY-FDPOS contains the length of string W_FIELD2 if the comparison is true. If the comparison is false, SY-FDPOS contains the length of the offset of characters that do not occur in both strings W_FIELD1 and W_FIELD2. In the previous example, the value of SY-FDPOS is 6.

For more information on this, check out this reference: http://help.sap.com/saphelp_nw04/ helpdata/en/fc/eb3516358411d1829f0000e829fbfe/content.htm.

The opposite operator of CO is CN. It is equivalent to NOT <CO *logical expression*>.

CA (Contains Any)

The CA (contains any) operator checks to see whether any letter in W_FIELD1 is also in W_FIELD2. In the following example, the logical expression is true because W_FIELD1 and W_FIELD2 share the common letter D:

```
MOVE 'ABCD' TO W_FIELD1.
MOVE 'DEFG1' TO W_FIELD2.
IF W_FIELD1 CA W_FIELD2.
WRITE 'At least one letter in field 1 matches at least one letter in field 2.'.
ENDIF.
```

The comparison is case sensitive. The opposite operator of CA is NA. It is equivalent to NOT <CA *logical expression*>.

CS (Contains String)

The CS (contains string) comparison operator checks to see whether FIELD2 is contained in FIELD1. The following logical expression is true, as the letters EC appear in FIELD1 and FIELD2:

```
DATA:  W_FIELD1(4) TYPE C,
W_FIELD2(2) TYPE C.
MOVE    'ABCD' TO W_FIELD1.
MOVE    'BC'       TO W_FIELD2.
IF W_FIELD1 CS W_FIELD2.
WRITE 'Field 2 is a part of Field 1. '..
ENDIF.
```

The comparison is not case sensitive, and spaces can be ignored.

If FIELD2 contained the letters BD in this example, however, the expression would be false, because FIELD1 contains those letters, but not in that order.

For CS, the system field SY-FDPOS is set to the number of the position of the first character of FIELD1. In this case, SY-FDPOS would contain the value 2. The opposite operator of CS is NS. It is equivalent to NOT <CS *logical expression*>.

CP (Contains Pattern)

For the last string comparison operator, CP (contains pattern), a few special characters must be defined:

*	Stands for any string.
+	Stands for any character.
#	Means take the next character literally, which means that #* equals the literal asterisk (*), rather than the wildcard.

These special characters allow you to search for strings very loosely inside fields:

```
DATA:  W_FIELD1(4) TYPE C,
MOVE   'ABCD' TO W_FIELD1.
IF W_FIELD1   CP   '*A++D*'.
WRITE 'Field 1 contains those letters!'.
ENDIF.
```

Note

If you're doing lengthy comparisons through a large table, avoid using CP and CS, as they take quite a bit of processing time.

This example searches W_FIELD1 for the letters A and D with any two letters between them and finds that they do exist two letters apart. Thus, the case is true, and the output is written to the screen.

The opposite operator of CP is NP. It is equivalent to NOT <CP *logical expression*>.

When you're getting your data from the database, it's preferable to search by string/pattern comparison there, rather than waiting until the data is inside the program. Let the SQL statement and the database do as much work as possible for you. SQL and the SELECT statements for the database are discussed in Chapter 8, "Using SAP SQL to Access Database Tables."

NESTING STATEMENTS

CASE statements can be nested inside CASE statements and inside IF statements, and IF statements can be nested in other IF statements and in CASE statements. The nesting offers a powerful tool; however, as nesting grows more complex, so does the difficulty of following what the program is doing. Be careful to map your logic step by step when using either of these statements or any combination of both of them.

A general rule of thumb is to avoid nesting three or more levels deep. Nesting a CASE statement inside an IF statement inside another IF statement? Try to figure out a better way to sort out your data—your program has become much too precise. On the other hand, here's a good example of nesting:

```
PARAMETERS:  ANSWER(4) TYPE C,   "Do you want a gift for Christmas?
GIFT(10)     TYPE C.   "What do you want?
IF ANSWER = 'YES'. CASE GIFT.
WHEN 'TOY'.
WRITE 'You want a toy'. WHEN 'BIKE'.
WRITE 'You want a bike'. WHEN OTHERS.
WRITE 'I don't know what you want.'. ENDCASE. ELSE.
WRITE: 'BAH HUMBUG!'.
ENDIF.
```

This example checks to see whether the user wants a gift for Christmas. If he answers yes, the code checks what he wants and outputs it to the screen. If the user says he doesn't want a gift, the program outputs some humor.

SUMMARY

ABAP/4 uses three conditional comparison operators. Use the CASE statement if the value of the field is known. The IF statement can be widely used for any comparisons, but it is generally used when comparing two fields. ON CHANGE OF is discussed in Chapter 6.

Remember to put the logical expression or case that's likeliest to be true at the top of your conditional structure so that the program won't waste time checking code that's not useful. By planning ahead and keeping good habits with your programs, you'll develop good code first and not have to fix bad code later. In SAP, the initial emphasis is to get the system up as fast as possible and then to stabilize it once it's running. If you take a few extra minutes or hours planning now, it could save you days in the future.

CHAPTER 5

USING THE LOOPING COMMANDS

IN THIS CHAPTER

- Using the DO Loop Command
- Using the WHILE Loop
- Using the LOOP Statement

SAP's looping commands play an important role in processing the data obtained from the relational tables. In SAP, large sets of data are processed. The looping commands allow programs to upload, download, or even process data record by record. To upload data in the most efficient way from the database, programs should use the SELECT * statement, which is a part of the SAP SQL. This statement is covered in subsequent chapters. At all other times when data needs to be processed, the looping commands will be used.

In ABAP/4, the three main looping commands are DO, WHILE, and LOOP. The DO command is used to repeat a process a certain number of times or until an error is encountered. The WHILE command repeats the process enclosed by the WHILE and ENDWHILE commands as long as a logical expression remains true. The LOOP command loops through internal tables to process each record contained in the table. The LOOP command can also be used to process field groups (which are discussed in Chapter 10, "Advanced Data Outputs").

USING THE DO LOOP COMMAND

The DO loop is used in ABAP/4 to process a set of commands enclosed by DO and ENDDO. The general syntax of the command is as follows:

```
DO [ N TIMES].
<commands>
ENDDO.
```

N is a numeric value that can also be represented dynamically by a field. If N TIMES is added to the DO command, commands are repeated N times, even if an error occurs; commands can be any set of ABAP/4 commands that are syntactically correct.

For example, this code will write 66 lines to the page and then terminate:

```
DO 66 TIMES.
  WRITE: / 'This loop pass is number ', sy-index.
ENDDO.
```

The output is as follows:

```
This loop pass is number 1
This loop pass is number 2
This loop pass is number 3
...
...
This loop pass is number 66
```

The system field, SY-INDEX, automatically stores the number of the current loop pass. When you use the READ and MODIFY commands, you'll rely on SY-INDEX heavily, along with an index when you process internal tables. The N field can also be a numeric variable.

Note

You must be careful to differentiate between the system fields, SY-TABIX and SY-INDEX. SY-INDEX is incremented during specific looping commands such as DO and WHILE, whereas SY-TABIX is incremented when operations are performed on internal tables. SY-TABIX refers to the current record in the internal table. So, while looping through an internal table, SY-TABIX is incremented, but SY-INDEX is not.

To read through an internal table, one possible way is to read the table line by line until the last line. This code illustrates how you can use a DO loop that has only the number of passes that the table has lines:

```
TABLES:  mseg.
DATA:    BEGIN OF inttab OCCURS 50.
         INCLUDE STRUCTURE mseg.
```

```
DATA:    END OF inttab.
DATA:    w_lines TYPE i.
SELECT * FROM mseg INTO TABLE inttab
WHERE matnr LIKE '4%'.
DESCRIBE TABLE inttab LINES w_lines.
DO w_lines TIMES.
  READ TABLE inttab INDEX sy-index.
  WRITE: / inttab-mblnr, inttab-mjahr, inttab-zeile.
ENDDO.
```

This code reads certain records from the material master table, MSEG, into an internal table with the same structure as MSEG. Once the table is populated from the SQL statement, you use the DESCRIBE TABLE command to put the total number of records from internal table INTTAB into the field W_LINES. Then the DO command loops only that number of times, reading each record one by one and printing each of them to the screen. If the number of records inside an internal table is known, it's preferable to use the DO N TIMES command to process the command lines, rather than using the WHILE loop. (However, the LOOP AT command is preferable when dealing with internal tables. See the later section "Using the LOOP Statement" for details.) The previous example is used to demonstrate how the DO loop can be set with a dynamic variable.

Exiting the Loop

If the N TIMES isn't added, an EXIT or STOP command must be incorporated somewhere inside commands. If neither EXIT nor STOP is incorporated, the program enters an endless loop. The program then encounters a runtime error if run online, as the system won't let an application run for more than 15 minutes (depending on how the system is configured). If the program is run in the background (as a batch job), the job associated with the program must be terminated by a system operator.

An EXIT command is preferable because the program begins with the subsequent line after the ENDDO statement when EXIT is executed. If a STOP command is called, the END-OF-SELECTION event is triggered. A general way to exit a DO...ENDDO statement is to incorporate an IF...ENDIF statement that checks the value of the system error status (SY-SUBRC):

```
DO.
    <COMMAND…>
  IF SY-SUBRC <> 0.
    EXIT.
  ENDIF.
ENDDO.
```

If the commands produce a result that changes the system variable, SY-SUBRC, to be a value other than zero, then the EXIT command is executed.

The SY-INDEX system field can also be used to invoke an EXIT command. The following example will exit the DO loop once the SY-INDEX reaches 10 iterations.

```
DO.
  IF sy-index = 10.
    EXIT.
  ENDIF.
ENDDO.
```

When to Use DO Loops

A good example of when it's preferable to use a DO command is when the program reads in data from an external flat file:

```
PARAMETERS: p_file(60) DEFAULT  '/users/programmer/dataset.txt' LOWER CASE.
DATA:   BEGIN OF inttab OCCURS 1000,
     text(255),
          END OF inttab.
OPEN DATASET p_file FOR INPUT IN TEXT MODE ENCODING DEFAULT.
DO.
  READ DATASET p_file INTO inttab.
  IF sy-subrc <> 0.
    EXIT.
  ENDIF.
  APPEND inttab.
  CLEAR inttab.
ENDDO.
```

Because the program doesn't know how long the data file is, in order to read it into memory, the program continues indefinitely until no more data is found (SY-SUBRC <> 0). The program then exits from the DO loop.

Nesting DO Loops

One important piece of information to note is that DO loops can be nested. Nesting loops means including loops within loops. Although nesting increases the risk of endless loops, it also adds more flexibility to what the program can accomplish.

The following program shows a nested DO loop. The final ENDDO statement is reached when the commands within it are completed 66 times. These commands include a loop of writing text five times for every loop pass:

```
DO 66 TIMES.
  DO 5 TIMES.
    WRITE:'THIS IS A SAMPLE PROGRAM.'.
  ENDDO.
  WRITE    'THIS WILL BE WRITTEN ONLY 66 TIMES'.
ENDDO.
```

The result of running this program is an output of THIS IS A SAMPLE PROGRAM. 330 times and 66 lines of THIS WILL BE WRITTEN ONLY 66 TIMES.

USING THE WHILE LOOP

The WHILE loop executes the commands enclosed by the WHILE and ENDWHILE statements until the logical expression associated with the WHILE statement becomes false. The general format for the WHILE statement is as follows:

```
WHILE <logical expression>.
    <Commands...>
ENDWHILE.
```

The WHILE command uses the same comparison operators and logical expressions as the IF...ENDIF statement. The WHILE command is preferable when considering the performance of the programs. The loop continues until the logical statement is found to be untrue. In a DO loop, the loop executes one more time to do the check; a WHILE loop terminates exactly as the statement is found to be untrue. The program exits the loop if a false statement is found. Again, you can use any set of ABAP/4 commands.

The following code reads through the internal table INT_TAB line by line (by the index—that is, the index refers to a specific line number in the table) and transfers one field from the internal table to a working field, W_FIELD:

```
DATA: w_index LIKE sy-tabix
CLEAR w_index.
WHILE sy-subrc = 0.
  w_index = w_index +  1.
  READ TABLE int_tab INDEX w_index.
  MOVE int_tab-field1 TO w_field.
ENDWHILE.
```

If the internal table contains 100 records, on the 101st loop pass, an error occurs (SY-SUBRC = 4). The program exits the loop and executes the command after ENDWHILE.

Note

It's possible to put an EXIT command inside a WHILE loop, but it's preferable to make the exit part of the logical expression.

Nesting WHILE Loops

As with DO, WHILE loops can be nested. Take care that a nested loop doesn't cause the logical expression in the outer loop to change unintentionally. Check all conditions for single-pass loops as well as nested loops to make sure that the conditions are "airtight" for the loops to be executing. An example of a problematic nested loop might be one where the first WHILE loop is reading an internal table and the logical expression uses the system field SY-TABIX. If the second WHILE loop also reads another internal table, the SY-TABIX value will change back and forth between the two loops and will cause confusion within the program.

Using the LOOP Statement

The LOOP command is used to loop through internal tables and for extracting from field groups (see Chapter 10). The general syntax for the LOOP command is:

```
LOOP [AT internal table [WHERE logical expression]]
   <commands...>
ENDLOOP.
```

The LOOP command by itself is used to process field groups (covered in Chapter 10).

When the program processes internal tables, it must read a table line into the header line of the table and then process that line. A good way to read these lines is with the LOOP AT internal table command. This command copies the values of the item data into the header data for manipulation by the user, one item at a time. This command is explained in much more detail in Chapter 6, "Working with Internal Tables."

When to Use the LOOP Command

This miniature program loads an internal table (INT_TAB) with data and appends 100 fields into the table. Then, to loop through the table, it utilizes the LOOP AT INT_TAB command to read the internal table's fields line by line and outputs them to the page (code shown later in this section):

```
DATA:    BEGIN OF int_tab OCCURS 100,
           field1(5) TYPE n,
           field2(5) TYPE c,
         END OF int_tab.
DO 100 TIMES.
  MOVE sy-index TO   int_tab-field1 .
  MOVE 'ABODE1' TO int_tab-field2.
  APPEND int_tab.
  CLEAR int_tab.
ENDDO.
LOOP AT int_tab.
  WRITE:/ int_tab-field1, int_tab-field2.
ENDLOOP.
```

The comparative latter code using the DO loop is much more complicated:

```
DO.
  READ TABLE int_tab INDEX sy-index.
  IF sy-subrc <> 0.
    EXIT.
  ENDIF.
  WRITE: / int_tab-field1,    int_tab-field2.
ENDDO.
```

If the two codes are compared, the LOOP code is much less complicated, and the DO loop code is processed one more time than the LOOP code. The LOOP code finishes as the last record is read from the table and processed. The DO loop is blind to how many records there are in the table, so the table is read one more time. An error is indicated in SY-SUBRC, and then the loop terminates.

Looping Selectively Through Internal Tables

Another great feature of the LOOP command is the LOOP AT <INTERNAL TABLE> WHERE logical expression addition. By defining a logical expression at the end of the LOOP command, the program can specify which lines of the table it reads. For the following example, assume that the internal table that's defined has already been filled with data from the database:

```
DATA:    BEGIN OF int_tab OCCURS 1000,
           gsber LIKE bseg-gsber,    "country code
           belnr LIKE bseg-belnr,    "document number
           text1(50) TYPE c,         "text
         END OF int_tab.
```

```
*..the table is filled with data..
LOOP AT int_tab WHERE gsber = '01'.
  WRITE int_tab-text1.
  WRITE int_tab-belnr.
ENDLOOP.
```

Although there may be 1,000 or more records in this table, only the ones with the country code (GSBER) of '01' will be displayed. This addition is a very efficient way of displaying only information related to certain criteria—a very important capability when processing reports or interfaces.

Another addition to the LOOP command is LOOP AT <INTERNAL TABLE> FROM <VALUE 1> TO <VALUE2>. <VALUE1> and <VALUE2> can be set dynamically by being defined as variables or statically as predefined numbers. This addition to the LOOP AT command allows the program to loop through only a certain portion of an internal table. This addition is very useful, especially when an internal table contains thousands of records.

```
DATA:     BEGIN OF int_tab OCCURS 1000,
            gsber LIKE bseg-gsber,     "country code
            belnr LIKE bseg-belnr,     "document number
            text1(50) TYPE c,          "text
          END OF int_tab.
*..the table is filled with data..
LOOP AT int_tab FROM 2 TO 10.
  WRITE int_tab-text1.
  WRITE int_tab-belnr.
ENDLOOP.
```

Now, if you are really feeling confident in your abilities, combine the last two additions in one statement, which results in the following:

```
DATA:     BEGIN OF int_tab OCCURS 1000,
            gsber LIKE bseg-gsber,     "country code
            belnr LIKE bseg-belnr,     "document number
            text1(50) TYPE c,          "text
          END OF int_tab.
*..the table is filled with data..
LOOP AT int_tab FROM 2 TO 10 WHERE gsber = '01'.
  WRITE int_tab-text1.
  WRITE int_tab-belnr.
ENDLOOP.
```

By combining both statements, the internal table is selectively read only from records 2 to 10 where the country code (GSBER) is equal to '01'.

SUMMARY

Three commands in ABAP/4 are used to loop through data:

- The DO loop is useful when the number of loop passes is known or when an EXIT or STOP command is part of the commands in order to prevent an endless loop.

- The WHILE loop contains a logical expression along with the WHILE command. All commands included between WHILE and ENDWHILE are executed as long as that logical expression remains true.

- The LOOP command is used to loop through internal tables in order to automatically read the data line by line.

It's essential that you understand the subtle differences between these commands and when to use one rather than the other. For example, you need to know that you can put an EXIT command inside a WHILE loop, but that the preferred method is to make the EXIT part of the logical expression. Remember that SY-INDEX is incremented for the DO and WHILE commands and that SY-TABIX is incremented for the LOOP command.

Quite a bit of looping deals with internal tables, which are discussed in depth in the next chapter.

CHAPTER 6

WORKING WITH INTERNAL TABLES

IN THIS CHAPTER

- Understanding the Structure of an Internal Table
- Defining a Table
- Manipulating Data in Tables
- Refreshing Tables
- Using Other Table Commands

In every implementation of SAP, the necessity to process multitudes of records predominates most systems. To store these records, you use internal tables. *Internal tables*—data structures declared in ABAP/4 code—are a very important part of ABAP/4 programming. They are used in 90 percent of every piece of code that's put into production, so you must devote careful attention to learning how to use and—more important—how *not* to use internal tables in your programs.

For example, keep in mind the following points about internal tables:

- Internal tables have the same general structure as database tables, but initially contain no records.
- Internal tables are very useful in applications where they're generally used to keep data in an organized structure while the data is manipulated in the program. Internal tables store data in the same manner as database tables, except that the data is held in

current memory rather than stored on disk somewhere. The data is used by the current program and disappears after the program ends. The data is generally extracted from various database tables and appended or added to the internal table.

■ Internal tables don't have primary keys as database tables have, but they can be read with a key in a different manner than database tables are read.

■ Because internal tables are held in the current program's memory space, the access time to read and process the data stored inside the internal tables is significantly less than a read of a database table. However, the available memory restricts how much space is allotted to these tables, so there's a tradeoff when dealing with the internal tables. Also, internal table processing uses CPU time. You, as the programmer, must weigh whether it's beneficial for the database or for the CPU to do the work in your data processing.

■ There are additional commands to loop through internal tables and process individual records one by one.

This chapter introduces internal tables and explains how to declare them in the data declarations. Reading from, writing to, and modifying the data in the tables are topics covered in later parts of the chapter. The final section deals with looping through internal tables in order to process records and sort the internal tables.

Tip

If you read any of the chapters in this book twice, make sure that this chapter is one of them. If internal tables are used correctly in your programs, you'll be called a "performance guru." If you don't understand internal tables and use them incorrectly, you'll be known as the programmer who slows down the system.

Understanding the Structure of an Internal Table

An internal table consists of the same structure as a database table. The table has a header record and individual item records. Figure 6.1 shows how an internal table looks in the ABAP/4 debugger. The record with the angle brackets (>>>) is the header record, and the numbered records are the item records. Table 6.1 shows an example of the structure of an internal table.

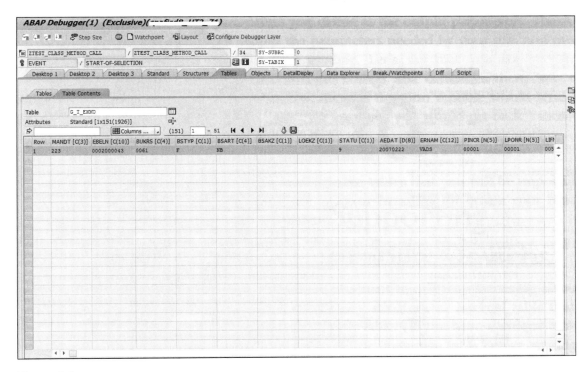

Figure 6.1
An internal table in the ABAP/4 debugger.

Table 6.1   A Sample Table Structure

FIELD1	FIELDS	FIELDS	FIELDX
Header			
Item1			
Item2			
Item3			
Item4			

The *header record* is a temporary "holding" record for the internal table. The header record space holds a copy of whichever item record has been read or modified, as well as any new record being added to the table. The header record is where data is stored before it's written to the table or after it's read from the table. When a program loops through the table, the current record is also stored in the header record. The header record is the record that's processed when the table is referenced in the program. The *item records* are the records already stored in the internal table. When an item record is read—either by a direct read or by looping through the table—a copy of the item record is made to the header record.

DEFINING A TABLE

The general format for defining a table is used in the data declaration part of the ABAP/4 code. After the REPORT statement and the TABLES declaration, the internal table is declared. Here's the general format:

```
REPORT ZSAMPLE1.

TABLES: VBFA, BSEG.
DATA: BEGIN OF <internal table name> OCCURS <number of records>,
        FIELD1   TYPE C,
        FIELD2 LIKE MSEG-MATNR,
        FIELDX(5) TYPE P,
     END OF internal table name.
```

The internal table name can be any name, but a typical naming convention is to name the internal table INT_name, where name is a general description of the table. The INT part of the table name will remind you many lines down in the program that the data structure you're dealing with is an internal table. An example of a bad table name would be naming an internal table MATERIAL that listed material numbers along with plant and quantity data. A better name would be INT_MATERIAL. Using MATERIAL for the name could get confusing when editing the code at a later date.

Another way to declare an internal table is to "include" an existing structure in the Data Dictionary in the internal table. There are two ways to accomplish this task. The first format is:

```
DATA: BEGIN OF INT_STPO OCCURS 100.
        INCLUDE STRUCTURE STPO.
DATA: END OF INT_STPO.
```

The benefit of this format is that you can include extra fields in your internal table. An example of extra fields is:

```
DATA:   BEGIN OF INT_STPO OCCURS 100.
        INCLUDE STRUCTURE STPO.
DATA:   EXTRA_FIELD1(20),
        EXTRA_FIELD2(20).
DATA: END OF INT_STPO.
```

Determining the Number of Records

Number of records is at minimum zero and at maximum a parameter set by your system administrators. A general rule is that you shouldn't have more than 100,000 records allocated to internal tables in your entire program. This number defines how much memory is allocated from the system to your application.

Caution

Don't just pick a random number out of the air and give that number to your internal table. The consequences of underestimating the number of records is a performance issue with your program. It's better to pick a number that's too small than a number that is too big:

- If the number you choose is too small, each record that's appended to the table after that maximum number is stored in the paging area of memory. This memory area is slower to respond than allotted memory claimed by your program, and therefore the program runs a little slower.

- If the number is too large, the program fails to initiate and won't run. If the number is very large, it impedes the performance of other applications running on the system. The extra records are stored in the paging area rather than in the memory allocated to the internal table.

Another way to estimate the number of records is to write the program and find out how many records are generally extracted from the database. Then go back into the code and adjust the number of records to reflect an accurate number. This last suggestion is a tough one, because most development environments or instances don't have a good data copy of the current production system. Talk to your system administrator to find out the current status of the system.

A typical program with an internal table would follow this structure:

```
REPORT ZSAMPLE.
TABLES: vbfa,
        vbap,
        bkpf,
        bseg.
```

```
PARAMETERS:   p_vbeln LIKE vbap-vbeln,
              p_gjahr LIKE bkpf-gjahr.

DATA:      BEGIN OF int_tab OCCURS 1000,
               vbeln LIKE vbap-vbeln,        "document number
               gjahr LIKE bkpf-gjahr,        "fiscal year
               bukrs LIKE bkpf-bukrs,        "company code
               text(50) TYPE c.             "text
DATA:      END OF int_tab.
DATA:      w_flag.      "flag

START-OF-SELECTION.
<DATA SELECTION CODE.......>
```

Code shows what would appear in a typical program. The internal table represents fields that will be copied from the tables listed and then manipulated later in the program. The words at the end of each LIKE statement are descriptive remarks. The quotation marks (") denote a comment that begins to the right of the quotation mark.

Using Field Strings

Field strings are useful for a variety of purposes. They can be used as keys to search large internal tables for information. (This application of a field string is discussed in the later section, "Using the WITH KEY Addition with READ.")

Field strings consist of multiple fields, just like internal tables. In fact, a field string is best represented in structure by one record of an internal table. However, field strings differ from internal tables in that field strings are only one record in length. Field strings contain no header record; there's only one item record. The manner in which a field string is declared is very similar to how an internal table is declared:

```
DATA: BEGIN OF F_STRING,
    FIELD1,
    FIELD2,
    FIELDS,
    FIELDX,
DATA: END OF F_STRING.
```

The structure of a field string is similar to that of a regular data field because there's only room for one piece of data; however, it's also the same as an internal table in that it can contain information about multiple fields.

You can fill a field string and then move it into an internal table where you can append, delete, or modify it. This application of the field string uses it as the data of a single record. The field string, once filled, is then moved to the internal table's header record, where it's processed against the table.

The following program selects data from the user table ZZUSERS and places the information in the field string F_STRING. Assume that ZZUSERS contains all the data needed for this program to work (it's a fictitious table created for the purpose of this example only). Once the data is read from the program, the program uses the area code of the telephone number to determine the area in which the user lives and places the appropriate city in the field. If the area code isn't one of the three cities the program checks, the record isn't added to the internal table:

```
TABLES: zzusers.
DATA:    BEGIN OF f_string,
         name(10)    TYPE c,
         address(50) TYPE c,
         phone(10)   TYPE c,
         area(20)    TYPE c.
DATA: END OF f_string.
DATA: BEGIN OF int_table OCCURS 100,
         name(10)        TYPE c,
         address(50)     TYPE c,
         phone(10)       TYPE c,
         area(20)        TYPE c.
DATA: END OF int_table.

START-OF-SELECTION.
  SELECT * FROM zzusers WHERE name LIKE 'A%'.
    MOVE zzusers-name      TO f_string-name.
    MOVE zzusers-address   TO f_string-address.
    MOVE zzusers-phone     TO f_string-phone.

CASE zzusers-phone+0(3).
  WHEN '202'.
    MOVE 'WASHINGTON DC'     TO F_STRING-AREA.
  WHEN '310'.
    MOVE 'los angeles'      TO F_STRING-AREA.
  WHEN '916'.
    MOVE    'sacramento'    TO F_STRING-AREA.
  WHEN OTHERS.
    MOVE    'undetermined'  TO F_STRING-AREA.
ENDCASE.
```

```
IF F_STRING-AREA NE 'undetermined'.
  APPEND F_STRING TO INT_TABLE.
ENDIF.
CLEAR F_STRING.

ENDSELECT.
```

The same result is achieved by moving the data to the internal table's header record and appending or clearing the record, if the area is determined or undetermined, respectively. The use of a field string keeps the data transfer uncomplicated. The data is transferred to the internal table only if the condition is finally met. The APPEND statement is used to move all fields from the structure to the corresponding fields of the internal table.

Field strings are used in the same general manner in field groups (see Chapter 10, "Advanced Data Outputs").

Including Structures

When internal tables or field strings are declared in the top part of the ABAP/4 program, the structure of each must be defined according to the requirements of the program specifications. Sometimes the structures are very similar to tables already existing in the Data Dictionary. Rather than type 15–30 lines declaring all the same fields, the table's structure can be defined with the existing structure:

```
TABLES:    TABLE.
DATA:    BEGIN OF INT_TABLE OCCURS 100.
INCLUDE STRUCTURE
  TABLE. DATA:    END OF
  INT_TABLE.
```

The INCLUDE STRUCTURE TABLE command takes the preexisting structure and incorporates it into the structure of the internal table. TABLE can be any table (pooled, transparent, cluster, internal) defined already in the Data Dictionary. To check whether the table that will be included exists, check the Data Dictionary for that table. The table to be included also must be declared in the TABLES statement at the top of the program.

Notice the syntax of the table declaration. A period follows the first BEGIN OF... line; in a regular declaration, you use a comma. The INCLUDE STRUCTURE line must exist on its own, so the previous line of code must end in a period so that line is executed. (If this syntax is incorrect, a syntax check on the program highlights the problem.)

By including the structure of the preexisting table, you accomplish two tasks:

- If future releases of SAP include changes in the table structure, or if the existing table is modified, the code needs to be changed. When you define fields individually in the program, the code needs to be changed if the new table change affects the program. If the table is included as a structure, however, the program becomes dynamic and uses the current structure defined in the Data Dictionary.

- The most obvious benefit of typing INCLUDE STRUCTURE is the time savings. Instead of typing multiple lines, you just type one. This benefit is secondary, as the first benefit has more substance—but in the SAP environment, where time is definitely a big factor, this command allows you to save time without sacrificing quality.

Extra fields can be declared in the internal table along with the preexisting structure. They are simply declared before or after the INCLUDE STRUCTURE statement:

```
TABLES:   BKPF.
DATA:     BEGIN OF INTJTABLE OCCURS 100,
F_YEAR1 LIKE BKPF-GJAHR,
F_YEAR2 LIKE BKPF-GJAHR.
INCLUDE STRUCTURE BKPF. DATA:
F_YEAR3 LIKE BKPF-GJAHR. DATA:     END OF
INT TABLE.
```

There are other additions to the include syntax that allow for even more flexibility, such as the addition of AS and RENAMING WITH SUFFIX.

```
TYPES: BEGIN OF t_fields,
       extra_field1(20),
       extra_field2(20),
       END OF t_fields.
DATA BEGIN OF fields.
  INCLUDE TYPE t_fields AS one RENAMING WITH SUFFIX _xtra1.
  INCLUDE TYPE t_fields AS two RENAMING WITH SUFFIX _xtra2.
  ...
DATA END OF fields.
```

By specifying the name ONE after the addition AS, you can address all components of the defined structure T_FIELDS.

With the addition RENAMING WITH SUFFIX, every individual component is renamed by adding the suffix, thus the naming conflicts between components of the same name will not occur.

Manipulating Data in Tables

Once you define an internal table, you should use it to its fullest capacity. SAP provides a strong set of commands for manipulating the data in tables. The commands are discussed in detail in the following sections, but here's a brief overview:

- You can move the data field-by-field to the internal table, or one record at a time—or you can add data to the table by appending it with the APPEND command. Using the COLLECT command, on the other hand, you can append new data and collect the same data together.

- If the data already exists and you need to change it, that's the time for the MODIFY command.

- Deleting a record? Use DELETE.

- When the data is in the internal table, you use the READ command to read the table.

- You clear an internal table with REFRESH or CLEAR. The differences are discussed shortly. REFRESH purges the entire table, and CLEAR clears the header record.

Moving Data into a Table

Initially, an internal table is just a structure consisting only of a blank header record. To fill the table, you must move data into the table. This data transfer is accomplished either by moving individual fields over to the header record or by moving a complete data record via a field string or from an existing record in another table. After the data is moved into the header record, the record can then be appended to the table and a new item record created. This section explains the differences between moving fields, corresponding data fields, or complete records over to the new internal table.

Moving Data Field-by-Field

The data can be transferred one field at a time until the record is full. If the data is coming from numerous sources, this method is usually the only option and is unavoidable. The positive point to this method is that it provides a good accounting of which data has been moved into the table. If a field is coded to be moved directly into the table, you can count on the fact that the data exists in the correct field in that internal table:

```
TYPES:   BEGIN OF ty_tab,
         name(10) TYPE c,
         age TYPE i,
         occupation(15) TYPE c.
```

```
TYPES: END OF ty_tab.
DATA: int_tab TYPE TABLE OF ty_tab INITIAL SIZE 100.
DATA: s_tab LIKE LINE OF int_tab.
DATA: field1(10) TYPE c VALUE 'ROBERT1',
      field2(3) TYPE n VALUE '36',
      field3(15) TYPE c VALUE 'Entertainer'.
CLEAR s_tab.
MOVE field1 TO s_tab-name.
MOVE field2 TO s_tab-age.
MOVE field3 TO s_tab-occupation.
APPEND s_tab TO int_tab.
```

The structure S_TAB and the first line of the internal table INT_TAB now contain the following data:

```
Field1      Field2       Field3
ROBERT      36           ENTERTAINER
```

If you add this record to the internal table, an item-level record is created exactly like the structure record. The structure record still contains the same data values until the data is cleared with a CLEAR statement, which overwrites it with different values.

Note

Because the WITH HEADER LINE addition is now obsolete, there are additional steps that are required to append a record into an internal table. The previous example uses a structure for capturing the data and then an APPEND statement to load the data into the internal table.

The INITIAL SIZE n statement predetermines the number of records that are available for the internal table. This has taken the place of the OCCURS n statement.

Moving Data with MOVE-CORRESPONDING

A faster method of moving data is using the command MOVE-CORRESPONDING. Use this command if the fields in the internal table are defined as being LIKE fields in the database table from which the data is being moved.

Caution

Be careful not to define different records as LIKE the same field; otherwise, the application won't move the data in the manner you expected. Instead, the application moves the same field from the database to both fields in the internal table.

In the following example, the fields BKPF-VBELN, BKPF-BUKRS, and BKPF-GJAHR are moved into the fields INT_TAB-FIELD1, INT_TAB-FIELD2, and INT_TAB-FIELDS, respectively:

```
TABLES bkpf.

TYPES:   BEGIN OF ty_tab,
         field1 TYPE bkpf-belnr,
         field2 TYPE bkpf-bukrs,
         fields TYPE bkpf-gjahr.
TYPES:   END OF ty_tab.

DATA: int_tab TYPE TABLE OF ty_tab INITIAL SIZE 100.
DATA: s_tab LIKE LINE OF int_tab.

START-OF-SELECTION.

  SELECT * FROM bkpf WHERE gjahr = '2010'.
    MOVE-CORRESPONDING bkpf TO s_tab.
    APPEND s_tab TO int_tab.
    CLEAR s_tab.
  ENDSELECT.

END-OF-SELECTION.
```

The APPEND S_TAB TO INT_TAB and CLEAR S_TAB commands are used to copy the BKPF data to the item level.

MOVE-CORRESPONDING takes up more CPU time than moving the data field-by-field or moving an entire record at a time into an internal table. The command is designed to be convenient for the programmer, but the convenience of the programmer over the overall system performance must be weighed when writing applications. All the fields defined inside the internal table also must be properly mapped to their associated fields in the database tables.

Note

When using MOVE-CORRESPONDING, make sure that no two fields in the internal table are defined as being like the same database field, or you'll get duplicate data. For example, if you defined an internal table with two fields named W_DOCN1 and W_DOCNO2 as being like BKPF-BELNR, the field BKPF-BELNR would be moved to both of those fields.

Data can be transferred from one record to another as long as the fields match. A typical application of this method is the transferring of a field string to an internal table:

```
TYPES:   BEGIN OF ty_tab,
         name(10) TYPE c,
         age TYPE i,
         occupation(15) TYPE c.
TYPES:   END OF ty_tab.
```

```
DATA: int_tab TYPE TABLE OF ty_tab INITIAL SIZE 100.
DATA: f_string LIKE LINE OF int_tab.

CLEAR f_string.
MOVE 'JOHN' TO f_string-name.
MOVE '100' TO f_string-age.
MOVE 'SALESMAN' TO f_string-occupation.
APPEND f_string TO int_tab.
```

A type-match error would occur in this example because the processor would see the field string moving a character into an integer field. If both the field string and the internal table contained only fields that contained only characters, the characters of the field string would be moved into the fields of the internal table, regardless of position. For example's sake, suppose that the field string and the internal table from the preceding example contained only fields of type C (all-character fields). The contents of the field string would be as follows:

```
F_STRING-NAME = JOHN
F_STRING-AGE = 100
F STRING-OCCUPATION = SALESMAN
```

The contents of the internal table after moving the field string to it would be

```
INT_TAB-NAME = JOHN
INT_TAB-OCCUPATION = 100
INT TAB-AGE =    SALESMAN
```

The program takes the characters from the field string and fills each field of the internal table individually until each field is filled, and then the next character is put into the next field—until the entire content of the field string is copied over or the internal table has no more room.

Appending Data to a Table (APPEND)

The APPEND command is used to add a record to an internal table. Once all the fields have been moved to or copied to the structure, the APPEND command copies the contents of the structure to a new item record at the end of the internal table. Here's the syntax:

```
SELECT * FROM <database table>.
MOVE-CORRESPONDING <database record> to <structure>.
APPEND <structure> to <internal table>.
CLEAR <structure>.
ENDSELECT.
```

The structure fields are filled with the corresponding fields from the database table record. Then the APPEND command is issued, and the record is copied from the structure to a new item record in the internal table.

Adding the CLEAR command after the APPEND command is a good programming habit. CLEAR clears the structure of any values, thus ensuring that no old data is transferred to new records. Get used to typing this command along with the APPEND, MODIFY, COLLECT, and DELETE commands.

The following tables illustrate what happens to values when you use these commands. Figure 6.2 shows the original values; Figure 6.3 shows the changed values after using APPEND; Figure 6.4 shows the changes after using CLEAR.

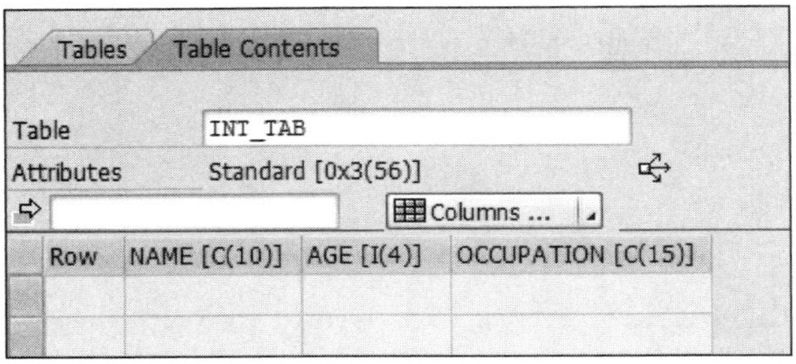

Figure 6.2
Internal table values before using the APPEND and CLEAR commands.

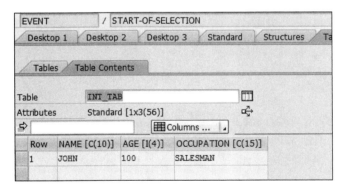

Figure 6.3
Internal table values after using APPEND.

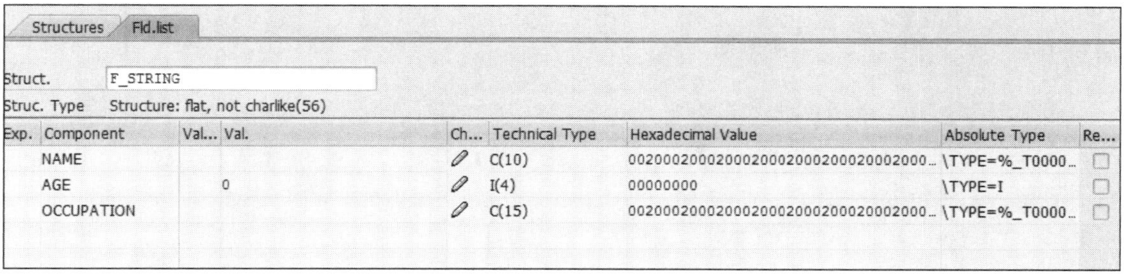

Structures	Fld.list						
Struct.	F_STRING						
Struc. Type	Structure: flat, not charlike(56)						
Exp.	Component	Val...	Val.	Ch...	Technical Type	Hexadecimal Value	Absolute Type	Re...
	NAME			✎	C(10)	0020002000200020002000200020002000...	\TYPE=%_T0000...	☐
	AGE		0	✎	I(4)	00000000	\TYPE=I	☐
	OCCUPATION			✎	C(15)	0020002000200020002000200020002000...	\TYPE=%_T0000...	☐

Figure 6.4
Internal table values after using CLEAR.

The APPEND command copies the contents of the structure and places it in a new item-level record in the internal table. The CLEAR command clears the contents of the structure. APPEND is used to add additional fields to the end of the internal table.

Caution

You can copy duplicate records to the internal table, but that's strongly discouraged. If the internal table is copied to the database, a database error occurs. Duplicate records can't exist at the database level.

Modifying Records (READ and MODIFY)

To change the value of a record or a field inside a record, the index or record number of the contents of that record must be determined, altered via a work-area structure, and then copied back to the same record number from which the original values were read. These steps must be followed because otherwise it is impossible to change an existing record; no other method is available.

The first step is to determine the SY-TABIX (line number) of the record to be read and/or modified. A READ statement is generally issued for this purpose. The READ statement copies a specified record to a work-area structure that will be used to modify the record in the internal table. This is the syntax:

```
CLEAR f_string.
READ TABLE int_tab WITH KEY name = 'JOHN' INTO f_string.
t_tabix = sy-tabix.
```

After the READ statement is issued, the item record is copied to the work-area structure F_STRING by using the WITH KEY statement.

```
READ TABLE int_tab WITH KEY name = 'JOHN' INTO f_string.
```

Another option is to use the SY-TABIX value with the READ statement. This example performs a read on the specific line of an internal table. The item will also be copied into a work-area structure for later processing.

```
CLEAR f_string.
READ TABLE int_tab WITH KEY name = 'JOHN' TRANSPORTING NO FIELDS.
t_tabix = sy-tabix.
READ TABLE int_tab INTO f_string index t_tabix.
```

Figure 6.5 shows how the table values have changed after using the READ command.

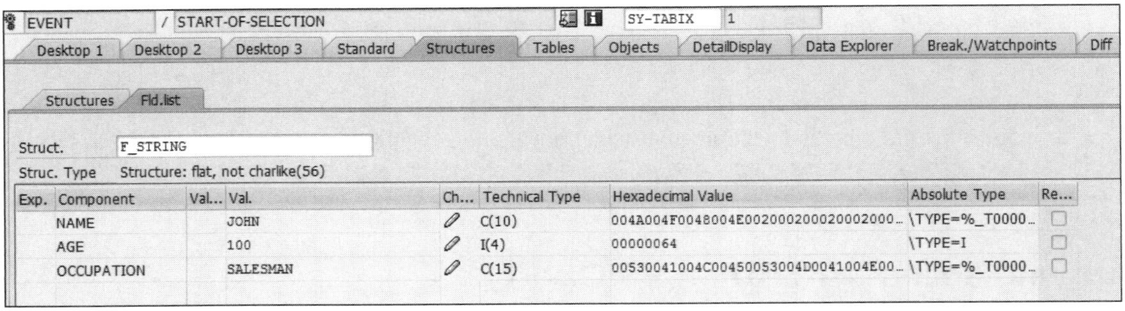

Figure 6.5
Contents of the table values after using READ.
Source: SAP AG or an SAP affiliate company. All rights reserved.

The same results would have been achieved had you issued this command:

```
READ TABLE INT_TAB into F_STRING INDEX 1.
```

The INDEX addition specifies which record at the item level is copied into the work area structure. The number specified can be a variable. Now that the record you want to manipulate is in the structure, you can change the contents of one of the fields to fit your specifications:

```
MOVE 'EEE' TO F_STRING-FIELD1.
```

Note

After the READ statement, if no record is found, SY-SURBC will be set to a value other than 0. Check Chapter 19, "ABAP Workbench (Debugger)," for more information on debugging.

With the record changed, you can issue a command to copy the new record over the old record at the item level:

```
MODIFY int_tab INDEX 1 FROM f_string.
CLEAR f_STRING.
```

Figure 6.6 shows what happens to the table values from Figure 6.5 after applying the MODIFY statement. The results of the CLEAR command for the work area structure are shown in Figure 6.7.

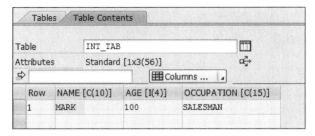

Figure 6.6
Contents of the table values after using MODIFY.

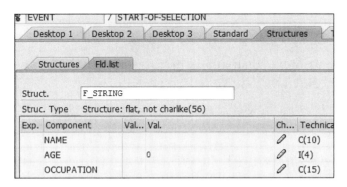

Figure 6.7
Contents of the table values after using CLEAR.

The MODIFY command copies the contents of the work area structure back to the item level with modifications. Even if the record is unaltered, the contents replace the old contents of the item record. As with the APPEND command, good programming practice is to use the CLEAR command directly after MODIFY. Using the CLEAR command ensures that the contents of the structure are fresh for the next new record. It's also possible to modify records using the INDEX addition that was introduced along with the READ command:

```
MODIFY <internal table> INDEX SY-index from <structure>
```

The addition of the INDEX feature copies the contents of the header record to the item record specified by index, which is the number of the record at the item level that's copied to the structure.

Deleting Records (DELETE)

Deleting a record from an internal table is essentially like using the MODIFY command, except for the fact that the record isn't changed; it's deleted. Here's the syntax:

```
DELETE <internal table>  [INDEX index].
DELETE <internal table> FROM <structure>.
```

The DELETE command compares the contents of the structure record with the contents of the item records and deletes the record if it matches exactly. If the INDEX addition is used, the record number at the item level specified by index is deleted.

New additions to the DELETE command allow you to delete duplicate records in internal tables as well as deleting certain records. To delete duplicate records, use the following syntax:

```
DELETE ADJACENT DUPLICATES FROM internal table COMPARING <fields>.
```

You must specify the internal table as well as the fields that will be compared to determine if records are duplicates. If no fields are specified, the entire record is compared (all fields).

To delete specific records, there are two different new commands. The first one is:

```
DELETE internal table WHERE <logical expressions>
```

Simply, if the logical expression is satisfied by the record, the record is deleted. The other way to delete specific records is to specify a range of records to delete. The syntax is:

```
DELETE internal table FROM <index1> TO <index2>.
```

The indexes are the beginning and ending record numbers of the block of records to be deleted.

A field key in your internal table can also be used to delete a row with the corresponding parameter value.

```
DELETE TABLE <table name> WITH TABLE KEY <key field> = <parameter value>.
```

The parameter value can be a selection screen parameter, a variable, or a constant value.

Collecting Records (COLLECT)

Sometimes users want a report or extract that summarizes certain data. If your program is gathering data at the item level from a database table, it would be useful for the application to add the same data together rather than having a long list of data that must be processed later. The COLLECT command is used for this task. COLLECT compares non-numeric fields in the header record against the non-numeric fields in the item-level record. If an exact match is found, the numeric fields are added to the field. Basically, if all the fields that are non-numeric (for example, characters) match another record, the numeric fields are added together, and the result is one record in the table, rather than two.

Here's the syntax for the COLLECT command:

```
COLLECT <work area structure> into <internal table>.
  CLEAR <work area structure>
```

Figure 6.8 shows an example internal table. Figure 6.9 shows the same table after running the COLLECT command.

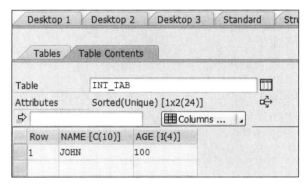

Figure 6.8
An internal table before running the COLLECT command.

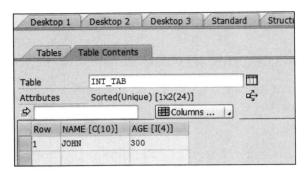

Figure 6.9
The same table after running the COLLECT command.

The COLLECT command consolidates data. In this example, the number for CARS was changed so that the value field increased by 100. Essentially, the work area structure record was added to the item record.

Caution

Be careful when choosing COLLECT versus MODIFY; the two commands produce very different results.

Clearing the Structure Record (CLEAR)

The CLEAR command completely clears the record of the structure. A good programming rule is to clear the structure after a record has been appended, deleted, modified, or collected into an internal table. The syntax is very simple:

```
CLEAR <structure>.
```

The CLEAR command sets all the fields defined in the data section to blanks or zeros, depending on the data type. The CLEAR command can also clear individual fields from within a structure or clear the individual fields themselves:

```
CLEAR structure-field name.
```

This use of the CLEAR command clears only the specified field, rather than the entire contents of the structure.

Earlier it was mentioned that good programming practice is to clear the work area structure after appending, modifying, deleting, or collecting into an internal table. If, in the next loop through the process, the program doesn't pick up a certain field from some location, using CLEAR guarantees that the previous record's data isn't left inside the structure fields that are processed against the table. Rather than process incorrect data, it's better to process blank data. You can always enter data in blank fields later. Incorrect data has to be found, analyzed, and then changed. If the structure record is cleared after every APPEND, MODIFY, DELETE, or COLLECT into an internal table, no data from the previous record is processed against the table again.

Caution

When you CLEAR a statement directly on an internal table, this process clears all the data in the internal table.

REFRESHING A TABLE (REFRESH)

To remove all the item records of an internal table—thus resetting it to its initial value—use the REFRESH command:

```
REFRESH internal table.
```

Essentially, the REFRESH command completely purges the internal table of any data. One warning though is to make sure you CLEAR the table as well, because refresh does not purge the header line. In a BDC session (covered in Chapter 17, "Writing a BDC Program"), there are many times when an internal table is submitted to the database, refreshed, and then filled again.

Reading Internal Tables

Once a table is filled with data by a read from the database tables, a function call, or from an external data file, the program can read the internal table one record at a time. Internal tables are managed more efficiently by the system and read faster than database tables.

Caution

Don't depend on internal tables for everything, of course, or the application will take up too much of your server resources.

To read an internal table, you use the READ command. READ can be used to read a table to find certain records or to read a certain record number. The search on the internal table can be sequential or direct. *Sequential searches* check individual records one by one until the desired record is found. *Direct searches* use a keyed index to read a particular record specified by the application. The generic syntax for the READ statement is as follows:

```
READ internal table [INDEX index]   [WITH KEY key [BINARY SEARCH]].
```

`internal table` is the name of the internal table defined in the data declaration section of the program. The `INDEX` addition allows the program to read the exact record number specified by the field index, which is a numeric data field. The `WITH KEY` addition lets the application search through the internal table to find a record where the key field or field string matches the first fields in the internal table. If the `WITH KEY` addition is used, the search time can be decreased if the `BINARY SEARCH` command is also used. The internal table must be sorted using the `SORT` command by the key fields. A binary search is equivalent to a direct read on a table at the database level. However, one of the stipulations for a binary search to be possible is that the internal table must be sorted by the key fields by which you're reading the table.

If the `READ` command is used without any of the additions, the records in the internal table are read one by one.

Note

The `SY-TABIX` system field contains the value of the record number currently being read or processed.

This sample program reads an external file into an internal table. Once all the records have been transferred from the external file, the internal table is read one record at a time and written to the screen, along with the record number (in `SY-TABIX`):

```
PARAMETERS:     p_data(50) TYPE c.
TYPES:   BEGIN OF ty_tab,
         field1(10)     TYPE c,
         field2(20)     TYPE c,
         field3(10)     TYPE c,
         field4(4)      TYPE n.
TYPES: END OF ty_tab.

DATA: int_tab TYPE TABLE OF ty_tab INITIAL SIZE 10000.
DATA: f_string LIKE LINE OF int_tab.
DATA: t_index TYPE sy-tabix.

START-OF-SELECTION.
* DATA TRANSFER FROM EXTERNAL FILE
  OPEN DATASET p_data FOR INPUT IN TEXT MODE ENCODING DEFAULT.
  DO.
    READ DATASET p_data INTO f_string.
    APPEND f_string TO int_tab.
    CLEAR int_tab.
```

```
    IF sy-subrc <> 0.
      EXIT.
    ENDIF.
  ENDDO.
  CLOSE DATASET p_data.
* TABLE READ
  WHILE sy-subrc = 0.
    CLEAR f_string.
    READ TABLE int_tab INTO f_string INDEX sy-tabix.
    WRITE: / sy-tabix, f_string.
  ENDWHILE.
```

SY-SUBRC has a value other than zero when all of the records have been read.

This example illustrates that the READ command, if used by itself, reads one record at a time in order. Rather than using READ by itself, however, you could use LOOP AT to process one record at a time. The READ command is powerful and very useful, but it should be used with its two additions. The INDEX addition allows the application to read a certain record number, and the WITH KEY addition lets you search the table for records that match a certain criteria and then processes them.

Using INDEX with READ

The INDEX addition to the READ command enables the application to read a certain record from the internal table. The internal table name must be specified, and the index must be specified. You must use one of the two additions required as part of the INDEX WITH READ logic.

You either must move the contents of the record into the work area structure:

```
READ internal table INTO <work area structure> INDEX index.
```

Or you can read the record without moving the contents to a work area structure:

```
READ internal table INDEX index TRANSPORTING NO FIELDS.
```

This addition is used when there is no need for further processing of the data read from the internal table.

internal table is the name of the internal table specified in the data declaration part of the application, and index is a numeric data field, also specified in the data section, that has a value ranging from 1 to the last record number of the table. If index is specified, and the number is greater than the number of records in the table, SY-SUBRC is set to 4 (or not to zero), which indicates that no record was retrieved.

How does the application know which record it wants to read? The answer is that the index is usually determined from onscreen interactive reporting, in which a list is displayed and the user double-clicks an item to get a more detailed description of that item. The commands you use to get the value of the index are the AT events (described in Chapter 14, "Writing a Report").

Using the WITH KEY Addition with READ

If the table is read via a key, specific records can be pulled rather than reading each individual record one at a time. The syntax of the command changes to add the key at the end of the READ statement.

```
READ internal table WITH KEY key.
```

The first part of the READ statement is the same. The WITH KEY addition specifies certain records with the key, which is a data field or a field string that the application compares against the record to find specific records in the internal table. If key is a data field, it's the first field in the table. If key is a field string, the number of fields specified in the field string are the first fields of the internal table. A field string can be used to specify the first few fields as the key in the table:

```
TYPES: BEGIN OF ty_tab,
         city(10)          TYPE c,
         state(2)          TYPE c,
         zip(5)            TYPE c,
         name(15)          TYPE c,
         address(20)       TYPE c,
         phone(10)         TYPE c.
TYPES: END OF ty_tab.

DATA: int_tab TYPE TABLE OF ty_tab INITIAL SIZE 10000.
DATA: int_key TYPE TABLE OF ty_tab.
DATA: f_tab LIKE LINE OF int_tab.
DATA: f_key LIKE LINE OF int_key.
DATA: w_key(10)    TYPE c.


**CODE TO FILL INTERNAL TABLE**
*---------------------------------------------*
*LOOP #1
*---------------------------------------------*
CLEAR w_key.
```

```
MOVE 'NEW YORK' TO w_key.
WHILE sy-subrc = 0.
  READ TABLE int_tab INTO f_tab WITH KEY w_key.
  IF sy-subrc = 0.
    WRITE: f_tab.
  ENDIF.
ENDWHILE.
*--------------------------------------------*
*LOOP #2
*--------------------------------------------*
CLEAR f_key.
MOVE 'NEW YORK' TO f_key-city.
MOVE 'NY' TO f_key-state.
MOVE '99999' TO f_key-zip.

WHILE sy-subrc = 0.
  READ TABLE int_tab INTO f_tab FROM f_key.
  IF sy-subrc = 0.
    WRITE  f_tab.
  ENDIF.
ENDWHILE.
```

In the first loop, the internal table is searched only by the first field, which is the city (NEW YORK). The records with the city NEW YORK are written to the screen. In the second loop, the same internal table is read with a different key. The key in the second loop is a field string with several fields specified: Only the records with the city NEW YORK, the state NY, and the ZIP code 99999 are read from the table and written to the screen.

By using a field string as a key, you can make the search criteria more specific, rather than just searching by one field at a time and then checking to see whether the other fields contain the required data. An alternative to reading the table via a key is looping through the table where certain criteria are met. This feature of the LOOP command is discussed in a later section of the chapter.

Conducting Binary Searches

A read through a table with thousands of records in a sequential search is very time consuming, especially on large systems. If the table contains more than a thousand records, the search must be changed from a sequential search to a direct search. To make the search direct, the table must be sorted by the key, and the search must be binary. To make this change, you use the BINARY SEARCH feature:

```
READ TABLE internal table into <work area structure>
  WITH KEY key BINARY SEARCH.
```

The key must be specified as described in earlier sections. A binary search must have certain criteria specified to the internal table. A binary search on an internal table must be specified with a key, either by an individual data field or by the data fields that make up the field string:

```
SORT internal table BY field1 field2 fields fieldN.
```

Once the table is sorted, the records can be searched using the binary search. To illustrate the performance benefit of using the binary search over the regular sequential search, a search with three key fields through an internal table with 30,000 records would take six hours with a regular sequential search and five minutes with a binary search.

USING OTHER TABLE COMMANDS

There are a few "utility" commands that don't fit any specific categories of commands. These are very useful commands, and we can't leave the topic of table commands without reviewing them briefly.

Determining Table Properties (DESCRIBE)

The DESCRIBE command allows the application to find out specific information about the internal table. DESCRIBE can determine how many lines are in the table as well as the parameter that was defined for the OCCURS statement in the data definition section:

```
DESCRIBE internal table [LINES lines] [OCCURS occurs].
```

DESCRIBE must be used with one of the additions LINES or OCCURS, and internal table is the name of the internal table as defined in the data declaration portion of the program. If the LINES statement is used, the numeric field LINES is filled with a number representing the total number of item records in the internal table. If the INITIAL SIZE addition is used, the numeric field's initial size is filled with the defined value, along with the internal table in the data declaration part of the program:

```
TYPES: BEGIN OF ty_tab,
        field1(10)   TYPE c,
        field2(10)   TYPE c.
TYPES: END OF ty_tab.
```

```
DATA: int_tab TYPE TABLE OF ty_tab INITIAL SIZE 10.
DATA: f_tab LIKE LINE OF int_tab.
DATA:  w_occurs TYPE   i,
       w_lines TYPE i.
START-OF-SELECTION.
  DO 100 TIMES.
    CLEAR f_tab.
    MOVE 'abcdefg' TO   f_tab-field1.
    MOVE '12345' TO f_tab-field2.
    APPEND f_tab TO int_tab.
    CLEAR f_tab.
  ENDDO.
  DESCRIBE TABLE int_tab OCCURS w_occurs LINES w_lines.
END-OF-SELECTION.
```

The value of W_OCCURS in the end is 10, as defined in the data declaration portion of the program. However, the value of W_LINES is 100 because the DO loop ran 100 times and put 100 records in the table. These values are useful to make sure that an index value is not too large, or that the available memory of the internal table isn't exceeded.

Sorting Records with the SORT Command

The SORT command was mentioned earlier in several examples. Essentially, the internal table can be sorted by its fields in ascending or descending order:

```
SORT internal table   [ASCENDING/DESCENDING]   by field1   field2 fields.
```

internal table can be sorted by its fields. The fields specified after internal table indicate which is the primary sort key, secondary sort key, and so on. You can specify up to 50 keys, using either ascending or descending order. ASCENDING specifies that the lowest value is at the top and the highest value is at the bottom. DESCENDING uses the opposite order. If no order is specified, ascending order is the default.

Looping with LOOP AT and LOOP AT WHERE

Looping commands are explained in other chapters, but the LOOP AT command applies directly to internal tables. LOOP AT moves the contents of the item-level records into a work-area structure or a field symbol, where it can be processed. This is the syntax:

```
LOOP AT internal table into <work area structure> / <field-symbol>,
  processing commands
ENDLOOP.
```

The LOOP AT WHERE statement is essentially the same as the LOOP AT statement, except that the WHERE clause specifies which records are to be moved up to the header level. The WHERE clause is used in the same context as with the SELECT statement:

```
LOOP AT internal table into <work area structure> / <field-symbol
   WHERE field1 conditional operator value AND field2 conditional operator value.
 processing commands
ENDLOOP.
```

Using ON CHANGE OF Inside a Loop

When looping through an internal table, to process a command once for each set of records would be very useful. ON CHANGE OF allows your programs to accomplish this task.

```
ON CHANGE OF <field> [or <field n>]
<commands>
ENDON
```

Let's say you have 30 records, 10 of which are for U.S. companies, 10 for Brazil, and 10 for Germany. You want to add the total revenue for each country and display it in a report.

```
TYPES: BEGIN OF ty_tab,
       revenue TYPE i,
       country(10) TYPE c.
TYPES: END OF ty_tab.

DATA: int_tab TYPE TABLE OF ty_tab INITIAL SIZE 20.
DATA: f_tab LIKE LINE OF int_tab.
DATA: w_revsum TYPE i,
      w_country(10).
SORT int_tab BY country.
LOOP AT int_tab INTO f_tab.
  ON CHANGE OF f_tab-country.
    WRITE:/10 w_country, 30 w_revsum.
    w_country = f_tab-country. w_revsum = 0.
  ENDON.
  w_revsum = w_revsum + f_tab-revenue.
ENDLOOP.
WRITE:/10 w_country, 30 w_revsum.
```

The program first sorts all the records of the internal table so that each country's records are grouped together. The program next loops through the internal table and adds the revenue in the variable, W_REVSUM. When a new country is encountered in the loop, the previous country's data is output to the screen, and the variables for the country and revenue are initialized. Notice after the loop that one more WRITE statement is included. The purpose of this statement is to print out the last portion of the data.

The output of this small program would look as follows:

```
BRAZIL      12540
GERMANY     345789
USA         24345
```

In summary of this command, the ON...ENDON statement allows applications to process a command once for a certain set of records inside an internal table.

SUMMARY

This chapter has discussed how internal tables are declared, used, and manipulated in ABAP/4 programs. After reading this chapter, you should know how to declare the internal table—field-by-field, or by including database structures in the declaration. You should also now be familiar with reading, modifying, and appending to an internal table.

Internal tables are very important in programming for SAP. Because data in SAP is stored in large database tables, the data must be handled in a table format in the programs. Internal tables enable programmers to do this task.

CHAPTER 7

WORKING WITH THE DATA DICTIONARY

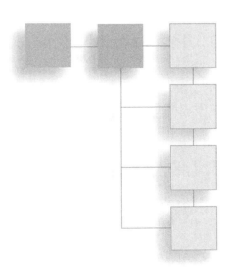

IN THIS CHAPTER

- Data and Structure Definitions
- Organizing Your Data
- Data Dictionary Tools

The ABAP developer must acquire several talents to become proficient. The most important is learning how to code in ABAP. The second most important is learning how to navigate through all of SAP's tables and data structures. Learning the Data Dictionary is very important. A programmer might be able to program an extract, report, or interface, but if the code is accessing data from the wrong place or table type, performance can suffer severely.

Something to realize early on in your ABAP learning experience is that the data from one table is available in several other tables as well. In a typical mainframe environment, the data is available from one place only. In SAP, by accessing smaller tables or one of the better table types, the programmer can accommodate the needs of the users and create efficient code at the same time. This chapter demonstrates how to find the data you need from the tables and how to look for it in other places besides the very large tables.

The Data Dictionary is a very large and important topic. This chapter describes how the Data Dictionary is related to coding in ABAP. It provides a general overview, with enough technical information to make the reader comfortable and knowledgeable in how to navigate through the millions of records contained in SAP's tables and views. An entire book could be written on how to use the Data Dictionary. This chapter covers the Data Dictionary from a programmer's perspective, showing you how to use it effectively only in programming ABAP.

DATA AND STRUCTURE DEFINITIONS

The importance of knowing SAP terms must be emphasized here because the complexity of the system forces people to work together. In order to work together, everyone needs to be able to speak the same language. Because a team of SAP implementation experts consists of BASIS (system administrators), ABAP programmers, functional analysts, and end users, the importance of communication can't be over emphasized. SAP is a fully integrated system, and in order to implement this system, the teams working together must be fully integrated as well.

Tables

The term *table* usually refers to either a database table used to store information permanently or a memory structure that is created by program execution that exists only as long as the program runs. There are four important table types in SAP: *cluster, transparent,* and *pool* tables are all *database tables* that exist permanently as part of the database. The fourth type, *internal tables,* exists in memory only and is defined on two levels. On one level they're local to programs that ABAPers create, and on the second level they represent empty structures that can be defined in the Data Dictionary for reuse (sometime referred to as a *structure*).

An *internal table* is a memory object that holds data. It usually consists of one header line and multiple item lines. Table 7.1 shows a blank table that contains no data. (It's shown here just as an example of table structure.)

Table 7.1 Blank Table with No Data

	Name	City	Phone
Header			
Item			

© 2014 Cengage Learning.

The *header line* holds the data that has been currently read by the program. The item lines hold each individual line of data in that data. The data is broken down into fields, which hold data for each related item. Table 7.2 shows an example.

Table 7.2   A Sample Table (INFO) Containing Data

Header	Name	City	Phone
Header	BOB	LAS VEGAS	(411) 555-1212
Item1	BOB	LAS VEGAS	(411) 555-1212
Item2	GARETH	NEW YORK	(555) 123-4567

© 2014 Cengage Learning.

The table called `INFO` contains two records, each with three fields. You will notice that when referring to a specific field within a table the nomenclature used is `<Table Name>-<Field Name>`. The fields, `INFO-NAME`, `INFO-CITY`, and `INFO-PHONE` each contain information for each individual record.

In this example, two records exist, one for `BOB` and another for `GARETH`. Any number of records can exist, and you can control if duplicate records are allowed. If duplicates are forbidden, then if you try to add another record with the same data in `Item1`, you'll get an error message saying that you're trying to add a duplicate record to the table. This `duplicate-records` error is applicable to both database and internal tables.

Certain fields can be defined as *key fields*. When all these fields are specified, they define a unique record for that table. No two records can have the same key fields. When all the key fields are specified during the reading of data, the read on the table becomes much faster, and database access time decreases. All the fields together make up the primary key. When someone refers to reading a table using the primary key, they mean reading the table specifying all of the key fields.

Transparent Tables

A *transparent* table is simply a Data Dictionary table that maps to a single physical table at the database level.

Pool Tables

Pool tables look like separate tables in the SAP Data Dictionary, but they're really all one huge table at the database level. So you might have rows from T001, T001W, and T023 all mixed together. Part of the key is the table name, so when you want a row from T001, it's added to your WHERE clause by the system.

Cluster Tables

Cluster tables are no longer used, but if you have an older SAP installation a few are left over from previous versions of SAP (versions 2.2 and earlier). They look like two or more tables in SAP, but at the database level they're really only one. They differ from pool tables in that they're part of a parent-child relationship, like PO header and PO lines (no longer in 2.1). But there's no real parent table: every child row duplicates all the parent information, so you don't need to do a join to get parent and child info. It wastes space and is slow to insert data, but very fast for SELECT statements because no join is done.

Internal Tables

An *internal table* is a structure defined in the Data Dictionary that contains no records, or a structure defined inside an ABAP program that initially contains no records. The structure has fields defined, but no data is stored in the table. The programs that use the internal tables populate them. Usually, the internal tables are used with function modules or as structures to hold data for input or output to external files. The internal tables defined in the Data Dictionary are usually predefined to be used with a function module, or as a structure to be filled for a *Batch Data Session* (BDC).

The internal tables defined inside ABAP programs are specified by the programmer and are typically used for data manipulation, sorting, or collecting. Searches can be done through these tables (once they are filled) with the READ command, which can specify a key, depending on how the internal table was defined by the programmer. A read on an internal table is generally a sequential search, unless the table is presorted, read by a key, and the search is defined as a binary search. The read then becomes a direct read. All these commands are covered in Chapter 6, "Working with Internal Tables."

Views

In addition to the different types of tables just discussed, there is another way to access database information from ABAP called *views*. *Views* are defined in the Data Dictionary and can combine multiple database tables that have been joined. The definition of the join conditions is done once when the view is created in the Data Dictionary and then reused by any program that pulls data from the view. Views have the same properties as transparent tables but contain much more data, and their primary keys are shared.

ORGANIZING YOUR DATA

The information in the Data Dictionary is organized in a structured manner. On the top of the structure is the table. Next is the domain, then the data element, and finally the field.

Let's use document numbers as an example to explain how the information is organized. The document numbers themselves would be the domain. A data element might be a sales order number. A particular field might specify the exact sales order for a specific table. By attributing a domain, data element, and field name to each piece of data, SAP has created a very clear picture of where data can be found. Unlike mainframe systems where the data is found in only one place, the data in SAP usually resides in several different tables. By searching the tables by domain or by data element, you can find common fields across multiple tables.

Domains

A *domain* is an object used to describe the type of field in which the data is stored. Examples of domains could be document numbers, short texts, dates, or markers. An analogous example in the real world might be the domains cars, boats, and trains. As you progress down the structure, the descriptions of the data and the fields become more and more specific.

Data Elements

A *data element* is a more specific description of what resides inside the domain. The example of document numbers, short texts, dates, and markers would focus down to invoice numbers, shipping text, billing dates, and timing data, respectively. In regard to the real world example, the data elements associated with cars would break down to Ford, Jeep, Toyota, Porsche, and so on. Again, as you progress down the tree, the descriptions become more and more specific. Data elements are very important in that they're specific enough to search tables for certain fields, but general enough to still find the data across all the tables. If you searched by domain, you would find that your search results would be much too general to mean anything, and if you searched by field, they would be too specific; the data wouldn't be constant across tables. Fields will have different field names across different tables; however, data elements and domain names will be the same if the same data is contained in that space.

Fields

Fields are the base description of where data resides. The notation for a field is usually preceded by the table to which it belongs. An example would be the billing document header table BKPF. If you were to look at one of the key fields, you would find that invoice numbers, or VBELN, would be one of the primary fields in this table. The notation for this field would be BKPF-VBELN. The name VBELN is specific to this table. In another table, a field with the same data might be called VBELN_VAUF. However, the data element for both fields would be the same, as would the domain name.

Using the car example, the field name would be the models of cars for that manufacturer. An example for Ford would be trucks and sedans. Fields are need because you may need to use the same data element more than once in a table. For example a table of sales order-related data might have a sales order document number, but it might also need to store a link to a related sales order document. They are both sales order document numbers and thus will have the same data element and same domain. But you need to be able to define two different fields to store both pieces of data in a single table.

Data Dictionary Tools

This section describes several of the transactions that you can use to search for data and check its integrity.

General Table Display (se16 and se17)

General Table Display is one of the main utilities that helps you find actual data in the database. The purpose of this transaction is to display the data from a selected table. By using this utility, you can compare the data that the program has read from the tables with the actual data in the tables to determine whether your selection criteria are correct.

To access the General Table Display utility, enter /nse17 in the command box in the top-left corner of the screen (see Figure 7.1).

Type the table name in the box and then press Enter or click the green checkmark next to the command line to display the specified table (see Figure 7.2).

A list of fields appears down the left column of the screen. The boxes enclose the descriptions of each field. Next to each field is a blank input box for data selection. Next to that column is a one-character entry box. This box marks fields that will be displayed when the transaction is executed. The keyed fields have an X already in that box. Next to that is another box for input, which is also blank. This box is the *sorting book*. Three buttons appear at the top of the screen, marked Execute, Choose All, and Delete Selection.

The fields containing an X are the fields that will be displayed once the Execute button is clicked.

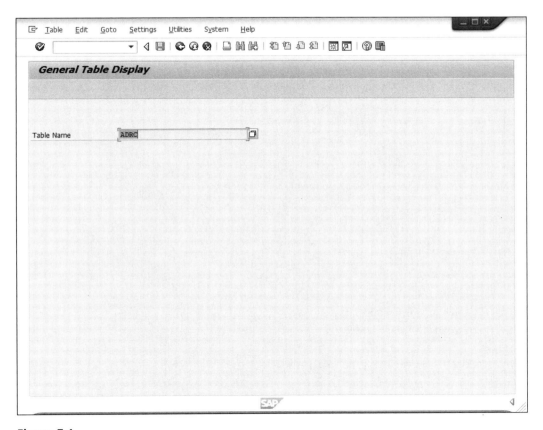

Figure 7.1
The initial screen of the General Table Display.

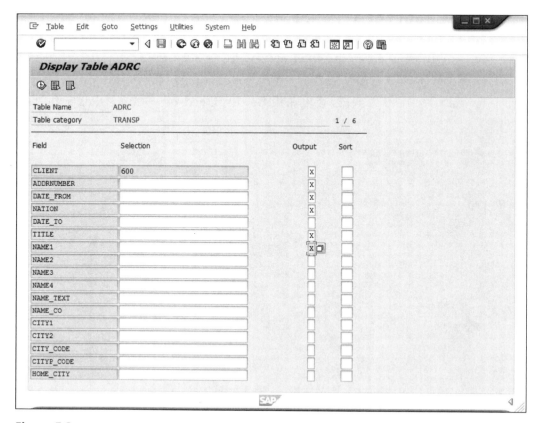

Figure 7.2
In this screen, you specify table or view count to see.

The second box, used to specify criteria for data selection, is probably the most important box on the screen. In this criteria box, you can enter a value to be matched against the records in the database. If a match is found, that record will be returned. If the second box is left blank, no filter will be applied by the database query for that field, and all records will be returned.

You always try to use some criteria when doing a query unless you are confident the database table holds very little data. Otherwise, not only would a search of this magnitude hinder the database, but it would be worthless in regard to what you would want to see. A better search would limit one of the fields so that a small number of data records is displayed. See Figure 7.3.

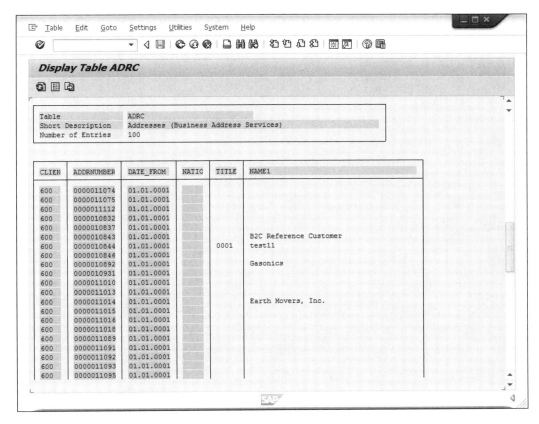

Figure 7.3
The output of ADRC.

Use Table 7.3 as a sample table to illustrate how a data display would work.

Table 7.3   A Sample Table Called ROLODEX

Name	City	Telephone Number
Bob	New York	(303) 555-1212
Gayle	San Francisco	(415) 555-1212
Kathleen	New York	(303) 411-5555
Jim	New York	(303) 555-1234
Susan	Rocklin	(916) 411-5678

© 2014 Cengage Learning.

On the se16 or General Table Display screen for the ROLODEX table, the following output would be displayed by default:

```
NAME    X
CITY    X
PHONE   X
```

If you wanted to display all the people who lived in New York, you would enter **New York** in the second column adjacent to the CITY field:

```
NAME    X
CITY       New York     X
PHONE
```

The output would be as follows:

```
Bob       New York
Kathleen     New York
Jim     New York
```

Notice that only the name and the city are output to the screen. In the initial selection screen, no X appears next to the PHONE field. If you click the green arrow button (Back) and put an X in the PHONE row, the phone numbers will also be listed.

A special ability of the second column is that you can use conditional operators along with the values. If you just enter a value in that box, the database assumes the "equal to" operator. You can also use other operators, as indicated in Table 7.4.

Table 7.4 Conditional Operators

Conditional Operator	Meaning
Greater than	>
Less than	<
Greater than or equal to	>=, =>
Less than or equal to	<=, =<
Not equal to	<>, ><

© 2014 Cengage Learning.

All of these operators are used in the same context as with the IF statement described in Chapter 4, "Using Conditional Operators."

In version 3.0, SAP replaced the old se16 transaction with a new version. The old se16 transaction is the se17 transaction just described. The new and improved se16 command allows for a little more flexibility when searching directly through database tables. The initial screen is still the same, as shown in Figure 7.4.

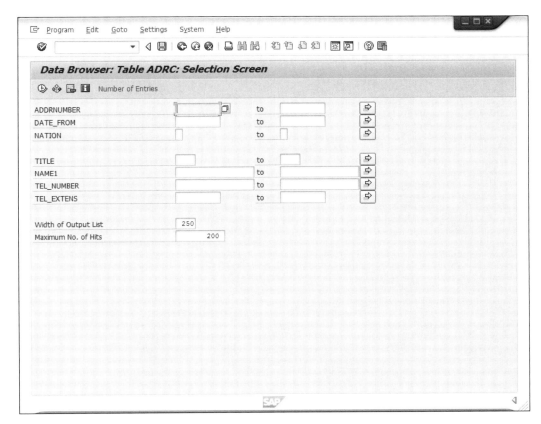

Figure 7.4
The initial screen of the se16 transaction.

After entering the table name, ADRC in this case, press the Enter key or click the green checkmark. This action brings you to the second screen where a selection screen is displayed. Each field in the table has a select-options range next to it. Values can be entered into these ranges in the format that is described in Chapter 1, "Data Types and Definitions." The se17 command's options were a little cryptic, as described in the previous section. The new commands may appeal more to new users of SAP as they are more intuitive. As shown in Figure 7.4, the width of the output list can now be set, as well as the maximum number of hits against the database. Figure 7.5 shows the new interface for choosing which database fields will be included in the selection criteria.

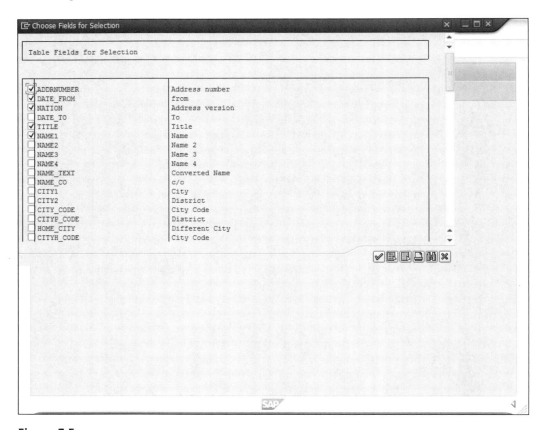

Figure 7.5
Table Selection screen for transaction se16.

The fields represented by `select-options` can be chosen by the user. If you follow the menu path Settings > Fields for Selection, SAP brings up a list of fields with check boxes beside them, as shown in Figure 7.6.

Figure 7.6
Selection screen for fields to be displayed.

Click on the fields you want to select against, and then click on the green check (Copy) button in the left corner. This action brings you back to the original screen shown in Figure 7.4. Enter your specifications for the table and then execute. A list of the data from the table is returned to the screen, as shown in Figure 7.7.

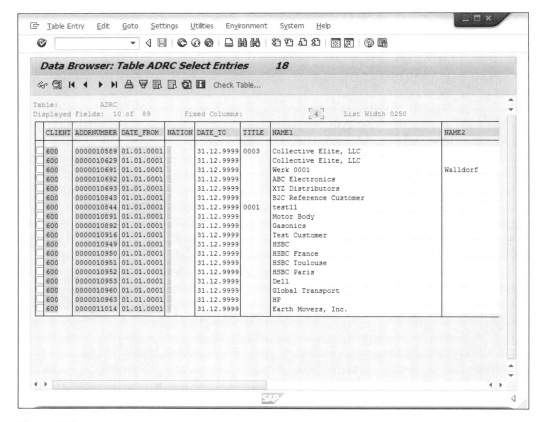

Figure 7.7
The output of `ADRC` when using se17.

By double-clicking on a line in the output list, a screen displaying all the values of that record appears in the next screen. This output is displayed in Figure 7.8. This is a useful screen for viewing individual data per record. Notice that, in the initial selection screen and this last screen, the fields have been displayed as field names, which are a bit cryptic. SAP allows you to change the display to show the field descriptions rather than following the menu path Settings > User Parameters. Select descriptions rather than field names to display the tables in a format that is easier to understand.

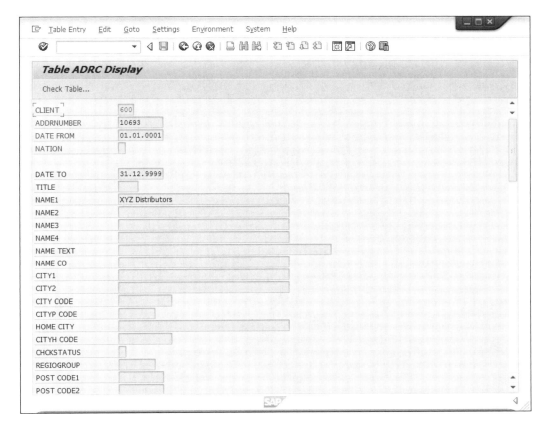

Figure 7.8
Display of one record after double-clicking an output record from the General Table Display.

Displaying Fields, Data Elements, and Domains (se15)

A useful Data Dictionary tool of the information systems feature is searching for tables with a certain field, data element, or domain. Certain fields exist in several tables, as do data elements and domains. If a certain field in the program specification is from one table, you may want to find another table that has the same field with related data. A good example of this instance is with the table ADRC, which can grow very large due to the number of address records it holds. Another table that holds related data is ADCP.

How would you find ADCP if you didn't have experience with that table? This section deals explicitly with that challenge. The Data Dictionary's *information system* enables you to search for tables, fields, data elements, domains, and text throughout SAP's tables. To get to the screen, you can enter the fast transaction se15 (see Figure 7.9).

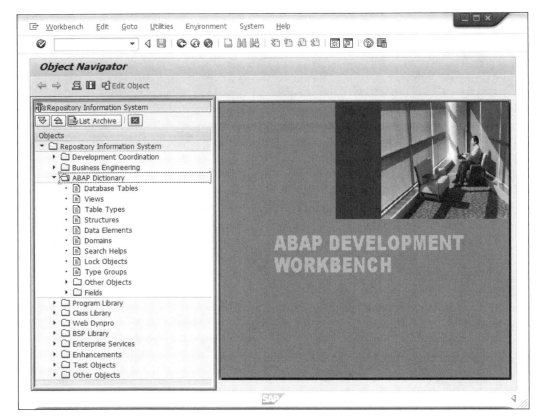

Figure 7.9
From this screen, you can search for many types of Data Dictionary objects.

This example uses the ADRC example as its model. To find another field in another table that holds the same data as a field in ADRC, you must first display the fields in ADRC. Double-click on Database Tables and enter **ADRC** as the table name. Then click the Execute button (see Figure 7.10). A row for ADRC should appear, and you will need to double-click the name. All of the fields are now displayed on the screen (see Figure 7.11).

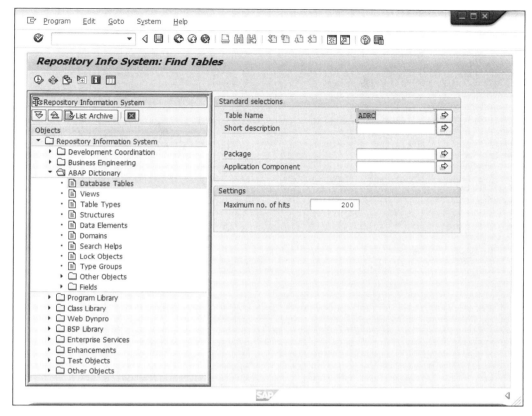

Figure 7.10
Here, you can select the database table you want to view.

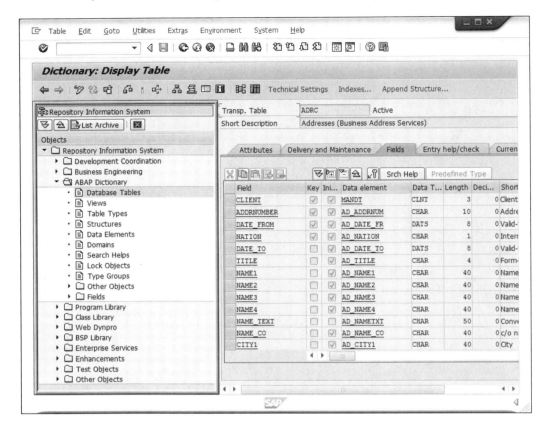

Figure 7.11
In this screen you see all the fields contained in the ADRC table.

On the screen, find the field you want and look for its corresponding data element. For example, try the address number, AD_ADDRNUM. Now double-click on AD_ADDRNUM in the Data Element column. This opens a new screen for that data element.

From there, you can use the menu path Utilities > Where Used List to bring up a search screen. Make sure the option Table Fields is selected and execute the transaction (see Figure 7.12). This tells the system to go look for all tables that have fields defined with the data element AD_ADDRNUM in them (see Figure 7.13).

A list of tables comes up, along with the fields that are associated with that data element. Data elements always correspond to the similar data, so any of the tables that appear will hold the same type of data as ADRC for that particular field.

Figure 7.12
This screen allows you to select what types of objects to search against.

Now, you must only go through that list of tables and find the related data you are interested in. Table ADCP, for example, will hold the relationship from a "street address" object to a "person" object in the SAP database. The ability to search across the Data Dictionary is very powerful and provides many options to help you learn how SAP stores and manages business data. Searches can be done in the same way, looking for table names that use specific field names, domains, or text.

Note

Text is always a very long and tedious search and should be avoided if possible. Sometimes you have no choice, however, so do what you need to do to get the data for the client.

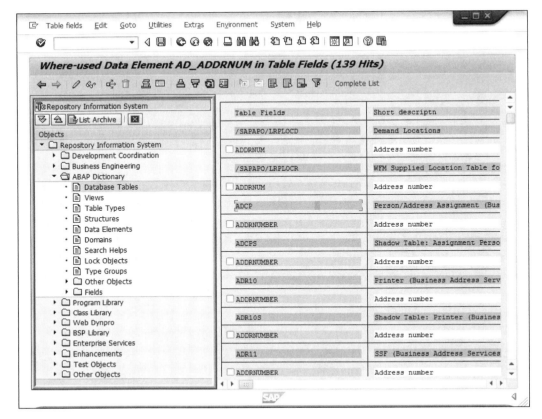

Figure 7.13
This screen displays the results of your search for AD_ADDRNUM.

SUMMARY

This chapter explained what makes up the data structures of the database, as well as the tools used to search through that data. It's very important that you understand the difference between pool, cluster, transparent, and internal tables. The information system and General Table Display were discussed in this chapter; these tools and definitions are central to your understanding of SAP before you begin programming. We strongly recommend that you become familiar with them before proceeding with any further education in development.

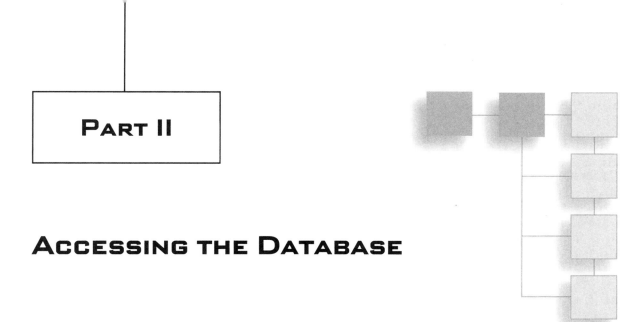

PART II

ACCESSING THE DATABASE

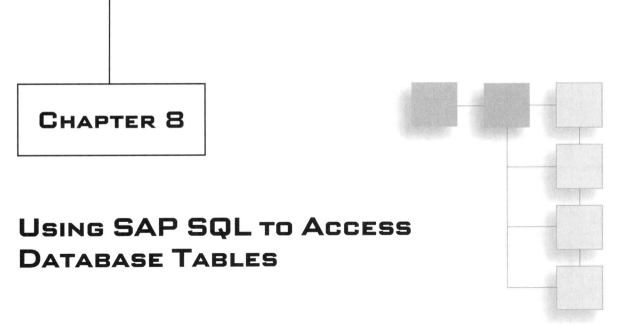

CHAPTER 8

USING SAP SQL TO ACCESS DATABASE TABLES

IN THIS CHAPTER

- Using SQL to Access Tables and Views
- Using SQL with Transactions
- Reading Data from the Database (SELECT)
- Updating Tables (UPDATE)
- Inserting Data (INSERT)
- Deleting Rows (DELETE)
- Learning Advanced Techniques

The primary reason that Enterprise Applications systems such as SAP ERP or CRM exist is to track and manipulate data. Like many modern applications, SAP stores this information in a relational database. In order to write any practical ABAP program, you must be able to access this database.

One of the most important ways to read or manipulate the database is through *Structured Query Language,* also known as SQL. SQL is an industry standard that can be used to access any compliant relational database. This chapter discusses the ABAP version of SQL, which is used to access the SAP database. The command set of SAP SQL is a limited subset of the standard version of SQL. Even if you already know SQL, it's important to become familiar with SAP's flavor of SQL because of its limitations.

Note

In this chapter, the term SQL refers to SAP SQL.

Although SAP SQL is a central topic in ABAP programming because it accesses the data that SAP exists to track and manipulate, it comprises only four commands, as listed in Table 8.1.

Table 8.1 SAP SQL Commands

Command	Description
SELECT	Reads data from a table or view.
UPDATE	Changes data in a table.
INSERT	Adds a new row of data to the table.
DELETE	Removes a row or rows of data from a table.

© 2014 Cengage Learning.

Because SELECT is used on both SAP and user-created tables, it's the most important and useful of the commands, and I'll cover it first, followed by UPDATE, INSERT, and DELETE.

USING SQL TO ACCESS TABLES AND VIEWS

As explained in Chapter 7, "Working with the Data Dictionary," a relational database is composed of many tables, each of which holds a specific set of data. A table is a physical object found in the database. The data in these tables can be thought of as a matrix of values. In a table of parts data, for example, individual fields containing data such as part numbers and part descriptions make up the columns of the matrix, whereas individual entries such as the entry for a steel bolt make up a row of the matrix.

SQL allows a programmer to read rows, insert new rows, or change existing rows of data. In addition to tables, SAP supports views, which are a logical—not physical—sets of data. In general, views combine data from several tables into a single logical object. For example, SAP uses one table for material data and another table to contain the description of the material. This setup allows a single type of material to have descriptions in multiple languages—English, French, and German, for example. You could create a view in the database to combine the material table and description table into a single view in which all of the information could be accessed together. Because a view is only a logical object, however, you can read but not change or add to the data in the view. To add a new part or change the English description, you must access the separate physical tables that provide the information for the view.

Note that views and tables appear virtually identical to the programmer; they're both objects in the SAP Data Dictionary.

Using SQL with Transactions

A major difference between the SAP database and generic relational databases is the fact that SAP applications provide thousands of built-in tables designed to support the business purpose of the application. In addition to these SAP tables, users can create their own tables through the Data Dictionary.

The SAP application is composed of thousands of transactions; these transactions can be called from an ABAP program in order to change data in SAP tables. However, although SQL can be used to *read* data from both SAP and *user-created* tables, it should be used to change or insert data only in user-created tables, not SAP tables. The SAP tables support the SAP application. In general, a program shouldn't be manipulating data in SAP tables by using SQL. In some special cases, SQL is used to make small changes to data in SAP tables, but this should be done only by programmers experienced not only in ABAP but also in the details of the SAP application—those who know the impact these changes will have in SAP.

For example, suppose that you want to write a program to change the stock-on-hand quantity of a material. This quantity is stored in the SAP table MARD. You could use SQL to simply go in and change the quantity field in the table. But don't forget that SAP is an integrated package of financial, manufacturing, and human resources applications. If the quantity of a material has increased, it must have been purchased from a vendor. And if it was purchased from a vendor, there must be an invoice for payment. Accounts need to be credited and debited. The simple act of receiving new material can have a cascade effect throughout SAP. Simply using SQL to increase a single field in a single table isn't enough.

Now, if the program had called transaction FB02, material receipt, this transaction would have taken care of all the possible effects of receiving material. (Calling SAP transactions is discussed in Chapter 17, "Writing a BDC Program.") So it's important to remember only to *read* data from SAP tables.

Reading Data from the Database (SELECT)

Reading information from the database is probably the most common activity in ABAP. It's done in reports to extract the data to be formatted, interfaces to send data to external systems, and interactive programs to provide information to users. Because it's so common and can take up so much processing time, knowing the SELECT command backward and forward may be the most fundamental skill in ABAP programming. In this first section, the basic form of the SELECT command is described. Later in the chapter you will explore the more advanced techniques.

Here's the basic form:

```
SELECT * FROM tab [WHERE condition].
ENDSELECT.
```

SELECT is a looping command, as you can see by the presence of the ENDSELECT command. When a SELECT is issued against a table, it returns all rows of data contained in that table, one at a time. So the first row returned is available for processing during the first pass of the loop. The second row is available during the second pass of the loop, and so on, until all rows have been read from the table. If no data is found, the code within the SELECT loop won't be executed.

Now for an example of the SELECT command in action. This piece of code reads from table T001, which contains information on company codes, the smallest business unit in SAP for the purposes of external reporting. The company codes will be read and printed along with a description:

```
TABLES T001.              "Company Code
SELECT * FROM T001.       "Get all fields from T001
WRITE:    /, T001-BUKRS.  "Company Code
WRITE    T001-BUTXT.      "Company Code Name
ENDSELECT.
```

The TABLES statement is always required when using this form of the SELECT statement to retrieve data. It defines a work area where the data returned is stored, and thus you can use the table fields in your code, as in the previous example where T001-BUKRS appears.

A fictional company called Acme Tools might produce the following output for the preceding piece of code:

```
0100 Corporate
0200 Acme North America
0400 Acme Asia
0300 Acme Europe
```

The Company Code table has many more fields than just BUKRS and BUTXT, and any of those fields could be used in the SELECT loop. SAP returns all data in the table; it's up to the programmer to decide which fields to use. Notice that the rows aren't returned in any particular order. When using the basic version of SELECT, SAP SQL doesn't allow the programmer to specify which fields of a table are returned by the SELECT. The command always returns *all* fields in a table. When the data is returned, it also isn't returned in any predictable order. (There is an option for processing the data in a certain order, which is discussed in the section titled "Using ORDER BY to Sort Data.")

The return code SY-SUBRC tells you whether data has been returned. If one or more rows of data are returned to the SELECT loop, SY-SUBRC will be equal to 0 after the ENDSELECT command has executed. If no rows are returned and the loop isn't executed, SY-SUBRC will be set to 4.

When data is returned, it's available through the table work area. Thus, the fields can be used through the *table-field* notation, just like an internal table or record variable. As noted previously, don't forget that all tables must be declared via the TABLES command before they're used in your program. (See Chapter 7 for more information about the TABLES command.)

Also, remember that each row is available for only one pass of the SELECT loop, so be prepared to store data in variables or internal tables if it will be needed later.

Using WHERE to Limit the Data Returned with SELECT

The basic SELECT command reads all data contained in a table and returns it to the program. But this isn't always what you want the program to do. A table can contain tens of thousands of rows of data. The program may be interested in only a tiny subset of that data. The question is, how do you limit the amount of data to only what you need? The mechanism used to do this in SQL is the WHERE clause. The WHERE clause allows the program to specify which rows of data are to be returned by the SELECT command.

In the earlier example for Acme Tools, the code printed all company codes. But what if the requirements had specified that the code for Corporate, 0100, was not to be printed? You could use the IF command to prevent display of Corporate if you know that the code for Corporate is 0100:

```
TABLES T001.           "Company Code
SELECT * FROM T001.    "Get all fields from T001
IF T001-BUKRS > '0100'.  "Don't Print Corp
```

```
  WRITE:     /, T001-BUKRS.   "Company Code
  WRITE T001-BUTXT.           "Company Code Name
ENDIF.
ENDSELECT.
```

Using IF would prevent code 0100 from being printed, so the program would be correct. But it wouldn't be efficient.

It's critical to remember that reading data from the database is very time consuming. Everything should be done to minimize the amount of data being read. In this case, you read a row of data, the company code, which you know you aren't going to use. So instead of using an IF statement to exclude this data after reading it from the database, use a WHERE clause to prevent it from being read in the first place. Using a WHERE clause, the Acme Tools code would look like this:

```
Tables T001    "Company Code
SELECT * FROM T001 WHERE BUKRS >   '0100'.
WRITE:     /,  T001-BUKRS.   "Company Code
WRITE T001-BUTXT.          "Company Code Name
ENDSELECT.
```

Here's the output:

```
0200 Acme North America 0400 Acme Asia
0300 Acme Europe
```

In this case, the WHERE clause tells SAP to go to the T001 table and return all rows of data where the field BUKRS is greater than 0100; thus, the corporate row is never returned to the program and won't be written out.

Preventing a single row from being read from the database won't speed up a program by any measurable degree, obviously, but it's easy to imagine another scenario. A second program might read and summarize thousands of financial transactions for the three Acme companies. If the WHERE clause is used to exclude the thousands of transactions with a company code for Corporate, a significant performance boost would be seen.

Using Operators with WHERE

There are several ways that the condition of the WHERE clause can be assembled. Here's one:

```
WHERE field operator var.
```

When specifying a field in the WHERE clause, the field name is used alone—you don't use the *table • field* format used in other statements. The basic operators available for use are the same ones seen in the IF statements (see Table 8.2). Either the abbreviated form or the symbol can be used, but we recommend that you choose one form and stick to it to improve readability.

Table 8.2 Basic Logical Operators You Can Use

Description	Logical Operator
Greater than	>
Less than	<
Greater than or equal to	>=, =>
Less than or equal to	<=, =<
Not equal to	<>, ><

© 2014 Cengage Learning.

Using AND and OR with WHERE

Here's another version of the WHERE syntax:

```
WHERE condition AND condition2  ...  AND conditionN.
```

For a row to be selected in this version, all the conditions in the list must be true. These individual conditions can include any of the options listed here. The AND operator can be combined with the OR operator, in which case the list is evaluated from left to right (unless parentheses are used).

Here's a version with OR:

```
WHERE condition! OR condition2  ...  OR conditionN.
```

In this version, for a row to be selected, any one of the conditions in the list must be true. For example, the statement

```
SELECT * FROM T001 WHERE BUKRS >    '0100'   OR BUKRS =    '0000'.
ENDSELECT.
```

The next example mixes OR with the BETWEEN statement:

```
SELECT * FROM T001 WHERE BUKRS BETWEEN    '0000'   AND    '0500' OR
  BUTXT <> 'CORPORATE'.
ENDSELECT.
```

BUKRS is the field used in the first condition, and BUTXT is used in the second, showing how you can mix multiple table fields in one WHERE clause.

The OR operator can be combined with AND in forming a WHERE clause. Just be careful of the order of precedence. The WHERE clause is evaluated from left to right, and you may need to use parentheses to ensure the statements you want are evaluated correctly.

Using NOT with WHERE

The following syntax line shows how you can use NOT with WHERE:

WHERE field [NOT] BETWEEN var1 AND var2.

This condition is true if the contents of field are greater than or equal to var1 and less than or equal to the contents of var2—unless modified by the NOT, in which case the opposite is true.

Note

The AND in this example is part of the BETWEEN operator and shouldn't be confused with the AND operator.

Another option for NOT:

WHERE field [NOT] IN (var1,var2,...,varN).

The condition is true if the value of field is equal to any of the variables in the list—unless modified by the NOT, in which case the opposite is true.

Now try this one:

WHERE field [NOT] LIKE string.

This operator allows you to compare a portion of the field to a character string. The string may contain wildcard characters for the comparison. The underscore (_) is a wildcard that can stand for any single character. The percent sign (%) is a wildcard that stands for any group of characters. These two wildcards can be used in the string in any combination. For example:

```
SELECT * FROM T001 WHERE BUTXT LIKE '%AMERICA'
   OR BUTXT LIKE 'ADVANCED%MANUFACTURING'.
ENDSELECT.
```

The first condition would be true for any company with a name ending in AMERICA—thus, NORTH AMERICA and SOUTH AMERICA would be selected, but CORPORATE wouldn't. The second condition would be true for any company with a name starting with ADVANCED and ending in MANUFACTURING—thus, ADVANCED FLIGHT MANUFACTURING would be selected, but CENTRAL MANUFACTURING wouldn't.

Here's one last version. Check it out:

```
WHERE field [NOT] IN sel.
```

The condition is true if the value of `field` passes the conditions in the `SELECT-OPTION` or range `sel`. A `SELECT-OPTION` is a variable type covered in Chapter 1, "Data Types and Definitions." It's a parameter that allows the users to enter a set of one or more conditions at runtime. A *range* is also a variable type, but the programmer must populate it with a set of one or more conditions. These conditions, which act identically regardless of which of the two variable types is used, can be an inclusive or exclusive list, range, or single value. Basically, anything a programmer could define in a `WHERE` clause, the user or programmer can specify in a single range or `SELECT-OPTION`. See Chapter 1 for more details on `SELECT-OPTION`s and ranges.

Note

To work properly, the `SELECT-OPTION` or range should be defined with the same data type as the database field.

WHERE Clause Examples

Next, here are some examples of using a `WHERE` clause.

This first example demonstrates the use of several common operators such as equal, greater than, and less than. The table being read, `EKPO`, contains information on purchase orders:

```
TABLES EKPO.
SELECT * FROM EKPO WHERE EBELN > '0005000000'
          AND WERKS = 'P002'
          AND AEDAT < '19961201'.
ENDSELECT.
```

In the next example, the `SELECT` statement reads from `EKPO` and uses `IN` and `BETWEEN` to restrict the rows returned. Notice that the first `IN` operator is a list, and the second `IN` operator uses a `SELECT-OPTION`. In the case of the `IN SELECT-OPTION`, the user can enter as many conditions as needed, and the programmer doesn't need to write any code to process it. The system evaluates the `SELECT-OPTION` and returns only those rows that meet the criteria entered by the user:

```
TABLES EKPO.
SELECT-OPTIONS S_AEDAT FOR EKPO-AEDAT.
```

```
SELECT * FROM EKPO WHERE EBELN BETWEEN '0005000000' AND '0005500000'
                        AND WERKS IN ('P002', 'P0031', 'P0051', 'P008')
                        AND AEDAT IN S_AEDAT.
ENDSELECT.
```

The following example uses parentheses and the OR operator to limit the rows returned. This could have been done instead with the IN operator; OR and IN have the same effect in this case:

```
SELECT * FROM EKPO WHERE ( EBELN = '0005000000' OR EBELN = '0005000001'
  OR EBELN = '0005000002' )
AND WERKS = 'P002' AND AEDAT < '19961201'.
```

Using the IN operator, this SELECT could be rewritten as follows:

```
SELECT * FROM EKPO WHERE EBELN IN ('0005000000', '0005000001', '0005000002')
                        AND WERKS = 'P002' AND AEDAT < '19961201'.
```

Options for the SELECT Command

The SELECT command has several options that you can use to modify the SELECT behavior, as described in the following sections.

Inserting Records Into an Internal Table (INTO TABLE)

When the INTO TABLE option is used, no ENDSELECT is required because all rows are inserted into the internal table specified by the programmer. Any data already in the internal table is lost. Here's the syntax:

```
SELECT * INTO TABLE itab FROM tab.
```

Caution

To avoid unpredictable results, make sure that the internal table you specify has the same structure as the database table from which you're selecting.

Appending Selected Records to a Table (APPENDING TABLE)

When the APPENDING TABLE option is used, no ENDSELECT is required because all rows are appended into the internal table specified by the programmer. In this case, any data already in the internal table is saved. Otherwise it's identical to using INTO TABLE. Here's how you use APPENDING TABLE:

```
SELECT * FROM tab APPENDING TABLE itab.
```

Selecting a Single Row (SELECT SINGLE)

You can use the `SELECT SINGLE` option when you want a single row of data. No `ENDSELECT` is needed because only one row is returned:

```
SELECT SINGLE * FROM tab WHERE where clause.
```

This is a very fast way to return a single row of data—for example, if you have a part number and want to look up the description for that single part.

When using this form, in order to correctly specify a single row, the `WHERE` clause should include all the key fields. As discussed in Chapter 7, the primary key is the field or group of fields that uniquely identifies all rows in a table. So if all key fields are in the `WHERE` clause, only one row is returned. For example, if a table uses a key of `NAME` and `ID`, the `WHERE` clause would have to be:

```
WHERE NAME = 'SMITH' AND ID = ' 19943'.
```

This would return only one row of data because only one row in the table has the combination of `SMITH` and `19943`. If you do not fully specify the unique key that corresponds to a single record in the table, SAP will return the first record that matches the partial key. The row returned is random, so make sure you use the full key when using `SELECT SINGLE` to ensure that the correct data is chosen.

When you know that one and only one row of data will always be returned, use this option to improve performance over a `SELECT` loop.

Using ORDER BY to Sort Data

You can add `ORDER BY` to any of the other options except the `SELECT SINGLE` option. Using `ORDER BY` returns the results of a `SELECT` loop or fills the specified internal table in ascending order. The order can be determined by any field; if a table has a `LASTNAME` field, `ORDER BY LASTNAME` will return rows to the `SELECT` loop starting with `ADAMS`, `BORNE`, `DWELL`, and so on.

Use the following format:

```
SELECT * FROM tab [WHERE where clause] ORDER BY field1 field2 ... fieldn.
```

The following version returns the results of a `SELECT` loop or fills the specified internal table in ascending order by the primary key of the table. If the primary key consists of more than one field, then they're ordered left to right:

```
SELECT * FROM tab [WHERE where clause] ORDER BY PRIMARY KEY.
```

SELECT Examples

The following are several examples of the different options for use with the SELECT command.

The first example demonstrates the INTO TABLE option by selecting a set of rows out of the table BSEG (Financial Documents) and inserting it into an internal table:

```
DATA BEGIN OF INT_BSEG OCCURS 1000.
   INCLUDE STRUCTURE BSEG.        "Duplicate the table BSEG DATA
DATA END OF INT_BSEG.
TABLES BSEG.
SELECT * INTO TABLE INT_BSEG
  FROM BSEG WHERE BUKRS = 'SEUR1'      "Company Code
  AND GJAHR = '1995'.      "Document Year
```

Notice no ENDSELECT is needed when using INTO TABLE statement.

The next example demonstrates the use of SELECT SINGLE. The table being read is MARD, which stores information on the inventory quantities of materials. The key fields for this table are MATNR (material number), WERKS (plant), and LGORT (storage location). Remember that to use SELECT SINGLE, the entire key must be specified, so in this example parameters are defined, and the SELECT uses them to look up a quantity and output it:

```
TABLES MARD.
PARAMETERS: P_MATNR LIKE MARD-MATNR,
  P_WERKS LIKE MARD-WERKS,
  PJ.GORT LIKE MARD-LGORT.
SELECT SINGLE * FROM MARD WHERE MATNR = P_MATNR
  AND WERKS = P_WERKS
  AND LGORT = PJ.GORT.
***Once again an ENDSELECT is not required
***because only one row will be returned
IF SY-SUBRC = 0. "Only output if select succeeds
  WRITE: 'Quantity on hand is', MARD-LABST.
ELSE.
  WRITE 'Material does not exist at plant/location given.'.
ENDIF.
```

UPDATING TABLES (UPDATE)

The UPDATE command in SAP SQL enables the programmer to change data within a database table. As stated earlier, this command isn't normally used to change data in SAP tables—only in user-defined tables. For the appropriate tables, this is a common activity. User tables often contain information that indicates when certain events occurred or will occur in the future.

The syntax for the UPDATE command comes in two different versions:

```
UPDATE tab [SET field1 = [field1 + ]var1    ... fieldN = [fieldN + ]varN]
    [WHERE condition].
UPDATE tab [FROM TABLE itab].
```

Using SET with UPDATE

In the first version of UPDATE, the SET option tells the system which of the fields to change. The WHERE clause limits the rows to be changed, just like a WHERE clause in a SELECT statement limits the rows being read.

For example, suppose that you have a user table called ZJOB_LOG with a key field called Job_Id and these values:

```
Job_Id       Start        Doc#
WEEKLYGL     06/01/15     0054001000
AREXT        06/08/15     0073000500
APIMP        07/01/15     0030100000
```

The following statement is issued:

```
UPDATE ZJOB_LOG SET START = '08012015' DOC# = DOC# +100.
```

The table would now contain these values:

```
Job_Id       Start        Doc#
WEEKLYGL     08/01/15     0054001100
AREXT        08/01/15     0073000600
APIMP        08/01/15     0030100100
```

Notice that the statement affected all rows. In the Start field, all rows were set to a constant value. The field Doc#, on the other hand, changed based on an equation.

This next statement demonstrates the effect of a WHERE clause:

```
UPDATE ZJOB_LOG SET START = '12312015' WHERE JOB_ID =   'APIMP'.
```

The table would now contain these values:

```
Job_Id       Start        Doc#
WEEKLYGL     08/01/15     0054001000
AREXT        08/01/15     0073000600
APIMP        12/31/15     0030100100
```

Notice that only one row was affected by this statement because only one row met the requirements of the WHERE clause.

It's also possible to issue an UPDATE without a SET or WHERE option:

```
UPDATE tab [FROM TABLE itab].
```

Remember this syntax line from a few paragraphs ago? In this case, the system looks at the values in the work area for the table and tries to find a row in the database that matches the values in the primary key field(s) of the work area. If found, it updates all fields in the table with the data in the work area. For example, suppose that a program needs to process 100 financial records every week, and the table called ZJOB_LOG exists to keep track of the next time this job needs to run and the next document in the list to be processed.

The following code updates this table with the correct information:

```
TABLES ZJOB_LOG.     "User defined table for batch jobs
*** ZJOB_LOG Contains three fields:
*** Jobid, C(8), Job Identifier, Primary Key
*** Start1, D, Start Date
*** Doc, C(12), Next Document
*** Get today's information
SELECT * SINGLE FROM ZJOB_LOG WHERE JOBJD = 'WEEKLYGL'
  AND START1 = SY-DATUM.
  <Process Data>
*** Update Job Log
ZJOB_LOG-START1 = ZJOB_LOG-START1 + 7.     "Schedule Next Job
ZJOB_LOG-DOC = ZJOB_LOG-DOC + 100.     "Set Next Document
UPDATE ZJOB_LOG.
IF SY-SUBRC <> 0.
  WRITE:  /,  'Error on Log Update!'.
ENDIF.
```

Because the UPDATE command here is issued with no SET or WHERE option, SAP uses the values in the work area for ZJOB_LOG and updates the row with the same key as the work area. In this case, the SELECT command populates the work area with the row where Job_Id is equal to WEEKLYGL. The field Start is changed to today's date plus seven days, and the Doc# field is increased by 100. Because Job_Id isn't changed, the UPDATE statement changes the same row that was originally selected.

In general, it's better if the update is issued with an explicit WHERE clause instead of using the work area, because it's easier to follow. This next piece of code has the same effect as the one just examined, but notice how much easier it is to read:

```
TABLES ZJOB_LOG.        "User defined table for batch jobs
***
*** ZJOB_LOG Contains three fields:
*** Job_Id, C(8), Job Identifier, Primary Key
*** Start1, D, Start Date
*** Doc, C(12), Next Document
DATA v_start type D. "Temp variable for date

*** Get today's information
SELECT SINGLE * FROM ZJOB_LOG WHERE JOB_ID = 'WEEKLYGL1'
  AND START1 = SY-DATUM.
  <Process Data>
v_start = ZJOB_LOG-START1 + 7.

*** Update Job Log
UPDATE ZJOB_LOG SET START1 = V_START DOC = DOC + 100
  WHERE JOB_ID = 'WEEKLYGL'.
IF SY-SUBRC <> 0.
  WRITE: /, 'Error on Log Update'.
ENDIF.
```

This example uses the SET option and the WHERE clause to explicitly spell out what's changing. This is much easier to follow than the mysterious UPDATE ZJOB_LOG, which tells the reader nothing more than the fact that something is changing about ZJOB_LOG.

Using the FROM TABLE Option with UPDATE

In the second version of UPDATE, there's an option called FROM TABLE that allows the programmer to submit an internal table with the same structure as the database table to be updated. No SET or WHERE clause is allowed with this option because the system takes the value stored in the primary key field(s) of the internal table and updates each corresponding row in the database table based on the value(s) stored in the internal table. If a row is present in the internal table with a key that isn't found in the database table, it's ignored, and processing continues with the next row in the internal table.

Suppose you want to reset the job log table. All interfaces should be set to run tomorrow, starting at the first appropriate document number. In SAP, most transaction-based data (for example, invoices, journal entries, and purchase requests) uses a document number as part of the key. Each transaction type can have a different valid range of document numbers—such as 0500000000 through 0650000000. This next example demonstrates how to accomplish this objective:

```
TABLES ZJOB_LOG.
DATA     BEGIN OF ILOG OCCURS 10.    "Internal Table
  INCLUDE STRUCTURE ZJOB_LOG.        "Same Fields as zjob_log
DATA     END OF ILOG.

*** Initialize Internal Table
ILOG-JOB_ID = 'WEEKLYGL'.
ILOG-START1 = SY-DATUM + 1.    "Set date to tomorrow
ILOG-DOC = '0050000000'.
APPEND ILOG. "Add record to Int Table
ILOG-START1 = SY-DATUM + 1.    "Set date to tomorrow
ILOG-JOB_ID = 'AREXT'.
ILOG-DOC = '0060000000'.
APPEND ILOG. "Add record to Int Table
ILOG-JOB_ID = 'APEXT'.
ILOG-START1 = SY-DATUM + 1.
ILOG-DOC = '0030000000'.
APPEND ILOG.

*** Update values in zjog_log
Update ZJOB_LOG FROM TABLE ILOG.
```

Now suppose that ZJOB_LOG contained these values when this piece of code was run:

JobId	Start	Doc#
WEEKLYGL	08/01/14	0054001100
AREXT	08/01/14	0073000600
MMEXP	12/31/16	0020100100

If you ran the code and today's date was May 2, 2015, here's what you'd get:

JobId	Start	Doc#
WEEKLYGL	05/03/14	0050000000
AREXT	05/03/14	0060000000
MMEXP	12/31/15	0020100100

Notice that the third row didn't change because none of the rows in the internal table have a value for Job_Id that matches MMEXP. Also, the row in the internal table with a Job_Id of APEXT doesn't have any effect because no row in the database matches it.

The UPDATE command gives the programmer a great deal of flexibility in changing values in a database table. Always make it obvious what data is being changed by explicitly spelling it out with SET and the WHERE clause.

INSERTING DATA (INSERT)

The INSERT command enables the programmer to add new data to a database table. As with UPDATE, the INSERT command shouldn't be used to add data to an SAP table—only to user-defined tables. This command isn't used as much as UPDATE because users manually entering data populate many tables. Each row in a database table must have a unique primary key. If a non-unique row is inserted into the table, the command fails and SY-SUBRC is set to 4. If the command succeeds, SY-SUBRC is set to 0, as usual.

Here are two possible formats for the INSERT command:

INSERT INTO tab VALUES rec.

INSERT tab [FROM TABLE itab].

The two different versions of the INSERT command are much like the versions of the UPDATE command. In one case, the data being added is provided explicitly; in the other, it's taken from the table work area or from an internal table.

Inserting Explicit Data

In the first option, the row to be inserted is first placed into a record called rec that should have the same structure as the database table into which you're inserting. This is much akin to the SET option of the UPDATE command, where the new values are explicitly spelled out. Here's an example of this first version:

```
TABLES ZJOB_LOG.
DATA BEGIN OF LREC          .         "Log Record
   INCLUDE STRUCTURE ZJOB_LOG. "Same Fields as zjob_log
DATA END OF LREC.
*** Initialize Internal Table
LREC-JOB_ID = 'WEEKLYGL'.
LREC-START1 = SY-DATUM + 1.
LREC-DOC = '0050000000'.
INSERT INTO ZJOB_LOG VALUES LREC. "Insert Data
IF SY-SUBRC <> 0.
   WRITE: /, 'Error! Duplicate Row Exists'.
ENDIF.

LREC-JOB_ID = 'AREXT'.
LREC-START1 = SY-DATUM + 1.      "Set date to tomorrow
LREC-DOC = '0060000000'.
INSERT INTO ZJOB_LOG VALUES LREC. "Insert Data
```

```
IF SY-SUBRC <> 0.
  WRITE: /, 'Error! Duplicate Row Exists'.
ENDIF.

LREC-JOB_ID = 'AREXT'.
LREC-START1 = SY-DATUM + 1.    "Set date to tomorrow
LREC-DOC = '0090000000'.
INSERT INTO ZJOB_LOG VALUES LREC.         "Insert Data
IF SY-SUBRC <> 0.
   WRITE:   /,   'Error!     Duplicate Row Exists'.
ENDIF.
```

If ZJOB_LOG is empty when this piece of code is run, the first two rows of data would be inserted successfully into the table. But the third INSERT command would fail because it attempts to insert data with a value for Job_Id (AREXT) that had already been inserted. Even though the Doc# fields contain different values, the command fails because Job_Id is a duplicate.

Inserting Data with FROM TABLE

The second variation of the INSERT command allows you to use the table work area to insert new data into the table:

```
INSERT tab [FROM TABLE itab].
```

Much like the version of the UPDATE command that uses the table work area, it can be a little bit difficult to understand what's going on.

The FROM TABLE option acts just like the option of the same name in the UPDATE command. The system uses the values in the specified internal table and inserts the data into the database. Like UPDATE, if one row fails, in this case because of a duplicate key, it doesn't cause the entire command to fail. Those rows without duplicates are successfully inserted.

Deleting Rows (DELETE)

DELETE lets you remove rows of data from a database table. As stated earlier, this command isn't normally used to delete data in an SAP table—only in user-defined tables. Like INSERT and UPDATE, DELETE comes in two primary varieties:

```
DELETE tab WHERE condition.
```

```
DELETE tab [FROM TABLE itab].
```

The two different versions of the DELETE command are much like the versions of the UPDATE command. In one case, the data being removed is provided explicitly; in the other, it's taken from the table work area or from an internal table.

Using WHERE with DELETE

In the first version of DELETE, the row to be deleted is explicitly spelled out through use of the WHERE clause. Unfortunately, if you want to delete all rows from a table, you need to supply a WHERE clause that's true for all rows. A good one to use specifies an empty string:

```
WHERE primary key <>  ''
```

This is always true because primary keys can't be empty. If the command deletes at least one row from the specified table, the return code in SY-SUBRC is set to 0. If no rows are deleted, the return code is 4.

Here's an example of the first version of the DELETE command:

```
TABLES ZJOB_LOG.
DELETE FROM ZJOB_LOG WHERE START1 < SY-DATUM.
```

Suppose that table ZJOB_LOG contains these values before this piece of code is run and assume today is January 24th, 2014:

```
Job_Id      Start         Doc#
WEEKLYGL    01/01/14      0054001100
AREXT       02/01/14      0073000600
MMEXP       12/31/13      0020100100
```

After running the code, here's what's left:

```
Job_Id      Start         Doc#
AREXT       02/01/14      0073000600
```

If you needed to make sure that all rows were deleted from the table every time, the following piece of code would accomplish just that:

```
TABLES ZJOB_LOG.
DELETE FROM ZJOB_LOG WHERE JOB_ID <> ''.
```

Because Job_Id is the key for the table, it will never be blank—thus, every row will meet the criteria for the WHERE clause and be deleted.

Deleting Multiple Rows with FROM TABLE

The second variation of the DELETE command allows programmers to delete multiple rows using an internal table or using the table work area to specify a single row to be deleted:

```
DELETE tab [FROM TABLE itab].
```

Much like the version of the UPDATE command that uses the table work area, it can be confusing when someone else is trying to understand your program. The FROM TABLE option acts similarly to the option of the same name in the UPDATE command. The system uses the values in the key field(s) to determine which rows to delete from the database. The non-key values are simply ignored.

Like UPDATE, if one row of the internal table fails, in this case because of a row with a matching key, it doesn't cause the entire command to fail. Rows with matches are successfully deleted, and failed rows are ignored.

LEARNING ADVANCED TECHNIQUES

In addition to the basic forms of SQL statements previously shown, SAP SQL also supports greatly enhanced functionality for the SELECT command. The syntax of the command has become much more complicated, so I will present a number of examples. Don't forget to take advantage of the online help in SAP if you need help with some of the details of the syntax.

By taking advantage of these enhancements, tremendous performance improvements can be made in ABAP programs. The most important enhancement is the ability to limit the amount of data retrieved from the database. With the basic version of SELECT, if you read data from a table with 100 fields, you always returned all 100 fields even if you were only interested in two of them. The advanced version of the SELECT command has the option of specifying which fields should be returned from the database, thus allowing the programmer to cut down unnecessary database and network activity.

Using Explicit Field Lists

Here's the advanced form of the SELECT command:

```
SELECT [SINGLE]  *|f1 f2 f3 6 [target] FROM tab [WHERE condition].
ENDSELECT.
```

The section of the command following the word SELECT is referred to as the field list. In the basic version, the field list was always an asterisk. In order to improve performance, instead of using the * to indicate a return of all fields of a table, you should explicitly list each field you want to be returned. When you are using an explicit field list, the target clause becomes very important. You must ensure that each field read has somewhere to be placed. The target can be one of a couple options:

```
INTO [CORRESPONDING FIELDS OF] rec
INTO (var1, var2, var3, varx)
INTO [CORRESPONDING FIELDS OF] TABLE tab
APPENDING [CORRESPONDING FIELDS OF] TABLE tab
```

You must specify a target when using an explicit field list. The one easy way to do this is to place the results into the corresponding fields in the work area of the table from which the data is selected. For example:

```
SELECT PLNUM MATNR PLWRK INTO CORRESPONDING FIELDS OF PLAF FROM PLAF.
ENDSELECT.
```

The nice thing about this approach is that programs written under older versions of ABAP can very easily be enhanced to improve their performance. Suppose an older program used this piece of code:

```
TABLES VBAK.
SELECT * FROM VBAK.
   WRITE:   /, VBAK-VBELN, VBAK-AUTLF, VBAK-AUART.
ENDSELECT.
```

This is not very effective because the table VBAK has over 70 different fields, yet only three of them are being used. By making a simple change to the SELECT statement performance, it can be improved without changing the bulk of the code.

```
TABLES VBAK.
SELECT VBELN AUTLF AUART INTO CORRESPONDING FIELDS OF VBAK FROM VBAK.
   WRITE: /, VBAK-VBELN, VBAK-AUTLF, VBAK-AUART.
ENDSELECT.
```

By using the advanced version, simple changes such as these can be made to programs, resulting in a general performance improvement across the system.

The other common approach is to define one or more variables and use them as the target, as in this example.

```
TABLES VBAK.
DATA: XVBELN LIKE VBAK-VBELN, XAUART LIKE VBAK-AUART.
SELECT VBELN AUART INTO (XVBELN, XAUART) FROM VBAK.
   WRITE: /, XVBELN, XAUART.
ENDSELECT.
```

Notice that there is no space between the variables and the beginning and ending parentheses of the INTO clause. This exact syntax is required, and if a space is present it will result in a syntax error.

The next two examples are functionally identical, but the second is more efficient. The first is written using basic SAP SQL commands, and the second is written with advanced enhancements.

```
>>>> stopped

REPORT ZCTEST.
TABLES: VBAK,VBAP, VBUP, PLAF.
DATA: BEGIN OF INT_DAT OCCURS 2000, VBELN LIKE VBAK-VBELN,
   AUART LIKE VBAK-AUART, IHREZ LIKE VBAK-IHREZ, AUTLF LIKE VBAK-AUTLF,
   POSNR LIKE VBAP-POSNR, KWMENG LIKE VBAP-KWMENG, MATNR LIKE VBAP-MATNR,
   PLNUM LIKE PLAF-PLNUM, PSTTR LIKE PLAF-PSTTR,
END OF INT_DAT.
SELECT-OPTIONS: S_VBELN FOR VBAK-VBELN DEFAULT '0600000000' OPTION GE, S_ERDAT
  FOR VBAK-ERDAT DEFAULT '20140101' OPTION GE.

* Read from sales order
SELECT * FROM VBAK WHERE VBELN IN S_VBELN
   AND ERDAT IN S_ERDAT.

* Read from sales item
SELECT * FROM VBAP WHERE VBELN = VBAK-VBELN AND UEPOS = '000000'.

* Read current item status
SELECT * FROM VBUP WHERE VBELN EQ VBAP-VBELN
   AND POSNR EQ VBAP-POSNR.
   CHECK VBUP-LFSTA NE 'C'.         "Delivery stat - Complete

* Read all planned order associated with the item
SELECT * FROM PLAF WHERE KDAUF EQ VBAP-VBELN
   AND KDPOS EQ VBAP-POSNR.
   INT_DAT-VBELN   =   VBAK-VBELN.
   INT_DAT-AUART   =   VBAK-AUART.
   INT_DAT-IHREZ   =   VBAK-IHREZ.
   INT_DAT-AUTLF   =   VBAK-AUTLF.
   INT_DAT-POSNR   =   VBAP-POSNR.
   INT_DAT-KWMENG  =   VBAP-KWMENG.
   INT_DAT-MATNR   =   VBAP-MATNR.
   INT_DAT-PLNUM   =   PLAF-PLNUM.
   INT_DAT-PSTTR   =   PLAF-PSTTR.
```

```
* Save results in internal table
APPEND INT_DAT.
ENDSELECT.
ENDSELECT.
ENDSELECT.
ENDSELECT.
```

Here is the second example featuring the advanced SAP SQL.

```
REPORT ZCTEST2.
TABLES: VBAK,VBAP, VBUP, PLAF.
DATA: BEGIN OF IVBAK OCCURS 1000,
  VBELN LIKE VBAK-VBELN,
  IHREZ LIKE VBAK-IHREZ,
  AUTLF LIKE VBAK-AUTLF,
  AUART LIKE VBAK-AUART,
END OF IVBAK.
DATA: BEGIN OF IVBAP OCCURS 10,
  VBELN LIKE VBAP-VBELN,
  POSNR LIKE VBAP-POSNR,
  KWMNG LIKE VBAP-KWMENG,
  MATNR LIKE VBAP-MATNR,
END OF IVBAP.
DATA: BEGIN OF IPLAF OCCURS 10,
  PLNUM LIKE PLAF-PLNUM,
  PSTTR LIKE PLAF-PSTTR,
END OF IPLAF.
DATA: BEGIN OF INT_DAT OCCURS 2000,
  VBELN LIKE VBAK-VBELN,
  AUART LIKE VBAK-AUART,
  IHREZ LIKE VBAK-IHREZ,
  AUTLF LIKE VBAK-AUTLF,
  POSNR LIKE VBAP-POSNR,
  KWMENG LIKE VBAP-KWMENG,
  MATNR LIKE VBAP-MATNR,
  PLNUM LIKE PLAF-PLNUM,
  PSTTR LIKE PLAF-PSTTR,
END OF INT_DAT.

SELECT-OPTIONS: S_VBELN FOR VBAK-VBELN DEFAULT '0600000000' OPTION GE,
S_ERDAT FOR VBAK-ERDAT DEFAULT '20140101' OPTION GE.
SELECT VBELN AUART IHREZ AUTLF
  INTO CORRESPONDING FIELDS OF TABLE IVBAK
  FROM VBAK
```

```
    WHERE VBELN IN S_VBELN
    AND ERDAT IN S_ERDAT.
LOOP AT IVBAK.

* Loop at sales items
    SELECT VBELN POSNR KWMENG MATNR
    INTO CORRESPONDING FIELDS OF TABLE IVBAP
    FROM VBAP
    WHERE VBELN = IVBAK-VBELN
    AND UEPOS = '000000' .
LOOP AT IVBAP.
    SELECT COUNT(*) FROM VBUP
    WHERE VBELN EQ VBAP-VBELN
    AND POSNR EQ VBAP-POSNR
    AND LFSTA EQ 'C'.         "Delivery stat – Complete
    CHECK SY-DBCNT = 0.
    SELECT PLNUM PSTTR INTO CORRESPONDING FIELDS OF TABLE IPLAF
    FROM PLAF WHERE KDAUF EQ VBAP-VBELN
    AND KDPOS EQ VBAP-POSNR.
LOOP AT IPLAF.
    INT_DAT-VBELN  =  IVBAK-VBELN.
    INT_DAT-AUART  =  IVBAK-AUART.
    INT_DAT-IHREZ  =  IVBAK-IHREZ.
    INT_DAT-AUTLF  =  IVBAK-AUTLF.
    INT_DAT-POSNR  =  IVBAP-POSNR.
    INT_DAT-KWMENG =  IVBAP-KWMNG.
    INT_DAT-MATNR  =  IVBAP-MATNR.
    INT_DAT-PLNUM  =  IPLAF-PLNUM.
    INT_DAT-PSTTR  =  IPLAF-PSTTR.
    APPEND INT_DAT.
ENDLOOP.
ENDLOOP.
ENDLOOP.
```

As these two examples show, with the advanced enhancements you have much more control of database access in ABAP. In this case, you only require the information from nine fields out of the three tables accessed. In the first example, you must retrieve all data from those three tables (over 200 fields) even though you only require nine. So in the second example, you use explicit field lists to limit the fields returned to only those required. This provides a huge savings in terms of network utilization.

Also in the second example, you use the INTO TABLE option to fetch a single array of data instead of using a SELECT loop. Retrieving data as a single array can be more efficient in many situations. SAP has difficulty with multiple-nested SELECT loops such as those in the first example. When a program is executing, as long as a SELECT loop is being processed, the application server must hold an open connection with the database server. When you have several nested SELECT statements, such as in the first example, multiple connections must be held open.

By using the INTO TABLE option, the program retrieves all requested data from the database at once and places it into an internal table. The programmer must use a LOOP command to loop through the internal table. Of course, if you know you will be looping through millions of rows of data, you do not want to wait for all of them to be transferred at once and then try to loop through all that data on the application server. In cases where large amounts of data are to be processed, it is better to use a SELECT loop.

Using Aggregate Functions to Process Data

In addition to allowing you to specify individual fields, you can also use aggregate functions on fields. An aggregate function performs a certain mathematical function against an array of records. So, instead of returning all the records in the array, the database returns only the result of the mathematical function. The most common aggregate function is summation. Using the sum function on a quantity field, for example, would return the sum of the quantity of all records to be returned instead of the records themselves. When using aggregates, you use an explicit field list with the exception of the COUNT(*) aggregate. The syntax for using an aggregate is:

```
SELECT SINGLE funct( f1 ) [AS v1] funct( f2 ) [AS v2] ...
  INTO <target> from tab.
```

The addition of the SINGLE keyword may be used here because you know the aggregate always returns a single row. The target clause is required as in any case where an explicit field list is used. The AS option allows you to give a name to the aggregate function. Later I will demonstrate the use of AS with the INTO CORRESPONDING FIELDS option.

Here is a simple example of the use of aggregates. In this case, you get the sum of the weight of all items in a delivery as well as the minimum and maximum weights of an item in the delivery.

```
TABLES LIPS.    "Delivery Items
DATA:  XSUM LIKE LIPS-NTGEW, XMAX LIKE LIPS-NTGEW, XMIN LIKE LIPS-NTGEW.
SELECT SINGLE SUM(  NTGEW )  MAX(  NTGEW )  MIN( NTGEW )
  INTO (XSUM,  XMAX,  XMIN)
  FROM LIPS
  WHERE VBELN =    '9234322'.
```

If you want to use the INTO CORRESPONDING FIELDS option, you must use AS to rename the aggregate fields. By default, SAP does not recognize that NTGEW and SUM(NTGEW) are the same field. But if you use AS, you can rename the aggregate field back to NTGEW, as seen in this example:

```
TABLES LIPS.
SELECT SINGLE SUM( NTGEW ) AS NTGEW
  INTO CORRESPONDING FIELDS OF LIPS
  FROM LIPS
  WHERE VBELN = '9234322'.
```

Using GROUP BY to Subtotal Data

In this case, the field LIPS-NTGEW will show the sum of all the records returned by the SELECT instead of a single value. Aggregates can also be used to generate subtotals instead of only totals. In this case, multiple rows are returned, one for each subtotal. Subtotals are created by placing the field you want to subtotal in the field list and by adding an option called GROUP BY to the end of the SELECT statement. Here is the syntax:

```
SELECT f1  f2  ...  funct( f3 )  funct( f4 )  ...
  INTO <target> from tab [<where clause>]
  GROUP BY f1 f2  ...
ENDSELECT.
```

Notice that in this case, the SINGLE keyword is not used. This is because you may get more than one subtotal; so a SELECT loop must be used instead. You can, of course, use any of the target options previously discussed. So if you use INTO TABLE, the results are placed into an internal table, and a SELECT loop is not required. Here is an example that returns the same aggregates as the first, but this time the plant (WERKS) subtotals them.

```
TABLES LIPS. "Delivery Items
DATA: XSUM LIKE LIPS-NTGEW, XMAX LIKE LIPS-NTGEW, XMIN LIKE LIPS-NTGEW.
data: xwerks like lips-werks.
SELECT WERKS SUM( NTGEW ) MAX( NTGEW ) MIN( NTGEW )
  INTO (XWERKS, XSUM, XMAX, XMIN)
  FROM LIPS
  WHERE VBELN = '9234322'
  GROUP BY WERKS.
ENDSELECT.
```

Aggregates are very powerful and take full advantage of SAP applications multi-tier architecture to balance the processing load between the database and the application servers.

If you needed to sum a million rows in the past, you would have had to select those million rows, transfer them to the application server, and add them one at a time. This is slow and unnecessarily eats up a lot of network bandwidth. Using aggregates, the summation takes place very quickly at the database level, and a single value is transported back to your program on the application server. The use of aggregates does increase the load on your database, but under normal conditions, the efficiency of aggregates is well worth it.

The following is a short program demonstrating the use of aggregates. The purpose of this program is to print a list of the total quantities of each material required by a planned order. It accepts the entry of a sales order number by the user and retrieves all planned orders associated with the sales orders entered. In SAP, a sales item can have one or more planned orders that tell how to build the item being sold. Each planned order is made up of the hierarchy of parts needed to make up the finished product. Within the planned order, a part may appear more than once. For example, a certain screw might secure the base of a chair as well as each armrest. This program reads the entire planned order and sums all of the parts in order to present a subtotal of the quantity required for each part.

```
REPORT ZCRLTST.
TABLES: VBAP, "Sales Items
  PLAF,
  RESB.
DATA: BEGIN OF IDAT OCCURS 50,
  MATNR LIKE RESB-MATNR,
  BDMNG LIKE RESB-BDMNG,
END OF IDAT.
SELECT-OPTIONS S_VBELN FOR VBAP-VBELN.
SELECT VBELN POSNR INTO CORRESPONDING FIELDS OF VBAP
  FROM VBAP WHERE VBELN IN S_VBELN
  AND UEPOS EQ '000000'.

*   Write Order and Item numbers
WRITE: /, VBAP-VBELN, VBAP-POSNR.
SELECT PLNUM RSNUM INTO CORRESPONDING FIELDS OF PLAF
  FROM PLAF WHERE KDAUF = VBAP-VBELN
  AND KDPOS = VBAP-POSNR.

*   Write Planned order number
WRITE: / PLAF-PLNUM.
SELECT MATNR SUM( BDMNG ) AS BDMNG
  INTO CORRESPONDING FIELDS OF TABLE IDAT
  FROM RESB
  WHERE RSNUM = PLAF-RSNUM
```

```
   AND SHKZG NE 'S'
   AND POSTP EQ 'L'
   AND DUMPS NE 'X'
   GROUP BY MATNR.
LOOP AT IDAT.

*  Write material and quantity
   WRITE: / IDAT-MATNR, IDAT-BDMNG.
ENDLOOP.
ENDSELECT.
ENDSELECT.
```

Using INNER JOIN to Access Multiple Tables

In standard SQL, the programmer can retrieve data from multiple tables at the same time. This is referred to as a table join and is also part of the syntax of the SAP SELECT command. In order to perform a table join, the tables must have a relationship that tells the database how to combine the data from the multiple tables into a single result set. For example, two tables, one with header data and the second with item data, might be joined to retrieve both head and item data at the same time.

Without using a join in the program, it would have to retrieve all the header data, then retrieve all the item data, and then combine it. The other option to access this type of related data in a single database read is through the creation of Data Dictionary–defined views. A view can include data from multiple tables, but views are Data Dictionary objects and must be set up ahead of time.

The benefits of a join are typically in performance because data comes from multiple database tables in a single read. This allows the developer to reduce the number of database calls and leverage the power of the server.

When performing a join, it is very important to correctly define the relationships between the two tables. A mistake can cause no data to be returned or, even worse, duplicate rows that are in error. With this caveat in mind, here is the syntax of the SELECT command with the INNER JOIN option.

```
SELECT tab1~f1 tab1~f2 tab2~f3 ... INTO (target)
   FROM (tab1 inner join tab2 on tab1~key1 = tab2~key1
   AND tab1~key2 = tab2~key2 ...
   inner join tab3 on tab1~key1 = tab3~key1
     AND tab1~key2 = tab3~key2 ...)
   [WHERE whereclause] [ORDER BY tab1~f1 tab2~f2 ...].
```

The syntax of this form of the SELECT command is very different from a standard SELECT. As you can see, the table name and field name are not separated by a dash (-) but instead by a tilde (~). With this option it is possible to select from more than two tables, but it is very important to choose the correct main table. The main table is the table in the FROM clause of the SELECT. The other tables are referred to as join tables. The main table must have a relationship with all of the join tables. If the relationships in the join are not specified correctly, the SELECT will return incorrect data and may cause a tremendous load on the system and result in incorrect results.

In this first example, you select data from two tables. The first is PLAF, which holds data about planned orders. The second is VBAP, which holds data about sales items.

The planned orders are associated with a sales item, so the join relationship is the order number and item number.

```
TABLES: PLAF, VBAP.
DATA: XVBELN LIKE VBAP-VBELN,
  XPOSNR LIKE VBAP-POSNR,
  XMATNR LIKE VBAP-MATNR,
  XPLNUM LIKE PLAF-PLNUM.
SELECT VBAP~VBELN VBAP~POSNR VBAP~MATNR PLAF~PLNUM
  INTO (XVBELN, XPOSNR, XMATNR, XPLNUM)
  FROM ( PLAF INNER JOIN VBAP ON PLAF~KDAUF = VBAP~VBELN
  AND PLAF~KDPOS = VBAP~POSNR )
  WHERE VBAP~VBELN = '1231311'
  ORDER BY VBAP~MATNR.
ENDSELECT.
```

This last example demonstrates joining three tables. Notice in this case that, instead of using a SELECT loop, you use the INTO TABLE option to place the results of the SELECT directly into an internal table.

```
REPORT ZCTEST1.
TABLES: VBAK,      "Sales Order Header
  VBAP,     "Sales Item
  VBUK.     "Document Status
DATA: BEGIN OF IDAT OCCURS 100,
  VBELN LIKE VBAK-VBELN,
  POSNR LIKE VBAP-POSNR,
  MATNR LIKE VBAP-MATNR,
  LFGSK LIKE VBUK-LFGSK,
END OF IDAT.
```

```
SELECT VBAK~VBELN VBAP~POSNR VBAP~MATNR VBUK~LFGSK
   INTO CORRESPONDING FIELDS OF TABLE IDAT
   FROM ( VBAK INNER JOIN VBUK ON VBAK~VBELN = VBUK~VBELN
   INNER JOIN VBAP ON VBAK~VBELN = VBAP~VBELN )
   WHERE VBUK~LFSTK <> 'C' "Documents not complete
   ORDER BY MATNR.
LOOP AT IDAT.
   WRITE:  /, IDAT.
ENDLOOP.
```

The use of the INTO TABLE option demonstrates that any of the common SELECT options will also work with the INNER JOIN option.

All of these enhancements demonstrated add a great deal of power and flexibility to ABAP. It is important to take advantage of them in both new and existing programs when you have the opportunity.

SUMMARY

This chapter has been an introduction to SAP SQL. Later in the book, when you get into detailed business cases and examples, you'll be able to see clearly the importance of SAP SQL. Almost every program makes use of SAP SQL to some extent, especially the SELECT command.

The GET command is a second method used to read information from the database, the pros and cons of which are detailed in Chapter 13, "Working with Logical Databases." Because the database is the heart of SAP, the SAP SQL commands that give a programmer access to that heart are of paramount importance.

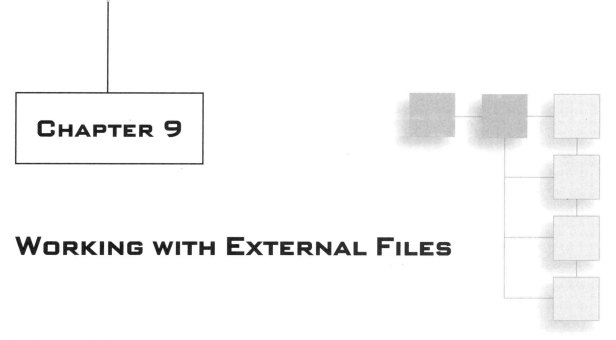

CHAPTER 9

WORKING WITH EXTERNAL FILES

IN THIS CHAPTER

- Data Mapping
- Establishing the Path and File Name
- Opening the File (OPEN DATASET)
- Adding a System Message (MESSAGE)
- Sending a Command to the Server (FILTER)
- Writing the Data to the Server (TRANSFER)
- Reading the Data from the Data File (READ)
- Closing the File (CLOSE DATASET)

This chapter deals with how ABAP code imports and exports external files from and to the application server. The application server is the machine on which all the compiled code is executed, and the format of the file is either ASCII text or binary.

The importance of external files can be highlighted by two examples:

- When SAP is implemented, the old system isn't just shut off and SAP started up. SAP is too large and complex a system for that, so SAP is brought online piece by piece, with pieces of the old system being replaced by the new pieces of SAP. To maintain this coexistence between the old system and SAP, some data must be shared between the two systems. The data is generally transferred in text format in a file that's either produced by the old system and read into SAP or produced by SAP and copied to the old system. Transferring files between systems allows the SAP implementation to progress step by step with relatively few growing pains.

■ The second important purpose of external files is for additional processing by one of the users. Essentially, the user might not want a hard copy (paper copy) version of the data in a report, so in addition to the paper copy, an electronic version is created. The electronic version can be imported into third-party software such as Microsoft's Excel spreadsheet or a form-generation tool such as Fantasia. The electronic copy allows users to process the data in a custom format that SAP might not supply. Also, the file can be attached to an email message and read by a number of users, rather than having copies printed and sent throughout the company. The electronic version essentially saves paper and allows users to utilize third-party software tools to analyze the data from SAP.

External files can be read or written directly using ABAP/4 code or processed using one of SAP's included function modules. These function modules can read and write external files to and from the application server as well as directly to the user's PC. These helpful functions are discussed in the latter portion of this chapter.

Data Mapping

When data is transferred from a system to SAP or vice versa, the source of the data and its final destination must be determined. *Data mapping* is the term used to describe the "travel plans" of the data being transferred. One of the primary purposes of coding ABAP is coding *interfaces*. An interface is the regular transfer of data from an older system to SAP, or vice versa.

This chapter is more concerned with the format of the output data. The term *format* refers to the fact that all fields pulled from SAP or brought in from an outside file should be of type C, character fields. Particular attention must be paid to the length of these fields, incoming or outgoing.

The best way to achieve good mapping from one system to another is to construct an internal table that has the desired format for the incoming or outgoing data. To accomplish this task, ask a functional analyst for a sample file that will be used by the program.

Then mark the separate fields and count how many spaces each field takes and define them as type `C` (character). Examine the following "file":

```
apple   fruit    500 -
banana - fruit    600 -
squash - vegetable    20
```

To hold this data in an internal table, you must count the spaces for each field. The first field can be identified as description, or `DESC` for short, and it holds 10 characters. The second field can be characterized as `TYPE`, and it is called just that. It holds 15 characters. The last field is regarded as the quantity, or shortened as `QTY`. It holds 7 characters. Now that you've specified the lengths and what kind of data each field holds, you can create an internal table that will hold each record (shown next):

```
DATA:    BEGIN OF INT_TAB OCCURS 100,
DESC(10) TYPE C,    "description
TYPE(15) TYPE C,    "type
QTY(7) TYPE C.    "quantity
DATA:    END OF INT_TAB.
```

This internal table is now set to read data from an external text file. If you put data into this internal table, on the other hand, it could be written as an external text file. This practice of setting up a structure to hold the incoming or outgoing data is a very good idea in order to separate fields from each other and to keep the incoming or outgoing data in a consistent format.

When setting up tables for data transfer, remember these two rules:

- All the fields in the internal table must be character fields to make sure that the right number of spaces from the data is read in or written out. Character fields will read in the defined number of spaces; some other fields won't. Character fields always work, so stick with them for transferring data. Once the data is read into SAP, the character field can be transferred to another field that's more appropriate. For example, the `QTY` field can be transferred to a field of type `I` (integer), which would allow for quantitative analysis on the field.

- The second rule is essentially mentioned in the first rule. Make sure that the right number of spaces is used to define the fields in the internal table. Get a preview copy of the file and count the spaces for each field. Although the process may seem tedious, it gives you results that are accurate and reliable.

This preliminary data mapping saves time and avoids headaches later on during data processing. The first goal is to get the data in or out cleanly. If no mistakes are encountered in the transfer process for the incoming or outgoing data, you can count on data integrity when the time comes to process the data.

Establishing the Path and File Name

The first actual step of accessing an external text file is establishing the path and file name of that file. The path and the file name should be declared as separate parameters in the data declaration section of your code. A separate data field should also be created to store the concatenation of the path and file name.

Here's an example:

```
PARAMETERS:    P_PATH(50) TYPE C lower case,
P_FILE(20) TYPE C lower case.
DATA:    W_DATA(70) TYPE C.
MOVE P_FILE TO W_DATA+50(20).
CONDENSE W DATA NO-GAPS.
```

The screen that this code would generate is shown in Figure 9.1.

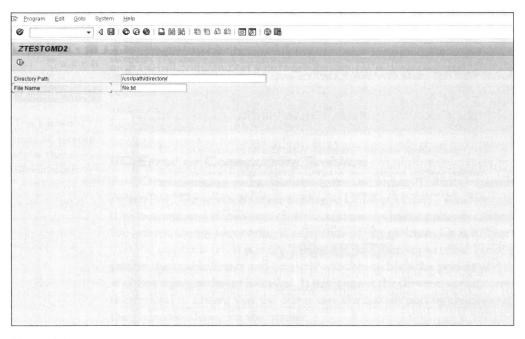

Figure 9.1
The sample selection screen for path and file name input.

Let's say that the path entered is /users/finance/. The file name will be audit.txt. The path is moved to the data field, W_DATA. The file name is moved to the offset position in W_DATA, starting at the 50th position. The CONDENSE / NO-GAPS code then removes all spaces between the path and the file name to make W_DATA contain the full path and file name for that file.

Tip

By using parameters for the path and the file name, you've made the program modular. The program can change as path structures or file names change, so it should never be hard coded into the program.

OPENING THE FILE (OPEN DATASET)

Once the full path and file name are stored in one field, a command is issued to open that file for reading, writing, or appending. To open the file, use the OPEN DATASET command:

```
OPEN DATASET path plus filename FOR   [[OUTPUT,INPUT,APPENDING]
[IN   [TEXT MODE ENCODING <linefeed>, LEGACY BINARY MODE,
          LEGACY TEXT MODE]]
```

The following sections discuss the options used with the OPEN DATASET command.

Marking a File for Output (FOR OUTPUT)

In OUTPUT mode, the program opens the file (if it exists) and writes over it or creates the file (if it doesn't exist).

If the following code is executed, a zero-length file appears in the directory specified by /users/zuser/ on the application server that's running the program. The file name is abap.txt:

```
DATA:    W_PATH(40) TYPE C VALUE '/users/zuser/abap.txt'.
OPEN DATASET W PATH FOR OUTPUT.
```

Note

If the path is incorrect, or if the path is protected, SY-SUBRC is set to be greater than 0. Generally, it's a good rule of thumb to make the path and the file name separate parameters to be entered at runtime. That way, if the path changes, the program can adapt.

Because the file has no data transferred to it in the current program, it's "zero-length." If you don't want to overwrite your previous week's file with the same name, make the new file name dynamic by incorporating the date or some other variable. In case of a system shutdown or catastrophe, keeping data on hand from previous weeks is a good idea in order to restore the system.

Marking a File for Input (FOR INPUT)

To read an external file, the FOR INPUT addition is needed at the end of the OPEN DATASET statement. The file must already exist on the application server in the specified path.

To see this command in action, look at the following sample code—it's explained later in the section called "Reading the Data from the Data File (READ)":

```
DATA:    END OF INT TAB.
DATA: W_DATASET(50) VALUE '/users/abap.txt'
OPEN DATASET W_DATASET FOR INPUT IN LEGACY TEXT MODE.
 DO.
   IF SY-SUBRC <> 0.
EXIT
ENDIF.
READ DATASET W_DATASET INTO INT_TAB.
APPEND INTJAB.
CLEAR INTJAB. ENDDO. CLOSE DATASET W DATASET
```

Selecting a Transfer Mode (IN TEXT MODE/IN BINARY MODE)

When text is transferred to a file, it can be transferred in one of three ways: using TEXT MODE with specified encoding, using LEGACY TEXT MODE, or using LEGACY BINARY MODE. In legacy text mode, the data is transferred line by line or field by field, with a carriage return inserted into the file after each line or field transferred. The data displayed from a text file would appear in the following format, if printed out:

```
12345
67890
11   12    13    14     15
```

After each line (five numbers), a carriage return is inserted in the text file, and the next piece of data appears on the next line.

If data is transferred in legacy binary mode, no carriage return is inserted after each field or line. The data keeps adding to the file as it progresses. The file from the preceding section would appear in the following format if written in binary mode:

```
1 2 3 4 5 6 7 8 9 10 11 12 13 14 15
```

No carriage return is inserted after each line, so the data appears line after line.

If your system is Unicode compliant (most systems these days are), for text mode, you would choose to use TEXT MODE with the specified encoding. The encoding types are:

- DEFAULT
- UTF-8
- NON-UNICODE

DEFAULT lets the system choose. If the system is Unicode compliant, then it will use UTF-8. If it is not, then it will use NON-UNICODE. If you know that a specific file is or is not Unicode, then you would choose UTF-8 or NON-UNICODE, respectively.

The general rule is that if the data is written in legacy binary mode, you need to make sure that the other program reads the file in legacy binary mode. The same rule applies for legacy text mode. Generally, write the file and read the file in the same mode to avoid problems when dealing with external files.

Tip

Check what the file looks like when it's printed. If it looks like a binary file (no carriage returns), read the file in binary mode. If it looks like a text file (carriage returns present after each line), read the file in text mode.

Writing to the End of a File (FOR APPENDING)

The FOR APPENDING addition to the OPEN DATASET command opens a file for the purpose of writing at the end of the file. The file must exist for the program to write to the end of the file; if the file doesn't exist, a new file is created. No example for this command is really necessary. If a file exists, records are added to the end of the file. If it doesn't exist, a new file is created. Otherwise, this addition to the OPEN DATASET command acts just like the addition FOR OUTPUT.

Indicating the Start of the Read (AT POSITION)

The AT POSITION addition to the OPEN DATASET command specifies a file position at which the read starts (counting from the start of the file). The next read or write will start at this position. The general syntax for this addition is as follows:

```
OPEN DATASET FOR INPUT AT POSITION position number.
```

The position is a byte marker and is marked explicitly as a number; position number can be any number from 0 to the end of the file. Obviously, you can't specify a position before the start of the file.

Adding a System Message (MESSAGE)

The MESSAGE command places a system message from the operating system into the field msg. This data field must be declared in the data declaration portion of the program; the field is generally of type character with a length of around 60 to 80 spaces:

```
DATA:   W_DATASET(50) VALUE  '/users/abap.txt',
W_MESSAGE(100),
W_RECORD(100).
OPEN DATASET W_DATASET FOR INPUT IN TEXT MODE MESSAGE WJESSAGE.
DO.
 IF SY-SUBRC <> 0.
WRITE W_MESSAGE.
EXIT.
ENDIF.
READ DATASET W_DATASET INTO W_RECORD.
ENDDO.
CLOSE DATASET W_DATASET.
```

Let's say, for example, that the file doesn't exist. If you try to open a file that doesn't exist, a system error message is placed in W_MESSAGE and displayed. When programs fail, it's nice to have a message indicating why—in this case, whether opening the file was or wasn't a problem. The more messages in your program, the easier it is to decipher what's causing a problem (assuming the messages are meaningful).

Sending a Command to the Server (FILTER)

The FILTER command allows SAP to issue an operating system command to the application server, provided that the application server is running a UNIX or Windows NT operating system. The general syntax for this command is:

```
OPEN DATASET dataset FOR OUTPUT FILTER filter command.
```

filter command can be any UNIX or NT command. For example, the value of filter command could be zip. The file would then be saved and *zipped* (compressed). When you need to open the file and read it again, you can use a FILTER command equal to unzip. The file is then *unzipped* (uncompressed) and read into SAP.

The FILTER command can be used with the OPEN DATASET command for output and for input.

WRITING THE DATA TO THE SERVER (TRANSFER)

TRANSFER is the command used to write the data from SAP to the opened data file on the application server. Logically, the TRANSFER command is associated with the OPEN DATASET *dataset* FOR OUTPUT command. Following is the general syntax:

TRANSFER field TO path and filename.

path and filename is the same as the dataset name used to open the file, and field can be any data field declared in the data declarations portion of the program. The field can be an internal table name as well as just a field name.

The following program first reads all of the records from the financial accounting detail table, BSEG, into an internal table, INT_TAB. Then, once all the records have been transferred, the file is opened for output. The LOOP AT command loops through to read all the records of INT_TAB. As each record is read, it's transferred to the file:

```
TABLES: BSEG.
DATA:    BEGIN OF INT_TAB OCCURS 1000.
         INCLUDE STRUCTURE BSEG.
DATA:    END OF INT_TAB.
DATA:    W_DATASET(50) VALUE '/users/abap.txt'.
SELECT * FROM BSEG INTO TABLE INTJAB WHERE
GJAHR = '2014'.
OPEN DATASET W_DATASET FOR OUTPUT IN TEXT MODE.
     LOOP AT INT_TAB.
     TRANSFER INT_TAB TO W_DATASET.
     ENDLOOP.
CLOSE DATASET W_DATASET.
```

After all the records have been processed, the file is closed with the CLOSE DATASET command, which is covered in the later section called "Closing the File (CLOSE DATASET)." If the transfer was not successful for some reason, SY-SUBRC will have a value other than zero in it.

Essentially, the TRANSFER command takes a data field or internal table record and writes it to an external file, providing that the file has been opened for output.

READING THE DATA FROM THE DATA FILE (READ)

The READ command is used to read the data from the opened data file on the application server into SAP. The READ command transfers the current line of the file, or just the right number of characters if the read is done in binary mode, into the field or internal table record. The general syntax of the READ statement used with external files is this:

```
READ path and filename INTO fieldname.
```

path and filename refers to the dataset that was opened using the OPEN DATASET command FOR INPUT, whereas fieldname can refer to any field or internal table record that was declared in the data declaration portion of the program (just like with the TRANSFER command).

If the file is opened in text mode, the line is transferred to the field or internal table record. If the line exceeds the number of spaces for either, the end of the line is dropped off. If the file is opened in binary mode, only the number of spaces allocated to the field or to the internal table record is transferred from the file. While binary mode sounds better, it's just a better idea to count out exactly how many spaces each field will take in the file and make your field(s) of an internal table match those spaces. In binary mode, it's possible to read half of a piece of data into one field and the other half into another field.

The following program reads in the data file that's output just above the code. Notice that the internal table has been precisely configured to read in just the right number of letters to fill the records properly. After the data is declared, the dataset is opened, and the reading process begins:

```
DATAFILE
Doolittle          Bob        Truck Driver
Smith              Sally      CEO
Morgan             Stephanie  Lawyer

DATA:    BEGIN OF INT_TAB OCCURS 10,
            LAST(19),
            FIRST(10),
            OCCUPATION(15).
DATA:    END OF INT_TAB.

DATA: W_DATASET(50) VALUE ' /users/abap.txt'.
OPEN DATASET W_DATASET FOR INPUT IN TEXT MODE.
DO.
IF SY-SUBRC <> 0.
  EXIT.
ENDIF.
```

```
  READ DATASET W_DATASET INTO INTJAB.
  APPEND INT_TAB.
  CLEAR
  INT_TAB.
ENDDO.
```

```
CLOSE DATASET W_DATASET.
```

Because the program essentially is "dumb" and doesn't know how many records are in this file, the IF statement tells the program to exit if an error is encountered. An error is encountered if the program attempts to read a record that doesn't exist. An error is denoted by the system field SY-SUBRC not being equal to 0. Each time the data is read into the internal table record, it must be appended to the table. Then the header record of the internal table is cleared in preparation for the next input. The CLEAR statement makes sure that no duplicate records are copied to the file.

Closing the File (CLOSE DATASET)

The final command issued is CLOSE DATASET:

```
CLOSE DATASET path plus filename.
```

This command closes the file. It must be used after writing, appending to, or reading the file.

Summary

In every SAP implementation, moving files to and from external systems is very important. SAP systems are not brought up at 100 percent; normally, part of the system is brought up and is run in parallel with the old system. For this to happen, external files must serve as communications between the new and old systems. This chapter covered how to read, write, and modify these files. External files are used extensively in Chapter 16, "Writing a Data Extract," and Chapter 17, "Writing a BDC Program."

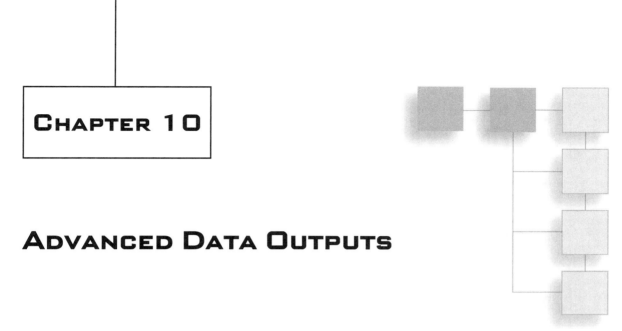

CHAPTER 10

ADVANCED DATA OUTPUTS

IN THIS CHAPTER

- Processing Events in ABAP/4
- Hiding Field Contents with `HIDE`
- Using Field Groups as an Alternative to Internal Tables

This chapter defines the commands in ABAP that cover events, interactive reporting, and a substitute for internal tables. Whereas all three of these topics are very important in your development as an ABAPer, it's important that you have a good grasp of the fundamentals presented in the previous chapters before launching into these areas. If you're a bit shaky on some of the topics covered in the chapters before this one, please reread the chapters.

These are the major topics covered in this chapter:

- *Events* are markers in code that define when the code following the `EVENT` label will be executed. For example, `AT USER-COMMAND` is an event that specifies what code to run after a user clicks a button or presses a function key Other events determine what the output might be on the selection screen, as well as when the data selection process would start.

- The `HIDE` statement, used in conjunction with events and the `WRITE` statement, allows interactive reporting. In interactive reporting, the report is written to the screen.

The user can double-click a certain line to get more information or to process a certain line of information.

■ Generally, interactive reporting is handled by developing module pools using the screen and menu painter, but it's possible to use ABAP commands in the editor screen to do a little interactive reporting. Module pools are a different type of program developed in SAP. They are developed using the screen and menu painter— editors outside of the ABAP/4 editor that's introduced in this book. The generation of screens and menus is not covered in this book.

■ Field groups is another method used to store data. Field groups enable you to store more data than in internal tables and to sort and process the records in a new and efficient fashion. Contractors debate whether field groups are faster or slower than internal tables in regard to access time, but the superior storage capacity is a definite plus for field groups.

You don't need to read this chapter in order; read any sections, in any order that interests you. Again, make sure that you have a good basic understanding of topics from previous chapters; otherwise, comprehending these new and advanced topics might be difficult.

PROCESSING EVENTS IN ABAP/4

Events are markers that define certain code that is to occur at certain times in the program. They help define how your programs should run. Certain events governed by the AT command, for example, are used extensively in interactive reporting. Other events, such as INITIALIZATION and START-OF-SELECTION, define at what times the data selection occurs or what default values appear on the selection screen before the program is run. Basically, the events tell the application server when to process certain parts of code. Events govern the timing of the program.

The events covered in this chapter include:

```
INITIALIZATION.
START-OF-SELECTION.
END-OF-SELECTION.
AT USER-COMMAND.
AT LINE-SELECTION.
AT PFfunction key number.
AT SELECTION-SCREEN.
AT NEW field.
AT END OF  field.
```

```
AT FIRST.
AT LAST.
AT field-group.
```

Setting Initial Values (INITIALIZATION)

The INITIALIZATION event occurs after the data declaration portion of the program. The code under this event defines the initial values of the parameters and SELECT-OPTIONS before the initial selection screen appears. Here's an example:

```
REPORT ZABAPER.

TABLES: MARC,
MARD,
MSEG,
VBFA.

PARAMETERS:   P_NAME LIKE SY-UNAME,
P_DATE LIKE SY-DATUM.
SELECT-OPTIONS: S_MATNR FOR MSEG-MATNR.
INITIALIZATION.
  P_NAME = SY-UNAME.
  P_DATE = SY-DATUM   -   1.
  S_MATNR-LOW = '1'.
  S_MATNR-HIGH =    '10'.
  S_MATNR-OPTION = 'BT' .
  S_MATNR-SIGN = 'I'.
  APPEND S_MATNR.
  CLEAR S_MATNR.

START-OF-SELECTION.
  WRITE 'START OF PROGRAM'.
```

Before the selection screen comes up, in the code between the two events INITIALIZATION and START-OF-SELECTION, the parameters for the username, date, and the selection-screen range for material number are all blank (see Figure 10.1). However, if you include the code lines shown, the new selection screen appears with values already filled in (see Figure 10.2).

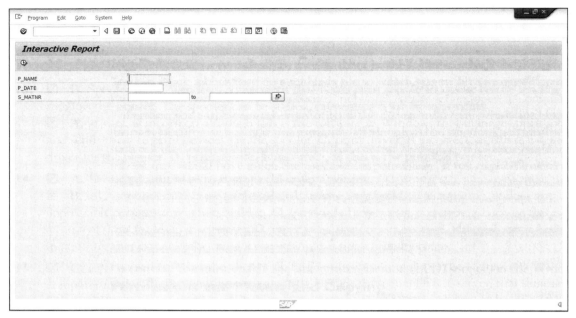

Figure 10.1
The selection screen with parameters and SELECT-OPTIONS initialized, but without values.

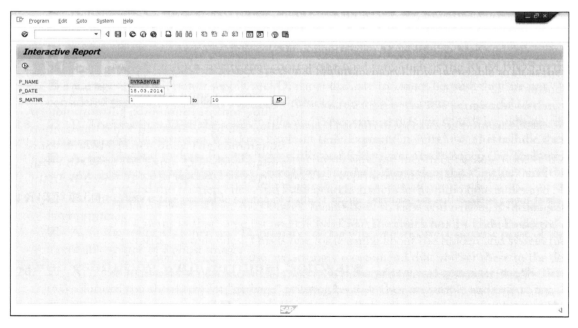

Figure 10.2
The selection screen with parameters and SELECT-OPTIONS initialized, with values.

Essentially, the code that appears after the event INITIALIZATION and before the next event, usually START-OF-SELECTION, is used to define the default or initial values of the PARAMETERS and SELECT-OPTIONS. The difference between defining default values in the actual PARAMETER definition, using the DEFAULT addition, and defining the value after the INITIALIZATION event is that the default values can be calculated with INITIALIZATION. The values defined after the INITIALIZATION event are also present in background processing, where the application is run in background mode. Background mode is used when a program is not run online, but in a batch. The program is scheduled to run automatically without a user clicking an Execute button, and the INITIALIZATION values appear automatically in the selection screen.

Using the START-OF-SELECTION and END-OF-SELECTION Markers

The START-OF-SELECTION event defines the code that will be processed initially—before any logical database access. This means that when the GET command is executed to utilize logical databases, the data extraction from that logical database occurs by looping through the code defined between the START-OF-SELECTION and END-OF-SELECTION markers. (See Chapter 13, "Working with Logical Databases," for details.)

Essentially, the START-OF-SELECTION and END-OF-SELECTION combination marks the place in the code that the data is read from the database and processed. The START-OF-SELECTION event also marks when another event has ended, such as INITIALIZATION.

In the following example, the INITIALIZATION event is performed first. The selection screen appears next. After the data is entered or changed, the next piece of code to run is the code that appears after the START-OF-SELECTION event:

```
REPORT ZABAPER.

TABLES:

MARC, MARD, MSEG, VBFA.

PARAMETERS:

P_NAME LIKE SY-UNAME, P DATE LIKE SY-DATUM.

SELECT-OPTIONS: S_MATNR FOR MSEG-MATNR.
INITIALIZATION.
P_NAME = SY-UNAME.
P_DATE = SY-DATUM - 1.
S_MATNR-LOW = '1'. S_MATNR-HIGH = '10'.
     S_MATNR-OPTION = 'BT'. S_MATNR-SIGN = 'I'.
APPEND S_MATNR. CLEAR S_MATNR.
START-OF-SELECTION.
```

```
WRITE 'START OF PROGRAM'.
PERFORM SAMPLE_SUBROUTINE.
END-OF-SELECTION.
FORM SAMPLE_SUBROUTINE.
ENDFORM.
```

START-OF-SELECTION and END-OF-SELECTION, like INITIALIZATION, help with the timing of the code being run in ABAP. The code after END-OF-SELECTION is triggered after all logical database records are read or after a STOP command is executed somewhere in the code.

Triggering Code with an AT Event

There are certain times when events can trigger certain code to run. These events are governed by the AT event command. The event is defined by the commands that follow the AT event. If the specified event occurs (for example, a function key is pressed), the code after the AT event command is executed. The ENDAT command defines the end of the code that must be executed if the event occurs.

The following sections explore some of the events used with AT event.

Executing User Commands (AT USER-COMMAND and AT LINE-SELECTION)

The USER-COMMAND event is used in interactive reporting. The code between the AT USER-COMMAND and the ENDAT command is executed when the user enters data into the OK code field (the upper-left entry field on the screen where you enter transactions) or when a function key is pressed. The data entered into the OK code field is stored in the system field SY-UCOMM.

The following code generates a crude report onscreen. If the user selects a line with the cursor and types DETA for detail, the program checks the detail table BSEG for the details associated with that document number and prints them to the screen. If no data is found, a message is printed saying NO DATA FOUND. Finally, if the user types END, the message END OF REPORT is written to the screen:

```
REPORT ZABAP2.
TABLES:  BKPF,
BSEG.
START-OF-SELECTION. SELECT * FROM BKPF.
WRITE BKPF-BELNR.
HIDE BKPF-BELNR.
ENDSELECT.
 END-OF-SELECTION.
```

```
AT USER-COMMAND.
CASE SY-UCOMM.
WHEN    'DETA'.
SELECT * FROM BSEG WHERE    BELNR = BKPF-BELNR.
IF SY-SUBRC <> 0.
WRITE    'NO DATA FOUND'.
ELSE.
WRITE BSEG-BELNR.
ENDIF.
ENDSELECT.
WHEN    'END'.
WRITE    'END OF REPORT'.
ENDCASE.
```

The AT LINE-SELECTION command defines the code that's executed after a user double-clicks a line or presses the F2 function key:

```
REPORT ABAP3.
TABLES:   BKPF,
BSEG.
START-OF-SELECTION.
GET BKPF.
WRITE BKPF-GJAHR.
HIDE BKPF-GJAHR.
END-OF-SELECTION.
AT LINE-SELECTION.
CHECK BKPF-GJAHR <> ' '.

SELECT * FROM BSEG WHERE GJAHR = BKPF-GJAHR.
IF SY-SUBRC <> 0.
WRITE    'NO DATA EXISTS FOR THAT FISCAL YEAR'.
ENDIF.
WRITE BSEG-GJAHR.

ENDSELECT.
```

The HIDE command in this example temporarily stores the contents of the fields displayed to the screen. (See the later section "Hiding Field Contents with HIDE" for details.) The CHECK statement makes sure that a valid line is selected (a line is selected that contains data from BKPF).

Essentially, the LINE-SELECTION event is specific to the double-click or the F2 function key. The function key can be changed, but that should be a rare occurrence—you have to use screen and menu painter logic that isn't covered in this book.

Controlling Function Keys (AT PF Function Key Number)

The event AT PF function key number governs function keys that the user would press in interactive reporting; the function key number is a number from 1 to 24. The number can't be a variable. Essentially, a report is displayed, and then the processor "waits" for the user to press a function key. When this function key is pressed, the code after the AT command is executed. Here's a very simple version of code demonstrating this event:

```
REPORT ZABAP

MESSAGE-ID ZZ.

TABLES:

PBIM, PBED.

SELECT  *  FROM PBIM WHERE MATNR LIKE    '64%'.
WRITE PBIM.
ENDSELECT.
AT PF8.
MESSAGE I999 WITH 'FUNCTION KEY 8 IS PRESSED'.
AT PF9.
MESSAGE I999 WITH 'FUNCTION KEY 9 IS PRESSED'.
```

This code checks the independent requirements table, PBIM, for all material numbers beginning with 64 and writes them to the screen. The AT commands aren't related precisely to the first code, but they exemplify exactly what the AT PF function key number command does. The code after the AT command could be any code, including the interactive reporting code demonstrated in the preceding sections. Any commands that represent the code after the AT command can be executed after the function key is pressed.

Processing Screen Input (AT SELECTION-SCREEN)

The AT SELECTION-SCREEN event is processed after the selection screen from a program is processed. For example, the selection screen is brought up onscreen, and the user enters the data and then clicks the Execute button. Before any code starts, the code after the AT SELECTION-SCREEN command is executed. Generally, this AT command is used to check for errors so that the user can reprocess the screen if the initial data input was invalid. Here's an example:

```
REPORT ZABAP
MESSAGE-ID ZZ.
PARAMETERS:      P_NAME LIKE SY-UNAME.
AT SELECTION-SCREEN.
IF P_NAME = ' '.
```

```
MESSAGE I999 WITH   'Please enter some data'.
 ENDIF.
WRITE:    'The current user is', P_NAME.
```

If the user doesn't enter any data but clicks the Execute button anyway, then 'Please enter some data' message pops up, and the selection screen is reprocessed.

Triggering Events with Field Changes (AT NEW Field and AT END OF Field)

The AT NEW field command covers a field changing in an internal table. If a new value is encountered in the field, the commands after the AT command are executed.

The following program loops through the internal table INT_PBIM, created by a data extract from the database table PBIM. Every time a new material number appears, the program writes NEW MATERIAL NUMBER. Essentially, if a new value appears in the field, the AT event is triggered.

```
REPORT ZABAP. TABLES:    PBIM.
DATA:    BEGIN OF INT_PBIM OCCURS 1000.
INCLUDE STRUCTURE PBIM. DATA:
END OF INT_PBIM.
SELECT * FROM PBIM INTO TABLE INT_PBIM.
LOOP AT INT_PBIM.
AT NEW MATNR.
WRITE 'NEW MATERIAL NUMBER'.
ENDAT.
WRITE INT_PBIM.

ENDLOOP.
```

The AT END OF field command is almost exactly the same as the AT NEW field—except that the event is triggered after the last encounter of the value in the field. This code waits until the last instance of a material number is reached and then writes a message to the screen indicating how many instances of that material number were processed:

```
REPORT ZABAP.
TABLES:    PBIM.
DATA:    BEGIN OF INT_PBIM OCCURS 1000.
INCLUDE STRUCTURE PBIM.
DATA:    END OF INT_PBIM.
DATA:    W_INDEX LIKE SY-TABIX.
SELECT * FROM PBIM INTO TABLE INT_PBIM.
LOOP AT INT_PBIM.
W_INDEX = W_INDEX + 1.
```

```
AT END OF MATNR.
WRITE: W_INDEX,    ' INSTANCES OF    ',    INT_PBIM-MATNR.
CLEAR W_INDEX.
ENDAT.
Write INT_PBIM.
Endloop.
```

Note

> The AT field-group command, although it's one of the AT commands, is covered in the section on field groups, called "Using Field Groups as an Alternative to Internal Tables." (You need to understand field groups before AT field-group will make sense to you. To explain the purpose and use of this event here would be putting the cart before the horse.)

Hiding Field Contents with HIDE

The HIDE command stores the contents of a field in memory, if the line is selected via cursor position. The syntax for this command is pretty simple:

```
HIDE field.
```

If a line is double-clicked or selected and then a function key is pressed, field is populated with the data from the current line holding that field. For example, if a selected line has the three fields—name, address, and phone number—and a HIDE ADDRESS command has been issued, the address on the selected line is put into the field address.

The following program loops through the customer data table, KNA1, and prints the customer's name to the screen. When the program is finished, the user selects a line and double-clicks. The program then writes the customer number of that line to the screen.

```
REPORT ZABAP.
TABLES:  KNA1.
SELECT  *  FROM KNA1.
WRITE KNA1-NAME1.
HIDE KNA1-KUNNR.
ENDSELECT.

AT LINE-SELECTION.
CHECK KNA1-KUNNR <>    '    '.
WRITE KNA1-KUNNR.
```

Using Field Groups as an Alternative to Internal Tables

Field groups combine fields from the data declaration portion of the program into one group; in other words, several fields are grouped together under one `field-group` name. At runtime, the `INSERT` command is used to define which data fields are assigned to which field group. There should always be a `HEADER` field group that defines how the extracted data will be sorted; the data is sorted by the fields grouped under the `HEADER` field group.

Defining Field Groups

The syntax for defining the field groups is very simple:

```
FIELD-GROUPS:       field group 1, field group 2.
```

Now look at an example of how a `field-group` is defined and which fields are assigned to it:

```
REPORT:  ZABAP.
DATA:  NAME(10)   TYPE C,
ADDRESS(50)  TYPE C, PHONE(10)  TYPE C.
FIELD-GROUPS:HEADER,
ITEM.
INSERT NAME INTO HEADER. INSERT ADDRESS
 PHONE INTO ITEM.
```

Every time the `HEADER` is referenced, it points to the data field `NAME`. Also, if you attempt to sort the data extract, it will be sorted by the field `NAME`, which is the only field in the field group `HEADER`. Make sure you always define a header because this is the group that `SORT` works from. To store a lot of records, the data must be copied to a storage area using the `EXTRACT` command (see the next section).

Extracting Data

As the data fields are populated, you'd probably like to save them. To do this, you use the `EXTRACT` command. The `EXTRACT` command copies the contents of the fields to a sequential dataset in the paging area of memory. The syntax of the field is:

```
EXTRACT field group
```

This command takes all the values of all the fields and copies them to a place in memory. As you move through the new data, each record is copied to memory. (Take a look at the last example in this chapter for a complete description and demonstration of how the entire process works.)

Sorting the Records (SORT)

The SORT command sorts all the records by the HEADER field group. The syntax for this command is just this:

```
SORT.
```

Because no internal table is referenced by the SORT command, the processor takes the SORT command and points it at the field groups. The SORT command is very simple.

It's possible to sort by a field group other than HEADER. If you want to do this, type the following command, specifying the field group you want to use:

```
SORT BY field group.
```

The program sorts all the records by the fields contained in field group.

Copying Records to Fields with LOOP

The LOOP command is similar to the SORT command. The general syntax is

```
LOOP.
ENDLOOP.
```

The LOOP command essentially copies the records found in the paging area of memory, one by one, to the current fields in memory. As each pass of the loop is processed, a new record is copied to those fields.

Triggering an Event with a New Value (AT field-group)

The AT field-group command is an event that triggers when a new value is encountered in the referenced field group. The code following the AT statement and enclosed by the ENDAT statement is executed if a new value is found in field group.

```
REPORT ZABAP
DATA:      Name(10)       TYPE C,
           ADDRESS(10)    TYPE C,
           CITY(30)       TYPE C,
           PHONE(10)      TYPE C.

FIELD-GROUPS:    HEADER, DATA.
INSERT NAME INTO HEADER.
```

```
INSERT ADDRESS CITY PHONE       INTO DATA.
NAME = 'BOB'.
ADDRESS =       '1900 PENNSYLVANIA AVENUE'.
CITY =          'WASHINGTON DC'.
PHONE =         '212-555-2345'.
EXTRACT HEADER.
EXTRACT DATA.
ADDRESS =       '789 LOS HOLTAS DRIVE'.
CITY =          'NEW HAVEN'.
PHONE =         '314-555-8934'.
EXTRACT DATA.
NAME = 'SKIP'.
ADDRESS =       '134 LOS COLTAS ST'.
CITY =          'MARYSVILLE'.

PHONE = '893-555-1245'.
EXTRACT HEADER.
EXTRACT DATA.
ADDRESS =       '9999 HENLEY STREET'.
CITY =          'REGENTS STREET'.
PHONE =         '987-555-1212'.
EXTRACT DATA.
NAME = 'ANNA' .
ADDRESS =       '3290 CITY DR.'.
CITY =          'SLIDELL'.
PHONE =         '916-555-1212'.
EXTRACT HEADER.
EXTRACT DATA.

SORT.
LOOP.
AT HEADER.
WRITE: / NAME. ENDAT.
AT DATA.
WRITE:/ ADDRESS, CITY, PHONE.
WRITE:/.
 ENDAT.

ENDLOOP.
```

The program defines the field groups and the data in the data declaration portion of the program. Then, as the data is copied to the fields, copies of the data are made to the paging area by the EXTRACT command. Notice that the HEADER isn't always extracted at the same time as the DATA is extracted. If the records are unchanged in the header, there's no reason to extract that data again because the extract on the DATA field group copies all the information.

The onscreen output of this data would be:

```
ANNA
3290 CITY   SLIDELL         916-555-12

BOB
1900 PENNS WASHINGTON DC    212-555-23

789 LOS HO NEW HAVEN        314-555-89

SKIP
134 LOS CO MARYSVILLE       893-555-12

9999 HENLE REGENTS STREET   987-555-12
```

As the code loops through the fields copied to the paging area, the data is displayed to the screen. On encountering a new name, the program outputs that name with the addresses, phone numbers, and cities associated with that name. Then another new name is found and output to the screen, along with all the pertinent information associated with that name. Notice in the previous example that there can be multiple DATA fields linked to a HEADER.

Summary

This chapter discussed the advanced techniques in creating output—working with events related to selection screen initialization and interactive reporting. Working with events such as AT enables you to make the selection screen more dynamic and easier for the user to use. The HIDE command lets you print fields to the screen and save other fields in memory, waiting for the user to call them up via a function key or by some other means of selection.

This chapter also introduced the concept of field groups as an alternative to internal tables. Because field groups are stored in the paging area of memory and can hold much more information than internal tables, this is a very useful feature of ABAP/4.

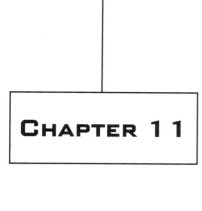

CHAPTER 11

ADDING SUBROUTINES
TO YOUR PROGRAM

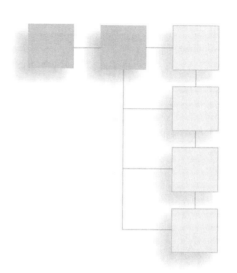

IN THIS CHAPTER

- Executing Subroutines (PERFORM)
- Defining Subroutines (FORM)
- Understanding the Scope of Local and Global Variables
- Looking at Form Examples

Like all modern programming languages, ABAP/4 allows the programmer to break programs into self-contained blocks of code. These blocks of code are often referred to as *subroutines*. The practice of breaking down a large program into smaller subroutines offers many advantages:

- Because the subroutines are self contained, they can be debugged independently of each other.
- Changes in one subroutine don't affect any other part of the program.
- The overall complexity of a program can be hidden by breaking it into smaller pieces that may be easier to understand.

ABAP/4 calls the most basic type of a subroutine *a form*. Forms can be explicitly defined in a program or can be made available to a program by use of the INCLUDE command. Forms are defined using the FORM command and invoked with the PERFORM command. A program can pass data to and from a form with parameters, variables, or constants, which are included in the PERFORM statement and can be used inside the form. With ABAP/4, parameters can be constants, variables, records, or internal tables.

A final subroutine issue is *variable scope*. The *scope* of a variable determines whether a subroutine can access that particular variable.

Using the information in this chapter, you should be able to use subroutines to develop large, complex programs while still maintaining readability and efficiency.

Note

With the newer versions of SAP and the introduction of object oriented ABAP programming (to be discussed in Chapter 23, "Object Oriented ABAP"), the use of subroutines are considered obsolete and only used outside of classes or in non-Unicode programs. Although subroutines are still available to support older programs, the use of new syntax elements is advised when building new programs.

Executing Subroutines (PERFORM)

The PERFORM command executes a form that has been defined in the program by using the FORM command. The PERFORM statement can occur in the code prior to the physical location of the form—that is, a form doesn't need to be defined before you can use it with PERFORM.

The basic syntax for the PERFORM command is as follows:

```
PERFORM form      [USING        p1   p2   p3   ...]
[CHANGING     p1    p2   p3   ...]
[TABLES       itab1   itab2   itab3   ...].
```

When a PERFORM is issued, the system executes the named form and then continues execution with the next command following the PERFORM.

You use forms to break up programs into logical groups. For example, here's a program to write a simple report:

```
***     Report ZOFIM000
***     02/01/97
REPORT ZOFIM000 LINE-SIZE 132 MESSAGE-ID ZZ.
TABLES:     ...   "Table List Goes Here
DATA:       ...   "Global Variables Go Here
*** Start Execution
PERFORM   INITIALIZATION.
PERFORM   EXTRACT_DATA.
PERFORM   PROCESS_DATA.
PERFORM   PRINT_DATA.
```

```
\ *** End Program
*** Forms
FORM INITIALIZATION.
"Forms Go Here
```

Instead of an imposing list of raw code, someone looking at the program for the first time can immediately see the structure of the program. If a change needs to be made to the selection criteria for the report, you could tell immediately that the EXTRACT_DATA form is the section of the program where you need to look. The value of using this modular approach to programming can't be overstated.

The TABLES, USING, and CHANGING Parameters

Data can be explicitly passed to and from a form with the USING and TABLES options. USING passes a single variable to a form. The CHANGING option has nearly the same effect (it's discussed later, in the forms section). If the value of the parameter is changed during the execution of the form, that new value is passed back on completion of the form when using the CHANGING option or is immediately changed with the USING option. The TABLES option passes an internal table—with all its rows of data—to the form. As is the case with USING, if any of the rows in the internal tables are changed during the execution of the form, the new values are immediately changed. For example:

```
REPORT ZOMMR00 LINE-SIZE 80.
TYPES:    BEGIN OF ty_matl_extract,
          matl#(18),    "Material Number
          matl_qty(8), "Material Plant
          plant(4),     "Plant
        END OF ty_matl_extract.
DATA: matl_extract TYPE STANDARD TABLE OF ty_matl
      extract INITIAL SIZE 1000.
DATA WS_RETURN_CODE LIKE SY-SUBRC.   "Return Code *** Start Execution
PERFORM INITIALIZATION.
PERFORM EXTRACT_DATA TABLES MATL_EXTRACT
USING WS_RETURN_CODE.
IF WS_RETURN_CODE <> 0.
EXIT.   "Quit Program if Error
ENDIF.
PERFORM process_data TABLES matl_extract
USING    ws_return_code
```

```
'PART2'    ws_temp2    var2
'PART3'    ws_temp3    var3
'PART4'    ws_temp4    var4
'PART5'    ws temp5    var5.
```

Use the colon notation to improve readability when executing several PERFORMs at the same time with different parameters.

DEFINING SUBROUTINES (FORM)

Now that you have seen a few simple examples of the PERFORM command in action, it's time to turn to the FORM command. This command defines the statements that make up a form. The block of code beginning with FORM must conclude with the statement ENDFORM.

Note

A form can't be defined in another form, but *recursive calls,* or a form that calls itself, are allowed. Also, you can declare new variables in a form, but this data is reinitialized each time the form is called—unless it's a recursive call, which can be a drag on performance.

The syntax for the FORM command is rather lengthy:

```
FORM form            [TABLES    itab1 itab2 itab3 ...]
[USING p1    [TYPE typ]    p2 p3   ...]
[USING VALUE(p1)    [TYPE typ]    VALUE(p2)    VALUE(p3)...]
[CHANGING VALUE(p1)    [TYPE typ] VALUE(p2)    VALUE(p3)...]
[p STRUCTURE struct].
```

Forms should be grouped together at the end of the program, one after another. The only statement that can be placed after a FORM...ENDFORM block is another FORM statement. The name of a form can be up to 30 characters in length and should describe the purpose of the form.

This is a simple example of the use of a form:

```
PERFORM   PAGE_FOOTER.
PERFORM PAGE HEADER.
FORM PAGE_FOOTER.
WRITE:  1(10) SY-SUBRC, 72(6),
WS_PAGE#.
ENDFORM.
FORM PAGEREADER.
WRITE: 31(18) 'GL JOURNAL ENTRY'.
ENDFORM.
```

In this example, two simple forms print information for the header and footer of a page. They might be called hundreds of times in the execution of the program, and their purpose is very clear.

Using Parameters to Pass Data

The best way to make data available to a form to be used or changed is by passing it to the form as a parameter. Parameters must be defined in both the FORM and PERFORM commands. They are passed by location, so the first parameter listed in PERFORM is passed to the first parameter listed in FORM. Because of this scheme, you need to take care when using forms. It's very easy to make a mistake and get the parameters mixed up.

ABAP/4 does not require you to define a type for parameters in a subroutine, but it is advisable to do so. When you specify a data type for a form parameter, the ABAP/4 compiler can optimize the code it produces to handle the parameter in the most efficient way possible. Also, if you define a type for your parameters, the syntax check has a better chance to find errors made in the calling of forms.

The next sections discuss the types of parameters allowed in a form.

Passing Internal Tables by Reference (TABLES)

The TABLES parameter enables you to pass internal tables to subroutines by reference (you can't pass internal tables by value):

```
TABLES    itab1  itab2 itab3  ...
```

The TABLES parameter must always appear first in the FORM statement—before any USING or CHANGING.

To access any of the individual fields with the syntax *tab-field* (for example, MARD-MATNR), you must also use the STRUCTURE option. Without STRUCTURE, only line-oriented statements can be used, such as WRITE itab—you wouldn't be able to use WRITE itab-FIELD1. (See the section called "Indicating the Structure of the Incoming Parameter (STRUCTURE)" for details on using the STRUCTURE option.)

Passing Parameters by Reference or Value (USING)

This option defines the parameters p1, p2, p3, and so on that are passed to the subroutine when it's called by a PERFORM statement:

```
USING p1    [TYPE typ]  p2 p3   ...
```

The parameters are passed by reference, which means that any changes to the parameter during the execution of the subroutine immediately change the variable passed in by the PERFORM statement.

This option tells the system to define the parameters p1, p2, p3, and so on that are passed to the subroutine by value:

```
USING VALUE(p1)    [TYPE typ]   VALUE(p2) VALUE(pS)    ...
```

Passing by value means that any changes to the parameter during the execution of the subroutine won't affect the original variable.

Note

Reference parameters and value parameters can be combined in the same USING statement.

Returning Changes to the Original Variables (CHANGING VALUE)

The CHANGING VALUE option passes parameters by value, but it also transfers any change of a parameter value back to the original variables when ENDFORM is reached:

```
CHANGING VALUE(p1)    [TYPE typ]    VALUE(p2)   VALUE(pS)   ...
```

This is appropriate for recursive subroutine calls, for which the variable shouldn't be changed immediately—only when the subroutine ends. If the subroutine is canceled due to an error, no changes are made to the parameters specified by CHANGING VALUE.

Indicating the Structure of the Incoming Parameter (STRUCTURE)

The STRUCTURE option follows any parameter that refers to a record or an internal table. It tells the system what the field layout of the incoming parameter is going to be:

```
STRUCTURE Struct
```

You can reference any of the individual fields of that structure in the subroutine. STRUCTURE also allows you to pass both Data Dictionary structures and internal structures (for example, internal tables or records). If you are going to access any of the fields within the record, you must include the STRUCTURE option.

Here's an example:

```
TYPES:      BEGIN OF ty_rec,     "Record Variable
            f1(10)   TYPE c,
            f2(4)    TYPE n,
            f3(1)    TYPE c,
            END OF ty_rec.
```

```
DATA: ws_rec TYPE ty_rec.
TYPES: BEGIN OF ty_itab.
         INCLUDE STRUCTURE bseg.     "Financial Documents Table
TYPES: END OF ty_itab.
DATA: itab TYPE TABLE OF ty_itab INITIAL SIZE 1000.
DATA: f_itab LIKE LINE OF itab.
PERFORM test TABLES itab USING ws_rec.
*&---------------------------------------------------------*
*&      Form   TEST
*&---------------------------------------------------------*
*       text
*---------------------------------------------------------*
*       -->P_ITAB      text
*       -->P_REC       text
*---------------------------------------------------------*
FORM test TABLES p_itab STRUCTURE bseg
USING p_rec STRUCTURE ws_rec.

  LOOP AT p_itab INTO f_itab.    "This is allowed with or
                                 "without STRUCTURE
    WRITE:   / f_itab-belnr,    "This is allowed only with STRUCTURE
             p_rec-f1.
  ENDLOOP.
ENDFORM.                        "TEST
```

Without the STRUCTURE option, the subroutine can't access any of the individual fields in a record or internal table.

UNDERSTANDING THE SCOPE OF LOCAL AND GLOBAL VARIABLES

When we talk about the *scope* of a variable, we're referring to the areas of the program in which the variable can be used. ABAP/4 has only two types of scopes:

- Any variable defined in the main portion of a program is considered *global* and can be used anywhere in the program.

- Any variable defined in a subroutine is *local* and can be used only in that specific subroutine—nowhere else in the program.

Look at this code:

```
REPORT ZTEST1.
DATA:    GLOBAL1(10) TYPE C,    "These are global variables
GLOBAL2(10) TYPE C.
***Start Main Program
GLOBAL1 = 'TEST'. PERFORM FORM1.
***End Main Program
FORM FORM1.
DATA: W_FORM1(10) TYPE C,
    "These are local because they are defined in a form
W2__FORM1(10) TYPE C.   "These can only be used in this form
W_FORM1 = GLOBAL1.
    "This is allowed because GLOBAL1 is global
PERFORM FORM2 USING W_FORM1.
ENDFORM.
FORM FORM2 USING VALUE(PJ) TYPE C. "Notice the name is different
    "in the form
GLOBAL2 = P_1. "This works because P_1 is passed into this form
W2_FORM1 = GLOBAL2. "This would raise an error because W2_FORM1
    "is local to FORM1 and can only be used there
ENDFORM.
```

This example has two global variables and two forms. In the first form, two variables are defined. Because the variables are defined in a form, they're local in scope and can be used only in FORM1. To use the variable W_FORM1 in FORM2, it's passed in as a parameter.

This program would raise an error because W2_FORM1 is referenced in FORM2. To use the variable without raising an error, it should be passed to FORM2 as a parameter, in the same way as W_FORM1 is passed.

As you can see, variable-scope rules in ABAP/4 are fairly straightforward. It's best to limit the number of global variables used and stick with local variables, which are passed as parameters only to those forms that need to use them.

Persistent Local Variables (STATICS)

Instead of using the DATA command to define local variables within a form, the STATICS command can be used. The syntax of the STATICS command is identical to that of DATA, but the local variables defined by it persist after a form has been executed. When a local variable is defined with the data statement in a form, it is re-created each time the form is called. Re-creating the variable is slow, and any value held by the variable is lost. On the other hand, a variable defined with STATICS is not re-created the second time a form is called. It persists between PERFORM commands and retains its value much like a global variable does. Despite this persistence, the scoping rules of a local variable still are in effect, so the variable can be accessed only from the form it was defined in. The following examples show the difference between STATICS and DATA variables.

```
REPORT ZTEST.
PERFORM F1. PERFORM F1.
*Begin Forms FORM F1.
STATICS V1 TYPE I.
ADD 1 TO V1.
WRITE V1. ENDFORM.
```

Here is the output:

```
1   2
```

In this first example, the local variable V1 is defined by the STATICS command. The first time the form F1 is called, V1 is defined and initialized to a value of zero. After the ADD command, V1 has a value of one. The second time F1 is called, V1 is still equal to one, so after the ADD command, it is now equal to two.

```
REPORT ZTEST2.
PERFORM F1.
*Begin Forms
FORM F1.
DATA V1 TYPE I.
ADD 1 TO V1.
WRITE V1.
ENDFORM.
```

Here is the output:

```
1       1
```

In this second example, the local variable V1 is defined by the DATA command. The first time the form F1 is called, V1 is defined and initialized to a value of zero. After the ADD command, V1 has a value of one. The second time F1 is called, V1 is redefined and initialized to a value of zero. So, after the ADD command, V1 is now equal to one again.

LOOKING AT FORM EXAMPLES

In this section, you'll take a look at some examples of using forms in programs. Forms aren't *required* in any program, but they're a great way to improve them.

The first example demonstrates the difference between passing parameters by reference and passing by value:

```
REPORT ZTEST.

DATA:   var1 TYPE i,
        var2 TYPE i.
***Begin Main Program
var1 = 10.
var2 = 25.
PERFORM form1 USING var1 var2.
WRITE: var1, var2.
***End Main Program

*&---------------------------------------------------*
*&      Form    FORM1
*&---------------------------------------------------*
*       text
*----------------------------------------------------*
*       -->VALUE        text
*       -->(P1)         text
*       -->P2           text
*----------------------------------------------------*
FORM form1 USING p1 TYPE i value(p2) TYPE i.
   DATA local1 TYPE i VALUE 30.
   p1 = local1 + p2.
   PERFORM form2 USING local1 p1.
   p2 = local1.
ENDFORM.
                        "End FORM1
*&---------------------------------------------------*
*&      Form    FORM2
*&---------------------------------------------------*
*       text
*----------------------------------------------------*
*       -->VALUE        text
*       -->(P1)         text
*       -->P2           text
*----------------------------------------------------*
FORM form2 USING value(p1) TYPE i p2 TYPE i.
p1 = 50 + p2.
p2 = p1.
ENDFORM.
                        "End FORM2
```

This example is confusing on purpose. It's an example of mixing value and reference; the output would be 105 25. Despite the confusion, all you need to remember is that value parameters can't be changed in the subroutine; reference parameters can.

The next example shows how an internal table can be passed into subroutines. Remember that internal tables can be passed only by reference—not by value:

```
REPORT ZTEST.
TYPES:    BEGIN OF ty_itab,
          field1(10) TYPE c,
          field2 TYPE i,
          END OF ty_itab.
DATA: itab TYPE STANDARD TABLE OF ty_itab INITIAL SIZE 100.
DATA: wa_itab LIKE LINE OF itab.
DATA var1 TYPE i VALUE 5.
***Begin Main Program
CLEAR wa_itab.
wa_itab-field1 = 'ONE'.
wa_itab-field2 = 100.
APPEND wa_itab TO itab.
CLEAR wa_itab.
wa_itab-field1 = 'TWO'.
wa_itab-field2 = 200.
APPEND wa_itab TO itab.
CLEAR wa_itab.
wa_itab-field1 = 'THREE'.
wa_itab-field2 = 300.
APPEND wa_itab TO itab.
PERFORM form1 TABLES itab USING var1.
***End Main Program


FORM form1      TABLES ptab STRUCTURE wa_itab USING p1.
  CLEAR wa_itab.
  LOOP AT ptab INTO wa_itab.
    wa_itab-field2 = wa_itab-field2 * p1.
    MODIFY ptab FROM wa_itab.
    CLEAR wa_itab.
  ENDLOOP.
ENDFORM.              "form1
```

After the program is run, this would be the value of the internal table ITAB:

```
FIELD1    FIELD2
ONE       500
TWO       1000
THREE     1500
```

The next example demonstrates the use of the CHANGING parameter in a recursive function call. Remember that a recursive form is a form that calls itself. USING parameters can't be used with recursive functions because they change the value of parameters immediately. For recursive forms, the parameters should be changed only after the form has ended, which is exactly how CHANGING operates.

This example calculates N!, which is the classic example of a recursive subroutine. The answer to N! is calculated as 1*2*3*4*...* N—or, put another way, N * (N - 1)! Because the same function is used over and over again, it's perfect for a recursive form:

```
REPORT ZTEST.
DATA w_result TYPE i. "Result of Calculation
PARAMETER p_num TYPE i. "Number to be calculated
*** Begin Main Processing
PERFORM calc_power CHANGING p_num w_result.
WRITE: 'The answer is ', w_result.
*** End Main Processing
*** Form CALC_POWER
*** This form will calculate ! for the input
*** and return the result in output.
FORM calc_power CHANGING value(p_input) value(p_output).
  DATA: w_temp_in TYPE i, "Holds temp value for calculation
        w_emp_xit TYPE i. "Holds temp result of calculation
  IF p_input <> 1. "Call form until input is one
  w_temp_in = p_input   -   1.
    PERFORM calc_power CHANGING w_temp_in p_output.
  ELSE.   "Output is one when input is one
  w_emp_xit = 1.
  ENDIF.
  p_output = p_input * w_emp_xit.    "Calculate answer
ENDFORM.   "End CALC_POWER
```

When this program is run, it prompts the user to enter a number and then returns the result. So if a user enters 4, the result returned is 1*2*3*4 or 24. The program calculates this by passing the value 4 into the CALC_POWER form. In the form, the input value of 4 is multiplied by the result from calling itself—using 4−1 or 3 as the input value. Each time the form calls itself, the current values are saved. The form keeps calling itself until the input is 1, at which point the result is set to 1 as well, and the form ends, which causes the CHANGING parameter to be passed back to the calling form with the answer.

The use of recursion in forms isn't a common operation, but for some tasks like the example just shown, it can provide extremely elegant solutions.

This final example is another demonstration of recursion. In this case, you call the same form repeatedly to read the nested structure of a sales order. Within R/3, a sales order can be made up of multiple materials. In some cases, the materials may be part of a hierarchical structure. For example, the first material might be a car, and below that in the hierarchy would be an engine and below that a piston. In this example, you read the entire hierarchy and look up the product division of each material and then produce a report of materials sorted by the division.

```
REPORT ZC LINE-SIZE 132 LINE-COUNT 65 MESSAGE-ID ZZ.
TABLES: vbap,     "Sales Item Table
        mara.     "Material Master

TYPES: BEGIN OF ty_ord,
        posnr LIKE vbap-posnr,     "Sales Item
        matnr LIKE vbap-matnr,     "Material
        spart LIKE mara-spart,     "Division
      END OF ty_ord.

DATA: iord TYPE STANDARD TABLE OF ty_ord INITIAL SIZE 10.
DATA: wa_ord LIKE LINE OF iord.

PARAMETERS: p_vbeln LIKE vbap-vbeln,   "Sales Order
            p_posnr LIKE vbap-posnr.   "Sales Item
*    Begin Program
START-OF-SELECTION.
*    Get Top of Hierarchy from Input Parameters
   SELECT SINGLE matnr INTO wa_ord-matnr FROM vbap WHERE
                        vbeln = p_vbeln AND posnr = p_posnr.
   IF sy-subrc EQ 0.
     SELECT SINGLE spart INTO wa_ord-spart
     FROM mara WHERE matnr = wa_ord-matnr.
*Record top-level item
     wa_ord-posnr = p_posnr.
     APPEND wa_ord TO iord.
```

```
*Get all nested items
     PERFORM get_child_items USING p_posnr.
*    Print results
     SORT iord BY spart matnr.

     CLEAR wa_ord.
     LOOP AT iord INTO wa_ord.
       WRITE: / wa_ord-spart, wa_ord-matnr, wa_ord-posnr, p_vbeln.
       CLEAR wa_ord.
     ENDLOOP.
   ENDIF.

END-OF-SELECTION.

*&---------------------------------------------------------------*
*&      Form   GET
*&---------------------------------------------------------------*
*&      text
*---------------------------------------------------------------*
*      -->PARENT     text
*---------------------------------------------------------------*
*Get any lower level items
* -> HIGH ITEM
FORM get_child_items USING parent LIKE vbap-posnr.
*    UEPOS holds the parent item number
  CLEAR wa_ord.
  SELECT posnr matnr INTO CORRESPONDING FIELDS OF vbap
  FROM vbap WHERE vbeln = p_vbeln AND uepos = parent.
    wa_ord-posnr = vbap-posnr.
    wa_ord-matnr = vbap-matnr.
    SELECT SINGLE spart INTO wa_ord-spart
    FROM mara WHERE matnr = wa_ord-matnr.
*Record Current Item
     APPEND wa_ord TO iord.
*Get any children items of current item
     PERFORM get_child_items USING vbap-posnr.
  ENDSELECT.
ENDFORM.    " GET CHILD ITEMS
```

The output of this report might look like this:

```
A1    9123-A52    000010    6002300
A1    9123-B62    000050    6002300
A4    9143-A52    000020    6002300
B1    9223 -252   000040    6002300
B1    9124-Z52    000030    6002300
B1    9123-Z62    000100    6002300
B1    9223 -Z72   000090    6002300
B1    9123-Z54    000060    6002300
C2    9173-F52    000070    6002300
C2    9133-F52    000080    6002300
```

SUMMARY

The process of breaking down a large program into smaller, more manageable blocks of code is a standard programming technique. This technique is supported in ABAP/4 through the FORM and PERFORM commands. By breaking down programs into smaller subroutines, you make them easier to understand, maintain, and enhance. Instead of using global variables throughout a program, it's better to pass variables from one form to another as parameters. Variables can be passed by reference, where changes to the variable in the form are permanent, or by value, where variables can't be changed in the form. Programming examples in future chapters make extensive use of forms and parameters.

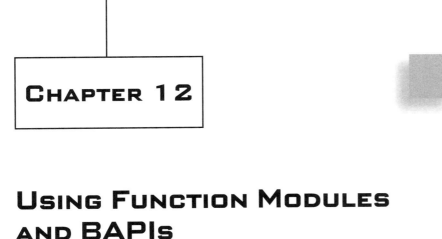

USING FUNCTION MODULES AND BAPIS

IN THIS CHAPTER

- Using the Function Modules Screen
- Creating a Custom Function Module
- Using Function Modules in ABAP Code
- Learning About Some Useful Function Modules

Imagine for a moment that you receive your first sheet of specifications for your first program—and then SAP America calls and says that they'll write half the code for you. Not only would you be ecstatic because there's less work to do, but you would also know that the code they provide has been tested extensively. To some extent, SAP has already done this by providing ready-to-use function modules along with their software package.

A *function module* is a separate program that can be called from your ABAP code to perform a specific task. Examples of such tasks include uploading and downloading files between the application server and your PC, calculating whether a date falls on a Sunday or a Monday, or perhaps rounding a number with decimals in it to the second place. The software provided by SAP comes with a library of pre-written programs that can be called to do these tasks, as well as a multitude of others.

These function modules are called by the ABAP code using the CALL statement. You, the programmer, provide the fields that hold the necessary information for the function module to do its work, as well as fields to receive the results of the work from the function calls. This chapter introduces you to the function module maintenance screen, where you can search for function modules by keywords, test function modules, examine what input and output parameters must be used, and view the source code SAP has used to program these function calls.

Note

> *Function calls* are the code that makes a "call" from the ABAP/4 code to the function module. The function module is the actual code and characteristics of the function module.

USING THE FUNCTION MODULES SCREEN

The Maintain Function Modules screen has quite a few features. To navigate to the screen, follow the menu path Tools > Applications > Development > Function Library button. The quick transaction code of se37 can be entered in the command line on top of any screen.

Within the Maintain Function Modules screen, you can view several features of the function module (see Figure 12.1). The screen has an input line to enter the function module name. By clicking one of the option buttons on the screen, you can display or modify the import/export parameters, the exceptions list, the documentation, the notes, the source code, and several other items of the selected module.

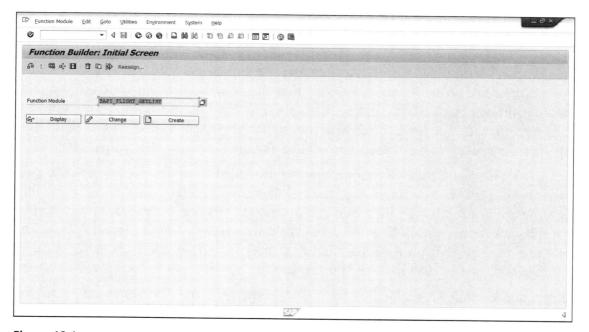

Figure 12.1
The Maintain Function Modules screen.

An important item to note is the import/export parameters, which represent the data that your ABAP/4 code sends into the function module and receives from the function module. Documentation provides important criteria for searching. The source code lets you view what the function module is doing when you call it.

Tip

Remember that the function module isn't magic; it's just another ABAP/4 program written by SAP or a third party to accomplish a certain task. You can gain a great deal of programming knowledge by viewing the code used in function modules. By clicking the Test button, you can run the function module in test mode with sample data to see whether it provides the output you need.

The hardest part about starting to learn ABAP/4 is that the lack of experience with the SAP system puts you at a disadvantage. Seasoned ABAPers have used many function modules and usually have some favorites that they use quite often in their programs. For your convenience, a list of favorite function modules used by the authors is provided at the end of this chapter. You should learn how these function modules work and how best to use them. For now, the next section demonstrates how to search for a function module that you need.

Searching for a Specific Function Module

To search for a function module, click the Find button on the Maintain Function Modules screen (se37). The Find Function Modules screen appears with a variety of search methods by which you can search for the desired function module (see Figure 12.2).

The best method to search for a function module is either by entering a string in the Function Name box along with asterisks (*) for wildcard characters or by entering keywords in the Short Description box (in the Search Documentation For section). After the processor returns a list, just double-click the desired function module to bring it up and analyze it.

Note

For a beginner ABAPer, there's no guarantee that a desired function module exists, but SAP has covered almost everything a programmer could desire. If the exact function module you need doesn't exist, maybe you can alter the output to fit the program specifications or alter the function module and make your own version of it to get the correct results.

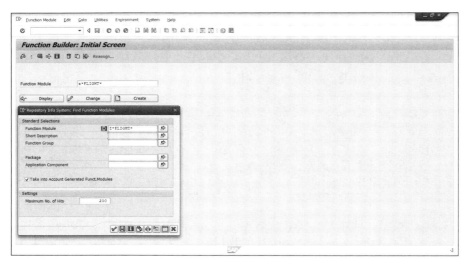

Figure 12.2
Searching the function modules. Enter your search criteria and click Execute.

Testing Individual Function Modules

At the Maintain Function Modules screen, you can click the Test button to test a function module. A screen appears in which you can enter sample input data, and the function module will show the output fields, using the sample data (see Figure 12.3).

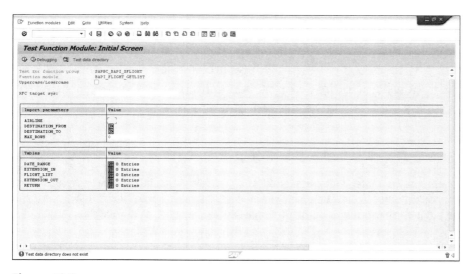

Figure 12.3
The test environment for the function module.

After filling in the list of input parameters, click the Execute button. The output parameters will be filled on the lower half of the screen.

CREATING A CUSTOM FUNCTION MODULE

If you find certain programs that you have created are using identical code, perhaps it's time that you develop your own function modules. It's a very simple process in which you create simple ABAP code and just define the input and output parameters.

Defining Input/Output Parameters

The first step is to open the Maintain Function Modules screen. Now you need to give a name to your function module. Pick any name that hasn't been used before, but be sure to start the name with the letter Z to denote that this function module was created by a third party. Type the desired name in the Function Module combo box.

When you eventually click the Create button to begin creating the function module (don't do it yet), the screen that appears will be related to your choice of option buttons below the function name. The two most important aspects of the function module are the import/export parameter interface and the source code. The third important aspect is the table fields, if you're using a table and defining the exceptions or errors.

To start creating your function module, enter the function module name and press the Create button. You will be asked to enter the function group and a short description (see Figure 12.4). A screen will then appear where you can define your import and export parameters. Type the names of your desired fields in these boxes. In the box to the right of each field, type the Data Dictionary or table fields in which to define these parameters. For example, if you typed `Year`, the field to the right of it might be `BKPF-GJAHR`, which represents the fiscal year field from the accounting header.

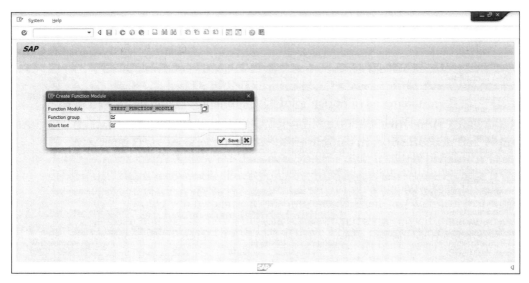

Figure 12.4
Creating a function module.

Create the export fields in the same way, and then click the Next Screen button or the green back arrow to work on the source code.

Import parameters are passed from the program to the function module. Their path is one way, from the program to the function module code. Export parameters are exactly the opposite. They are passed from the function module back to the program. Note in the code that the import parameters are listed under Exporting, and the export parameters are listed under Importing because the descriptions are relative to the variables. Table parameters are not restricted to one-way traffic. They are passed back and forth between the code and the function module.

Developing the ABAP Code

When you're ready to work on the source code for your function module, you reach it by using the Source Code button on the Maintain Function Modules screen. The ABAP/4 editor screen (se38) will open.

Because you've already defined the input and output parameters, these are defined as variables in your program—even though no formal data declarations are found in the source code. The procedure is very simple from here on. Just assume that the input parameters contain data, and manipulate the data in whatever way you need to obtain the output you want. Store that output in the parameters you define as the output parameters. The ABAP code that calls your program will output the parameters needed by your function module and receive the data from your function module. Let's say that you use the string-concatenate function module (which takes two strings and combines them into one). Your program would export the two strings, and the function module would send back one string. If you sent out ' abc' and ' def', for example, you would get back ' abcdef'.

Defining Tables and Handling Errors

The next part of the process allows you to define the tables that you will be importing or exporting with the function module and set up error-handling for errors your function module might encounter with data being input.

To define tables and errors, go back to the Maintain Function Modules screen and click the option button named Interface Table Parameters/Exceptions. Then click Create.

To define tables, simply list the name by which you want to call your incoming or outgoing table. Then type the name of a Data Dictionary structure or internal table that has already been defined, to define the structure of your table. (If you have a unique table, be sure to use the Data Dictionary to declare and define your new table before writing the function module.) This process is exactly the same as defining the import and export parameter interface, except that you are now declaring tables rather than fields.

Because this program will be a remote one, you need to define the possible errors that the program might encounter. For example, if your function module is a program to read in the name of a customer and output the address from the database, one error might be that the customer referenced by the code doesn't exist. The code used to raise the event that activates that error is the MESSAGE command with a unique addition for function modules. The syntax is as follows:

```
MESSAGE X number RAISING event.
```

X represents the type of message—E, A, I, or S—just like the regular MESSAGE command, number is the general message number, and event is the exception that you define. When this event is raised, the definition that associates that event with a number for the SY-SUBRC puts that number in the return code. This definition is set when you call the function under EXCEPTIONS. (See the next section on using function modules in ABAP/4 code.)

Simply brainstorm the most likely errors you will encounter and assign codes to them. The output of the SY-SUBRC (system return-code field) will be associated with these codes. 0 always represents a positive (no errors) result.

Tip

Try not to exceed five return codes so that the programmer doesn't get bogged down in return codes when using your function module.

Activating the Function Module

The final step in creating a function module is to click the Activate button. This step checks the function module for errors and compiles your ABAP code. If you encounter any errors, recheck your steps and your source code.

USING FUNCTION MODULES IN ABAP CODE

The first step in using function modules is to search through the function library (using the Find Function Modules screen) for the function module you want to use. For this example, you'll use the function module G_POSTING_DATE_OF_PERIOD_GET. This function module is actually an FI (finance) function module to get the ending date of the current fiscal period.

To insert a function into your code, click the Pattern button on the ABAP/4 Editor Edit Program screen while you are in the editor. In the resulting dialog box, click the Call Function option button and type the function module's name into the box (see Figure 12.5).

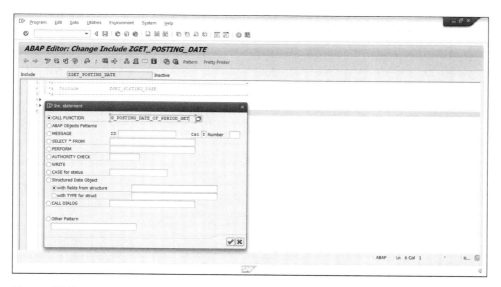

Figure 12.5
Inserting a function module in the code.

For this example, type G_POSTING_DATE_OF_PERIOD_GET and click OK. The code inserted into the program looks like this:

```
CALL FUNCTION            'G_POSTING_DATE_PERIOD_GET'
EXPORTING
     PERIOD    =
     VARIANT   =
     YEAR      =
IMPORTING
     TO_DATE   =
EXCEPTIONS
        PERIOD_NOT_DEFINED   =1
        VARIANT NOT DEFINED  =2.
```

It's up to you, the programmer, to fill in the appropriate fields in this template that SAP conveniently inserts into your program. Once your code is inserted, along with the incoming and outgoing variables, you can use the function module to get the data you need. In this case, the incoming data consists of the fiscal period, a fiscal year variant, and the current year. The fiscal year period is a unique key used by SAP to define when your fiscal year begins and ends.

The subsequent code demonstrates how a function call is coded into an ABAP/4 program:

```
REPORT ZABAP.
MESSAGE-ID 22.

PARAMETERS:
P_PERIOD(3)   TYPE N OBLIGATORY.

DATA:

W_VARIANT(2) TYPE C VALUE 'AM',
W_ENDDATE LIKE SY-DATUM,
W_YEAR(4) TYPE N.

MOVE SY-DATUM+0(4) TO W_YEAR.

CALL FUNCTION 'G_POSTING_DATE_OF_PERIOD_GET'
  EXPORTING
    PERIOD                = P_PERIOD
    VARIANT               = W_VARIANT
    YEAR                  = W_YEAR
  IMPORTING
    TO_DATE               = W_ENDDATE
  EXCEPTIONS
    PERIOD_NOT_DEFINED = 1
    VARIANT NOT DEFINED = 2.
```

```
CASE SY-SUBRC.
 WHEN 1.
MESSAGE E999 WITH 'PERIOD NOT DEFINED'.
WHEN 2.
MESSAGE E999 WITH 'VARIANT NOT DEFINED'. WHEN OTHERS.
SHIFT W_ENDDATE BY 4 PLACES CIRCULAR.
 ENDCASE.
WRITE W_ENDDATE.
```

The function module is now defined with input and output parameters, along with what the SY-SUBRC field will contain upon reaching the two exceptions defined.

Processing Input/Output Parameters

The program defines what the input data is by putting the appropriate data into the incoming fields. Notice that the parameter P_PERIOD is obligatory, meaning that the user can't get past the selection screen without entering a value into that field. The program then defines what the year and variant are, and the function module accepts these three values as the input parameters. Once processed, the code in the function module outputs the ending date into the output parameter, W_ENDDATE.

Defining Errors Encountered in Function Calls

If an error occurs in the function module, one of the two exception events is raised, and the SY-SUBRC field is populated with a value. The code after the function module then checks to see what the return code is and outputs an appropriate message relating to that code. If there are no errors, the program modifies the output from the function module and then outputs it to the screen. In a regular program, the output would be used to retrieve more data from the database or something of that nature, but to keep the examples concise, it's just output to the screen here.

Some Useful Function Modules

This set of function modules is used to download and upload files to and from your PC:

WS_DOWNLOAD	Automatically downloads a file to a PC.
WS_UPLOAD	Automatically uploads a file to a PC.
DOWNLOAD	Downloads a file, but prompts the user for name and path.
UPLOAD	Uploads a file, but prompts the user for name and path.

This function module works with fields and strings and manipulates them in useful ways:

STRING_CENTER	Transports a string into the target field in centered format.

This group of function modules generates random numbers:

QF05_RANDOM	Generates a random number.
QF05_RANDOM_INTEGER	Generates a random integer.
QF05_RANDOM_SAVE_SEED	Saves the initial value for the function modules.
ROUND	Rounds a number to the correct place.

Here are some other useful function modules:

DATE CONVERT TO FACTORYDATE	Intuitively, this function module converts a regular date to the factory date. Factory dates will take into account working holidays and special days.
FACTORYDATE CONVERT TO DATE	This is the reverse of the function module above.

Here is another function module:

SAPGUI PROGRESS INDICATOR	This function call is responsible for creating the little progress indicator on the bottom-left portion of the screen when programs are generated or a new transaction is compiled.

This function call can be added to your program to show the percent completion of the program. Be careful not to add this function module to programs that will be run over a modem line because the network time to ping the progress back and forth will extend the length of the program by hours, especially if the modem is 28.8Kbps or slower. See the following example subroutine for some useful code.

```
FORM STATUS_INDICATOR USING COUNT-MAX     TYPE I

COUNT-ACTUAL TYPE I.

TEXT TYPE C.

DATA: BEGIN OF PERCENT,

ACTUAL TYPE I,
DISPLAY(3),END OF PERCENT.

"jede 5. Lieferung
DATA: MOD TYPE I. DATA: STRING(80).
    MOD =COUNT-ACTUAL MOD 05. CHECK MOD = 0.
PERCENT-ACTUAL = 100 * COUNT-ACTUAL /
COUNT-MAX. WRITE PERCENT-ACTUAL TO PERCENT-

DISPLAY. STRING = TEXT.
REPLACE '&' WITH PERCENT-DISPLAY INTO STRING.

CONDENSE STRING.
CALL FUNCTION 'SAPGUI_PROGRESS_INDICATOR'

EXPORTING
PERCENTAGE = PERCENT-ACTUAL
TEXT =STRING
EXCEPTIONS
OTHERS = 1.

ENDFORM. " PROCESS_INDICATOR
```

For example, say you are displaying records in an internal table. A describe command gets you the total number of records in the table, and looping through the table, you know the current record by the system variable SY-TABIX. The text could consist of something to the effect of '& Percent. Pass the total number of records to the COUNT-MAX the current record number to the COUNT-ACTUAL, and the text to the text field. Put the call to this form inside the loop through the table, and the indicator will show up on the bottom, along with a changing percentage! Have fun with this one.

Summary

This chapter introduced and explained how to program with function modules—code already written by SAP—in your ABAP/4 projects. It showed how you can develop your own function modules and how to utilize them in code as well.

A function module has import fields supplied by the program to the function module. The function module takes these fields, uses them, and produces export fields to send back to the program. Function modules are very useful—why write extra code if it already has been written for you?

Several useful function modules were listed; once you start programming in ABAP/4, you'll want to explore these modules to find out just how useful they really are.

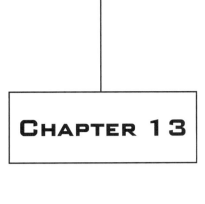

CHAPTER 13

WORKING WITH LOGICAL DATABASES

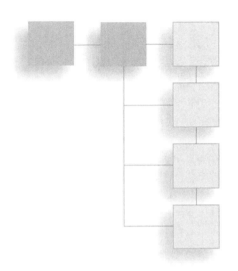

IN THIS CHAPTER

- Advantages of Logical Databases
- Using the GET Event to Retrieve Data
- Limiting Data with Logical Database Parameters

Chapter 8, "Using SAP SQL to Access Database Tables," introduced SAP SQL, a set of statements that allows the programmer to read and change data stored in the SAP database. In order to read data from a table, the SELECT command was used in that chapter. Another method that allows the programmer to read data from a table is using a logical database. A *logical database* is actually a separate program, usually written by SAP, although user-created logical databases are allowed. A logical database provides read-only access to a group of related tables to an ABAP/4 program. When a program that calls a logical database is run, the program behind the logical database runs as well. The logical database issues the SELECT commands and returns the data to the calling program.

ADVANTAGES OF LOGICAL DATABASES

SAP uses a relational database to store data. Therefore, in order to read a single business object, such as a purchase order, the programmer must read from several tables. These tables are typically assembled in a parent-child relationship, where a single parent record in one table has zero or more child records in another table. In this case, the purchase order header information is in the database table EKKO, and each line item of the purchase order is stored in the database table EKPO.

The programmer must know the primary key for each table and use the key values to read from each table. The logical database hides this complexity from the programmer because it knows how the different tables relate to each other and can issue the SELECT command with the proper WHERE clause to retrieve the data. Because you don't have access to the WHERE clause that the logical database uses, the logical database has its own selection screen with the typical criteria from which you might want the user to select. When you use a logical database in your program, this selection screen is called automatically, and the user can enter information to limit the data returned by the logical database. The developer can also use the CHECK command to limit what data the program processes, as described later in this chapter.

USING THE GET EVENT TO RETRIEVE DATA

SAP includes a number of events that a programmer can use to enable the processing of data from a logical database. An *event* is a keyword that defines a block of code to be executed when the system detects the appropriate occurrence. The most important event for logical databases is the GET table event.

GET isn't a command like SELECT or WRITE; instead, it's an event. It can be confusing because ABAP/4 has no ENDGET; all code following the GET keyword is considered part of the GET event until another event keyword is reached—such as a different GET table or an END-OF-SELECTION. The syntax of the GET event is:

GET table [LATE].

(You'll learn about the use of LATE in the next section.) Using events to access data in a logical database can be confusing at first, so let's start with a simple example. All logical databases have three-character identifiers; for example, the logical database for material is MSM. A logical database is composed of several tables that form a hierarchy. The logical database makes data from that hierarchy available to an ABAP/4 program. A portion of the hierarchy for the MSM logical database is made up of these tables:

MARAV (Material header)
MARM (Quantity unit)
MBEWV (View for logical database)
MVKE (Material Master: Sales Data)
MARCV (View table for the logical database MGM)
PROPF (Forecast parameters)
MARD (Material Master: Storage Location/Batch Segment)

MARAV is at the top of the hierarchy. Below it are MARM, MBEWV, MVKE, and MARCV. MARCV has two more tables below it: PROPF and MARD.

To access these tables via a SELECT command, the programmer needs to know how all these tables are related to each other. The material type is stored in MARAV, but the material location is in MARD, so to include both these values in a report would be a chore. When using a logical database, however, no knowledge of the relationships is required. Unfortunately, because ABAP/4 has no ENDGET command, reading code with multiple GET events can be confusing. You simply have to remember that a code block associated with an event ends with the next event statement, such as another GET or an END-OF-SELECTION:

```
REPORT ZOMMT00000.
TABLES: MARAV, "Material Header MARD.
    "Material Storage Location
START-OF-SELECTION.
WRITE: /, 'Extracting Materials and locations'.
WRITE: /, /, 'Material Number', 16 'Material Type'.
GET MARAV.
WRITE: /, /, (15) MARAV-MATNR,      "Material*
            16 MARAV-MTART.         "Material Type
GET MARD.
WRITE: /,    2(4) MARD-WERKS,       "Plant Code
            7 MARD-LGORT.           "Storage Location
END-OF-SELECTION.
WRITE: /, /, 'Report Complete'.
```

Note

Notice that nowhere in the program is the logical database MSM mentioned. Unfortunately, logical databases are assigned in the program attributes, not directly in the ABAP/4 code. If you see the GET event in the program, however, you know that the program is using a logical database.

Now suppose that this report is run for Acme Tools, which currently has only three materials in SAP, and those materials can be allocated to any of three plants. The output of the report would look something like this:

```
Extracting Materials and locations
Material Number       Material Type
0050000100            M001
PLNA                  0001
PLNA                  0002
PLEU                  0001
```

```
0050000200          M001
PLNA                0002
PLAS                0001
0050000300          T001
PLAS                0001
PLEU                0001
```

Report Complete

In the traditional top-down method of flow, you would expect a list of all the rows of data from MARAV, followed by all the rows of data from MARD. But events in a ABAP/4 program don't execute in a top-down manner; they execute when appropriate. When looking at a program that uses events, it's important not to try to read the code in a top-down manner. Each event is a separate subroutine that's executed when the system detects a certain condition.

In the example code, the logical database MSM reads data from the hierarchy of tables previously mentioned and makes this data available one row at a time. The first event triggered in the program is START-OF-SELECTION, which occurs just before any data is read. Next, the database is accessed by MSM. The first table in the hierarchy is MARAV, so the first row of this table is provided to the program triggering the GET MARAV event.

MSM continues to read through the tables in the hierarchy after MARAV—it reads from MBEWV, MVKE, MARCV, PROPF, and MARD, which again triggers an event in the program (GET MARD). For each record in MARD that's a child to the record read from the top of the hierarchy, MARAV, the GET MARD event is triggered.

When all rows have been read by MSM, control returns to MARAV. The program gets the next row. This action triggers the GET MARAV event, which prints the second material number.

From this point, the process repeats itself with the data being read from the tables lower in the hierarchy until all records that are children of the current MARAV record have been read. So the simple report is actually doing a great deal of work. This is often the case in ABAP/4, where much of the complexity is hidden from a programmer. But this also means that a simple mistake can produce wildly wrong answers. A simple GET statement may in fact access four or more database tables if the GET specifies a table at the bottom of a logical database hierarchy. The overhead of reading from all those tables isn't obvious from looking at a single statement.

Using GET LATE

The modifier LATE changes the conditions that trigger the GET event. Instead of being triggered when a new row is made available to a program by a logical database, it's triggered after all records lower in the hierarchy have been processed. So if your first example is changed to use GET LATE like this:

```
REPORT ZOMMT00000.
TABLES:   MARAV,   "Material Header
MARD.   "Material Storage Location
START-OF-SELECTION.
WRITE:    /,       'Extracting Materials and locations'.
WRITE:    /, /,    'Material Number', 16 'Material Type'.
GET MARAV LATE.
WRITE:      /,   (15) MARAV-MATNR,     "Material*
                  16 MARAV-MTART, /.   "Material Type
GET MARD.
WRITE:    /,   2(4) MARD-WERKS,        "Plant Code
                7 MARD-LGORT.          "Storage Location
END-OF-SELECTION.
WRITE:/,/'REPORT COMPLETE'
```

The resulting output would look like this:

```
Extracting Materials and locations
    PLNA 0001
    PLNA 0002
    PLEU 0001
0050000100          M001

    PLNA 0002
    PLAS 0001
0050000200          M001

    PLNA 0002
    PLAS 0001
0050000300          T001

REPORT COMPLETE
```

LIMITING DATA WITH LOGICAL DATABASE PARAMETERS

Each logical database has its own selection screen with parameters that can be used at runtime to enter a set of criteria for the data returned to the program. For example, the Financial Documents logical database, BRM, uses the screen shown in Figure 13.1.

When a user enters values into the selection screen, those values are used as criteria when the logical database returns data to the calling program. Only rows of data that meet the criteria specified by the user are returned.

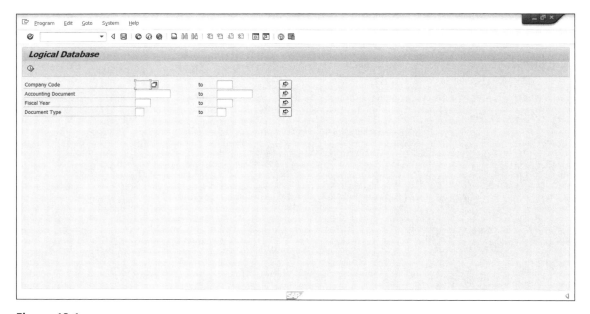

Figure 13.1
The selection for the logical database BRM.

If other parameters are present in the program using the logical database, they'll be added to the end of the selection screen. This works well for entering criteria at runtime, but what if a program is required to apply criteria to the rows processed—without a user entering criteria at runtime? The basic way to accomplish this is by using a CHECK statement.

CHECK includes a conditional statement; if that condition fails, CHECK acts like an EXIT statement. When a CHECK statement fails in a logical database, processing for the current table stops, and no subordinate table is read. For example, suppose that the report from the preceding example should list only data with a material type of 0001:

```
REPORT ZOMMT00000.
TABLES:   MARAV,   "Material Header
MARD.    "Material Storage Location

START-OF-SELECTION.
WRITE: /,    'Extracting Materials and locations'.
WRITE: /, /, 'Material Number', 16 'Material Type'.
GET MARAV.
CHECK MARAV-MTART = '0001'.
```

```
WRITE: /, /, (15) MARAV-MATNR,    "Material*
             16 MARAV-MTART.      "Material Type
GET MARD.
WRITE:      /,  2(4) MARD-WERKS,  "Plant Code
             7 MARD-LGORT.        "Storage Location
END-OF-SELECTION.
WRITE:  /,  /,    'Report Complete'.
```

This would produce the following output:

```
0050000300 0001
PLAS       0001
PLEU       0001
```

The records from table MARAV whose material type isn't 0001 are not processed. By the same token, the child records from table MARD for corresponding records aren't processed either.

The CHECK command seems simple—and it really is. Use it to limit the amount of data returned from the database. When you use a SELECT statement without a WHERE clause, it returns all rows from a single table. But when you use a GET event without a CHECK, the system must access all rows in that table, as well as all rows in all tables above it in the logical database hierarchy. This can be a serious drain on performance. Remember the first rule of client-server programming: Limit database access as much as possible to improve performance.

SUMMARY

Logical databases can be a convenient way of reading information from the database. Much of the complexity of a relational database is hidden from the programmer, resulting in programs that are simpler and easier to maintain. But this simplicity comes with a tradeoff in efficiency when using a logical database. Because the programmer has no access to the WHERE clauses that the logical database uses to retrieve data, in some cases a program using a SELECT statement may give you better performance.

In general, if you're reading a small number of records from large tables and can make use of indexes other than the primary key, SELECTs are more efficient. But if you use CHECKs at high levels in the table hierarchy to limit the amount of data being returned, logical databases can be efficient. Chapter 14, "Writing a Report," provides more examples of the tradeoffs from using SELECT versus logical databases.

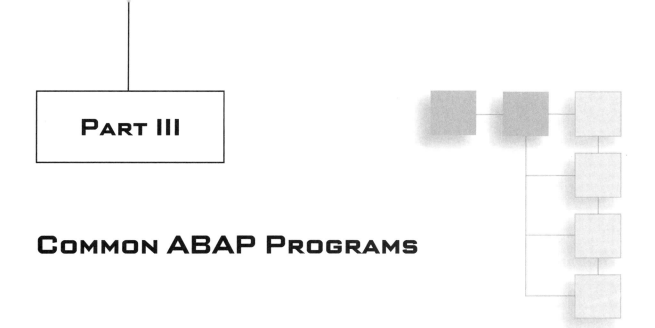

PART III

COMMON ABAP PROGRAMS

CHAPTER 14

WRITING A REPORT

IN THIS CHAPTER

- Determining the Functional Specifications
- Selecting Data
- Creating Organized Output
- Printing the Report
- Viewing the Complete Program

One of the most basic and complex tasks of a programmer is to write a program that reads data from the database tables, formats it, and displays it on the screen or in a document for the user. A program that does not create or update data but only reads data and displays it as output is referred to as a *report*.

Reports are one of the main programs written by ABAPers. Data extracts and BDC sessions (or interfaces) are the other two. These two programs are discussed in detail in this section of the book. The newest program is Web Dynpro, and it's covered in the next chapter.

To write a report, you follow these basic steps:

1. Review the functional specifications provided by the functional analyst. You must review this document closely.

2. After reviewing the functional specs, you determine your data sources and write the code.

Tip

You might assume that you would first define the data tables to hold the extracted data, but it's best to first attempt to code the `SELECT` statements to extract the data from the database tables. Once the SQL code is worked out, you have a better idea of how much data is coming in and in what format. Then you can define the data fields and internal tables that will be used to process the data.

DETERMINING THE FUNCTIONAL SPECIFICATIONS

Table 14.1 is an example of what you could expect in a functional spec. As an example, you'll use this spec to write a report in this chapter. This example is a very brief spec. Typically, they are much longer with much more intricate logic attached.

Table 14.1   Example Functional Specs

Report Name	Sales Report	
DESCRIPTION	This report selects sales orders that were created based on the date range specified in the selection screen. Retrieve the sales order line items for those sales orders and display the relevant information on the screen in the format specified here.	
FREQUENCY	This report will be run ad hoc by users. It can be run for wide date ranges in background.	
OUTPUT		
Column	*Table-Field*	*Description*
1	VBAK-VBELN	Sales Order Number
2	VBAK-ERDAT	Sales Order Create Date
3	VBAK-ERNAM	Username of person who created sales order
4	VBAP-POSNR	Sales Order Line Item Number
5	VBAP-MATNR	Sales Order Material Number
SORT CRITERIA	Sort the output by sales order number and then sales order line item number.	
SELECTION CRITERIA	VBAK-ERDAT Sales order create date/range (low to high).	

Review this spec and think to yourself what other questions you might need to finish the programming job. Typically, the spec is not as simple as this one. You might ask the functional analyst if there are any linkage tables for the output fields. You then would simulate querying the data using se16 and see if you have the right fields to query the tables. It might be that you need to use better key fields.

However, you must review the spec and verify that all the fields that are specified are correct. If they are not, review them with the functional analyst until you can find agreement.

SELECTING DATA

Data selection is a very important part of writing a report. It consists of a number of steps:

1. Choosing the tables from which the data will be pulled.

2. Determining the order in which the data will be selected.

3. Deciding whether an internal table or a field group is the best method for the report.

4. Specifying the data types that you plan to use for the data.

Choosing the Right Tables (Verifying the Functional Spec)

Back in the days of version 2.X with SAP, developers had to pay particular attention to the types of tables that they used in their programs. Today, most if not all tables are transparent. Pooled and cluster tables are very rare. So when we say choose the right table, we mean be as efficient as possible in your data access.

For this report, the two tables that are mentioned are related to each other. VBAK is the sales header table, and VBAP is the sales item table. VBAK has a key field of VBELN (the sales order number), and VBAP has two key fields called VBELN and POSNR (the sales order item number).

If the specs had mentioned delivery number or invoice number, then you would have to figure out how to link sales order number to those documents. Typically, there would be an additional table in the middle allowing you to find the relationship between those tables (that is, VBFA, sales document flow). For this particular example, you have the right tables.

Determining the Order of Data Selection

The order of data selection plays an important role in how efficient the code is for the report. For this report, it really is not that much of an issue. You know that the selection criteria is off VBAK, so you must query that first. Then, based on the data retrieved from VBAK, you get the corresponding entries in VBAP.

If you had chosen to get all entries in VBAP and then all the entries in VBAK where the date restriction was met, you would retrieve too many VBAP entries right up front.

When developing other programs, consider retrieving the tables that are most easily accessed (ones where you have most of the key fields) first or the tables where there are the most unique entries. Based on those tables, you can minimize the data retrieval on the other tables.

Field Groups versus Internal Tables

The last step before actually starting to code the report is to determine how many records will typically be retrieved, and whether an internal table or field group would be appropriate for the report. Use transaction se16 to query the tables you will access. If you find that the number of entries being returned is in the hundreds of thousands, consider using field groups. If it's less than that, internal tables are the way to go.

Specifying the Data Types

Now that you have determined the tables to use and that you will use an internal table, it is time to write some code. You first need to define the internal tables that contain the VBAK and VBAP fields:

```
TABLES:     VBAK,
            VBAP.

DATA: BEGIN OF LT_VBAK OCCURS 0.
DATA: VBELN LIKE VBAK-VBELN,
ERDAT LIKE VBAK-ERDAT.
DATA: END OF LT_VBAK.

DATA: BEGIN OF LT_VBAP OCCURS 0.
DATA:     VBELN LIKE VBAP-VBELN,
    POSNR LIKE VBAP-POSNR,
    MATNR LIKE VBAP-MATNR.
DATA: END OF LT_VBAP.
```

It is best to do the OCCURS 0 statement because SAP will take care of the memory for the internal tables. You also should specify the selection criteria for the report. For this report, it is simple. It is simply the create date for the sales order:

```
*Selection Screen
select-options: s_erdat for vbak-erdat.
```

Data Selection

Finally, you need to query the tables to get the data you need. In order to do this, you need to write SQL statements against VBAK and VBAP.

```
SELECT vbeln erdat ernam FROM VBAK into corresponding fields of table lt_vbak
    WHERE ERDAT in s_erdat.

SELECT vbeln posnr matnr from vbap into corresponding fields of table lt_vbap
for all entries in lt_vbak
    WHERE VBELN = lt_vbak-vbeln.
```

First, you query VBAK and get all the entries where the orders were created in the date range specified in the selection screen. Then you query VBAP using the data retrieved from VBAK as a filter. Note that you only select the specific fields that are required rather than the entire table (SELECT * FROM VBAK). When you're efficient with your SQL statements, you minimize memory usage and keep your programs quick and nimble.

CREATING ORGANIZED OUTPUT

Per the functional specifications, the program must sort the internal tables by sales order and then by sales order line item number.

```
sort lt_vbak by vbeln.
sort lt_vbap by vbeln posnr.
```

Setting Up Titles and Headers

Final formatting and output is probably the most tedious part of writing a report. By now, all the data should be organized nicely in internal tables that are ready to be processed onto a screen, email, or PDF. But you must write the code to output the data in a specific format.

The first task is to generate the header of the report. This code prints out the page number, the column headings, and the report tile for each new page. It is generally incorporated in a subroutine that is called when the code detects that the end of a page has been reached.

```
*&---------------------------------------------------------*
*&      Form   write_header
*&---------------------------------------------------------*
*       text
*---------------------------------------------------------*
form write_header.
  write:/55 'Sales Order Report'.
```

```
write:/  'Program',
         15 sy-repid.
write:/  'Date',
         15 sy-datum.
write:/  'Time',
         15 sy-uzeit.
skip.
uline.
write:/  'Order',
         15 'Date',
         30 'Name',
         45 'Item',
         55 'Material'.
uline.
```

PRINTING THE REPORT

The final step of the reporting process is to send the output to the printer. If the report is run online, once the data appears onscreen, you simply click the Print button that automatically appears on the menu bar.

If the program is executed in background mode or as a job, you must create a job print definition. First, type the name of your program in the ABAP Editor screen and click Execute. The selection screen appears. Enter the appropriate data and choose Program > Execute in Background. A screen appears that looks like Figure 14.1.

Type the printer name. To print immediately, select the Print Immed option. Deselect the option Delete After Print and select New Spool Request. Then click the Save button. A background job will be scheduled to run. Once it's finished, the report will automatically print at the printer station.

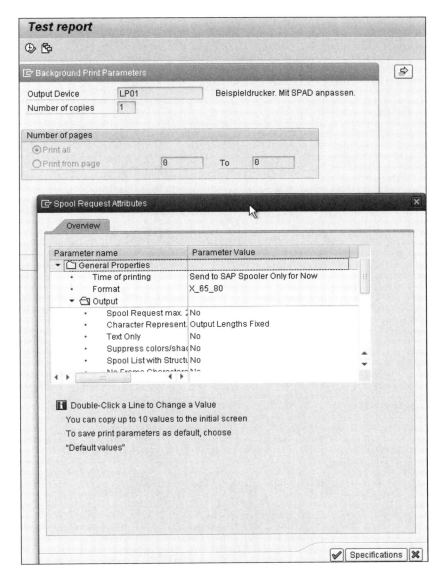

Figure 14.1
Defining the printer output for batch jobs.

VIEWING THE COMPLETE PROGRAM

This code represents the completed report in its full form, from start to finish. Separate pieces have been introduced through the chapter, so this last part of the chapter contains the code in its entirety:

```
*&---------------------------------------------------------------*
*& Report ZTESTGMD3
*&
*&---------------------------------------------------------------*
*&
*&
*&---------------------------------------------------------------*

REPORT ZTESTGMD3.

tables: vbak,
        vbap.

DATA: BEGIN OF LT_VBAK OCCURS 0.
DATA:    VBELN LIKE VBAK-VBELN,
ERDAT LIKE VBAK-ERDAT,
ERNAM like VBAK-ERNAM.
DATA: END OF LT_VBAK.

DATA: BEGIN OF LT_VBAP OCCURS 0.
DATA:    VBELN LIKE VBAP-VBELN,
  POSNR LIKE VBAP-POSNR,
  MATNR LIKE VBAP-MATNR.
DATA: END OF LT_VBAP.

* Selection Screen
select-options: s_erdat for vbak-erdat.

top-of-page.
  perform write_header.

start-of-selection.
  SELECT vbeln erdat ernam FROM VBAK into corresponding fields of table lt_vbak
        WHERE ERDAT in s_erdat.


  SELECT vbeln posnr matnr from vbap into corresponding fields of table lt_vbap
  for all entries in lt_vbak
        WHERE VBELN = lt_vbak-vbeln.

*Output
  sort lt_vbak by vbeln.
  sort lt_vbap by vbeln posnr.
```

```
loop at lt_vbak.
  loop at lt_vbap where vbeln = lt_vbak-vbeln.
    write:/   lt_vbak-vbeln,
          15 lt_vbak-erdat,
          30 lt_vbak-ernam,
          45 lt_vbap-posnr,
          55 lt_vbap-matnr.

  endloop.
endloop.




*&---------------------------------------------------------------------*
*&      Form write_header
*&---------------------------------------------------------------------*
*       text
*----------------------------------------------------------------------*
form write_header.
  write:/55 'Sales Order Report'.
  write:/   'Program',
        15 sy-repid.
  write:/   'Date',
        15 sy-datum.
  write:/   'Time',
        15 sy-uzeit.
  skip.
  uline.
  write:/   'Order',
        15 'Date',
        30 'Name',
        45 'Item',
        55 'Material'.
  uline.
endform.
```

Summary

Congratulations! You have just written your first complete ABAP program. The next three chapters cover the Web Dynpro, Data Extracts, and BDC programs. The level of complexity will increase, but the same basics will be used over and over. Be sure to refer back to prior chapters for reference if you get stuck.

CHAPTER 15

WEB DYNPRO

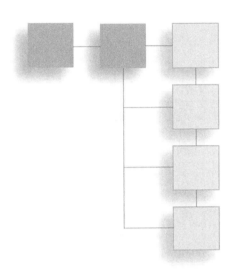

IN THIS CHAPTER

- Understanding the Areas of Web Dynpro
- Building a Simple Application
- Testing Your Web Dynpro Component

Web Dynpro for ABAP (WD4A, WDA) is the SAP standard user interface technology developed by SAP AG. Its intended use is for the development of web-based applications in the SAP ABAP environment, which utilizes SAP development tools and concepts. It provides a front-end web user interface to connect directly to a backend SAP R/3 systems to access data and functions for reporting. Web Dynpro for ABAP consists of a runtime environment and a graphical development environment with specific development tools that are integrated in the ABAP Workbench (SAP transaction se80).

Web Dynpro offers the following advantages for application developers:

- The use of graphical tools significantly reduces the implementation effort.
- Reuse and better maintainability by using components.
- The layout and navigation is easily changed using the Web Dynpro tools.

- User interface accessibility is supported.

- Full integration in the ABAP development environment.

ARCHITECTURE OF WEB DYNPRO

This section covers the architecture of Web Dynpro, including the development tools. Keep these points in mind as you read this section:

- Web Dynpro is the SAP NetWeaver programming model for user interfaces (UIs).

- Every Web Dynpro application is structured according to the Model View Controller (MVC) programming model:

  The model defines the interface to the main system and allows the Web Dynpro application access to system data.

  The view is responsible for showing the data in the web browser.

  The controller resides between the view and the model. The controller formats the model data to be displayed in the view, processes the user entries made by the user, and returns them to the model.

Web Dynpro Component

The component is the principal, global unit of the Web Dynpro application project. You have the ability to create any number of component views in a component and assemble them in any number of the corresponding Web Dynpro windows.

Creating a Web Dypro component is the initial step in developing a new Web Dypro application. Once the component is created, it acts as a node in the Web Dypro object list on the left side of the Web Dynpro builder window, underneath the Web Dynpro Components node. See Figure 15.1.

Note

Double-clicking the component name will display the component on the right side of the Web Dynpro builder screen. The component view will also display the administrative details for the application, which include the description, the name of the person who created it, the creation date, or the assigned development package.

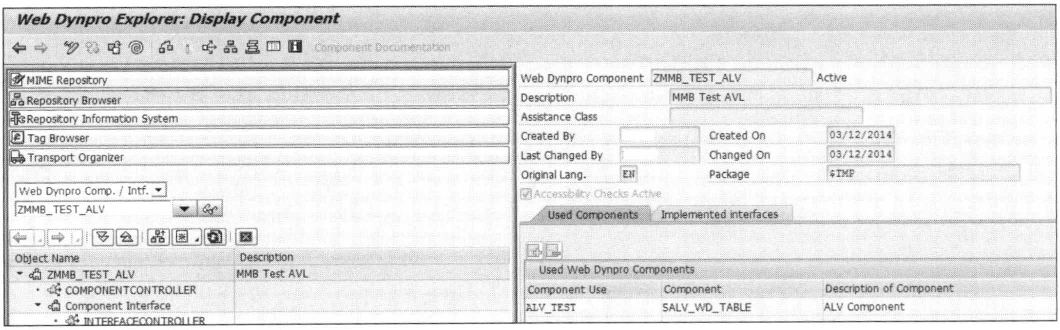

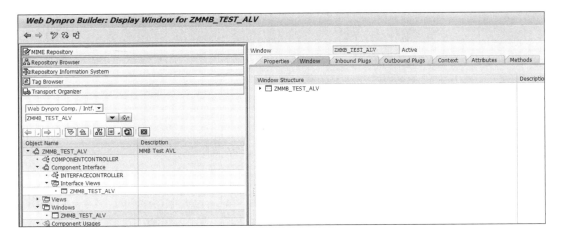

Figure 15.1
The Web Dynpro component.

Web Dynpro Window

At least one Web Dynpro window is contained in each Web Dynpro component. The Web Dynpro window embeds all the views that are displayed within the front-end web application. The window is processed in the window editors of the ABAP Workbench. The required navigation between the individual views can be set up in the window. See Figure 15.2.

Note

A window will contain the structure of all embedded views to be displayed and is linked to the Web Dynpro application via an interface view.

Figure 15.2
The Web Dynpro window.

Web Dynpro View

All the required layout and dialog elements are arranged in the Web Dynpro view. Examples of the layout and dialog elements include labels, values, and buttons that are used to display data and/or trigger events. The view contains a controller and a controller context in which the application data to be processed is stored in a hierarchical structure. This allows the linking of the graphical elements with the application data. See Figure 15.3.

Note

In order to create a Web Dynpro view for your component, you first need to select the Views node of the Web Dynpro component in the object list and then choose Create from its context menu. The View editor will appear on the right side of the Object Navigator in the tools area once the view has been created. You can now edit the graphical design of the view using the tools available in the Layout tab.

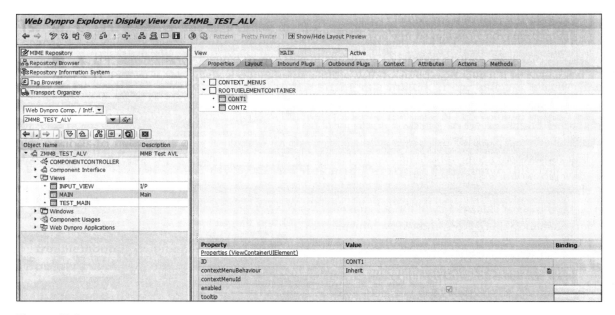

Figure 15.3
The Web Dynpro view.

Web Dynpro Component Controller

A Web Dynpro component controller is contained in each corresponding Web Dynpro component. A component controller is generated during the component creation and consists of context, events, and methods. The component controller is viewable within all views in a corresponding component in a WD application. The controllers can access context elements or methods of the component controller within different component views. For this purpose, the component controller usage is automatically created for every view controller.

Note

A Web Dynpro component controller is the main driver of exchanging data between different views of a given component. The SAP framework provides the instrument for the context mapping, which is a main tool to easily perform this data exchange.

Web Dynpro Programming Controller

In order to simplify the process of programs and to allow for data to be edited in context, attributes and methods are used within Web Dynpro applications. Action event handlers and cross-controller method calls are examples of program processes. See Figure 15.4.

Note

As you start to create a new Web Dynpro component, a component controller is generated automatically. The view controller is automatically created. Each window of a component contains a window controller, and you can create custom controllers for specific purposes.

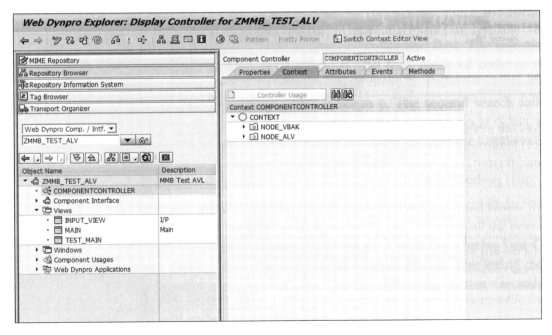

Figure 15.4
The Web Dynpro component controller.

Interface Controller

The Web Dynpro interface controller creates the interface of a component for the use in another component. The method logic is developed in the component controller. Once the interface flag is set for a given set of methods, events, and context nodes in the component controller, these elements are copied into the interface controller.

Web Dynpro Application

The important role of the Web Dynpro window is to establish the connection between the structured view group and a URL that will be called by the user of the Web Dynpro application. The Web Dynpro application calls only a single view on the screen at a time and calls the specified view as the default view within that given window. The user can navigate from this start view to other views in the flow. See Figure 15.5.

Note

The Web Dynpro application is the independent object in the object list of the ABAP Workbench. The interaction between the window and the application is created by the interface view of a given window. There is typically only a single interface view that is automatically assigned to each window of a component, with the interface view containing a plug by default.

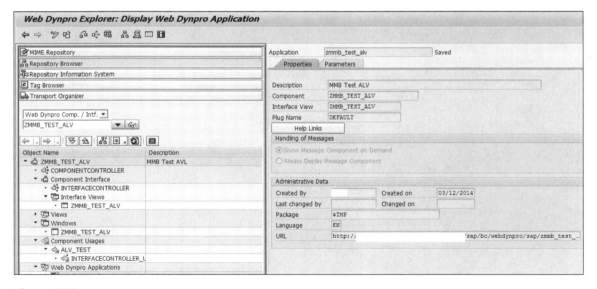

Figure 15.5
The Web Dynpro application.

Web Dynpro Application URL

The URL of a Web Dynpro application is automatically generated by the system. You can find the URL of your application in the Web Dynpro Explorer on the Properties tab.

The URL of a WD application has the following URL format:

```
<schema>://<host>.<domain>.<extension>:<port>/abc/klm/xyz/<namespace>
       /webdynpro/<application name>
```

- ■ `<schema>` stands for the URL schema (also known as protocol), which usually is the protocol `http` or `https` (if configured).

- ■ `Host` is the name of the application server that should execute the application. `Domain` with the extension comprises several hosts under a common name and can be an individual host or a network.

- ■ The `port` number can be omitted if the standard port 80 (`http`) or 443 (`https`) is used.

- ■ The `namespace` can be the standard namespace /SAP/ or customer namespaces.

- ■ The `application name` is the name of the web application as defined in the Web Dynpro explorer by the WD component.

BUILDING A SIMPLE APPLICATION

In this section, you learn how to develop a simple Web Dynpro application that accepts an input value from the user on the first screen and displays the value entered on the second screen. Follow these steps to try it out:

1. Go to transaction se80.
2. Select Web Dynpro Comp./Intf from the list, as shown in Figure 15.6.

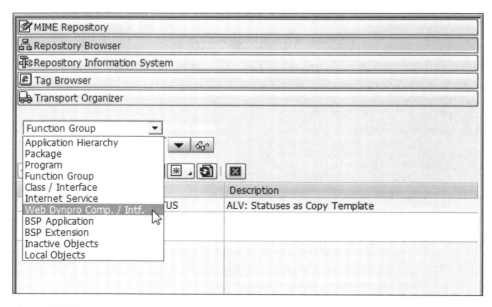

Figure 15.6
Selecting Web Dynpro Comp./Intf from the list.

3. Create a new WD component by the name ZTEST_WD4A_SAMPLE1 and assign it to the local object, as shown in Figure 15.7.

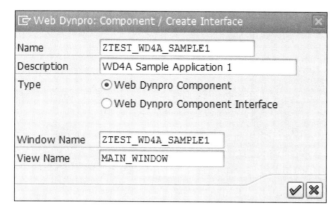

Figure 15.7
Creating a new WD component.

4. Right-click on the Web Dynpro component named ZTEST_WD4A_SAMPLE1 and create a view. See Figures 15.8 through 15.10 for this process.

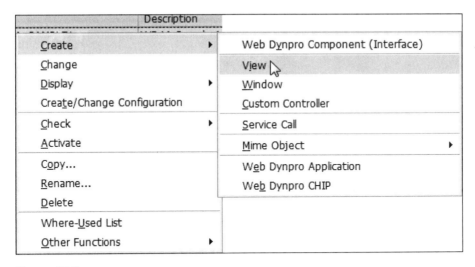

Figure 15.8
Right-click on the component and choose Create and View.

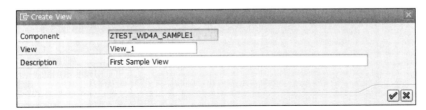

Figure 15.9
Enter the view name and a description and click on the green check box.

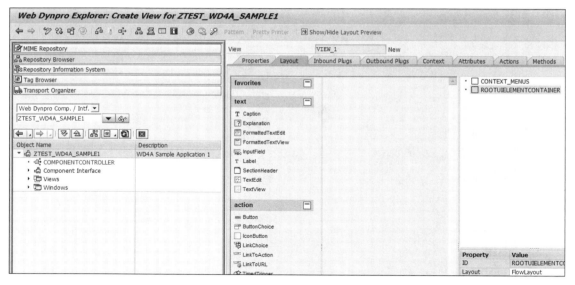

Figure 15.10
You can see that the view has been created.

5. Save the application and then double-click on the COMPONENTCONTROLLER.

6. Check if the application is in Change mode.

7. Create a node as shown in Figures 15.11 and 15.12.

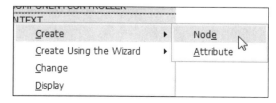

Figure 15.11
Create a node.

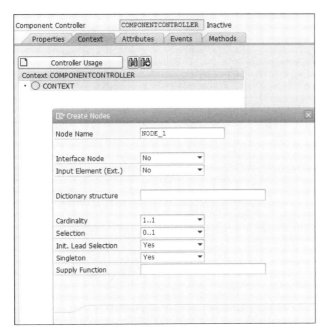

Figure 15.12
The Create Nodes dialog box.

8. Create an attribute for the node, as shown in Figures 15.13 and 15.14. Figure 15.15 shows the component controller with NODE_1.

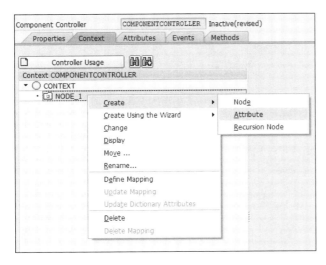

Figure 15.13
Create an attribute.

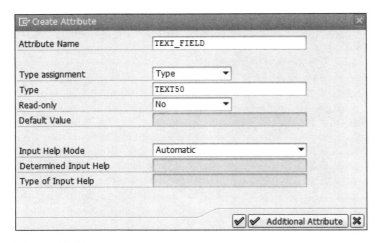

Figure 15.14
The Create Attribute dialog box.

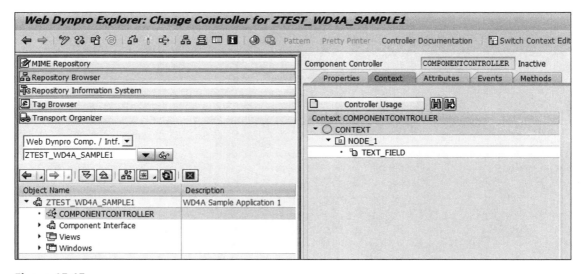

Figure 15.15
Component Controller contains a context with NODE_1.

9. Save the application and then double-click on the VIEW_1 view that you created earlier, as shown in Figure 15.16.

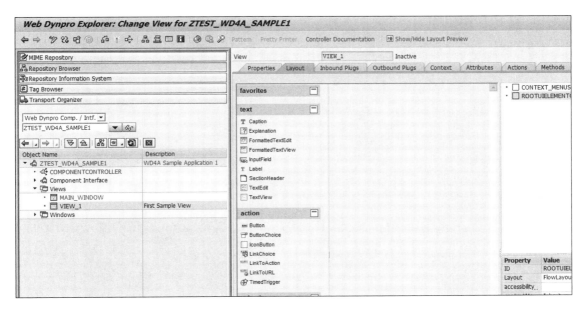

Figure 15.16
Changing the view.

10. In this step, you'll design the first screen of your application with the following elements:

   ■ A label for the text box

   ■ A text box as an input field

   ■ A button (for Execute)

11. Insert a new element by right-clicking the ROOTUIELEMENTCONTAINER within the Layout tab of VIEW_1 view and choosing Insert Element, as shown in Figure 15.17.

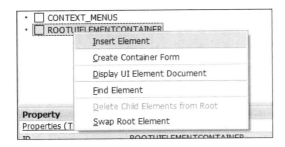

Figure 15.17
Inserting a new element.

12. Add the Label element with an ID of TEXT_LABEL, as shown in Figure 15.18.

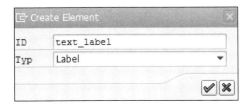

Figure 15.18
Inserting a Label element.

13. Add the Value element with an ID of TEXT_VALUE, as shown in Figure 15.19.

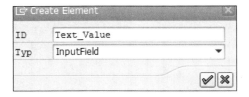

Figure 15.19
Inserting a Value element.

14. Finally, add the Button element with an ID of EXECUTE, as shown in Figure 15.20.

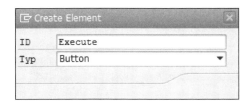

Figure 15.20
Creating an Execute button.

15. After inserting the elements onto the layout, change the values in the TEXT_LABEL, TEXT_VALUE, and EXECUTE property tabs, as shown in Figures 15.21 through 15.23.

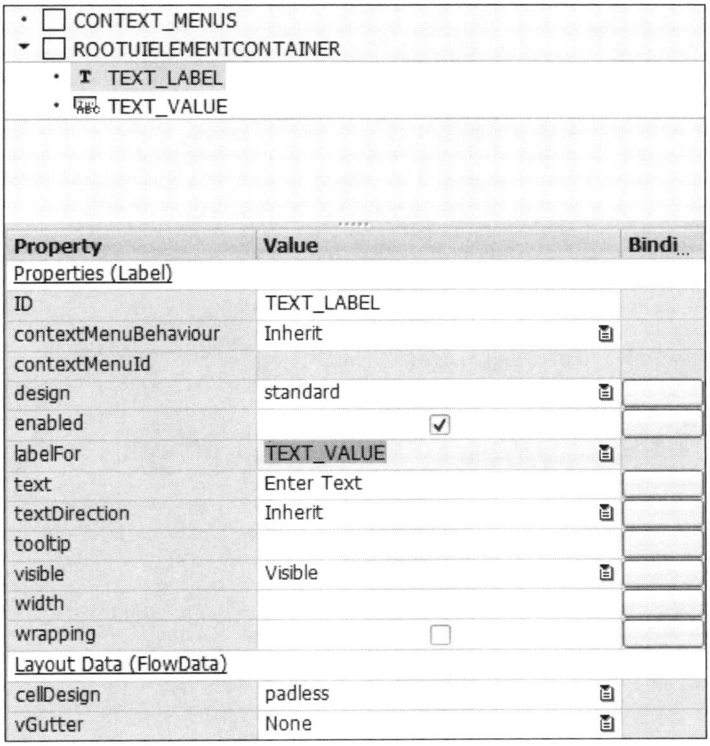

Property	Value		Bindi...
Properties (Label)			
ID	TEXT_LABEL		
contextMenuBehaviour	Inherit	🗐	
contextMenuId			
design	standard	🗐	
enabled	✓		
labelFor	TEXT_VALUE	🗐	
text	Enter Text		
textDirection	Inherit	🗐	
tooltip			
visible	Visible	🗐	
width			
wrapping	☐		
Layout Data (FlowData)			
cellDesign	padless	🗐	
vGutter	None	🗐	

Figure 15.21
Change the values in the property tabs for the new TEXT_LABEL element.

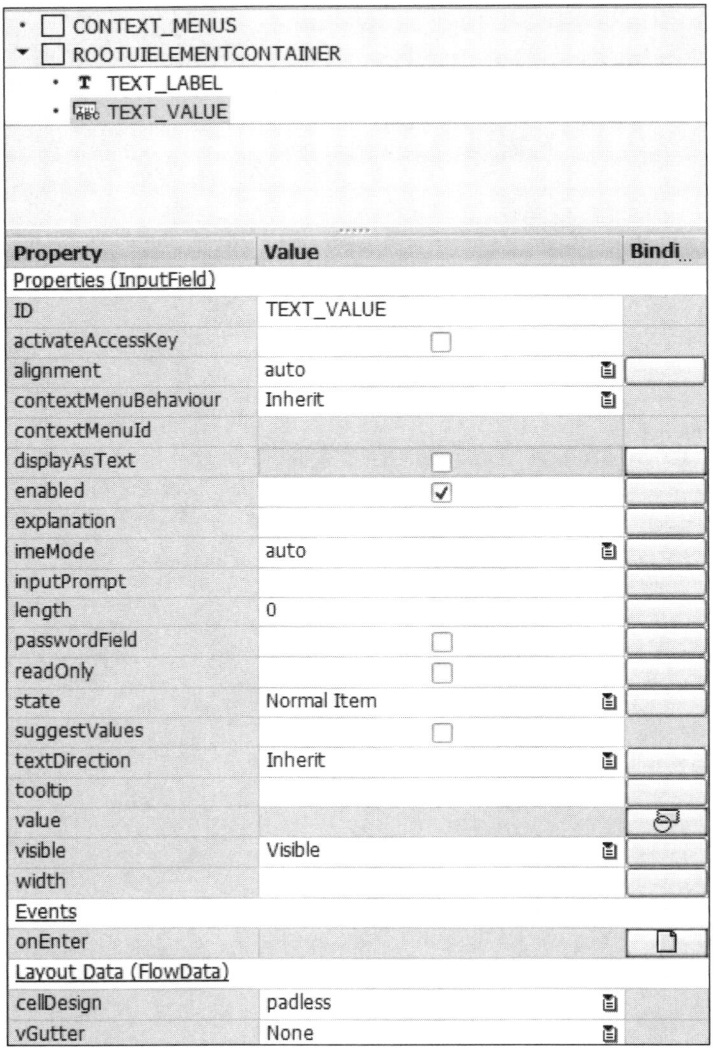

- ☐ CONTEXT_MENUS
▾ ☐ ROOTUIELEMENTCONTAINER
    • **T** TEXT_LABEL
    • TEXT_VALUE

Property	Value	Bindi...
Properties (InputField)		
ID	TEXT_VALUE	
activateAccessKey	☐	
alignment	auto	
contextMenuBehaviour	Inherit	
contextMenuId		
displayAsText	☐	
enabled	✔	
explanation		
imeMode	auto	
inputPrompt		
length	0	
passwordField	☐	
readOnly	☐	
state	Normal Item	
suggestValues	☐	
textDirection	Inherit	
tooltip		
value		
visible	Visible	
width		
Events		
onEnter		
Layout Data (FlowData)		
cellDesign	padless	
vGutter	None	

Figure 15.22
Change the values in the property tabs for the new TEXT_VALUE element.

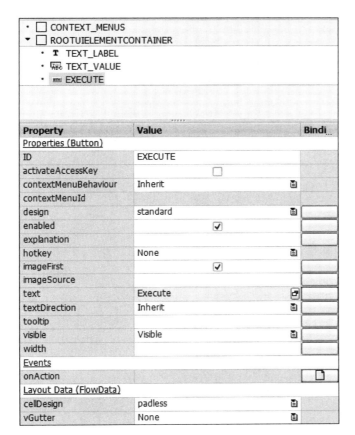

Figure 15.23
Change the values in the property tabs for the new EXECUTE element.

16. In the properties window of the EXECUTE element, do the following:

Change the text to Execute.

Click on Create for the property OnAction.

Enter execute for the Action and the Outbound Plug name, as shown in Figure 15.24.

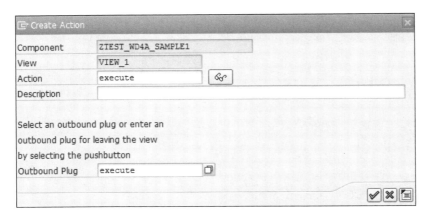

Figure 15.24
Name the Action and the Outbound Plug from this window.

17. Press OK when you see the Outbound Plug prompt.

18. The pop-up box shown in Figure 15.25 will display. Click Yes and continue.

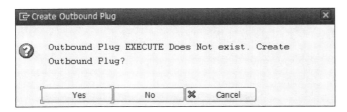

Figure 15.25
Choose Yes to create the new Outbound Plug.

19. Click on the Context tab. Drag and drop the node on the right side to the context on the left side.

20. Click on Yes when you're asked if the node should be copied and mapped. Figure 15.26 shows the node copied to the context of VIEW_1.

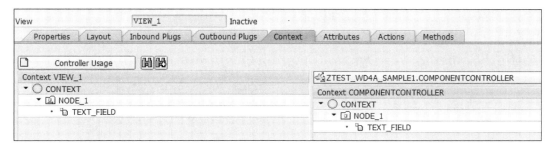

Figure 15.26
NODE_1 of the component controller copied to View_1 context.

21. Save the application.

22. Click on the Layout tab.

23. Double-click on the TEXT_FIELD. For the Value property, select the TEXT_FIELD attribute by clicking on the binding button, as shown in Figure 15.27.

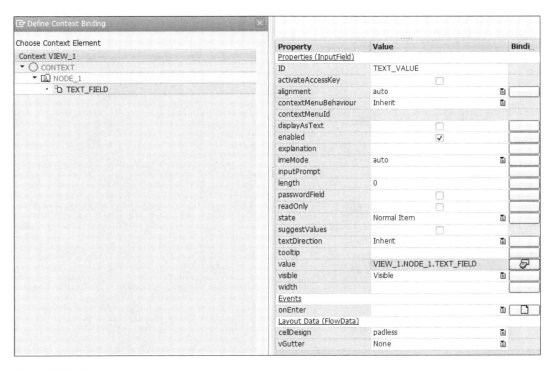

Figure 15.27
Binding created for the TEXT_FIELD element.

At this point, the first view has been designed and completed. The next series of steps shows you how to design the second application screen.

1. Right-click on the Web Dynpro component and create another view, called VIEW_2, as shown in Figure 15.28.

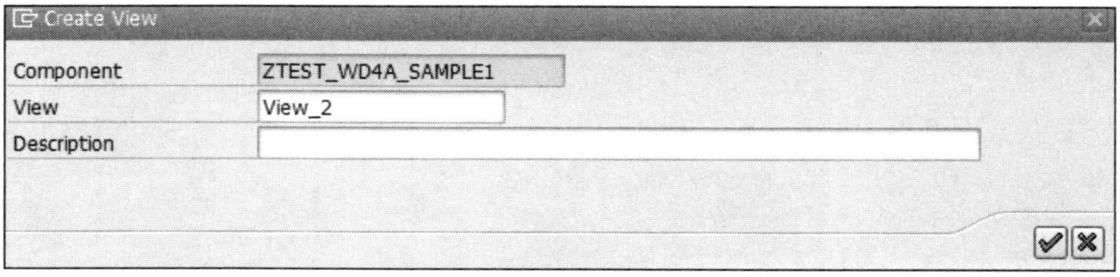

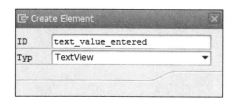

Figure 15.28
Creating the second view.

2. Create a Label element named Entered Text with type Label, as mentioned in the earlier step. See Figure 15.29.

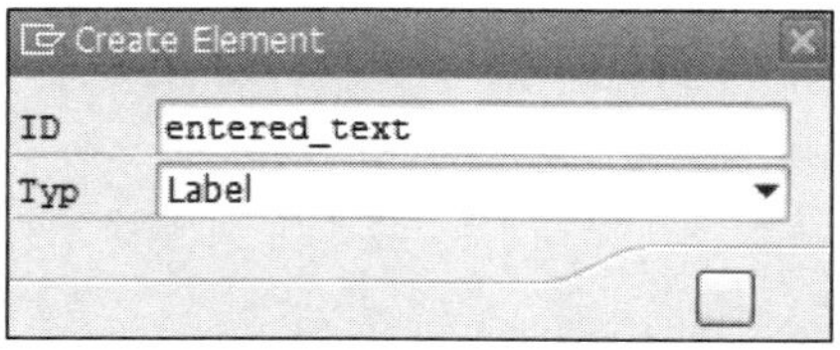

Figure 15.29
Creating a Label element.

3. Create another element named TEXT_VALUE_ENTERED with type TextView onto the layout, as shown in Figure 15.30.

Figure 15.30
Creating another element.

Ensure to match the property values as shown in Figure 15.31.

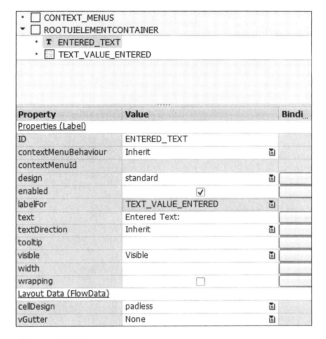

Figure 15.31
Make sure the property values match the ones shown here.

You would display the value entered on the first screen in an element called
TEXT_VALUE.

4. Click on the Context tab and map the nodes as in the earlier step. Drag NODE_1 to the
   VIEW_2 context, as shown in Figure 15.32.

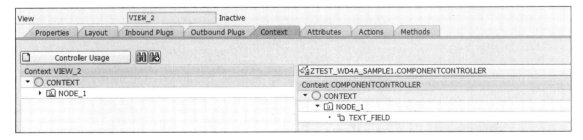

Figure 15.32
NODE_1 contained in the VIEW_2 context.

5. Go to the Inbound Plugs tab and create an inbound plug, as shown in Figure 15.33.

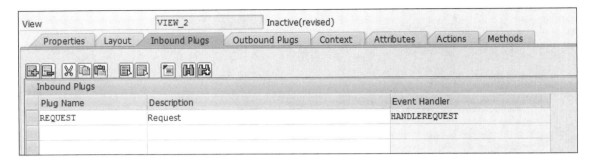

Figure 15.33
Creating an inbound plug.

6. Go back to the layout and then double-click on the element called TEXT_VALUE_ENTERED to open the properties. For the Text property, click on the binding button and select Name, as shown in Figure 15.34.

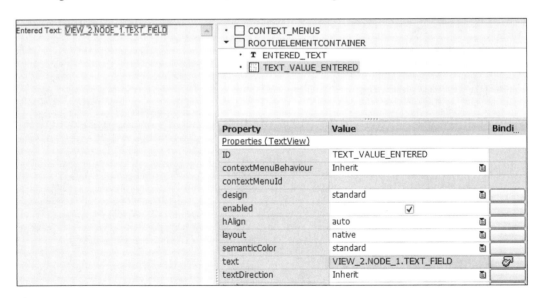

Figure 15.34
Binding for the TEXT_FIELD element in VIEW_2.

In these next series of steps, you'll embed the views you created into the window created in the first series.

1. Double-click on the window called MAIN_WINDOW.

2. Right-click on the window name and select Embed View, as shown in Figure 15.35.

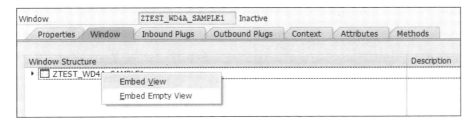

Figure 15.35
Choose Embed View to start the process.

Perform this step twice, once for VIEW_1 (see Figure 15.36) and again for VIEW_2 (see Figure 15.37).

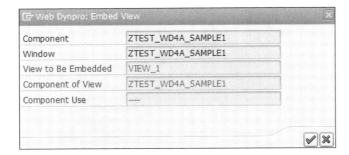

Figure 15.36
Embedding VIEW_1.

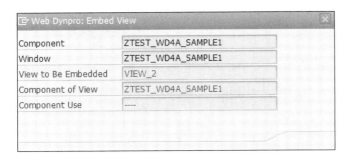

Figure 15.37
Embedding VIEW_2.

3. Embed both the views created earlier. Do not select the view called EMPTYVIEW, which is created by default.

4. Expand the tree. You should see something similar to Figure 15.38 when you do so.

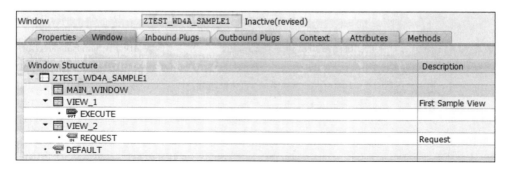

Figure 15.38
Expanding the tree.

5. Right-click on the EXECUTE element and choose Create Navigation Link, as shown in Figure 15.39.

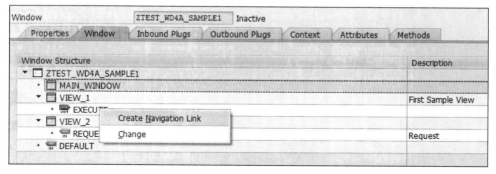

Figure 15.39
Creating a navigation link.

6. Select VIEW_2 for the Dest. View, as shown in Figure 15.40.

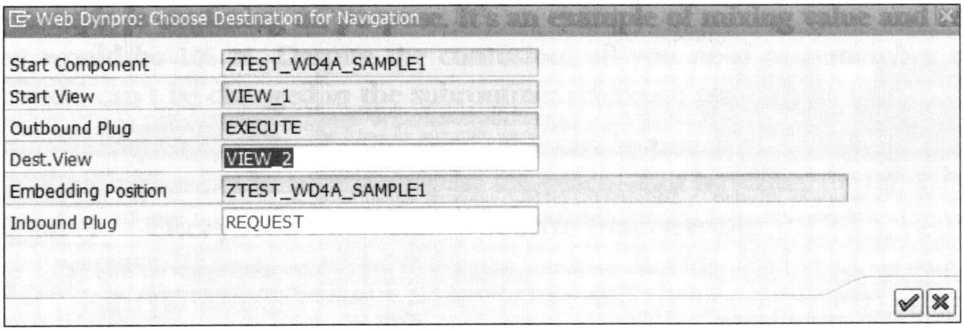

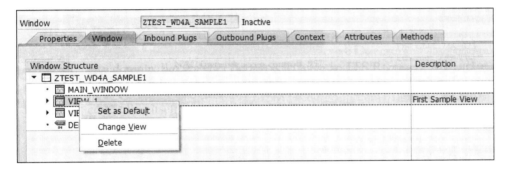

Figure 15.40
Choosing the destination view.

7. Now select the VIEW_1 and make it the default, as shown in Figure 15.41.

Figure 15.41
Making VIEW_1 the default view.

Save and activate the application. (When you're activating, select all the components related to this Web Dynpro application. Only when all the components are activated will the application execute.) Now your application is ready to execute.

TESTING YOUR WEB DYNPRO COMPONENT

In this section, you'll learn how to text the new component you created. Follow these steps to do so:

1. Right-click on the Web Dynpro component you created and choose Create > Web Dynpro Application, as shown in Figure 15.42.

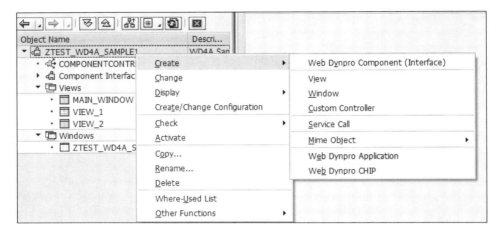

Figure 15.42
Creating the Web Dynpro application.

2. Without changing any values, press Save.

3. Execute your Web Dynpro application. You should see something very similar to Figure 15.43.

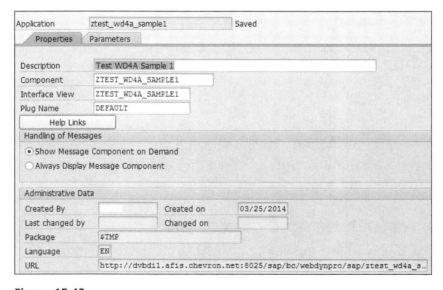

Figure 15.43
Complete attributes of the Web Dynpro application.

Summary

In summary, there are many SAP Workbench development tools that can be utilized when developing a Web Dynpro application. These tools are powerful and offer a great number of advantages to developers. These advantages include reuse and better maintainability by using components, easily changing the layout and navigation, and use of the full integration within the ABAP development environment. Although learning to develop a Web Dynpro application takes a considerable amount of effort and practice, the time required to gain that knowledge is worthwhile considering the reward of being able to create Web Dynpro applications for your company or customers.

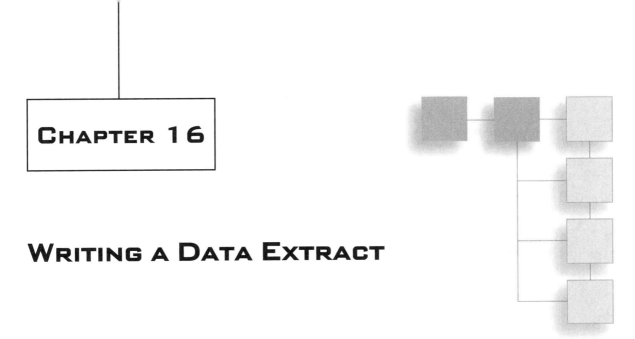

Chapter 16

Writing a Data Extract

In This Chapter

- Determining the Data to Be Extracted
- Extracting the Data
- Writing the Data to a File
- Transferring the File to the Target System
- Example Extracts

A *data extract* is a program that pulls data out of a system on a periodic basis so that it can be transferred to an external system for processing. In the case of SAP, data extracts are often used to keep legacy or other external systems in sync with SAP by passing data from SAP to those systems. For example, a legacy manufacturing system might need weekly extracts of material inventory levels from SAP. This chapter goes through the steps of designing and writing a data extract.

Steps in a Data Extract

Several steps are commonly used to design and write a data extract:

1. Determine what data to extract by looking for the database tables that hold the information.
2. Extract the correct data from those database tables identified.

3. Write that data—in the proper format—to a file.

4. Transfer the file to the target system.

Once each of these steps is complete, the final program can be scheduled for future use.

Determining the Data to Be Extracted

The first step in the process is to determine what data is to be extracted. You'll be given a set of program requirements that could range from "We need some information on materials" to a detailed breakdown of exactly which database tables, which fields in those tables, and the criteria to be used to determine which rows of data to select. Normally, the requirements you get will fall somewhere in the middle.

Usually the requirements are written by business analysts who have no knowledge of relational databases and will simply list the information they need in business terms.

So the requirements might call for extracting all purchase orders that include purchase order number, date, name of requester, and material numbers for items ordered. The programmer's job is to take those business terms and translate them into specific tables and fields in those tables.

Using Logical Databases to Find Tables

A number of ways exist in SAP to find the tables that hold the information you need. One of the simplest ways is to look at the logical databases SAP has already created for the business object that interests you. As discussed in Chapter 13, "Working with Logical Databases," a logical database is a group of tables that SAP has put together to allow a program to use the GET event to read information from the database. Simply look at the list of logical databases for the business object in which you are interested (see Figure 16.1). This list is found in the logical database information transaction, se36.

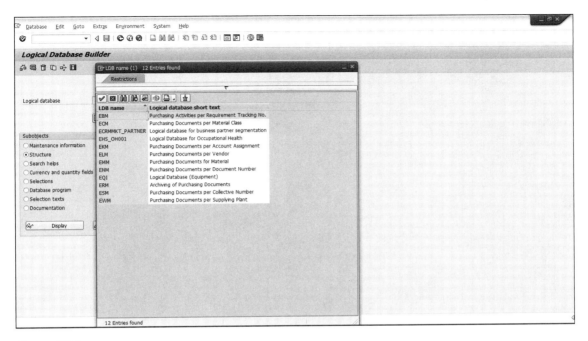

Figure 16.1
Some of the logical databases available.

For example, a logical database for purchase orders is EMM. By using the Display Structure button on the logical database information screen, you can view the table hierarchy that includes the database tables EKKO and EKPO. The structure gives descriptions for each table; from there, you can use the Data Dictionary to get a list of the individual fields in each table.

Using SAP Transactions to Find Tables

Another way to find the tables that hold the attributes of specific business objects is to look at the SAP transactions. As you may recall, a transaction is a group of screens used by end users to maintain or view data—so transactions will correspond to the business terms that the analysts use. SAP provides transactions for all business objects in the system. For sales orders, there are transactions to create, change, or view the sales orders. For example, the transaction VA03 displays a single sales order over several screens.

Remember that most fields on a screen correspond with a field in the database. The system provides the database field name in the Technical Information dialog box (see

Figure 16.2). To access the dialog box for a particular field, click the field, press Fl, and then choose Technical Information.

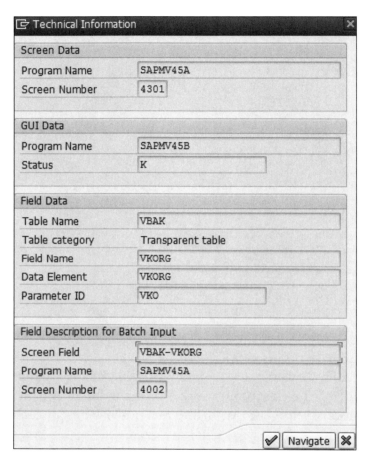

Figure 16.2
Technical Information screen for a database field.

Note

For some screen fields, the technical information won't provide a corresponding field in the database. In these cases, look at the other fields that appear on the screen and determine which database tables they come from. Most attributes of business objects can be found in three or four tables at most.

Choosing Specific Fields

Once the database fields have been mapped to the business requirements, you can determine which specific fields need to be read and whether there are any criteria to limit the number of rows. Periodic extracts of data normally don't want the same data read twice, so programs need criteria to limit the extract to new data only. All data entered into SAP is date stamped with the date of entry recorded in a database table; the date stamp is therefore often a good criterion.

Another possible criterion is the document number—a number that's assigned to most transactions and is incremented each time a new transaction occurs. For example, each time a new purchase order is created, the purchase order number (EKKO-EBAN) is increased. So if the last purchase order number extracted is saved, each time the program is run that last number can be recalled and used as a starting point.

Extracting the Data

Once the database tables and fields have been identified, you need to write a program to read the data. As you should know by now, you can read information from the database with either of two techniques:

- To read the tables directly, you use the SELECT command. In this case, the programmer must understand the relationships between the many tables.

- The second technique is to use a logical database and the GET statement. This is easier to use but often not as efficient as SELECT statements.

Regardless of the technique used, the fields will be read, and any criteria needed should be applied through a WHERE clause or CHECK statement.

Writing the Data to a File

After the information is read from the database, it needs to be written to a system file. The TRANSFER command moves data from SAP to a system file. The first step is to determine the directory path and name of the system file you'll use.

A common approach to naming such a file is to mix a static name with a date stamp so that each file has a unique name. For example, a daily extract of purchase order information might use a file name such as poextract.04.18.14; the next time the interface is run, the file name would be poextract.04.19.14. By using unique names, you avoid the possibility of overwriting a file that failed to transfer.

Once the file name is built, use the OPEN command to ready the file for writing.

When the information has been read from the database, the program can process or format the data. When giving the requirements for an extract, those requirements contain the necessary format for the extract file. The typical format is to specify each field by its position in the file. For example, the purchase order number might occupy the first 10 positions of a file, the creation date might be in the next eight positions, and so on. Another possibility is a format where each field is followed by a separator, such as a comma or a pound sign.

Caution

> When using separators, be very careful of long description fields because they may contain any type of character, including the separator. For example, the description of a part might be Bolt, steel, 7 inch. If you used the comma as a separator, the system would think that the description field was two different fields. Use the `REPLACE` command to remove any separators that might be in description fields before transferring them to the file.

Transferring the File to the Target System

After the system file has been built, the final step is to send that file to the target system. ABAP has the ability to create a system file and transfer data to and from it, but it has very limited ability to deal with the operating system. No ABAP command exists to move or copy files at the operating-system level; each SAP site must set up its own way of moving files into and out of SAP.

Some of the common techniques used are a daemon or the `CALL FUNCTION` command. A *daemon* is a program that runs in the background of the operating system, written in a low-level language such as C, watching for files and sending them to the proper target. As explained in Chapter 11, "Adding Subroutines to Your Program," the `CALL FUNCTION` command can be used to make operating system calls if your operating system is UNIX. For example, `CALL FUNCTION` can be used to execute the UNIX `rep` (remote copy) command to move files to another server. Because moving files into and out of SAP is such a common operation, all sites will have a solution to this problem. You should find this solution and use it in all your programs.

EXAMPLE EXTRACTS

In this section, you'll look at three examples of data extract programs:

- The first example extracts documents created by the SAP automated check runs and writes them to a file. SAP automatically creates checks for payments to vendors.

- The second example extracts purchase order information (*a purchase order* is an order to buy one or more items).

- The final example is an extract of material inventories.

In each example, the requirements are provided, followed by the ABAP program to accomplish them.

Check Payments

The first program, called ZCHECK, extracts documents created by the SAP automated check runs and writes them to a file. SAP automatically creates checks for payments to vendors and records these checks as financial documents in the BKPF and BSEG tables. For each document, a record is placed in BKPF with general information such as document number and date created. Then each line item of the document is placed in BSEG with information such as the amount, vendor, and general ledger account.

This data extract will be run by end users on demand and should allow the user to enter the following parameters:

- A range of document numbers

- A range of document dates

- A company code

- The path and file name of the output file

These checks can be identified by a document type (BKPF-BLART) of KZ and a payment indicator (BSEG-ZLSCH) of C. Once the check information is read, you can determine the bank account of the check by using the G/L Account (BSEG-SAKNR) to retrieve the bank ID (T042I-HBKID) and then the bank account (T012K-BANKN).

The output file should have the format shown in Table 16.1.

Table 16.1 ZCHECK Output File

Field Name	Position	Data Type	Length	Source: Table-Field
Check number	1	C	10	BSEG-BELNR
Date of issue "MMDDYY"	11	C	06	BSEG-VALUT
Bank account number	17	C	17	T012K-BANKN
Amount	34	C	11	BSEG-WRBTR
Name vendor	45	C	30	LFA1-NAME1
Filler	75	C	06	

© 2014 Cengage Learning.

Here's the program:

```
*&---------------------------------------------------------*
*& Report   ZCHECK
*&
*&---------------------------------------------------------*
*& Description : This program will extract Check
*& Documents on demand from the BSE6 table
*& which contains different financial documents.
*& Look ups will be done to retrieve the
*& vendor name and bank account of the check.
*&
*&---------------------------------------------------------*

REPORT ZCHECK      NO STANDARD PAGE HEADING LINE-SIZE 132
  LINE-COUNT 65 MESSAGE-ID ZZ.

TABLES : BSEG,       "Financial Documents Header
BKPF,  "Financial Documents Item
LFA1,  "Vendor Master
T042I, "Account determination
T012K. "House Bank Accounts

*Variables
DATA:
WS_BUF(15), "Temporary Buffer
WS_AMNT(11) TYPE N, "Temporary Field For Amount
WS_REC TYPE I VALUE 0. "Record Count

DATA: BEGIN OF REC_OUT OCCURS 0,   "Output File
```

```
CHECT(10),   "Check Number
ZALDT(6),    "Check Date
BANKN(18),   "Bank Account
AMNT(11),    "Check Amount
NAME1(30),   "Vendor Name
FILLER(6),
END OF REC_OUT.
* Select Options/Parameters
PARAMETERS: P_BUKRS LIKE BSEG-BUKRS OBLIGATORY.   "Company Code
SELECT-OPTIONS:  S_BUDAT FOR BKPF-BUDAT,  "Date Created
  S_BELNR FOR BKPF-BELNR.       "Document Number
PARAMETERS: P_FILE(45) OBLIGATORY LOWER CASE "UNIX Output File Name
  DEFAULT '/interfaces/outbound/checkdata.txt'.

* Main Processing
START-OF-SELECTION.
  PERFORM OPEN_DATASET.
  PERFORM EXTRACT_DATA.
  PERFORM CLOSE_DATASET.

*&---------------------------------------------------------*
*&      Form   OPEN_DATASET
*&---------------------------------------------------------*
*&        Open File to prepare for data
*---------------------------------------------------------*
FORM OPEN_DATASET.
****** build unix filename to write
  OPEN DATASET P_FILE FOR OUTPUT IN TEXT MODE
    ENCODING DEFAULT
    WITH SMART LINEFEED.
  IF SY-SUBRC NE 0.
    MESSAGE E999 WITH 'Error Creating File ' P_FILE.
  ENDIF.
ENDFORM.                        "OPEN_DATASET
"End Form   Open_Dataset


*&---------------------------------------------------------*
*&      Form   EXTRACT_DATA
*&---------------------------------------------------------*
* Read data from BKPF, financial documents header table,
* and BSEG, financial documents line items, then look up vendor
* name and bank account before transferring data to file.
*---------------------------------------------------------*
```

```
FORM EXTRACT_DATA.
*** Select Header Documents
   SELECT * FROM BKPF WHERE BELNR IN S_BELNR   " Check Document#
     AND BUDAT IN S_BUDAT   " Posting Date
     AND BUKRS = P_BUKRS    " Company code
     AND   BLART = 'KZ'.    " Doc Type
     SELECT * FROM BSEG WHERE BUKRS = BKPF-BUKRS   "Get Void Line Items
     AND BELNR = BKPF-BELNR
     AND GJAHR = BKPF-GJAHR
     AND ZLSCH = 'C'.       "Indicates Check
       CLEAR REC_OUT.
       WRITE BSEG-WRBTR USING EDIT MASK 'RR  '        "Get Amount
       TO REC_OUT-AMNT.
       PERFORM PAD_FIELD USING REC_OUT-AMNT.
       MOVE BKPF-BUDAT TO WS_BUF.        "get date 'DDMMYY'
       MOVE WS_BUF+4(4) TO REC_OUT-ZALDT.
       MOVE WS_BUF+2(2) TO REC_OUT-ZALDT+4.
       MOVE BSEG-BELNR(10) TO REC_OUT-CHECT.        "Check#
       SELECT SINGLE * FROM LFA1
       WHERE LIFNR = BSEG-LIFNR.
       MOVE LFA1-NAME1 TO REC_OUT-NAME1.

       SELECT * FROM T042I         "Get Bank Account
       WHERE UKONT = BSEG-HKONT.
         SELECT SINGLE * FROM T012K
         WHERE BUKRS = T042I-ZBUKR
         AND HBKID = T042I-HBKID
         AND HKTID = T042I-HKTID.
         IF SY-SUBRC EQ 0.
           MOVE T012K-BANKN(18) TO REC_OUT-BANKN.
           PERFORM PAD_FIELD USING REC_OUT-BANKN.   " Bank Account
         ELSE.
           MESSAGE E999 WITH T042I-HBKID T042I-HKTID
           'Bank Account missing from T012K'.
         ENDIF.
       ENDSELECT.
       TRANSFER REC_OUT TO P_FILE.   "Save Record to File
     ENDSELECT.
   ENDSELECT.
   ENDSELECT.
   WS_REC = WS_REC + 1.
ENDFORM.                    "EXTRACT_DATA
```

```
*&---------------------------------------------------------*
*&     Form   CLOSE_DATASET
*&---------------------------------------------------------*
*&     Close dataset and report totals
*---------------------------------------------------------*
FORM CLOSE_DATASET.
  CLOSE DATASET P_FILE.
  IF SY-SUBRC NE 0.
    MESSAGE E999 WITH 'Error Closing file ' P_FILE.
  ENDIF.
  IF WS_REC > 0.
    MESSAGE I999 WITH WS_REC 'records written to File.'.
  ELSE.
    MESSAGE I999 WITH 'No records found. No file created.'.
  ENDIF.
ENDFORM.   "End form Close Dataset

*&---------------------------------------------------------*
*&     Form   PAD_FIELD
*&---------------------------------------------------------*
*&     Pad number with leading zeros
*---------------------------------------------------------*
*&     -->P_NUM      text
*---------------------------------------------------------*
FORM PAD_FIELD USING P_NUM.
  SHIFT P_NUM RIGHT.
  WHILE SY-SUBRC = 0.
    REPLACE ' ' WITH '0' INTO P_NUM. "Zero Pad
  ENDWHILE.
ENDFORM.                 "PAD_FIELD
```

This first example demonstrates a simple extract program run at user demand. The following examples demonstrate more of the attributes for extracts.

Purchase Orders

The second program extracts information about new purchase orders created in SAP. It reads the Purchase Order Line Item table, EKPO. The tracking number, together with the purchase order number and purchase order line item number, is used to retrieve the material requisition number from table EBAN. The custom table ZOUT_DOC stores the last document number read during the last time the extract was run. After the extract is run, the last document read is replaced in the ZOUT_DOC table.

The following parameters are allowed:

■ Starting purchase order number

■ Ending purchase order number

■ Path and file name of output file

The user will supply a file name for the extract data set. Assume that the program won't have to transfer the file to an external system. Table 16.2 shows the format for the output file.

Table 16.2   ZPOEXT Output File

Field Name	Position	Length	Data Type	SAP table-field
PO number	1	10	C	EKPO-EBELN
PO line number	11	5	C	EKPO-EBELP
Request number	18	10	C	EKPO-EDNR
Request line number	28	5	C	EBAN-BNFPO
Item quantity	33	18	C	EKPO-MENGE
PO date	51	10	C	EKKO-AEDAT
Item description	61	40	C	EKPO-TXZ01
Item amount '0000000000'	101	10	C	EKPO-NETWR

© 2014 Cengage Learning.

Once the requirements have been determined, the next step is to develop the ABAP program to extract the data:

```
*&---------------------------------------------------------*
*& Report   ZPOEXT
*&
*&---------------------------------------------------------*
*&  Description : Extract New Purchase Order Data.
*& Read data from BKPF, financial documents header table, and
*& BSE6, financial documents line items, then look up vendor
*& name and bank account before transferring data to file.
*&
*&---------------------------------------------------------*
```

```
REPORT ZPOEXT                    NO STANDARD PAGE HEADING
  LINE-SIZE 132
  LINE-COUNT 65
  MESSAGE-ID ZZ.


TABLES :    ZOUT_DOC ,    "Interface Document Log
EKKO,    "Purchase Order Headers
EKPO,    "Purchase Order Line Item Detail
EBAN. "  Purchase Requisitions

* Variables    *
DATA:
WS_TEMP(18),         "Temp field for conversion
WS_AMOUNT(13) TYPE N,      "Temp Field for amount
 WS_MAX LIKE EKPO-EBELN,    "Max Doc# Processed
BEGIN OF REC_OUT,
EBELN LIKE  EKPO-EBELN,
EBELP LIKE  EKPO-EBELP,
BEDNR LIKE  EKPO-BEDNR,
BNFPO LIKE  EBAN-BNFPO,
MENGE LIKE  EKPO-MENGE,
AEDAT LIKE  EKKO-AEDAT,
TXZ01 LIKE  EKPO-TXZ01,
AMOUNT(10)  TYPE C,
END OF REC_OUT.
* Select Options/Parameters

PARAMETERS:
P_BELNR LIKE EKPO-EBELN, "Starting PO to process
P_LIMIT LIKE EKPO-EBELN   "Upper Limit of PO's to process
  DEFAULT '9999999999',
P_FILE(45) OBLIGATORY LOWER CASE    "UNIX Output File
DEFAULT '/interfaces/outbound/podata.txt'.
* Main Processing
INITIALIZATION.

START-OF-SELECTION.
  PERFORM OPEN_DATASET.
  PERFORM EXTRACT_DATA.
  PERFORM CLOSE_DATASET.
  PERFORM UPDATE_ZOUT_DOC.
****** End Program
```

```
*&---------------------------------------------------------*
*&       Form    OPEN_DATASET
*&---------------------------------------------------------*
*&       Prepare datafile
*----------------------------------------------------------*
FORM OPEN_DATASET.
  OPEN DATASET P_FILE FOR OUTPUT IN TEXT MODE
    ENCODING DEFAULT
    WITH SMART LINEFEED.
  IF SY-SUBRC NE 0.
    MESSAGE E999 WITH 'Error Creating File ' P_FILE.
  ENDIF.
ENDFORM. "End Form Open_Dataset

*&---------------------------------------------------------*
*&    Form    EXTRACT_DATA
*&---------------------------------------------------------*
*&    Extract Purchase Order data from SAP and transfer to file.
*----------------------------------------------------------*
FORM EXTRACT_DATA.
  IF P_BELNR IS INITIAL. "Look up next PO if parameter is blank
    SELECT SINGLE * FROM ZOUT_DOC        "Get First PO#
    WHERE ID = 'POEXT'.
    P_BELNR = ZOUT_DOC-BELNR.            "Assign Starting PO#
  ENDIF.
  WS_MAX = P_BELNR.   "Store Current PO#
* Extract new PO items
  SELECT * FROM EKPO WHERE
  EBELN <= P_LIMIT
  AND EBELN > P_BELNR.
  IF EKPO-EBELN > WS_MAX.
    MOVE EKPO-EBELN TO WS_MAX.           "Keep max PO# processed
  ENDIF.
  CLEAR REC_OUT.   "Clear Buffer
  MOVE EKPO-EBELN TO REC_OUT-EBELN.    "Get PO#
  MOVE EKPO-EBELP TO REC_OUT-EBELP.    "Get PO Line#
  MOVE EKPO-BEDNR TO REC_OUT-BEDNR.    "Requisition Number
  SELECT * FROM EBAN WHERE EBELN = EKPO-EBELN
  AND EBELP = EKPO-EBELP
  AND BEDNR = EKPO-BEDNR.
    MOVE EBAN-BNFPO TO REC_OUT-BNFPO.    "Get Requisition line#
  ENDSELECT.
```

```
   MOVE EKPO-MENGE TO REC_OUT-MENGE.        "Get Item Qty
   MOVE EKPO-TXZO1 TO REC_OUT-TXZO1.        "Get Item Description
   MOVE EKPO-NETWR TO WS_AMOUNT.            "Get Order Amount
   WS_AMOUNT = WS_AMOUNT * 100.             "Remove Decimal
   PERFORM PAD_FIELD USING WS_AMOUNT.       "Format Amount
   MOVE WS_AMOUNT to REC_OUT-AMOUNT.        "Save Amount
   SELECT SINGLE * FROM EKKO WHERE EBELN = EKPO-EBELN.
   MOVE EKKO-AEDAT TO REC_OUT-AEDAT.        "Get PO Transaction Date
   TRANSFER REC_OUT TO P_FILE.              "Write buffer to file
ENDSELECT.
ENDFORM.                      "EXTRACT_DATA

*&---------------------------------------------------------*
*&      Form   CLOSE_DATASET
*&---------------------------------------------------------*
*        Close Dataset and report any errors
*----------------------------------------------------------*
FORM CLOSE_DATASET.
  CLOSE DATASET P_FILE.
  IF SY-SUBRC NE 0.
    MESSAGE E999 WITH 'Error Closing file ' P_FILE.
  ENDIF.
ENDFORM. "End form Close Dataset

*&---------------------------------------------------------*
*&    Form   UPDATE_ZOUT_DOC
*&---------------------------------------------------------*
*&    Update ZOUT_DOC with last document processed
*----------------------------------------------------------*
FORM UPDATE_ZOUT_DOC.
  UPDATE ZOUT_DOC SET BELNR = WS_MAX       "Update Last Document
  WHERE ID = 'POEXT'.
  IF SY-DBCNT NE 1.   "If # of rows update <> 1 Raise Error
  MESSAGE E999 WITH 'Error Updating Table ZOUT_DOC'.
  ENDIF.
ENDFORM.   "End Form Update_ZOUT_DOC

*&---------------------------------------------------------*
*&      Form   PAD_FIELD
*&---------------------------------------------------------*
*&      Pad number with leading zeros
*----------------------------------------------------------*
```

```
*&      -->P_NUM        text
*--------------------------------------------------------*
FORM PAD_FIELD USING P_NUM.
  SHIFT P_NUM RIGHT.
  WHILE SY-SUBRC = 0.
    REPLACE ' ' WITH '0' INTO P_NUM. "Zero Pad
  ENDWHILE.
ENDFORM.                     "PAD_FIELD
```

Inventory Changes

SAP records changes to materials as *material movements*. Each movement is recorded in a material document in the MKPF and MSEG tables, much like the financial documents stored in the BKPF and BSEG tables discussed in the preceding sections. The type of movement can be determined by the document type.

This program reads through the material documents in the MSEG table. If a new document has a storage location MSEG-LGORT, it indicates that the available quantity has changed since the last time the extract has been run. Only one document needs to be reported for each combination of material, plant, and storage location because the program will look up the current quantity directly. Once all appropriate documents have been identified, extract the current material quantity from the MARD table. The last material document number read will be updated in ZOUT_DOC and used to restrict the search next time it's run to new documents.

The following parameters are allowed:

- Target system to which you're sending the extract
- User ID on the target system
- File name and path of target system

The user will supply the parameters at runtime. Assume that a custom function call has been written that will transfer the extracted file to the target system, called ZUNIX_FILE_TRANSFER. Table 16.3 shows the format for the output.

Table 16.3   ZMATEXT Output File Format

Field Name	Position	Length	Data Type	SAP table-field
Material number	1	18	C	MARD-MATNR
Plant	19	4	C	MARD-WERKS
Storage location	23	4	C	MARD-LGORT
Quantity	27	14	C	MARD-LABST
Material document	41	10	C	MSEG-MBLNR
Document year	51	4	C	MSEG-MJAHR
Document line number	55	4	C	MSEG-ZEILE

© 2014 Cengage Learning.

Here's the program:

```
*&---------------------------------------------------------*
*& Report   ZMATQTY
*&
*&---------------------------------------------------------*
*& Description: Extract Material Movements and Quantities.
*&
*&---------------------------------------------------------*
REPORT ZMATQTY
  LINE-SIZE 132   No Standard Page Heading
  LINE-COUNT 65
  MESSAGE-ID ZZ.

TABLES:   ZOUT_DOC,   "Interface Document Log
  MARD, "Material Quantity on Hand
  MSEG. "Material Movement Documents

DATA:
WS_DSN(85)   "Filename
  VALUE '/interfaces/outbound/matqty.txt',
WS_MAX LIKE   MSEG-MBLNR,   "Max Document Processed
WS_MBLNR LIKE MSEG-MBLNR.   "Starting Document

DATA: BEGIN OF ITAB OCCURS 0,
  MATNR LIKE MSEG-MATNR,
  WERKS LIKE MSEG-WERKS,   "Plant Code
```

```
  LGORT LIKE MSEG-LGORT,      "Storage Location
  LABST LIKE MARD-LABST,      "Material Quantity
  MBLNR LIKE MSEG-MBLNR,      "Document #
  MJAHR LIKE MSEG-MJAHR,      "Doc Year
  ZEILE LIKE MSEG-ZEILE,      "Doc Line#
END OF ITAB.


*    Select Options/Parameters
PARAMETERS: P_DEST(30),  "Target System for Extract
P_USER(30),   "User Id on Target
P_TARGET(85). "Target File and Path
SELECT-OPTIONS: S_WERKS FOR MSEG-WERKS,   "Plant Code
S_MATNR FOR MSEG-MATNR.       "Material Number

*    Main Processing
START-OF-SELECTION.
  PERFORM OPEN_DATASET.
  PERFORM EXTRACT_DATA.
  PERFORM CLOSE_DATASET.
  PERFORM UPDATE_ZOUT_DOC.


*&---------------------------------------------------------------*
*&      Form   OPEN_DATASET
*&---------------------------------------------------------------*
*&      Open dataset and check for errors
*---------------------------------------------------------------*
FORM OPEN_DATASET.
  OPEN DATASET WS_DSN FOR OUTPUT IN TEXT MODE
    ENCODING DEFAULT
    WITH SMART LINEFEED.
  IF SY-SUBRC NE 0.
    MESSAGE E999 WITH 'Error Creating File ' WS_DSN.
  ENDIF.
ENDFORM. "End Form Open_Dataset

*&---------------------------------------------------------------*
*&      Form   EXTRACT_DATA
*&---------------------------------------------------------------*
* Extract data and Transfer it to the internal table, itab.
* Movement Documents are read and stored in an internal table
```

```
* only if no other document for that Material, Plant, Location
* combination has not been read before.
*
* After all new documents have been read look up the current
* quantity from MARD.
* If documents have been read transfer file to target system.
*-------------------------------------------------------------*
FORM EXTRACT_DATA.
  SELECT SINGLE * FROM ZOUT_DOC          "Get First Document#
  WHERE ID = 'MATEXT'.
  WS_MBLNR = ZOUT_DOC-BELNR.   "Assign Starting PO#
  WS_MAX = WS_MBLNR.   "Save Max Document
*** Get Material Movement (Change) Documents
  SELECT * FROM MSEG WHERE MBLNR > WS_MBLNR
  AND LGORT NE '     '
  AND MATNR IN S_MATNR
  AND WERKS IN S_WERKS.
    IF MSEG-MBLNR > WS_MAX.
      MOVE MSEG-MBLNR TO WS_MAX.        "Keep max doc# processed
    ENDIF.
*    Insert Werks/Matnr into Itab if it is not already there
    READ TABLE ITAB WITH KEY MATNR = MSEG-MATNR
     WERKS = MSEG-WERKS LGORT = MSEG-LGORT
     TRANSPORTING NO FIELDS.
    IF SY-SUBRC NE 0.    "If no rows found append new data
    CLEAR ITAB.
      MOVE MSEG-MBLNR TO ITAB-MBLNR.
      MOVE MSEG-MJAHR TO ITAB-MJAHR.
      MOVE MSEG-ZEILE TO ITAB-ZEILE.
      MOVE MSEG-MATNR TO ITAB-MATNR.
      MOVE MSEG-WERKS TO ITAB-WERKS.
      MOVE MSEG-LGORT TO ITAB-LGORT.
      APPEND ITAB.
    ENDIF.
  ENDSELECT.
*** Get Quantities for selected materials
  LOOP AT ITAB.
    SELECT SINGLE * FROM MARD WHERE MATNR = ITAB-MATNR
    AND WERKS = ITAB-WERKS
    AND LGORT = ITAB-LGORT.
    IF SY-SUBRC EQ 0.
      ITAB-LABST = MARD-LABST.
      TRANSFER ITAB TO WS_DSN.       " Transfer Data to File
```

```
      ENDIF.
    ENDLOOP.
    IF SY-SUBRC <> 0.
      MESSAGE I999 WITH 'No Documents Found!'.
    ELSE.
***** Send the UNIX file to system specified at runtime
      CALL FUNCTION 'ZUNIX_FILE_TRANSFER'
        EXPORTING
          I_DEST_SYSTEM    =     P_DEST
          I_USER_ID        =     P_USER
          I_TARGET_FILE    =     P_TARGET
          I_FILENAME       =     WS_DSN
        EXCEPTIONS
          CAN_NOT_CONNECT  =  01
          SYNTAX_ERROR     = 02.
      IF SY-SUBRC = 0.
        MESSAGE I999 WITH 'Outbound transfer successful with'
        WS_DSN.
      Else.
        Message E999 WITH 'Outbound transfer failed with'
        WS_DSN 'ERROR' SY-SUBRC.
      ENDIF.
    ENDIF.
ENDFORM.    "END FORM EXTRACT DATA

*&---------------------------------------------------------------*
*&    Form   CLOSE_DATASET
*&---------------------------------------------------------------*
*&    Close Dataset and report any errors
*---------------------------------------------------------------*
FORM CLOSE_DATASET.
  CLOSE DATASET WS_DSN.
  IF SY-SUBRC NE 0.
    MESSAGE E999 WITH 'Error Closing file'.
  ENDIF.
ENDFORM. "End form Close Dataset

*&---------------------------------------------------------------*
*&       Form   UPDATE_ZOUT_DOC
*&---------------------------------------------------------------*
* Update ZOUT_DOC with last doc processed
*---------------------------------------------------------------*
```

```
FORM UPDATE_ZOUT_DOC.
  UPDATE ZOUT_DOC SET BELNR = WS_MAX    "Update Last Document
  WHERE ID = 'MATEXT'.
  IF SY-DBCNT NE 1.   "If # of rows update <> 1 Raise Error
    MESSAGE E999 WITH 'Error Updating Table ZOUT_DOC'.
  ENDIF.
ENDFORM. "End Form Update_ZOUT_DOC
```

SUMMARY

The data extract is one of the most common programs that is coded on an SAP system. No company uses SAP exclusively, so the ability to move information into and out of SAP, to integrate SAP into a heterogeneous network of systems, is critical. Data extracts are half of that equation. The other half, moving information into SAP, is addressed in Chapter 17, "Writing a BDC Program."

CHAPTER 17

WRITING A BDC PROGRAM

IN THIS CHAPTER

- Understanding the steps in a BDC Session
- Identifying Screens in a Transaction
- Building the BDC Table
- Submitting the BDC Table
- Example BDC Sessions

ABAP/4 has a programming technique for loading data into SAP, known as a *Batch Data Communications Session* or a *BDC session*. A BDC session is a combination of ABAP/4 programming and built-in SAP functionality. It simulates the act of a user entering data into an SAP transaction. The system takes the data from an ABAP/4 program and feeds it to an SAP transaction screen by screen, much like a user would. The programmer can choose to have SAP process a batch of several transactions immediately or at a later time. Also, a single transaction can be executed directly by the programmer with more control and better error handling.

Either way, several steps must be taken to design and program a BDC session. This chapter explains those steps and the options available to an ABAP/4 programmer who wants to use a BDC session to load data into SAP.

UNDERSTANDING THE STEPS IN A BDC

The first step in a BDC session is to identify the screens of the transaction that the program will process. Next, you write a program to build the BDC table that is used to submit the data to SAP. The final step is to submit the BDC table to the system in batch mode or as a single transaction through the CALL TRANSACTION command. Once these steps are completed, the program can be scheduled for periodic execution. The following sections examine the individual steps in the process, and then two examples are provided for you to review.

Identifying Screens in a Transaction

When a user enters data into SAP, he or she uses transactions for the data entry. Each transaction has several screens, identified by a program name and a screen number, into which that data is entered. Information on the current screen can be found by choosing the System > Status command from any menu (see Figure 17.1).

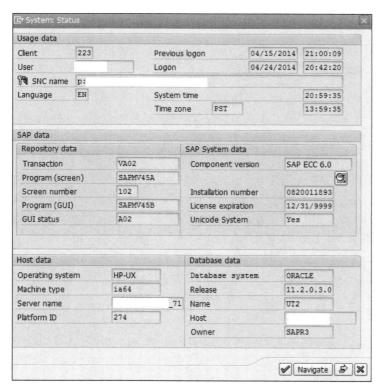

Figure 17.1
The System Status screen.

Each screen has fields that correspond to fields in the database. These field names are used when building the BDC table that submits the data to SAP. Clicking a screen field, pressing the Help key (Fl), and then clicking the Technical Info button (see Figure 17.2) can retrieve the field name.

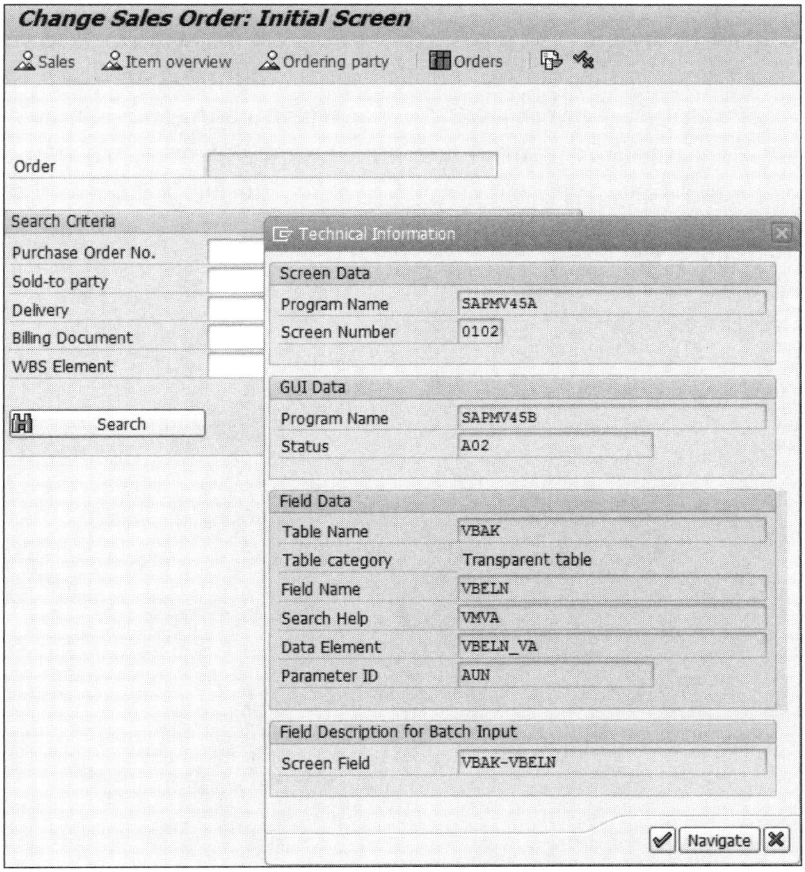

Change Sales Order: Initial Screen

Sales   Item overview   Ordering party   Orders

Order   [   ]

Search Criteria

Purchase Order No.   [   ]

Sold-to party   [   ]

Delivery   [   ]

Billing Document   [   ]

WBS Element   [   ]

Search

Technical Information

Screen Data

| Program Name | SAPMV45A |
| Screen Number | 0102 |

GUI Data

| Program Name | SAPMV45B |
| Status | A02 |

Field Data

Table Name	VBAK
Table category	Transparent table
Field Name	VBELN
Search Help	VMVA
Data Element	VBELN_VA
Parameter ID	AUN

Field Description for Batch Input

| Screen Field | VBAK-VBELN |

Navigate

Figure 17.2
Reviewing the technical information for a database field.

Screens also have function buttons that may bring up other screens. One function code may be called per screen—the most common being Fll (Save). To get a list of available function codes from any screen, right-click the screen. Submitting a function code is identical to submitting a value for a screen field. The value BDC_OKCODE is used in place of a field name, and the function code is used in place of the field value, in the form /XX, where XX is the number of the function code. So the last entry into all BDC tables, which is always to save the data, is the field name BDC_OKCODE and a field value of /11. In some cases you need to duplicate the act of a user selecting a field with the cursor. This can be done using the value BDC_CURSOR in place of the field name. Then place the name of the field you wish to select in the field value.

To design a BDC session, you need to map out the path of which screens will be used in the transaction, which fields must be populated, and which function buttons are used to move from screen to screen. For example, the transaction MK02, which changes a purchasing vendor, has several screens. The first screen number is 0100, and the program name for the screen is SAPMF02K. This screen has two fields, RF02K -LIFNR and RF02K-EKORG, plus several check boxes (see Figure 17.3). Once all screens are identified, the next step to write the program is to build the BDC table using that information.

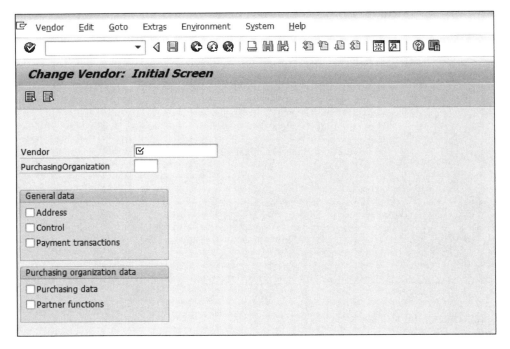

Figure 17.3
The initial screen of the change of vendor program.

A multiple-line field is a special kind of field that allows the user to enter multiple lines of data. For example, a screen might allow a user to enter several lines of text as a description. Each line would have the same field name, for example MARA-LTEXT. In order to populate data to this type of field, an index is added to the field name to indicate which line is to be populated by the BDC session. The first line of text would be populated as `MARA-LTEXT(1)`, the second as `MARA-LTEXT(2)`, and so on. Many times, only the first line is used in a BDC session, but if multiple lines are required, a counter should be used to track which line will be populated.

Usually a screen has several fields with multiple lines. For example, the screen to create a purchase order has fields for line number, material number, quantity, amount, and others. Each line corresponds to a separate item. Figure 17.4 shows an example of a screen that uses multiple lines for several fields. This screen allows multiple year/total U.S. dollar combinations to be entered.

Figure 17.4
An example of multiple-line fields.

Source: SAP AG or an SAP affiliate company. All rights reserved.

Building the BDC Table

The BDC table is an internal table with a specific structure that's filled with the data to be submitted. The program should fill the BDC table with values for fields, one row in the internal table per record. An additional record to provide information about the screen itself must precede the rows of field data. Table 17.1 shows the structure of the BDC table.

Table 17.1   BDC Table Structure

Field	Type	Description
program	Char(8)	Program name of transaction
dynpro	Char(4)	Screen number of transaction
dynbegin	Char(1)	Indicator for new screen
fnam	Char(35)	Name of database field from screen
fval	Char(80)	Value to submit to field

© 2014 Cengage Learning.

Before data for fields can be entered, a screen record is added to the BDC table with the program name in the program field, the screen name in the dynpro field, and an X in the dynbegin field, which tells the system that a new screen is beginning. Then a record is added for each field on the screen for which you want to submit data. For field records, the program, dynpro, and dynbegin fields should be left blank. Instead, the name of the field is placed in the fnam field, and the value for that field is placed in the fval field. For example, to submit data for the first screen of the Change Vendor transaction, the row of data added to the BDC table would have SAPMF02K in the program field, 0100 in the dynpro field, and X in the dynbegin field.

Once the fields are populated, the record should be appended to the table. The next record would be the data for the first field on the screen, Vendor. For this field, RF02K -LIFNR would be placed in the fnam field. The vendor number to be changed, for example 0010010, would be placed in fval, and the record would be appended to the BDC table. The next field to be entered is RF02K-EKORG, which will be populated with the value CNTL. Once all fields are populated for the first screen, a new screen is started in the same way as the first. The process repeats until all screens have been completed for this transaction. The final entry into the BDC table is always the function code Fll to save the completed transaction. Table 17.2 shows the values for this example, as they would be placed in the fields.

Table 17.2   BDC Table Values

program	dynpro	dynbegin	fnam	fval
SAPMF02K	0100	X	RF02K-LIFNR	0010010'
			RF02K-EKORG	CNTL
SAPMF02K	0200	X		

© 2014 Cengage Learning.

A typical BDC program may process three to six screens each, with anywhere from two to ten fields. The code to build the BDC table is straightforward, consisting mainly of MOVE and APPEND commands. Because the process to build the BDC table is repeated dozens of times, it's a good candidate for a subroutine.

Following are two examples of building a BDC table. The first example doesn't use forms:

```
REPORT ZBDCVEND.
*** Example to build part of a BDC table for the
*** Change Vendor Transaction

TYPES: BEGIN OF ty_bdc.   "BDC Table
       INCLUDE STRUCTURE bdcdata.
TYPES: END OF ty_bdc.
DATA: int_bdc TYPE STANDARD TABLE OF ty_bdc INITIAL SIZE 100.
DATA: wa_bdc LIKE LINE OF int_bdc.
*** Start of Main Program
*** Start Screen 100
CLEAR wa_bdc.
MOVE    'SAPMF02K' TO wa_bdc-program.
MOVE    '0100'  TO wa_bdc-dynpro.
MOVE    'X1'  TO wa_bdc-dynbegin.
APPEND   wa_bdc TO int_bdc.

CLEAR wa_bdc.
MOVE    'RF02K-LIFNR'  TO wa_bdc-fnam.
MOVE    '0010010' TO wa_bdc-fval.
APPEND   wa_bdc TO int_bdc.

CLEAR wa_bdc.
MOVE    'RF02K-EKORG' TO wa_bdc-fnam.
MOVE    'CNTL'    TO wa_bdc-fval.
APPEND   wa_bdc TO int_bdc.
*** And so on until the BDC Table is complete
```

This example shows the repetitive nature of building a BDC table; anything repetitive can usually be done better with a subroutine. In this next example, two forms are created. The first, BDC_SCREEN, is used when a new screen is to be started; the second, BDC_FIELD, is used when a new field is to be added to the BDC table:

```
REPORT ZBDCVEND.
*** Example to build part of a BDC table for the
*** Change Vendor Transaction

TYPES: BEGIN OF ty_bdc.    "BDC Table
      INCLUDE STRUCTURE bdcdata.
TYPES: END OF ty_bdc.
DATA: int_bdc TYPE STANDARD TABLE OF ty_bdc INITIAL SIZE 100.
DATA: wa_bdc LIKE LINE OF int_bdc.

*** Start of Main Program
*** Start Screen 100
PERFORM bdc_screen TABLES int_bdc
      USING 'SAPMF02K' '0100'.

PERFORM bdc_field TABLES int_bdc
      USING 'RF02K-LIFNR' '0010010'.

PERFORM bdc_field TABLES int_bdc
      USING 'RF02K-EKORG' 'CNTL'.
*** And so on until the BDC Table is complete
*** End of Main Program
*** Form BDC_SCREEN
*** This form takes two parameters and makes an entry into a BDC
*** table specified for a new screen.
FORM bdc_screen TABLES p_bdc STRUCTURE bdcdata USING p_program p_screen.
  CLEAR wa_bdc.        "Clears table work area
  wa_bdc-program = p_program.
  wa_bdc-dynpro = p_screen.
  wa_bdc-dynbegin = 'X1'.
  APPEND wa_bdc TO p_bdc.
ENDFORM.                     "BDC_SCREEN
*** Form BDC_FIELD
*** This form takes two parameters and makes an entry into a BDC
*** table specified for a new field

FORM bdc_field TABLES p_bdc STRUCTURE bdcdata USING p_name p_value.
  CLEAR wa_bdc.
  CASE p_value.
    WHEN ' '.    "Don't move if value is blank
    WHEN OTHERS. "Move value
```

```
    MOVE p_name TO wa_bdc-fnam.
      MOVE p_value TO wa_bdc-fval.
      APPEND wa_bdc TO p_bdc.
  ENDCASE.
ENDFORM.              "BDC_FIELD
```

Although you have to write two forms for this second example, the main portion of the program is made much simpler through the use of PERFORM and the colon notation. As you can imagine, if you had a program with six screens and 50 fields, the first method of building the BDC table would be quite complicated and unnecessarily verbose.

Submitting the BDC Table

Once the BDC table has been built, it needs to be submitted to SAP for processing. There are two ways to submit a BDC table. The first is through the CALL TRANSACTION command, which allows a single transaction to be processed by SAP. The second is to use the BDC_INSERT function, which allows multiple transactions to be processed. There are a number of factors to consider before deciding which technique to use to submit the BDC table.

Processing Data with CALL TRANSACTION

The CALL TRANSACTION command allows a single BDC table to be processed immediately by the system. The data in the BDC table is used to execute the transaction; the return code for the statement tells the program whether the transaction executed successfully. When using CALL TRANSACTION, it's the programmer's responsibility to handle failed transactions, but this method is a very efficient way to process transactions. The syntax for the command is as follows:

```
CALL TRANSACTION trans   [USING bdctab MODE mode]
                         [UPDATE upd] [MESSAGES INTO messtab].
```

The mode allows the programmer to control what happens when the BDC table is submitted. These are the possible entries:

A	Show all screens
E	Show only screens with errors
N	Show no screens

The A and E modes are normally used for debugging. When the program is executed in A or E mode, the screens from the transaction appear populated with data from the BDC table, and the user must step through each screen—and can correct errors, in some cases. Mode N is the only mode that can be used in a program that's run in the background, without user attention. In this case, no screens appear. If an error occurs, the transaction fails, and the return code is not 0. In addition to the return code, the system error message is available through a set of SY fields: SY-MSGNO, SY-MSGID, SY-MSGV1, SY-MSGV2, SY-MSGV3, and SY-MSGV4.

The update option controls how changes are made to the database. The values are A for asynchronous updates and S for synchronous updates. In the case of a synchronous update, the command will wait for changes to be made. For an asynchronous update, the command will not wait. This effect of this option varies with the exact transaction called.

The messages option will cause SAP to capture any error or success messages and place them in the internal table specified. See the second example for usage of the messages option.

This approach processes a single transaction faster than using BDC_INSERT (discussed in the next section). Because the results of the transaction are returned to the calling program, error handling can be implemented in the program. It may be possible to correct certain errors and resubmit the data, or a separate error report could be created. Also, it's possible to use CALL TRANSACTION without a BDC table. In this case, the current program is suspended, the transaction specified is brought up, and a user must enter data into the screens.

Processing Data with BDC INSERT

The second way to process a BDC session is by submitting it to the system for batch processing. With this method, several transactions can be processed together. But unlike CALL TRANSACTION, the data isn't processed immediately; instead, it's placed into the SAP batch queue for later processing. Thus, the results of processing a transaction aren't returned to the program that created the BDC session. (However, the SAP transaction sm35 allows users to view the results of a batch job that has been processed by the system.)

There are three SAP function modules that need to be called from the BDC program to submit the transactions for processing (the functions are executed with the CALL FUNCTION command, discussed in Chapter 11, "Adding Subroutines to Your Program"):

- BDC_OPEN_GROUP: This function opens the BDC session and must be called before any processing is done.

- BDC_INSERT: This function is called for each transaction in the batch. The BDC table is filled with data, as previously discussed for a transaction. Then the BDC_INSERT function is called and the BDC table is passed to it. This process is repeated for each transaction in the batch.

- BDC_CLOSE_GROUP: This final function closes the session and submits it to SAP for processing.

Using the BDC_OPEN_GROUP Function   The function module BDC_OPEN_GROUP opens a BDC session. A BDC session is a batch of several transactions that will be processed together. Only one session can be open at a time. The following parameters should be exported to the function when called:

CLIENT	The SAP client in which the session is processed. Usually left blank, which causes it to default to the current client.
GROUP	A name used to identify the BDC session to be processed. This name doesn't need to be unique.
HOLDDATE	Suspends processing of the BDC session until after this date has passed.
KEEP	Keeps the session in the system after processing until it's deleted by an administrator, when the field is set to X.
USER	The name used to execute the session in batch mode. You can't supply an online username for this field.

Using the BDC_INSERT Function   The `BDC_INSERT` function adds a transaction to the BDC session that's currently open. The following parameters should be exported to the function when called:

TCODE	The transaction code for the transaction that should be used to process the data in the BDC table being inserted. For example, MK02 for the change vendor transaction.
DYNPROTAB	The name of the internal table being used as the BDC table for the current program.

Using the BDC_CLOSE_GROUP Function   Use the `BDC_CLOSE_GROUP` function to close the current BDC session, once all transactions to be processed have been inserted. There are no parameters needed for this function. When the session is closed, it's ready to be processed by the system.

Example BDC Sessions

This section presents three examples of BDC sessions. These examples are for reference only—they won't run on just any SAP installation. Because SAP is so customizable, the screens for a given transaction can vary wildly between installations. For example, when creating a new vendor (a company from which materials may be purchased), Company X may need to supply a tax code, but at Company Y, no tax code field will even appear in the Create Vendor transaction. Thus, every company using SAP will write BDC programs based on their unique installation of SAP. This is great for programmers, because it means all BDC programs must be customized for each unique installation of SAP.

A BDC Program to Change a Vendor's Address

This first program changes address information for a vendor. The transaction that does this is MK02. (The transaction allows you to change much more information about a vendor than simply the address, obviously, but that's all this example program does.) There are two screens to this transaction that you'll be using. (Remember that the first step to writing a BDC session is to identify all screens, fields, and function codes that will be used.) Figure 17.5 shows the first screen for transaction MK02. Here the program must supply the vendor number that is to be changed and select the address box to indicate the type of data that you want to change.

The second screen looks like Figure 17.6. Here's where the address information goes. Once the information has been passed to the screen, the final step is to save the changes. All transactions use the function code Fll to save, and a save always ends a transaction. Using the Help system to identify the field name for each field would produce the list shown in Table 17.3.

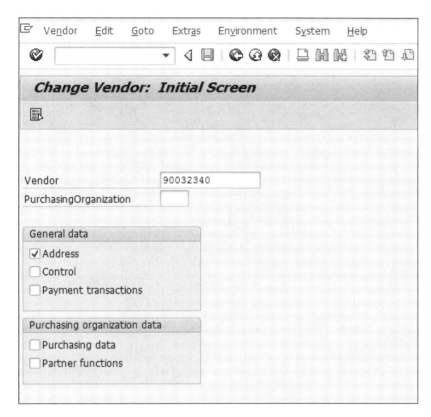

Figure 17.5
Change vendor, screen 1.

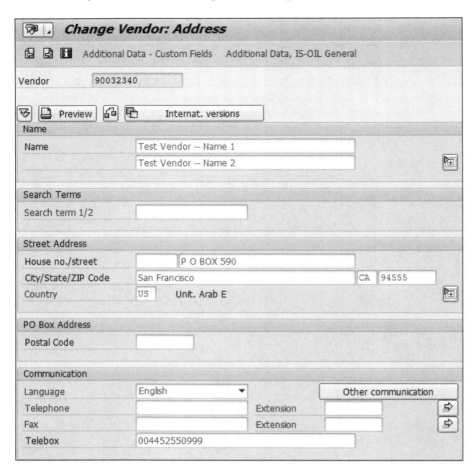

Figure 17.6
Change vendor, screen 2.

The program should read a data file and use the information to execute the Change Vendor transaction as many times as needed. The CALL TRANSACTION command should be used to submit each transaction for processing. All errors encountered during processing of the file should be written out in a report at the end of the program. The program reads the information to be loaded into SAP via the BDC session, from an external text file with the file format shown in Table 17.4.

Table 17.3   Field Names for the Change Vendor Transaction

Field Names for Screen 0100

Field	Contents
Vendor Number	RF02K-LIFNR
Purchasing Organization	RF02K-EKORG
Change Address Check Box	RF02K-D0110

Field Names for Screen 0200

Field	Contents
Vendor Name 1	LFA1-NAME1
Vendor Name 2	LFA1-NAME2
Vendor Name 3	LFA1-NAME3
Vendor Name 4	LFA1-NAME4
Vendor Street	LFA1-STRAS
Vendor City	LFA1-ORT01
Vendor Region	LFA1-REGIO
Vendor ZIP	LFA1-PSTLZ
Vendor Country	LFA1-LAND1
Vendor Phone 1	LFA1-TELF1
Vendor Phone 2	LFA1-TELF2

© 2014 Cengage Learning.

Table 17.4   Input File Format

Field Name	Position	Data Type	Length
Vendor Number	1	c	10
Purchasing Organization	11	c	4
Vendor Name 1	16	c	35
Vendor Name 2	51	c	35
Vendor Name 3	86	c	35
			(Continued)

Table 17.4   Input File Format (*Continued*)

Field Name	Position	Data Type	Length
Vendor Name 4	111	c	35
Vendor Street	146	c	35
Vendor City	181	c	35
Vendor Region	216	c	3
Vendor ZIP	219	c	10
Vendor Country	229	c	3
Vendor Phone 1	232	c	16
Vendor Phone 2	248	c	16

© 2014 Cengage Learning.

And here at last is the code for this example:

```
REPORT ZBDC_MK02 LINE-SIZE 80 LINE-COUNT 65 MESSAGE-ID zz.
*    Tables
*
*    None
*
*    Variables
*      .
**** BDC Processing
TYPES: BEGIN OF ty_bdc.   "BDC Table
       INCLUDE STRUCTURE bdcdata.
TYPES: END OF ty_bdc.
DATA: int_bdc TYPE STANDARD TABLE OF ty_bdc INITIAL SIZE 100.
DATA: wa_bdc LIKE LINE OF int_bdc.
**** Vendor In File
TYPES: BEGIN OF ty_vend,
lifnr LIKE rf02k-lifnr,
ekorg LIKE rf02k-ekorg,
name1 LIKE lfa1-name1,
name2 LIKE lfa1-name2,
name3 LIKE lfa1-name3,
name4 LIKE lfa1-name4,
stras LIKE lfa1-stras,
ort01 LIKE lfa1-ort01,
```

```
     regio LIKE lfa1-regio,
     pstlz LIKE lfa1-pstlz,
     land1 LIKE lfa1-land1,
     telf1 LIKE lfa1-telf1,
     telf2 LIKE lfa1-telf2,
     END OF ty_vend.

DATA: rec_vend TYPE STANDARD TABLE OF ty_vend.
DATA: wa_vend LIKE LINE OF rec_vend.

TYPES: BEGIN OF ty_error,
          msg LIKE sy-msgv1,
          lifnr LIKE lfa1-lifnr,
       END OF ty_error.
DATA: int_error TYPE STANDARD TABLE OF ty_error INITIAL SIZE 50.
DATA: wa_error LIKE LINE OF int_error.
DATA: lv_filename TYPE string.
*Parameters
PARAMETERS: p_infile(80) TYPE c LOWER CASE. "Input file name and path

AT SELECTION-SCREEN ON VALUE-REQUEST FOR p_infile.

   PERFORM get_filename_upload_file.
*Main Processing *
**
START-OF-SELECTION.
   PERFORM get_file_data.
   PERFORM process_file.

END-OF-SELECTION.
   PERFORM error_report.

*Form PROCESS_FILE*
*...
*This form will read the vendor file and build the BDC table *
*for each record. It will then submit each transaction and   *
*save any errors recorded.*
*
FORM process_file.

   PERFORM build_bdc.
   PERFORM submit_bdc.

ENDFORM. " PROCESS FILE

*Form BUILD BDC
*This form will build the BDC table for each transaction.
```

```
FORM build_bdc.
  REFRESH int_bdc.

  LOOP AT rec_vend INTO wa_vend.
*** Build *** Build Screen 100
    PERFORM bdc_screen TABLES int_bdc
    USING 'SAPMF02K' '0100'.

    PERFORM bdc_field TABLES int_bdc
    USING    'RF02K-LIFNR'  wa_vend-lifnr. "Vendor
    PERFORM bdc_field TABLES int_bdc
  USING    'RF02K-EKORG'  wa_vend-ekorg.  "Purchase Org
    PERFORM bdc_field TABLES int_bdc
  USING    'RF02K-D0110'  'X1'.      "Select Address
*** Build Screen 200
    PERFORM bdc_screen TABLES int_bdc
    USING 'SAPMF02K' '0200'.
    PERFORM bdc_field TABLES int_bdc
    USING    'LFA1-NAME1'  wa_vend-name1.  "Vendor Name1
    PERFORM bdc_field TABLES int_bdc
    USING    'LFA1-NAME2'  wa_vend-name2.  "Vendor Name2
    PERFORM bdc_field TABLES int_bdc
    USING    'LFA1-NAME3'  wa_vend-name3.  "Vendor Name3
    PERFORM bdc_field TABLES int_bdc
    USING    'LFA1-NAME4'  wa_vend-name4.  "Vendor Name4
    PERFORM bdc_field TABLES int_bdc
    USING    'LFA1-STRAS'  wa_vend-stras.   "Vendor Street
    PERFORM bdc_field TABLES int_bdc
    USING    'LFA1-ORT01'  wa_vend-ort01.   "Vendor City
    PERFORM bdc_field TABLES int_bdc
    USING    'LFA1-REGIO'  wa_vend-regio.  "Vendor Region
    PERFORM bdc_field TABLES int_bdc
    USING    'LFA1-PSTLZ'  wa_vend-pstlz.  "Vendor ZIP
    PERFORM bdc_field TABLES int_bdc
    USING    'LFA1-LAND1'  wa_vend-land1.  "Vendor Country
    PERFORM bdc_field TABLES int_bdc
    USING    'LFA1-TELF1'  wa_vend-telf1.  "Vendor Phone 1
    PERFORM bdc_field TABLES int_bdc
    USING    'LFA1-TELF2'  wa_vend-telf2.  "Vendor Phone 2

    PERFORM bdc_field TABLES int_bdc
    USING    'BDC_OKCODE'  '/11' .  "Save and End
    CLEAR wa_vend.

  ENDLOOP.
```

```
ENDFORM.     "BUILD BDC

*Form SUBMIT BDC
*This form will submit the BDC table using CALL TRANSACTION.
FORM submit_bdc.
CALL TRANSACTION 'MK02' USING int_bdc MODE 'N'.
IF sy-subrc <> 0. "If error record vendor and error msg
   MOVE sy-msgv1 TO wa_error-msg.
   MOVE wa_vend-lifnr TO wa_error-lifnr.
   APPEND wa_error TO int_error.
ENDIF.
ENDFORM.     "SUBMIT BDC

*Form ERROR REPORT
*This form will write out any errors to the screen.
FORM error_report.
WRITE 'Vendor Records with Errors!'.
WRITE: / 'VENDOR', ' ', 'ERROR MESSAGE'.
LOOP AT int_error INTO wa_error.
WRITE:/ wa_error-lifnr,    11 wa_error-msg.
ENDLOOP.

ENDFORM. "ERROR REPORT

*Form BDC_SCREEN
**. *
*This form takes two parameters and makes an entry into a BDC *
*table specified for a new screen.*
*.*
FORM bdc_screen TABLES p_bdc STRUCTURE bdcdata USING p_program p_screen.
   CLEAR wa_bdc.          "Clears table work area
   wa_bdc-program = p_program.
   wa_bdc-dynpro = p_screen.
   wa_bdc-dynbegin = 'X1'.
   APPEND wa_bdc TO p_bdc.
ENDFORM.                     "BDC_SCREEN
*_*
*Form BDC_FIELD
*_*
*This form takes two parameters and makes an entry into a BDC *
*table specified for a new field.   *
*   .*
FORM bdc_field TABLES p_bdc STRUCTURE bdcdata USING p_name p_value.
   CLEAR wa_bdc.
```

```
   CASE p_value.
     WHEN ' '.   "Don't move if value is blank
         WHEN OTHERS.   "Move value
         MOVE p_name TO wa_bdc-fnam.
       MOVE p_value TO wa_bdc-fval.
       APPEND wa_bdc TO p_bdc.
   ENDCASE.
ENDFORM.                            "BDC_FIELD

FORM get_filename_upload_file .
   DATA: v_title TYPE string,
         v_rc       TYPE i,
         int_filetab   TYPE filetable.

   v_title = 'WINDOW ' .

   CALL METHOD cl_gui_frontend_services=>file_open_dialog
     EXPORTING
       window_title      = v_title
       default_filename  = '*.txt'
       initial_directory = 'C:\'
       multiselection    = ' '   "No multiple selection
     CHANGING
       file_table        = int_filetab
       rc                = v_rc.


   READ TABLE int_filetab INTO p_infile INDEX 1.

ENDFORM.                            " GET_FILENAME_UPLOAD_FILE

FORM get_file_data .
   lv_filename = p_infile.

   CALL FUNCTION 'GUI_UPLOAD'
     EXPORTING
       filename             = lv_filename
       filetype             = 'ASC'
       has_field_separator  = 'X'
       header_length        = 0
       read_by_line         = 'X'
       dat_mode             = ' '
       codepage             = ' '
       replacement          = '#'
       check_bom            = ' '
```

```
TABLES
   data_tab                    = rec_vend
EXCEPTIONS
   file_open_error             = 1
   file_read_error             = 2
   no_batch                    = 3
   gui_refuse_filetransfer     = 4
   invalid_type                = 5
   no_authority                = 6
   unknown_error               = 7
   bad_data_format             = 8
   header_not_allowed          = 9
   separator_not_allowed       = 10
   header_too_long             = 11
   unknown_dp_error            = 12
   access_denied               = 13
   dp_out_of_memory            = 14
   disk_full                   = 15
   dp_timeout                  = 16
   OTHERS                      = 17.


 IF sy-subrc <> 0.

   MESSAGE ID sy-msgid TYPE sy-msgty NUMBER sy-msgno
           WITH sy-msgv1 sy-msgv2 sy-msgv3 sy-msgv4.

   ENDIF.


ENDFORM.                    " GET_FILE_DATA
```

Comparing Different Processing Techniques

This second example allows the programmer to compare three different techniques to process a transaction. The transaction that will be processed is the *Mass Changes of Planned Orders (Action Control)* or *MDAC*. A planned order is a plan to manufacture a product. It contains all the parts that make up the product, the quantities needed, and the dates when the product will be produced. Typically a planned order will have a start date and a finish date. The planned order action control transaction allows certain actions to be performed against a planned order. Some examples of actions available are: checking the availability of the materials required to determine a start date, un-committing the material reservation of a planned order, and exploding the bill of materials of a product to determine the parts required for a planned order. Transaction MDAC consists of one screen only. See Figure 17.7 for the MDAC screen.

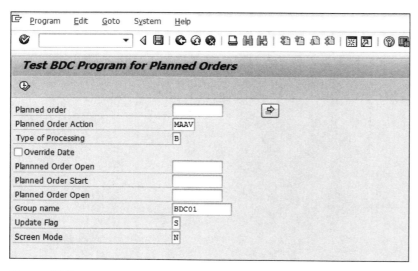

Figure 17.7
The initial screen of the program to change the planning costs.

The example program allows the person executing it to determine how the MDAC trans-action will be processed. You can choose from processing via CALL TRANSACTION or a BDC session. Also in the case of the MDAC transaction, there is a function module that per-forms the same activity. Some simple transactions like MDAC have an associated function call but not all. By allowing the user to choose how to process the transaction, the three techniques can be compared. For example, you might want to time each to see which technique gives you the best performance. Table 17.5 lists the fields we will be populating for screen one of transaction MDAC.

Table 17.5   Field Names for the Change Transaction

Field	Contents
Planned Order Number	PLAF-PLNUM
Total Qty	MDCD-GSMNG
Scrap Qty	MDCD-AVMNG
Production Version	MDCD-VERID
Sequence Number	MDCD-SEQNR
Open Date	MDCD-PERTR
Start Date	MDCD-PSTTR
Finish Date	MDCD-PEDTR
Action	T46AC-ACCTO

© 2014 Cengage Learning.

Here is an example BDC program that will update planned orders through the mass update transaction MDAC.

```
REPORT zcbdctst MESSAGE-ID zz LINE-SIZE 170 LINE-COUNT 58.

*   Tables
*
TABLES: plaf,        "Planned Orders
        t100.        "System Error Messages
*   None
*
*   Variables
*   .
**** BDC Processing

TYPES: BEGIN OF ty_bdc.   "BDC Table
       INCLUDE STRUCTURE bdcdata.
TYPES: END OF ty_bdc.
DATA: bd TYPE STANDARD TABLE OF ty_bdc INITIAL SIZE 200.
DATA: wa_bd LIKE LINE OF bd.

TYPES: BEGIN OF ty_xmdcd.        "Action Handler input
        INCLUDE STRUCTURE mdcd.
TYPES: END OF ty_xmdcd.
DATA: xmdcd TYPE STANDARD TABLE OF ty_xmdcd INITIAL SIZE 200.
DATA: wa_xmdcd LIKE LINE OF xmdcd.
```

```
TYPES: BEGIN OF ty_messtab.      "Message table for errors
          INCLUDE STRUCTURE bdcmsgcoll.
TYPES: END OF ty_messtab.
DATA: messtab TYPE STANDARD TABLE OF ty_messtab INITIAL SIZE 10.
DATA: wa_messtab LIKE LINE OF messtab.

DATA: ws_temp1 LIKE bdcdata-fval,      "Temp field for dates
      ws_temp2 LIKE bdcdata-fval.      "Temp field for quantities

FIELD-SYMBOLS: <fs_pln> TYPE any.

SELECT-OPTIONS p_pln FOR plaf-plnum NO INTERVALS. "Planned Order*
PARAMETERS: p_action LIKE plaf-mdacc DEFAULT 'MAAV', "Planned Order Action
            p_call DEFAULT 'B'.       "Type of Processing
*B - BDC Session C - Call Trasaction F - Function Call
PARAMETERS: p_oride AS CHECKBOX,   "Override dates in database
p_date1 TYPE d,          "Pin Order Open
p_date2 TYPE d,          "Pin Order Start
p_date3 TYPE d,          "Plan Order Finish
PARAMETERS: p_bdc LIKE apqi-groupid  DEFAULT 'BDC01'.  "Name Of BDC Session.
PARAMETERS: p_update DEFAULT 'S',    "Update Mode
            p_mode DEFAULT 'N'.      "Screen Mode
*   Begin main program

START-OF-SELECTION.
  IF p_call EQ 'B1'.
*   Process in a BDC session so open a new one
    CALL FUNCTION 'BDC_OPEN_GROUP'
      EXPORTING
        group                 = p_bdc
        keep                  = 'X'
        user                  = sy-uname
      EXCEPTIONS
        client_invalid        = 1
        destination_invalid   = 2
        group_invalid         = 3
        group_is_locked       = 4
        holddate_invalid      = 5
        internal_error        = 6
        queue_error           = 7
        running               = 8
        system_lock_error     = 9
        user_invalid          = 10
        OTHERS                = 11.
```

```
    IF sy-subrc NE 0.
      MESSAGE e999 WITH 'Error Opening BDC Session!'.
    ENDIF.
  ENDIF.
*Loop at planned order numbers entered by user

  LOOP AT p_pln.
    SELECT SINGLE * FROM plaf WHERE plnum = p_pln-low.
    IF sy-subrc NE 0.
      MESSAGE i999 WITH 'Pin Order does not exist:' p_pln-low.
*Skip this entry
      CONTINUE.
    ENDIF.
*Override dates in database if user requested
    IF p_oride NE space.
      plaf-pertr = p_date1.
      plaf-psttr = p_date2.
      plaf-pedtr = p_date3.
    ENDIF.

*Date Sequence must be correct if not blank
    IF NOT ( plaf-psttr IS INITIAL ) AND NOT ( plaf-pedtr IS INITIAL ).
      IF plaf-psttr >= plaf-pedtr.
        CLEAR plaf-psttr.
      ENDIF.
    ENDIF.

*"Should be Start < Finish

    IF NOT ( plaf-psttr IS INITIAL ) AND NOT ( plaf-pertr IS INITIAL ).
      IF plaf-pertr > plaf-psttr.      "Should be Open <= Start
        CLEAR plaf-pertr .
      ENDIF.
    ENDIF.

    IF p_call NE 'F'.
*       If this is not a function call then build BDC table
      PERFORM build_bdc.
    ENDIF.

    CASE p_call.
      WHEN 'C1'.
*Process via a call transaction immediately
        CALL TRANSACTION 'MDAC' USING bd
        MODE p_mode
```

```
      UPDATE p_update
      MESSAGES INTO messtab.
      IF sy-subrc EQ 0.
        WRITE: /, 'MDAC execute successfully!', p_pln-low.
      ELSE.
        WRITE: /, 'MDAC Failed!', sy-subrc, p_pln-low.
      ENDIF.
*        Print results from message table
      PERFORM print_results.
    WHEN 'B'.
*Process in batch via BDC session
      CALL FUNCTION 'BDC_INSERT'
        EXPORTING
          tcode           = 'MDAC'
        TABLES
          dynprotab       = bd
        EXCEPTIONS
          internal_error = 1
          not_open       = 2
          queue_error    = 3
          tcodejnvalid   = 4
          OTHERS         = 5.
      IF sy-subrc EQ 0.
        WRITE: /, 'BDC Insert successful!', p_pln-low.
      ELSE.
        WRITE: /, 'BDC Insert Failed!' , sy-subrc, p_pln-low.
      ENDIF.
    WHEN 'F1'.
*Process immediately via a call function, no BDC table required
*Fill XMDCD record for planned   order
      wa_xmdcd-psttr = plaf-psttr.     "Start date in planned ord
      wa_xmdcd-pedtr = plaf-pedtr.     "Finish date in planned ord
      wa_xmdcd-pertr = plaf-pertr.     "Opening date in planned ord
      wa_xmdcd-verid = plaf-verid.      "Production version
      wa_xmdcd-seqnr = plaf-seqnr.      "Sequence number order
      APPEND wa_xmdcd TO xmdcd.
*Call function to execute action immediately
      CALL FUNCTION 'MD_SET_ACTION_PLAF'
        EXPORTING
          iplnum          = p_pln-low
          iaccto          = p_action
```

```
                iaenkz          = 'X'
                imdcd           = xmdcd
             EXCEPTIONS
                error_message = 1.
          IF sy-subrc EQ 0.
            WRITE: /, 'Function Call successful!', p_pln-low.
          ELSE.
            WRITE: /, 'Function Call failed!', sy-subrc, p_pln-low.
          ENDIF.
      ENDCASE.
   ENDLOOP.
   IF p_call EQ 'B1'.
*    CLOSE BDC SESSION
      CALL FUNCTION 'BDC_CLOSE_GROUP'
         EXCEPTIONS
            not_pen       = 1
            queue_error = 2
            OTHERS        = 3.
      IF sy-subrc EQ 0.
        WRITE: /, 'BDC Close successful!'.
      ELSE.
        WRITE: /, 'BDC Close Failed!', sy-subrc.
      ENDIF.
   ENDIF.

*** Start Forms
*   Build BDC Table for current planned order   *
*    .*
FORM build_bdc.
* Clear header and internal table
   CLEAR bd. REFRESH bd.
*    Screen start.
   PERFORM bdc_screen TABLES bd USING 'SAPMM61P' '0300'.
   MOVE p_pln-low TO ws_temp2.
*    Customer purchase order number.
   PERFORM bdc_field TABLES bd
USING 'PLAF-PLNUM' ws_temp2.
*    Convert planned order total quantity to character field
   WRITE plaf-gsmng NO-SIGN LEFT-JUSTIFIED TO ws_temp2.
   PERFORM bdc_field TABLES bd
   USING 'MDCD-GSMNG' ws_temp2.
*    Convert planned order scrap quantity to character field
   WRITE plaf-avmng NO-SIGN LEFT-JUSTIFIED TO ws_temp2.
```

```
  PERFORM bdc_field TABLES bd
  USING 'MDCD-AVMNG' ws_temp2.
*   Convert Production version to character field
  WRITE plaf-verid NO-SIGN LEFT-JUSTIFIED TO ws_temp2.
  PERFORM bdc_field TABLES bd
  USING 'MDCD-VERIO' ws_temp2.
*   Convert Sequence Number to character field
  WRITE plaf-seqnr NO-SIGN LEFT-JUSTIFIED TO ws_temp2. PERFORM bdc_field TABLES bd
USING 'MDCD-SEQNR' ws_temp2.
*   Fill open date
  IF NOT ( plaf-pertr IS INITIAL ).
    WRITE plaf-pertr MM/DD/YYYY TO ws_temp1.
    PERFORM bdc_field TABLES bd
    USING 'MDCD-PERTR' ws_temp1.
  ENDIF.
* Fill Start Date
  IF NOT ( plaf-psttr IS INITIAL ).
    WRITE plaf-psttr MM/DD/YYYY TO ws_temp1.
    PERFORM bdc_field TABLES bd
    USING 'MDCD-PSTTR' ws_temp1.
  ENDIF.
*   Fill Finish Date
  IF NOT ( plaf-pedtr IS INITIAL ).
    WRITE plaf-pedtr MM/DD/YYYY TO ws_temp1.
    PERFORM bdc_field TABLES bd
    USING 'MDCD-PEDTR' ws_temp1.
  ENDIF.
  MOVE p_action TO ws_temp2.
*   Fill Planned Order Action
  PERFORM bdc_field TABLES bd
  USING 'T46AC-ACCTO' ws_temp2.
*   Execute Action
  PERFORM bdc_okcode TABLES bd USING '/81'.
ENDFORM.                    "BUILD_BDC
*&---------------------------------------------------------------*
*&      Form   PRINT_RESULTS
*&---------------------------------------------------------------*
*       text
*----------------------------------------------------------------*

*The power of Call Transaction is that it executes the BDC *
*in real time and the results can be captured in an internal *
```

```
*table. This allows you to give real-time feedback to the *
*person executing the transaction. The results are in *
*the form of system messages. Only the message id and number *
*are captured in the results table. A look up must be done   *
*using the table T100 to get the English text of the message.   *
*Both success and error messages will be captured. *
*This result's functionality is only found in Call Transaction   *
*
FORM print_results.
  DATA ws_text(100).   "English text of results
  LOOP AT messtab INTO wa_messtab.   "Loop at results table
*Get english text of current message
  SELECT SINGLE text INTO (ws_text)
  FROM t100 WHERE sprsl = sy-langu
  AND arbgb = wa_messtab-msgid AND msgnr = wa_messtab-msgnr.

*Some messages have variables. Replace the & with the variable
  REPLACE '&1' WITH wa_messtab-msgv1 INTO ws_text.
  REPLACE '&2' WITH wa_messtab-msgv2 INTO ws_text.
  REPLACE '&3' WITH wa_messtab-msgv3 INTO ws_text.
  REPLACE '&4' WITH wa_messtab-msgv4 INTO ws_text.

  WRITE: / wa_messtab-msgid, wa_messtab-msgnr, ws_text(100).
  CLEAR ws_text.
ENDLOOP.

CLEAR: messtab[].
ENDFORM.                    "PRINT_RESULTS

*&---------------------------------------------------------------*
*&      Form   BDC_OKCODE
*&---------------------------------------------------------------*
*       text
*---------------------------------------------------------------*
*      -->BD          text
*      -->OKCODE      text
*---------------------------------------------------------------*
FORM bdc_okcode TABLES bd STRUCTURE bdcdata
USING okcode LIKE bdcdata-fval.

  CLEAR bd.
  wa_bd-fnam  = 'BDC_OKCODE'.
  wa_bd-fval = okcode.
  APPEND wa_bd TO bd.

ENDFORM.                    "BDC_OKCODE
```

```
*Form BDC_SCREEN
**    .*
*This form takes two parameters and makes an entry into a BDC *
*table specified for a new screen.   *
*   .*
FORM bdc_screen TABLES p_bd STRUCTURE bdcdata USING p_program p_screen.
  CLEAR wa_bd.        "Clears table work area
  wa_bd-program = p_program.
  wa_bd-dynpro = p_screen.
  wa_bd-dynbegin = 'X1'.
  APPEND wa_bd TO p_bd.
ENDFORM.                      "BDC_SCREEN    ·
*   _*
*   Form BDC_FIELD
*   _*
*This form takes two parameters and makes an entry into a BDC *
*table specified for a new field.   *
*   .*
FORM bdc_field TABLES p_bd STRUCTURE bdcdata USING p_name p_value.
  CLEAR wa_bd.
  CASE p_value.
    WHEN ' '.   "Don't move if value is blank
      WHEN OTHERS.   "Move value
        MOVE p_name TO wa_bd-fnam.
      MOVE p_value TO wa_bd-fval.
      APPEND wa_bd TO p_bd.
  ENDCASE.
ENDFORM.                       "BDC_FIELD
```

You can use this example with any transaction. Simply replace the `build BDC` form with the
`BDC` table you want to test. Then you can compare the different ways to process a
transaction.

A BDC Program to Create Project-Planning Data

This final example creates planning data for a project in SAP. In SAP, a *project* is an object
against which you can charge costs. A project is broken down into one or more elements
in the *work breakdown structure* (WBS). A WBS element describes either a concrete task
or a partial one that can be further subdivided. A WBS element can have a planned budget
for use in forecasting future expenses. A typical project might be opening a new
manufacturing plant. This project has many tasks, each of which is assigned to a WBS
element. One such element is purchasing the land for the plant; this element has a

planned budget of one million dollars. It's this type of planned budget data that this program will be creating in SAP via a BDC session.

Once again the Help system is used to identify the field name for each field, producing the list shown in Table 17.6.

Table 17.6   Field Names for the Change Transaction

Field	Contents
Field Names for Screen 1	
Project Number	PROJ-PSID
WBS Element	PRPS-POSID
Field Names for Screen 2	
Amount	BPDY-WERT1

© 2014 Cengage Learning.

Figures 17.8 and 17.9 show the first and second screens for the transaction. Notice that the second screen uses multiple lines. In this case, the current year, 2014, is the third line; in order to populate it, the field would be `BPDY-WER1(3)`.

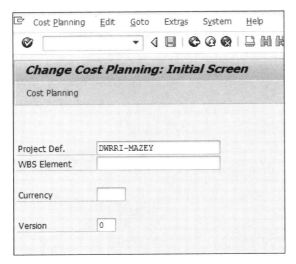

Figure 17.8
The first screen of the Change Cost Planning transaction.

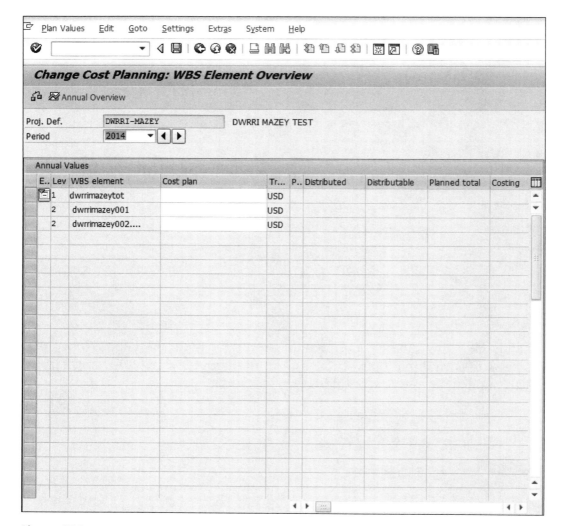

Figure 17.9
The second screen of the Change Cost Planning transaction.

The program should read a data file and use the information to execute the transaction as many times as needed.

This program demonstrates a technique to use both CALL TRANSACTION and BDC_INSERT to process the transactions. By using both, you get the speed of CALL TRANSACTION and the error handling of BDC_INSERT. The CALL TRANSACTION command can be used to submit each transaction for processing, but if an error is detected, the transaction should be resubmitted with BDC_INSERT. Thus, transactions without errors are processed quickly; those with errors get to use SAP's built-in error handling.

The program will read a text file with the file format shown in Table 17.7.

Table 17.7   Input File Format

Field Name	Position	Data Type	Length
Project Number	1	C	24
WBS Element	25	c	24
Project Plan Value	49	C	13
Project Plan Fiscal Year	62	c	4

© 2014 Cengage Learning.

Here's the BDC program using the flat file format to change the data:

```
*&---------------------------------------------------------------*
*& Report   ZPROJCO
*&
*&---------------------------------------------------------------*
*&
*&
*&---------------------------------------------------------------*
REPORT zprojco NO STANDARD PAGE HEADING LINE-SIZE 132 LINE-COUNT 65
MESSAGE-ID zz.

* Tables
*
* None
*
* Variables
* .
**** BDC Processing

TYPES: BEGIN OF ty_bdc.   "BDC Table
       INCLUDE STRUCTURE bdcdata.
TYPES: END OF ty_bdc.
DATA: int_bdc TYPE STANDARD TABLE OF ty_bdc INITIAL SIZE 100.
DATA: wa_bdc LIKE LINE OF int_bdc.
```

```
* Variables *
* *
**** Work fields used during BDC Processing
DATA: ws_index(2) TYPE n, "Index for Fields
      ws_bdc_created VALUE 'N',     "Flag For Errors
      ws_year(4)    TYPE n, "Temp year
      ws_wert1(14) TYPE c   VALUE 'BPDY-WERT1(   )'. "Plan Value
* Internal Tables *

**** Project Plan Value
TYPES:  BEGIN OF ty_proj,
         pspid    LIKE proj-pspid,    "Project Number
         posid    LIKE prps-posid,    "WBS Element
         wert1(21)   TYPE c, "Plan Value
         gjahr(4)    TYPE c, "Plan Year
         END OF ty_proj.


DATA: rec_proj TYPE STANDARD TABLE OF ty_proj.
DATA: wa_proj LIKE LINE OF rec_proj.

DATA: lv_filename TYPE string.
*Parameters
PARAMETERS: p_infile(80) TYPE c LOWER CASE. "Input file name and path

AT SELECTION-SCREEN ON VALUE-REQUEST FOR p_infile.

  PERFORM get_filename_upload_file.
*       Main Processing *
*       *
START-OF-SELECTION.
  PERFORM get_file_data.
  PERFORM process_file.

END-OF-SELECTION.
  PERFORM clean_up.


*Form BUILD BDC
*This form will build the BDC table for each transaction.

FORM build_bdc.
  REFRESH int_bdc.

  LOOP AT rec_proj INTO wa_proj.
*** Build First Screen
    PERFORM bdc_screen TABLES int_bdc
    USING 'SAPMKBUD' '200'.
```

```
      PERFORM bdc_field TABLES int_bdc
      USING 'PROJ-PSPID'      wa_proj-pspid.
      PERFORM bdc_field TABLES int_bdc
      USING 'PRPS-POSID'      wa_proj-posid.
      PERFORM bdc_field TABLES int_bdc
      USING 'BDC_OKCODE'      '/01'.
*** Build Second Screen
*** Calculate Index
      WRITE sy-datum(4) TO ws_year.
*** Current Year is always Line 3
      ws_index = 3 + wa_proj-gjahr - ws_year.

*** Build Amount using index
      ws_wert1 = ' BPDY-WERT1( )'.
      MOVE ws_index TO ws_wert1+11(2).
      PERFORM bdc_screen TABLES int_bdc
      USING 'SAPLKBPP' '200'.


      PERFORM bdc_field TABLES int_bdc
      USING ws_wert1 wa_proj-wert1.
      PERFORM bdc_field TABLES int_bdc
       USING 'BDC_OKCODE'    '/11'.

      CLEAR wa_proj.

    ENDLOOP.

ENDFORM.        "BUILD BDC

*Form SUBMIT BDC
*This form will submit the BDC table using CALL TRANSACTION.
FORM submit_bdc.
CALL TRANSACTION 'CJ40' USING int_bdc MODE 'N'.
IF sy-subrc <> 0. "If error record vendor and error msg
  PERFORM process_error.
ENDIF.
ENDFORM. "SUBMIT BDC

*Form BDC_SCREEN
** . *
*This form takes two parameters and makes an entry into a BDC *
*table specified for a new screen.*
* .*
```

```
FORM bdc_screen TABLES p_bdc STRUCTURE bdcdata USING p_program p_screen.
CLEAR wa_bdc.          "Clears table work area
wa_bdc-program = p_program.
wa_bdc-dynpro = p_screen.
wa_bdc-dynbegin = 'X1'.
APPEND wa_bdc TO p_bdc.
ENDFORM.                        "BDC_SCREEN
* *
* Form BDC_FIELD
**
*This form takes two parameters and makes an entry into a BDC *
*table specified for a new field. *
*.*
FORM bdc_field TABLES p_bdc STRUCTURE bdcdata USING p_name p_value.
  CLEAR wa_bdc.
  CASE p_value.
    WHEN ' '. "Don't move if value is blank
        WHEN OTHERS. "Move value
        MOVE p_name TO wa_bdc-fnam.
      MOVE p_value TO wa_bdc-fval.
      APPEND wa_bdc TO p_bdc.
  ENDCASE.
ENDFORM.                        "BDC_FIELD

*&---------------------------------------------------------------*
*&      Form   get_filename_upload_file
*&---------------------------------------------------------------*
*       text
*----------------------------------------------------------------*
FORM get_filename_upload_file .

  DATA: v_title TYPE string,
        v_rc      TYPE i,
        int_filetab   TYPE filetable.

  v_title = 'WINDOW ' .

  CALL METHOD cl_gui_frontend_services=>file_open_dialog
    EXPORTING
      window_title      = v_title
      default_filename  = '*.txt'
      initial_directory = 'C:\'
      multiselection    = ' '    "No multiple selection
```

```
   CHANGING
     file_table          = int_filetab
     rc                  = v_rc.


  READ TABLE int_filetab INTO p_infile INDEX 1.
ENDFORM.                    " GET_FILENAME_UPLOAD_FILE

*&---------------------------------------------------------------*
*&      Form   get_file_data
*&---------------------------------------------------------------*
*       text
*----------------------------------------------------------------*
FORM get_file_data .

  lv_filename = p_infile.

  CALL FUNCTION 'GUI_UPLOAD'
    EXPORTING
      filename              = lv_filename
      filetype              = 'ASC'
      has_field_separator   = 'X'
      header_length         = 0
      read_by_line          = 'X'
      dat_mode              = ' '
      codepage              = ' '
      replacement           = '#'
      check_bom             = ' '
    TABLES
      data_tab              = rec_proj
    EXCEPTIONS
      file_open_error       = 1
      file_read_error       = 2
      no_batch              = 3
      gui_refuse_filetransfer = 4
      invalid_type          = 5
      no_authority          = 6
      unknown_error         = 7
      bad_data_format       = 8
      header_not_allowed    = 9
      separator_not_allowed = 10
      header_too_long       = 11
      unknown_dp_error      = 12
```

```
     access_denied              = 13
     dp_out_of_memory           = 14
     disk_full                  = 15
     dp_timeout                 = 16
     OTHERS                     = 17.


  IF sy-subrc <> 0.

     MESSAGE ID sy-msgid TYPE sy-msgty NUMBER sy-msgno

              WITH sy-msgv1 sy-msgv2 sy-msgv3 sy-msgv4.

  ENDIF.


ENDFORM.                         " GET_FILE_DATA
```

```
*For an error a BDC session is created and the transaction    *
*is resubmitted to make use of SAP's built in error handling *

FORM process_error .
*** Open BDC Session Once Only
  IF ws_bdc_created = 'N'.
    CALL FUNCTION 'BDC_OPEN_GROUP'
      EXPORTING
        client        = sy-mandt
        group         = 'PLANNER'
        keep =
        'X'
        user =
        sy-uname
        ws_bdc_created
        =      'Y'.



  ENDIF.
*** Insert Error Transaction
  CALL FUNCTION 'BDC_NSERT'
    EXPORTING
      tcode      = 'CJ40'
    TABLES
      dynprotab = int_bdc.
```

```
    IF sy-subrc <> 0.
      MESSAGE e999 WITH 'BDC Error'.
    ENDIF.
*** Clear the BDC Table
    REFRESH int_bdc.

ENDFORM.                         " PROCESS_ERROR

**&---------------------------------------------------------------*
**&      Form   PROCESS_FILE
**&---------------------------------------------------------------*
**          text
**----------------------------------------------------------------*
FORM process_file.
**
*This form will read the vendor file and build the BDC table *
*For each record.
*   It will then submit each transaction and    *
*   save any errors recorded.
*   *
**.*
    DO.
      READ DATASET p_infile INTO wa_proj.
      IF sy-subrc <> 0.
        EXIT.
      ELSE.
        APPEND wa_proj TO rec_proj.
        CLEAR wa_proj.
      ENDIF.
    ENDDO.
    PERFORM build_bdc.
    PERFORM submit_bdc.

ENDFORM.                "PROCESS FILE

*&---------------------------------------------------------------*
*&      Form   CLEAN_UP
*&---------------------------------------------------------------*
*          text
*----------------------------------------------------------------*
*     This is for Closing the Inbound file of Project Plan Values *
*
FORM clean_up.
*** Close Inbound file
CLOSE DATASET p_infile.
```

```
IF sy-subrc <> 0.
  MESSAGE e999 WITH 'Error Closing' p_infile.
ENDIF.
*** Close the BDC Session if Needed
IF ws_bdc_created = 'Y1'.
  CALL FUNCTION 'BDC_CLOSE_GROUP'.
  IF sy-subrc <> 0.
    MESSAGE e999 WITH 'error closing bdc session'.
  ENDIF.
ENDIF.
ENDFORM.    "End Clean_Up
```

This is an excellent example of using both BDC_INSERT and CALL TRANSACTION to get the best of both techniques. The only drawback to this example is that transactions that are successfully processed aren't logged by SAP. Logging takes place only when using BDC_INSERT, and only errors are submitted this way. Of course, there's often no need to log successful transactions, only transactions with errors need to be logged.

Summary

Interfaces that use BDC sessions to load data into SAP are some of the most critical. At many SAP sites, the majority of programming done during an SAP installation is interface work. BDCs are a unique aspect of ABAP/4 and are very difficult to explain. They really do require hands-on experience to be done well. One thing to look out for is a transaction that behaves differently in a BDC session than it does when a user enters the data by hand. Transactions aren't supposed to act differently, but sometimes it happens. If unexpected errors are encountered when processing a BDC session, the best way to examine what's happening is by using mode A of CALL TRANSACTION, which displays all screens. If unexpected screens pop up during the processing of the BDC, they'll be displayed, and the program that builds the BDC table can be modified to compensate for them.

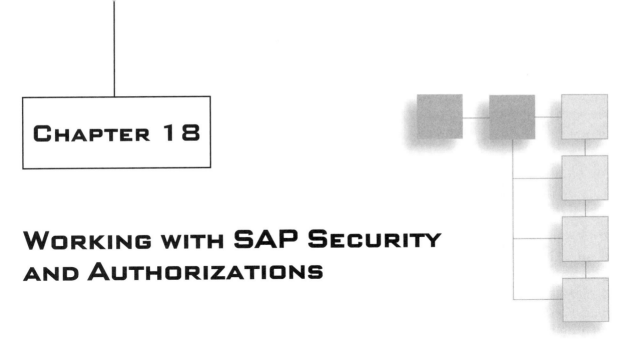

CHAPTER 18

WORKING WITH SAP SECURITY AND AUTHORIZATIONS

IN THIS CHAPTER

- Understanding the SAP Security Model
- Creating Authorization Objects
- Using the `AUTHORITY-CHECK` Command to Enforce Security

This chapter introduces some of the basics of SAP security. Like any complex system, SAP has multiple layers of security. This chapter covers the making of security checks from within ABAP programs. In SAP, user security is referred to as *authorizations*. The object that controls if an operation in the system is allowed is referred to as an *authorization object*. When the programmer makes an authority check against an authorization object, the system ensures that the user has the ability to perform that operation.

THE SAP SECURITY MODEL

Authorization checks control access to operations in SAP. A developer places authorization checks in programs when security is an issue. The system then searches the user's profile, maintained by the system administrator, to verify that the user has access to the object being checked. These authorization objects consist of up to 10 fields, which may contain specific values to be checked. You can contact the basis administrator of your system for more information. In order to make use of new authorization objects, you will need to ensure that object is incorporated into the security scheme that SAP basis team manages.

The Authorization Object

The authorization object grants the ability to perform some operation in the system. For example, the authorization object could be a requirement that only some people be allowed to view or maintain a list of suppliers with quality problems. This would be mapped to an authorization object with the name Z: SUPPPRB. When a program displays or changes data on the supplier list, a check should be made against the Z: SUPPPRB.

Authorization Fields

An authorization object can have up to 10 authorization fields. Each field is the equivalent of an SAP data element. (See Chapter 7, "Working with the Data Dictionary," for information about data elements.) For example, the supplier authorization just described—Z:SUPPPRB—might have two fields, one called REGIO and another called ACTVT. The REGIO field holds a region value and all suppliers are assigned to a region. The ACTVT field is used in many objects and holds activity values. In general, when ACTVT has the value 01, it indicates the ability to create data. An ACTVT of 02 indicates the ability to change data, and a value of 03 indicates the ability to display data.

The User Master Record

Each user in an SAP system has a master record that contains all authorizations that the user may perform. Your SAP basis administrator will manage these authorizations via a system of roles and profiles. Each authorization object can be mapped to one or more roles and profiles. Those roles and profiles are then assigned to individual users. As an ABAP developer, you will not need to worry about the relationships your administrator has set up with users, roles, and profiles. The system will take care of the details. All you need to be concerned with is checking the correct authorization object at the correct point in your code.

For example, a user might have the object Z: SUPPPRB and fields REGIO with the value USA and ACTVT with a value of 03. This indicates that the user could display suppliers for the USA region, but if this user attempts to execute a program that changes data in the USA region, the user would fail any authorization checks. This is not an automatic process—to enforce this security, the programmer must perform the authorization check correctly in the program.

CREATING AUTHORIZATION OBJECTS

When creating a custom authorization object, the first step is to create any custom authorization fields needed. Most of the time you will not need to create custom fields and will simply use fields created by SAP. Most major SAP data elements have corresponding authorization fields, including plant (WERKS), sales office (VKBUR), and activity (ACTVT). Be sure to check for an existing field before creating new ones. To view or create authorization fields, select Tools > ABAP Workbench > Development > Other Tools > Authorization Objs > Fields (see Figure 18.1).

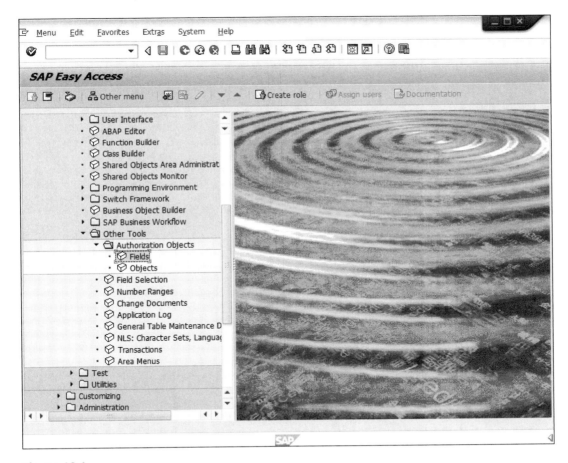

Figure 18.1
Creating an authorization, step 1.

Next, choose Create to create a custom field (see Figure 18.2) from the list of authorization fields.

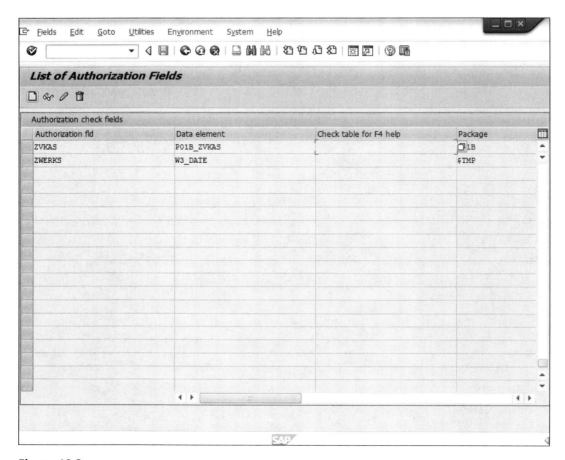

Figure 18.2
Authorization field list.

From this new screen, you create a new field. Enter a name and data element. Like all custom objects, the name should start with Z, as shown in Figure 18.3.

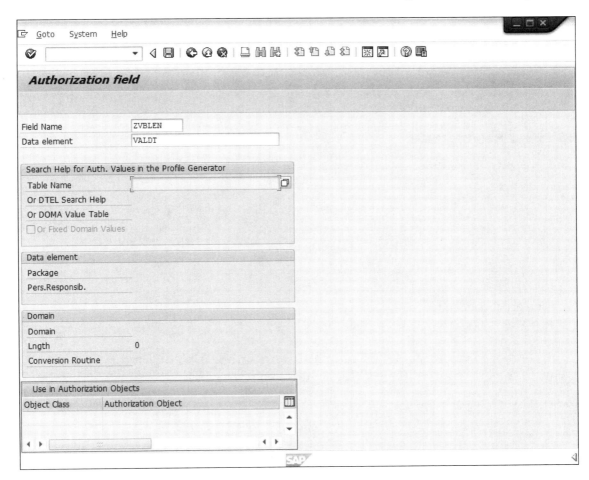

Figure 18.3
Creating a new authorization field.

After you create custom fields, it is time to create the object to hold them. Because SAP groups authorization objects into classes, you should create a custom class before you create a custom object. To create an authorization object class, select Tools > ABAP Workbench > Development > Other Tools > Authorization Objs > Objects. From this screen, choose Create > Object Class (see Figure 18.4).

Figure 18.4
Creating a new object class.

Once the class has been created, you can create an authorization object for the new class using Create > Authorization Object (see Figure 18.5).

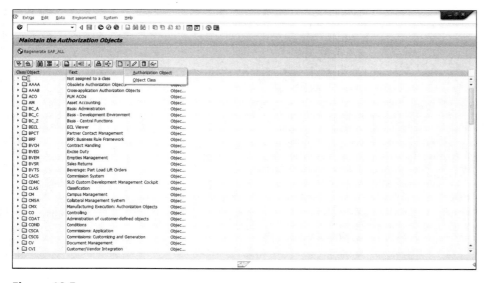

Figure 18.5
Begin creating a new authorization object.

This brings up the screen shown in Figure 18.6.

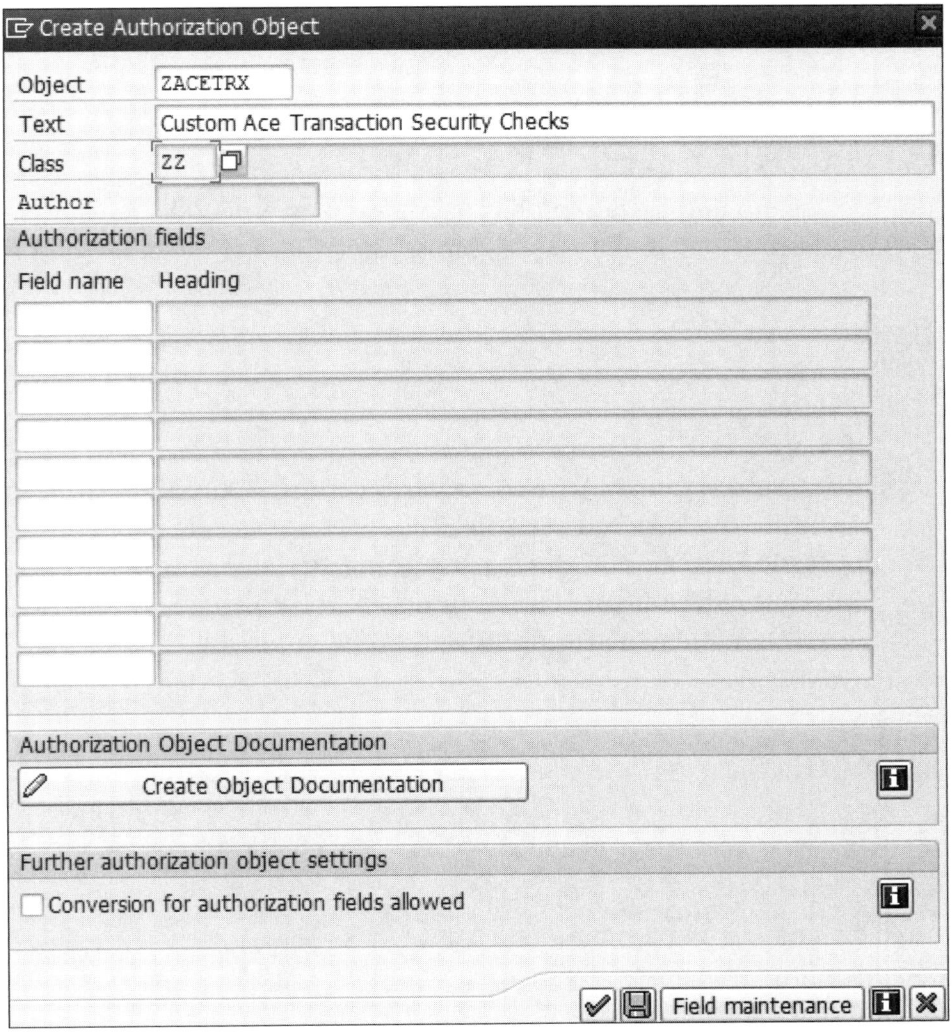

Figure 18.6
Create a new authorization object.

As shown in Figure 18.6, when creating an authorization object, it is required that you enter a name, descriptive text, the class, and the list of authorization fields that will be contained in the object. In the example shown in Figure 18.6, an object called ZACETRX is being created. This will contain the names of people who have authorization for a special transaction.

Once you create your authorization object, you are ready to add the checks to your programs.

USING THE AUTHORITY-CHECK COMMAND

You are now ready to use custom authorization objects in your programs. The AUTHORITY-CHECK command checks authorizations in ABAP programs. The syntax of the command is as follows:

```
AUTHORITY-CHECK OBJECT obj
ID name1 FIELD val|DUMMY ID name2 FIELD
Val|DUMMY
ID name10 FIELD val|DUMMY
```

You will be checking the val value against the user master record. If you do not want to check a field, you can substitute the keyword DUMMY for the FIELD val option. This causes the system to ignore the value of the field when performing the authorization check. When this command is performed, you can tell if the check is successful by a return code of the command. Any value other than zero indicates a failure. Table 18.1 contains a list of possible return codes.

Table 18.1 AUTHORITY-CHECK Return Codes

Return	Description
0	Check was successful.
4	Check failed because user is not authorized.
8	Number of fields submitted for check exceeds 10.
12	Object does not exist.
24	Field names listed in the check do not match the fields of the object.
28, 32, 36	System error.

© 2014 Cengage Learning.

Here are some simple examples of using the AUTHORITY-CHECK command:

```
AUTHORITY-CHECK OBJECT 'Z:CUST'
ID 'ACTVT' FIELD '01'.
IF SY-SUBRC NE 0.
```

```
  MESSAGE E999 WITH 'You are not authorized to use this program!'.
ENDIF.
AUTHORITY-CHECK OBJECT 'Z:PLANT'
ID 'WERKS' FIELD 'P100'
ID 'MATNR1   DUMMY
ID 'ACTVT'   FIELD   '02'.
IF SY-SUBRC NE 0.
  MESSAGE E999 WITH   'You are not authorized in Plant P100'.
ENDIF.
```

The following is a program featuring several of the concepts previously presented, including authorization checks, function modules, forms, and a BDC session. The purpose of this program is to change the delivery dates of items on a sales order. When a sales order is created in SAP, it is broken into two groups of information—a header record containing data and one or more records of item data. The sales order header holds a default delivery date that records when the customer wants the item delivered. In addition, each item on the order has its own delivery date. The delivery dates of each may vary in an order.

This program reads a file containing sales order numbers and dates. For each order, the system checks the user's authority for running the program to change the order. If the user has authority, a BDC session builds and then processes via the CALL TRANSACTION command. The results of each transaction is saved and reported back to the user at the end. Note that the authorization check is made before the processing of the sales order takes place. SAP has its own security on changing documents like sales orders; but in this case, a custom authorization object is checked.

```
*&----------------------------------------------------------*
*& Report ZCVDATE1
*&
*&----------------------------------------------------------*
*& Author: Bob Lyfareff
*& Date:   March 27,2014
*& Type: Program - Alter delivery date in sales items
* Description of function:
* This program will take a list of items and change the delivery
* date of all items on a sales order. It will change the delivery
* date in the sales order header back to the original date.
* The user's authorization will be checked by the system for
* each order to ensure the user has change authorization
* for the sales group (VBAK-VKBUR).
* The data will be changed using transaction VA02.
```

```
*&--------------------------------------------------------------*
REPORT ZCVDATE1 LINE-SIZE 132 LINE-COUNT 65 MESSAGE-ID ZZ.

TABLES: T100,          "Message Texts Table
VBAK.            "Sales Order Header Table
DATA: BEGIN OF INT_ORDER OCCURS 100,      "Input file with orders
LINE(120),
END OF INT_ORDER.


DATA: BEGIN OF INT_DATA OCCURS 100,
  VBELN LIKE VBAP-VBELN,
  DELDATE type D,
END OF INT_DATA.

"Data to be processed
DATA: BEGIN OF INT_RES OCCURS 200,
  VBELN LIKE VBAP-VBELN,
  POSNR LIKE VBAP-POSNR,
  MSGID LIKE BDCMSGCOLL-MSGID,
  MSGNR LIKE BDCMSGCOLL-MSGNR,
  MSGNUM LIKE SY-TABIX,
  SUBRC LIKE SY-SUBRC,
  SAV_TEXT(275),
END OF INT_RES.

DATA: BEGIN OF BD OCCURS 10.            "BDC Table
        INCLUDE STRUCTURE BDCDATA.
DATA: END OF BD.

DATA: BEGIN OF XBDCMSGCOLL OCCURS 10. "Transaction Messages
        INCLUDE STRUCTURE BDCMSGCOLL.
DATA: END OF XBDCMSGCOLL.

DATA: WS_TOTAL TYPE I,
  WS_VBELN LIKE VBAP-VBELN,
  FLG_ERR,
  WS_SUBRC(10),
  WS_TOP,
  ws_mode value 'n'.

parameters: p_file like rlgrap-filename default 'c:\pullin.txt1'.
```

```
*       Start Main Program
START-OF-SELECTION.
*       Open file and read records
  PERFORM INIT_DAT.
  LOOP AT INT_DATA.
    CHECK INT_DATA-VBELN NE SPACE.      "check order is not blank
    WS_TOTAL = SY-TABIX.   "Keep track of total
*       Build BDC table to change data
    CLEAR BD[].
    PERFORM BUILD_BDC.
*       Call transaction VA02 and record result
    PERFORM PROCESSITEM.
  ENDLOOP.
  WRITE: /, WS_TOTAL, 'Total Items Processed'(023).
*       Print Results Report
  PERFORM PRINT_RESULTS.

*&--------------------------------------------------------------*
*&      Form   INIT_DAT
*&--------------------------------------------------------------*
*       Read file and get orders and dates
*---------------------------------------------------------------*
FORM INIT_DAT.
* Use data file to get item list, read local PC file
  CALL FUNCTION 'WSUPLOAD'
    EXPORTING
      FILENAME              = P_FILE
      FILETYPE              = 'ASC1 TABLES'
      DATA_TAB              = INT_ORDER
    EXCEPTIONS
      CONVERSION_ERROR
      =1
      FILE_OPEN_ERROR       = 2
      FILE_READ_ERROR       = 3
      INVALID_TABLE_WIDTH = 4
      INVALIDJYPE           = 5
      NO_BATCH              = 6
      UNKNOWN_ERROR         = 7
      OTHERS                = 8.
  IF SY-SUBRC NE 0.
    MESSAGE E999 WITH 'Error opening PC file!' SY-SUBRC.
  ENDIF.
```

```
  LOOP AT INT_ORDER.
     CHECK INT_ORDER-LINE NE SPACE.
     CLEAR INT_DATA.
* Set Delivery Date
     INT_DATA-DELDATE = INT_ORDER-LINE+10(8).
* Set Sales Order
     INT_DATA-VBELN = INT_ORDER-LINE(10).
* Pad Sales order with leading zeros if needed
     SHIFT INT_DATA-VBELN RIGHT DELETING TRAILING SPACE.
     DO.
       REPLACE SPACE WITH '0' INTO INT_DATA-VBELN.
       IF SY-SUBRC NE 0. EXIT. ENDIF.
     ENDDO.
* Check that Order exists and get sales office
     SELECT SINGLE * FROM VBAK WHERE VBELN = INT_DATA-VBELN.
     IF SY-SUBRC NE 0.
       WRITE: / 'SAP Order#'(110), INT_ORDER-LINE(10), 'Not
Found'(111).
     ELSE.
* Check authorization to see if user has change authority
* for the Sales Office of this order
       AUTHORITY-CHECK OBJECT 'Z:SOOFF'
       ID 'VKBUR' FIELD VBAK-VKBUR
       ID 'ACTVT' FIELD '02'.
       IF SY-SUBRC EQ 0.
         APPEND INT_DATA.
       ELSE.
         WRITE: /, 'Failed to change order', VBAK-VBELN,
       / 'You do not have authorization to change Sales Office',
         VBAK-VKBUR.
       ENDIF.
     ENDIF.
   ENDLOOP.
ENDFORM.                       "INIT_DAT

*&---------------------------------------------------------------*
*&      Form   BUILD_BDC
*&---------------------------------------------------------------*
* Build BDC table for current order
*----------------------------------------------------------------*
FORM BUILD_BDC.
   DATA: WS_VDAT LIKE VBAK-VDATU, WS_TEMP(10).
```

```
*       Get Current delivery date
  SELECT SINGLE VDATU INTO (WS_VDAT)
  FROM VBAK WHERE VBELN = INT_DATA-VBELN.
* Screen start.
  PERFORM SCREEN TABLES BD USING 'SAPMV45A' '0102'.
* Fill sales document number
  PERFORM FIELD TABLES BD
  USING 'VBAK-VBELN' INT_DATA-VBELN.
* Move to first sales order screen
  PERFORM OKCODE TABLES BD USING 'UER2'.

* Screen start.
  PERFORM SCREEN TABLES BD USING 'SAPMV45A' '0400'.
* Select all sales items to be changed
  PERFORM OKCODE TABLES BD USING 'MKAL'.
* Screen start.
  PERFORM SCREEN TABLES BD USING 'SAPMV45A' '0400'.
* Function change delivery date in selected items
  PERFORM OKCODE TABLES BD USING 'SWLD'.
* Screen Start
  PERFORM SCREEN TABLES BD USING 'SAPMV45A' '0255'.
* Change delivery date to date found in input file
  PERFORM FIELD TABLES BD USING 'RV45A-S_ETDAT' INT_DATA-DELDATE.
* Move old delivery date to a text field to ensure proper format
  WRITE WS_VDAT TO WS_TEMP.
* Screen Start
  PERFORM SCREEN TABLES BD USING 'SAPMV45A' '0255'.
* Continue to next screen
  PERFORM OKCODE TABLES BD USING 'SUEB'.
* Screen Start
  PERFORM SCREEN TABLES BD USING 'SAPMV45A' '0400'.
* Restore original req date to header
  PERFORM FIELD TABLES BD USING 'RV45A-KETDAT' WS_TEMP.
* Screen Start
  PERFORM SCREEN TABLES BD USING 'SAPMV45A' '0400'.
* Save changes to sales order
  PERFORM OKCODE TABLES BD USING 'SAVE'.
ENDFORM.                         "BUILD_BDC

*&---------------------------------------------------------------------*
*&      Form PROCESSITEM
*&---------------------------------------------------------------------*
```

```
* Call transaction VA02 to change the sales order using the
* BDC table created earlier. Any success or error messages
* will be captured in a table for later use.
*------------------------------------------------------------*
FORM PROCESSITEM.
  CALL TRANSACTION 'VA02' USING BD
  MODE WS_MODE
  UPDATE 'S'
  MESSAGES INTO XBDCMSGCOLL.
* Save return code
  WS_SUBRC = SY-SUBRC.
  IF WS_SUBRC EQ 0.
* This will appear in the system log
    MESSAGE S999 WITH INT_DATA-VBELN 'Processed Successfully!'.
  ELSE.
* This will appear in the system log
    MESSAGE S999 WITH INT_DATA-VBELN 'Failed_due_to_Error!'.
  ENDIF.
* Loop at transaction messages table to record any errors
  LOOP AT XBDCMSGCOLL.
* Clear header of results table
    CLEAR INT_RES.
    MOVE: INT_DATA-VBELN   TO INT_RES-VBELN,   "Sales Order
      XBDCMSGCOLL-MSGID TO INT_RES-MSGID,    "Message ID
    XBDCMSGCOLL-MSGNR TO INT_RES-MSGNR,    "Message Number
      WS_SUBRC TO INT_RES-SUBRC,    "Return Code

      SY-TABIX TO INT_RES-MSGNUM. "For later sorting
* Table T100 holds the texts for error messages
    SELECT SINGLE * FROM T100 WHERE SPRSL = SY-LANGU
    AND ARBGB = XBDCMSGCOLL-MSGID
    AND MSGNR = XBDCMSGCOLL-MSGNR.
    INT_RES-SAV_TEXT = T100-TEXT.
* Replace & with the results stored in the MSGV# fields
    REPLACE '&' WITH XBDCMSGCOLL-MSGV1 INTO INT_RES-SAV_TEXT.
    REPLACE '&' WITH XBDCMSGCOLL-MSGV2 INTO INT_RES-SAV_TEXT.
    REPLACE '&' WITH XBDCMSGCOLL-MSGV3 INTO INT_RES-SAV_TEXT.
    REPLACE '&' WITH XBDCMSGCOLL-MSGV4 INTO INT_RES-SAV_TEXT.
    CONDENSE INT_RES-SAV_TEXT.
* Save messages for later reporting to results table
    APPEND INT_RES.
  ENDLOOP.
```

```
* Clear tables
  CLEAR: BD[], XBDCMSGCOLL[].
ENDFORM.                          "PROCESSITEM

*&---------------------------------------------------------------*
*&      Form   PRINT_RESULTS
*&---------------------------------------------------------------*
*        text
*----------------------------------------------------------------*
FORM PRINT_RESULTS.
* Sort by return code so successful transactions (subrc=0) come last
  SORT INT_RES BY SUBRC DESCENDING VBELN POSNR MSGNUM.
  WRITE /.
  ULINE.
  WRITE: / '******* Results of Processing *******'.
  ULINE.
  WRITE: /, 'Transactions With Errors:'.

  LOOP AT INT_RES.
    IF INT_RES-SUBRC EQ 0 AND WS_TOP = SPACE.
* When subrc = 0 successful transactions begin
      WRITE: /, 'Transactions Not Raising Errors:'.
      WS_TOP = 'X'.
    ENDIF.
    WRITE: / ' '.
    IF INT_RES-MSGNUM = 1.
* Print the order number of the first message
WRITE: /, 'SO', INT_RES-VBELN.
    ENDIF.
    WRITE: / INT_RES-MSGID,
    INT_RES-MSGNR,
    INT_RES-SAV_TEXT(100).
  ENDLOOP.
ENDFORM.                          "PRINT_RESULTS

*&---------------------------------------------------------------*
*&      Form   SCREEN
*&---------------------------------------------------------------*
*        Add BD entry for screen start
*----------------------------------------------------------------*
*        -->BD         text
*        -->PROGRAM    text
*        -->SCREEN     text
```

```
*------------------------------------------------------------*
FORM SCREEN TABLES BD STRUCTURE BDCDATA USING PROGRAM SCREEN.
  CLEAR BD.
  BD-PROGRAM = PROGRAM. BD-DYNPRO  = SCREEN. BD-DYNBEGIN = 'X' .
APPEND BD.
ENDFORM.                          "SCREEN

*&-----------------------------------------------------------*
*&      Form   FIELD
*&-----------------------------------------------------------*
*       text
*------------------------------------------------------------*
*       -->BD         text
*       -->FIELD      text
*       -->VALUE      text
*------------------------------------------------------------*
FORM FIELD TABLES BD STRUCTURE BDCDATA USING FIELD VALUE.
  CLEAR BD.
  BD-FNAM = FIELD. BD-FVAL = VALUE. APPEND BD.
ENDFORM.                          "FIELD

*&-----------------------------------------------------------*
*&      Form   OKCODE
*&-----------------------------------------------------------*
*       Create BD entry for a transaction code
*------------------------------------------------------------*
*       -->BD         text
*       -->OKCODE     text
*------------------------------------------------------------*
FORM OKCODE TABLES BD STRUCTURE BDCDATA USING OKCODE.
  CLEAR BD.
  BD-FNAM    = ' BDC_OKCODE'. BD-FVAL    = OKCODE. APPEND BD.
ENDFORM. " End Program
```

FORM INIT DAT

This first form initializes the data to be processed by the program. First it reads the PC file that holds the data to be processed into an internal table. Then it loops through that table and extracts the sales order number and the new delivery date. It compares the sales order number against the sales order table, VBAK, to make sure the order really exists in the system. Once it confirms the order number, it checks to see if the user has the authority to change sales orders based on the sales office (VBAK-VKBUR).

FORM BUILD_BDC

This is where the BDC session is built that will change the delivery date of items on the sales order. Also, the original delivery date is saved in the sales order header.

FORM PROCESSITEM

In this form, submitting the BDC via the `Call Transaction` command changes the date. Messages encountered during the transaction are saved in the `XBDCMSGCOLL` table. This table captures both success and failure messages. The data form is then transferred to the results table, which is later reported to the user.

FORM PRINT RESULTS

Here, both success and failure messages are reported to the user out of the results table.

SUMMARY

This is simply one aspect of the SAP security model, performing security checks via ABAP coding. To learn more about security and authorizations in SAP, consult your system administrator or books on SAP basis administration.

PART IV

ADVANCED TECHNICAL ISSUES

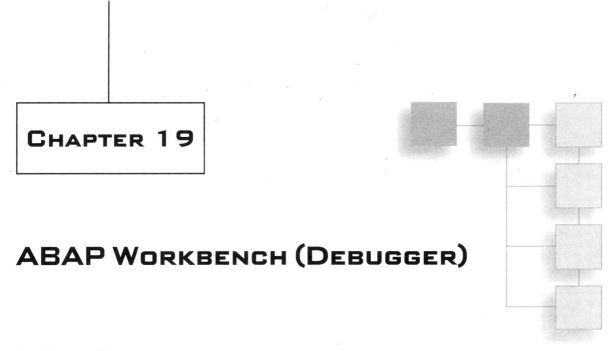

CHAPTER 19

ABAP WORKBENCH (DEBUGGER)

IN THIS CHAPTER

- Using the ABAP Debugger
- Learning Debugging Techniques

This chapter introduces the ABAP debugger and some techniques used to analyze programs. It also covers the methods used to enter debug mode—setting breakpoints, both manually and dynamically; a tour around the debug screen; and techniques to effectively debug your code.

THE ABAP DEBUGGER

The ABAP debugger is probably the most important development tool you'll utilize aside from the workbench. The use of the debugger allows for line-by-line execution, along with supervision over the contents of certain variables and internal tables in real time. The debugger gives you a different perspective on coding. It can be used to see what is happening in SAP transactions that are running or to analyze your programs that you are coding. In either case, what you view is ABAP code, and you are able to control its execution to a line-by-line process.

Entering Debug Mode

The first step to debugging code is to enter debug mode. There are three methods for accomplishing this task. The first method is formally entering debug mode from the editor. Another is the called the "slash h" method. The final method is setting breakpoints inside the code.

The first method is reached from the ABAP editor, either in the initial screen or in editor mode. Both paths are demonstrated in Figures 19.1 and 19.2.

Let's use some sample code to debug:

```
REPORT ZTEST.
WRITE:/  'This is my debugging test program'.
```

Via both of these methods, you would enter a screen that looks like Figure 19.3. Essentially, this figure introduces you to what the debugger looks like. This screen and all of its components are explained in the second section of this chapter, which covers the debugger's functionality. The debugger allows you process your ABAP code line by line.

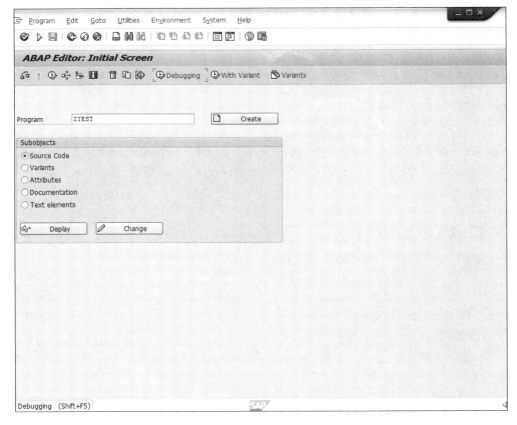

Figure 19.1
Click the Debugging button to execute a program in debug mode.

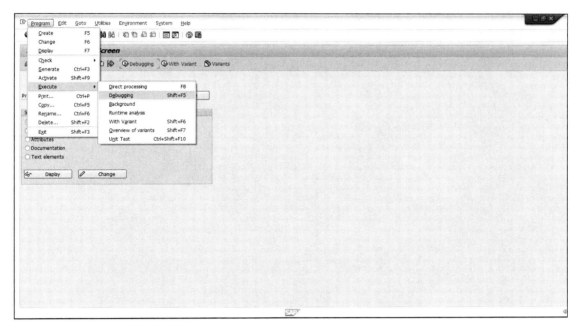

Figure 19.2
Follow the menu path to execute a program in debug made from the editor mode screen.

The se38 method does have some limitations. For example, you can only debug reports or programs that you can execute from the se38 screen. If you want to debug a transaction, you must use the "slash h" method or set a breakpoint. To enter debug mode anywhere in SAP, just type /h in the command box in the top-left corner of the screen (see Figure 19.4).

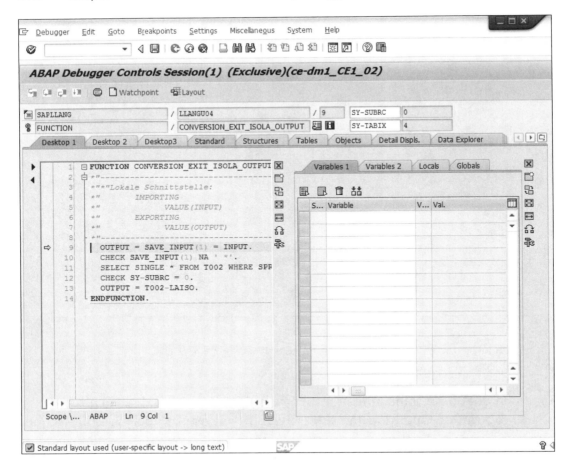

Figure 19.3
The initial debugging screen.

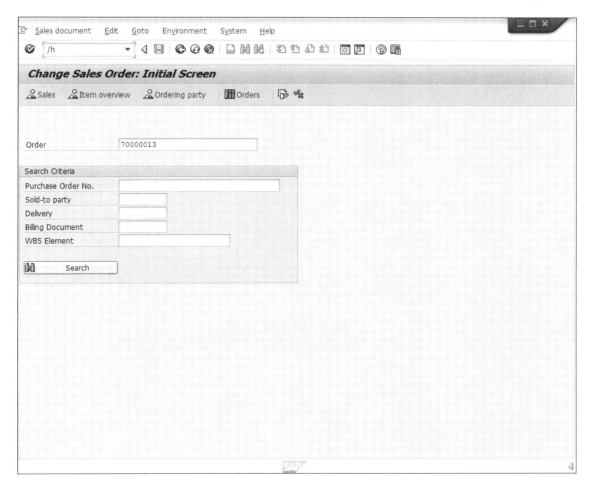

Figure 19.4
Type /h in the command box at the top-left side of the screen.

After pressing Enter on the keyboard, a message at the bottom-left portion of the screen says, "Debugging switched on" (see Figure 19.5).

At this point, proceed with pressing the buttons you usually would to continue in the transaction, but instead a second window will open with the code behind the transaction. The original window will continue to display the input and output of your program.

This allows you to debug the code in one window and view the results in real time in the second. This is a very handy feature, and you should spend some time moving between the two screens to get a feel for how they each respond.

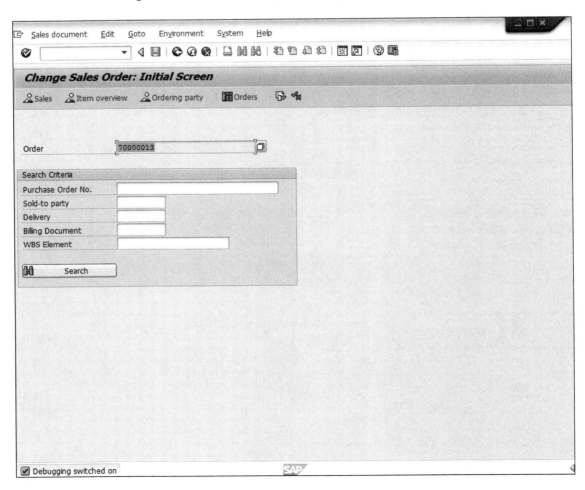

Figure 19.5
Debugging switched on.

Because this book's scope deals only with programs executable from the se38 screen, it does not cover specialized techniques used to debug transactions. Many of the methods can be used, however, for a deeper understanding of debugging. With that being said, all of the basic techniques and examples covered here can be used to debug online transactions. With this foundation you can focus on some of the additional functions that focus on transactions and custom screens created via the ABAP screen painter.

DEFINING THE DEBUGGER'S SCREEN

Now that you are in debug mode, what does this new screen mean to you? Debug mode is almost like a brand new transaction within the program you are running. This section gives you a tour of the screen and the most useful commands. Once you know your way around the debugging screens, you can move on to the debugging techniques section of this chapter, which covers a more strategic approach to tackling the debugging of your programs.

For consistency, please type the following program into your system and then debug it. If you follow these instructions, your screen should look exactly like the ones here.

```
REPORT ZTEST
*&-----------------------------------------------------------*
*& Report   ZTEST
*&
*&-----------------------------------------------------------*
*& Grab Sales Order Data for a batchuser
*&
*&-----------------------------------------------------------*
REPORT ZTEST .

TABLES: VBAK, VBAP.
PARAMETERS: P_DATUM LIKE SY-DATUM.

DATA: BEGIN OF INT_VBAK OCCURS 1000.
        INCLUDE STRUCTURE VBAK.
DATA: END OF INT_VBAK.

DATA: BEGIN OF INT_VBAP OCCURS 1000.
        INCLUDE STRUCTURE VBAP.
DATA: END OF INT_VBAP.

SELECT * FROM VBAK INTO TABLE INT_VBAK
  WHERE ERDAT = P_DATUM.
```

```
LOOP AT INT_VBAK.
  IF INT_VBAK-ERNAM = 'BATCHUSER'.
    PERFORM VBAP_DISPLAY.
  ELSE.
    WRITE:/  INT_VBAK-VBELN,
      15  'Not Relevant'.
  ENDIF.
ENDLOOP.



*&---------------------------------------------------------------*
*&      Form   VBAP_DISPLAY
*&---------------------------------------------------------------*
*         Display Results
*----------------------------------------------------------------*
FORM VBAP_DISPLAY.

  REFRESH INT_VBAP.
  SELECT * FROM VBAP INTO TABLE INT_VBAP
  WHERE VBELN = INT_VBAK-VBELN.
  LOOP AT INT_VBAP.
    WRITE:/  INT_VBAP-VBELN,
      11 INT_VBAP-POSNR,
      20 INT_VBAP-ARKTX.
  ENDLOOP.

ENDFORM.                      "VBAP_DISPLAY.
```

Use the Debugging button to execute this program from the ABAP editor (or se38 screen) and enter a date for your selection criteria. You should have a second window that looks like Figure 19.6. One thing to note is, because this program includes a user parameter that requires your input, the debugger window will not start in your source code. All reports that have user input (parameters or select-options) begin in a section of standard SAP code that will process user input. Only once you get past this standard code will you see your ABAP code.

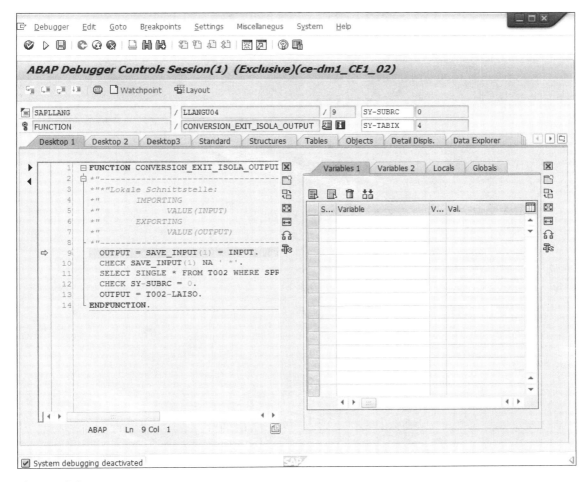

Figure 19.6
The initial debugging screen.

General Commands

The most useful and most frequently used functions of the debugging screen have been defined as buttons. The first four icons from the left—Single Step, Execute, Return, and Continue—are the most important. These four buttons allow you to move through the code in a controlled fashion.

Below the buttons you will see two panes. The first pane holds the source code tool that is the code currently being executed. The second pane defaults to a variable tool with a list of variables that will initially be empty. The tabs along the top of the screen allow you to flip between different views and different tools. The default described here is in the Standard tab.

The critical commands are explained and demonstrated in the next section. First we will define some of the screen areas. See Figure 19.7.

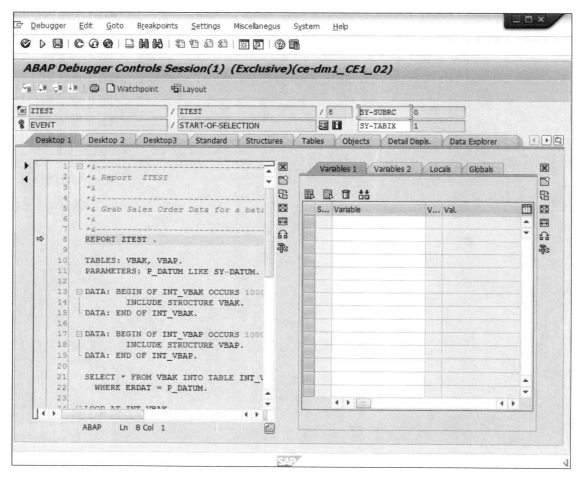

Figure 19.7
The initial debugging screen. Use this to reference the default buttons and areas of the debugging screen.

Focus on the Variables tool on the right of the screen. The second column holds the name of the variable, and the fourth column holds its value. You can track an unlimited number of variables at one time. Simply scroll down if you need to add more. Of course, you can always add or remove variables at any time. If you keep scrolling to the right, there is a button that looks like a pencil. This is an important button that you will use often. It enables you (if your system administrator gives you enough authority) to replace the contents of what is currently in the variable with something new. Of course this is a very dangerous feature on a production system; however, on a development system it is very useful. If you continue to scroll to the right you will find a column to view a variable's content in hexadecimal notation. We have not found this useful in our debugging, but you have that ability if you want.

At the top of the screen there are a few key pieces of information. From the left you will see the program name that is currently being executed. Next to that is the INCLUDE code file with the current line number that is in focus. Often these two items will be the same, but if you are breaking up your program into separate INCLUDE code files, they will differ. Below that on the left you find the type and name for the current module or event being executed. This is more important in complex transaction programming but can be helpful even in a simple report to remind you of the state of the program.

Next on the top-left of the screen, two system variables are displayed. SY-SUBRC is the return code of the last line of code executed. Viewing the results of the last piece of code executed is something you will want to do all the time when debugging, so having it displayed prominently at the top of the screen is helpful. Below that is SY-TABIX, which is the row number of the last internal table processed. Generally it will default to one most of the time. When you do process an internal table with a statement such as LOOP, it will change as you move through the table.

The ABAP debugger is very customizable. The descriptions here are for the default layout, but feel free to experiment on a layout that best meets your needs. You can have three separate custom debugger layouts access through the Desktop 1, 2, 3 tabs in addition to the Standard tab. Just click on one of the tabs and add/remove the tools as you see fit.

The Choose Command

There are several ways to insert a variable into the Variable tab on the lower-right column (refer to Figure 19.6). A variable is a regular data field, a parameter, a select option, a field in the header of a database table, or a field inside of an internal table. One way to insert a variable is to manually type the name of the variable. But who wants to do things the long way? The second method is to double-click on the variable in the code. The variable will appear in the next available blank row in the Variable tab. The value stored in the variable displays in the fourth column. You will probably find that double-clicking is the best method. See Figure 19.8.

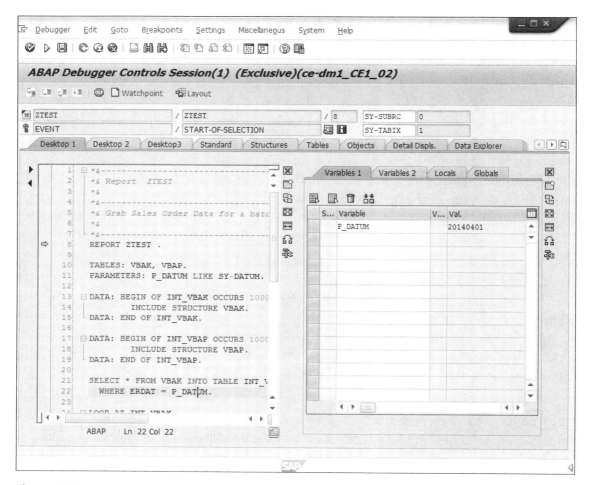

Figure 19.8
If you enter a variable in the second column, the value held in that variable is displayed in the fourth column.

To add a new dimension to the variable display, you can click on a variable in the variable tool. You are transferred to a new screen, which looks like Figure 19.9. This is the display details screen, which will give you more information about a data field. This screen can also be reached by clicking on the Detail Display tab of the debugging screen, but you will need to manually fill in the field name. So double-clicking from the first screen is the most effective way to go.

On this new tab, in addition to the variable's contents, administrative data regarding the variable also displays (for example, length, type, and so on).

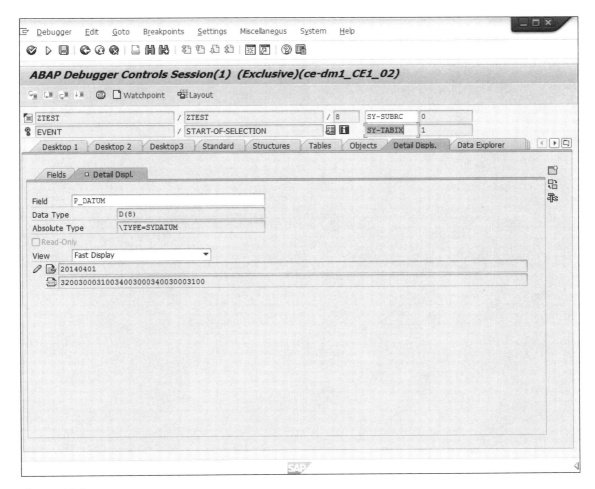

Figure 19.9
The Detail Display tab showing details about a variable.

If you type the name of an internal table in the Variables tool (Figure 19.7), the header record will not display in the fourth column. Instead you will see a message that this is a structure. This display is shown in Figure 19.10.

By double-clicking, you navigate to the Structures view tab, which will allow you to see the contents of the header record for an internal table or structured variable. See Figure 19.11.

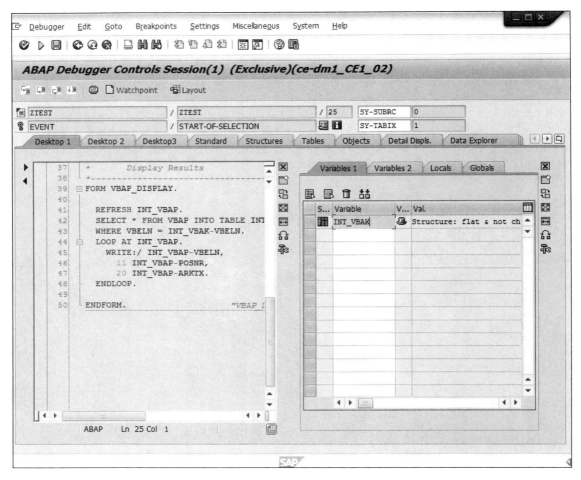

Figure 19.10
Internal table name with header display.

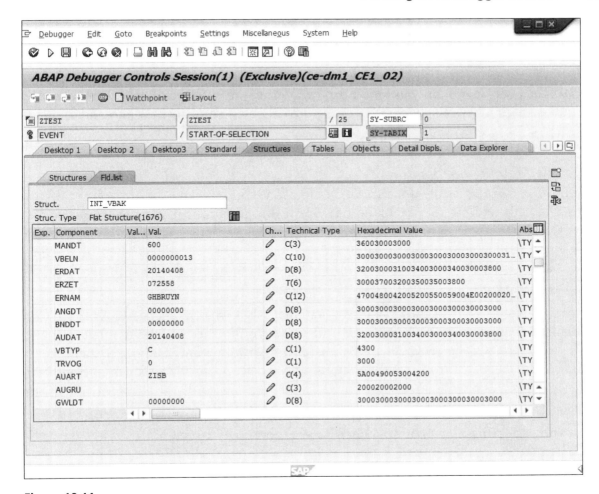

Figure 19.11
The Structures tab for an internal table.

The screen displays the structure view. Each field is named, and the contents of the header display in the fourth column. The type and length of each field display in the sixth column.

This view is a very useful one for structures or internal tables. Despite only displaying one structure, it does have a big advantage over other screens. You can view and edit all fields within the structure from this tab.

The Single Step Command

Right now, you are probably double-clicking like mad, but no values are in your variables. So the challenge is how to execute commands in the program to populate the variables with data. One of the solutions to this challenge is the Single Step command. Enter debug mode and navigate to Figure 19.7 (your initial screen). Notice where the yellow arrow marker is on the left side and press the Single Step button or press the F5 key. Initially, the marker resides next to the REPORT statement.

The marker resides next to the first SELECT statement, but what happened to all those DATA commands? The program declares those and passes you to the first executable command (in this case, the SELECT command). This is an important point. Only executable commands can be stepped through. Declarations such as the definition of a variable with the DATA, PARAMETER, or SELECT-OPTION command happen automatically and do not trigger the debugger to stop.

By pressing the Single Step button once more, the SELECT command executes, and the table INT_VBAK is populated with *X* number of records. You can type one of the INT_VBAK fields into the variable column or double-click on one of them to display the contents of that field. See Figure 19.12.

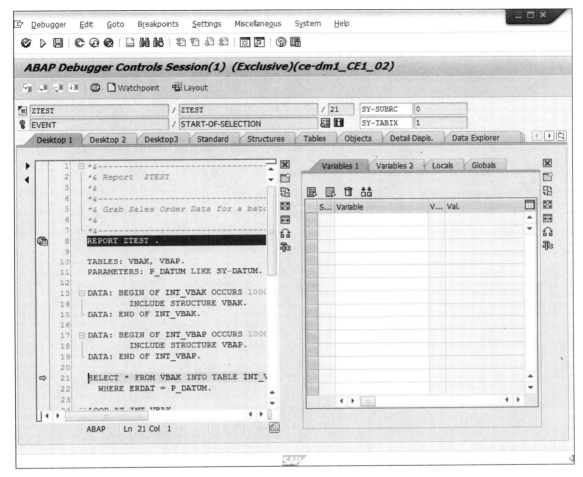

Figure 19.12
Similar to Figure 19.7 but after pressing the Single Step button.

Continue single stepping until you reach the IF statement. The BATCHUSER value is hard-coded into the program. Feel free to change this value. Or, put some debugging knowledge to work. You should be looking at a screen like Figure 19.13.

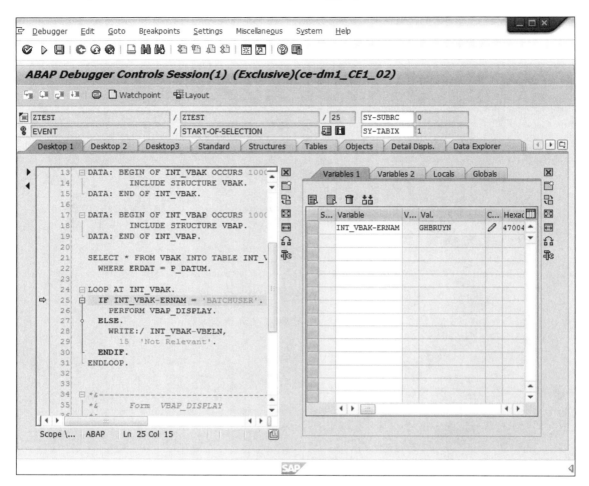

Figure 19.13
Screen showing the value of INT_VBAK-ERNAM as GHBRUYN.

The INT_VBAK-ERNAM field displays in the name column, and the GHBRUYN value displays in the value column. You want to have this logical statement be true, so delete GHBRUYN and type in BATCHUSER. You may need to press the Change button (looks like a pencil) to open the field for editing. You should see a screen like Figure 19.14.

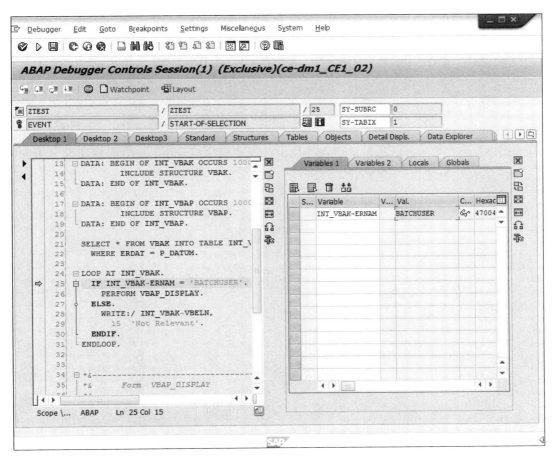

Figure 19.14
The `INT_VBAK-ERNAM` value has now been replaced with the value of `BATCHUSER`.

You have effectively replaced the value of the internal table field with another one. By single stepping, you can navigate to the PERFORM line, which will execute a subroutine. Because you are single stepping through the code, by clicking the Single Step button once more, you will find that you have navigated deeper into the code and down into the subroutine code itself. See Figure 19.15.

This rule holds true when executing outside programs, function calls, screens, or subroutines. Single stepping always takes you into the next piece of code. This fact differentiates the Single Step command from the EXECUTE (F6) button in that EXECUTE performs a call to any sort of subroutine as one single step. You can use EXECUTE with subroutines such as forms, functions, and modules. However, you cannot use EXECUTE with an INCLUDE file because an INCLUDE is not a subroutine. It is simply a way for you to organize your source code into separate code files. EXECUTE and SINGLE STEP act identically when you reach an INCLUDE statement in a program.

The EXECUTE Command

The EXECUTE command is very similar to the Single Step command, but there is one big difference. If you navigate down in the code where the subroutine is called with the PERFORM command and then click the Execute button, you see the difference in results. Whereas Single Step takes you into the subroutine code, the Execute button treats the entire subroutine as one command, and the yellow arrow marker moves from the PERFORM line directly to the next one, the ELSE line. See Figure 19.16.

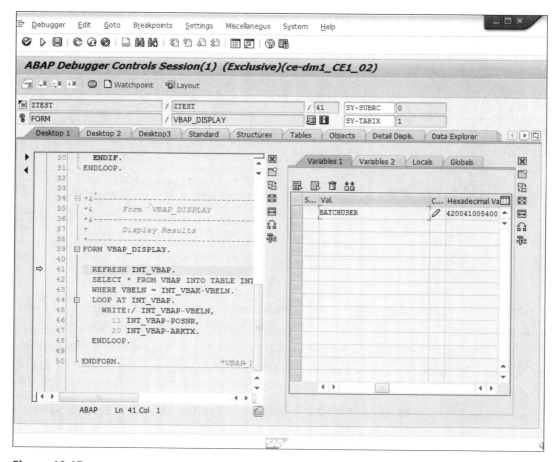

Figure 19.15
The debugger has navigated from the PERFORM statement into the actual subroutine.

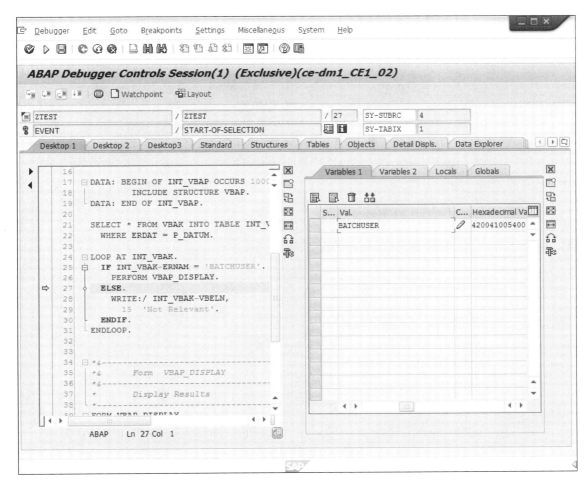

Figure 19.16
Using the EXECUTE button, you do not navigate into the subroutine, but rather proceed to the next step, in this case the ELSE statement.

This functionality is very desirable. For example, if you are 10 layers deep inside SAP code, there is no need for you to single step through this function module, especially if it is in a loop and is repeated several hundred or thousand times. Or if you have a large subroutine that is not relevant to the issue you are attempting to trace, you can skip it by using EXECUTE when you reach the routine instead of single stepping all the way through. The EXECUTE command is very useful in many different situations to bypass code that is not of interest to you.

The Continue Command

The next button is the Continue button. This button releases the program from running step by step to running freely through the code. The benefit is that the program stops if it reaches a manually set breakpoint or a hard-coded breakpoint in the code. To set a manual breakpoint in the code, you have two choices. Either double-click to the left of the line of code, and a stop sign icon appears to left of the code (see Figure 19.17), or click on the line of code at which you want to place a breakpoint and follow the menu path Breakpoints > Create Breakpoint (see Figure 19.18).

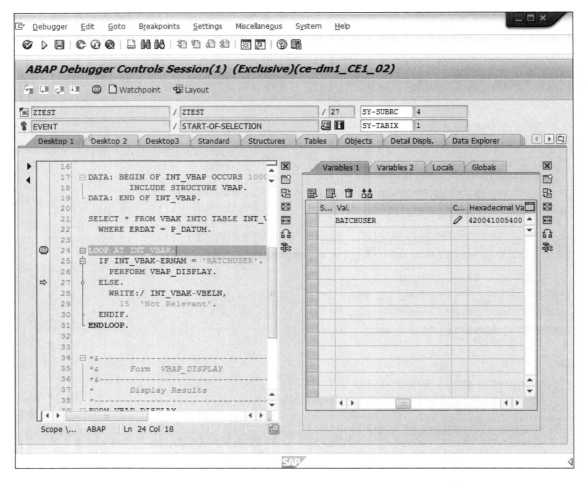

Figure 19.17
If you double-click to the left of a line of code, a stop sign appears, which represents a breakpoint.

Another method is to code a breakpoint into your code. The two commands are:

BREAK-POINT

and

BREAK <username>.

The more desirable of the two choices is the second one. If you are debugging code that is being used by other developers, you do not want them kicked into debug mode while they are running their programs. The second coding method is better because the breakpoint is triggered only if you are the one running the code (assuming the username you enter is your own). So, for example, put a breakpoint inside your code. BREAK <USERNAME> executes a global macro that has a breakpoint command in it, which is only triggered if the user, <USERNAME>, is running the code.

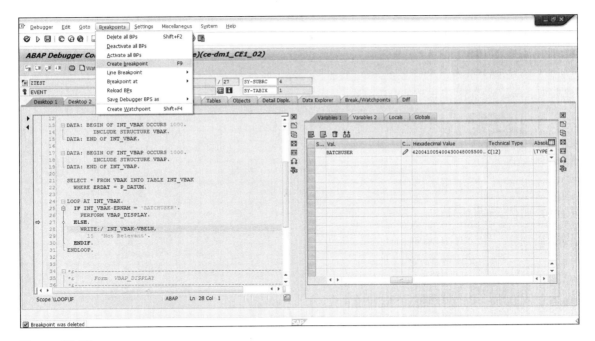

Figure 19.18
Another way to set a breakpoint is by using the Create Breakpoint menu command.

```
*------------------------------------------------------------*
*& Report   ZTEST2
*&
*&-----------------------------------------------------------*
*& Breakpoint Example
*&
*&-----------------------------------------------------------*
REPORT ZTEST2.
TABLES:  VBAK, VBAP.
PARAMETERS:    P_DATUM LIKE SY-DATUM.

DATA:  BEGIN OF INT_VBAK OCCURS 1000.
          INCLUDE STRUCTURE VBAK.
DATA: END OF INT_VBAK.

DATA: BEGIN OF INT_VBAP OCCURS 1000.
          INCLUDE STRUCTURE VBAP.
DATA: END OF INT_VBAP.


SELECT * FROM VBAK INTO TABLE INT_VBAK
  WHERE ERDAT = P_DATUM.

LOOP AT INT_VBAK.
  IF INT_VBAK-ERNAM =  'BATCHUSER'.
    BREAK GHBRUYN.
    PERFORM VBAP_DISPLAY.
  ELSE.
    WRITE:/INT_VBAK-VBELN, 15 'Not Relevant'.
  ENDIF.
ENDLOOP.


*&-----------------------------------------------------------*
*&      Form   VBAP_DISPLAY
*&-----------------------------------------------------------*
*       Display Sales Order Item
*------------------------------------------------------------*
FORM VBAP_DISPLAY.
  REFRESH INT_VBAP.
  SELECT * FROM VBAP INTO TABLE INT_VBAP
    WHERE VBELN = INT_VBAK-VBELN.
```

```
  LOOP AT INT_VBAP.
    WRITE:/ INT_VBAP-VBELN, 11 INT_VBAP-POSNR, 20 INT_VBAP-ARKTX.
  ENDLOOP.
ENDFORM.                      "VBAP_DISPLAY
```

In this example code, the breakpoint is placed into the code after the following line:

```
IF INT_VBAK-ERNAM =    'BATCHUSER'
```

This way, the program can execute in a normal fashion, and the debugging screen appears when a breakpoint is encountered. You will want to replace the name BATCHUSER with your username. When a breakpoint is encountered, either manually set or coded, the program halts at that point. The Continue button allows you to skip parts of code that you do not suspect of having problems. The Continue feature improves your efficiency in debugging programs.

The Return Command

Return is a fairly simple command. Imagine that you are debugging a program and the program calls a subroutine, which in turn calls a function module. You single step through the code and find yourself inside the function module code. By pressing the Return button, the debugger returns you and the yellow arrow to the next higher level point in the code stack (in this case to the point in the subroutine where the function module is called). If you press Return again, the debugger navigates you to the next higher level, which is the main program, and leaves you at the point just after the first subroutine is called. This command is especially helpful when debugging SAP code or transactional code because sometimes you can find yourself many layers deep inside code.

The Primary Screen

As you may have noticed already, when the second window opens with the debugger, the original window remains with the program executing. This can be very helpful as you work through the code because any output the program generates will be displayed in that first screen as normal. If a report is being run or a transaction and a WRITE command are executed, you see the output in regular report format. See Figure 19.19.

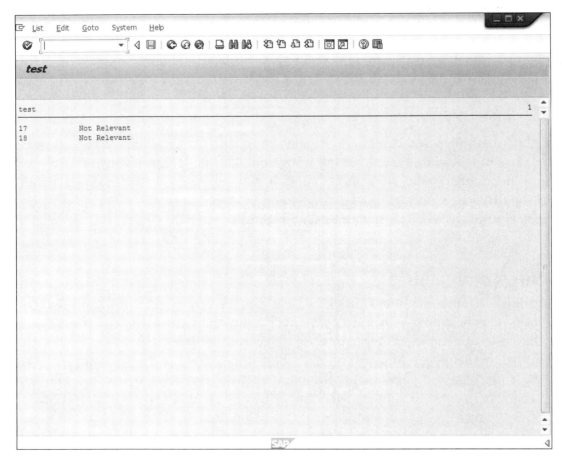

Figure 19.19
Output display shown as you are debugging.

Simply flip between the two windows as necessary to move between the code and the results.

Using Watchpoints

Watchpoints are used to dynamically set breakpoints in your code. If a variable (either the header of an internal table or any field) is marked as a watchpoint, the program halts in debug mode every time the value inside that field changes. For example, your program loops through a series of sales orders, printing the line items for each one. If you want to look for one particular sales order, or perhaps in another program see where a variable changes (on which line), you would put INT_VBAK-VBELN in the Variables tool of the initial debugging screen. See Figure 19.20.

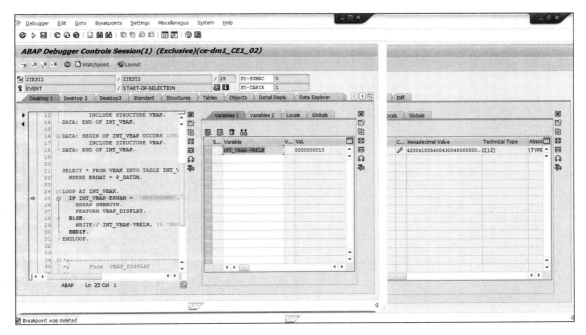

Figure 19.20
The initial debugging screen with the field INT_VBAK-VBELN shown in one of the variable columns.

Select the field with INT_VBAK-VBELN and click on the Watchpoint button at the top of the screen. Click on the green checkmark in the Watchpoint pop-up window and press Enter. See Figure 19.21 for illustration.

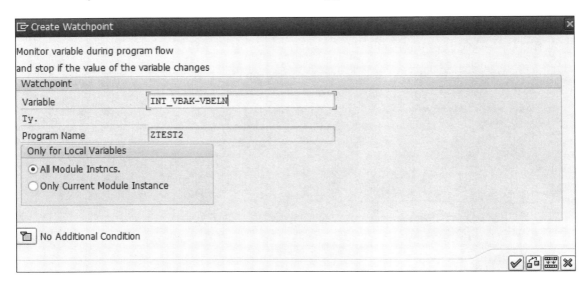

Figure 19.21
The Watchpoint entry window.

Click on the Program button to return to the main screen. Click on the Continue button. The program immediately stops at the line after the LOOP AT INT_VBAK. A message at the bottom of the screen reads "Watchpoint reached." See Figure 19.22.

If you click on the Continue button again, the program stops again at this line; however, the INT_VBAK-VBELN value has changed to the next value in the internal table.

If you forget or want to remove a watchpoint you previously set, you can use the Break/Watchpoint tab to edit all current watchpoints.

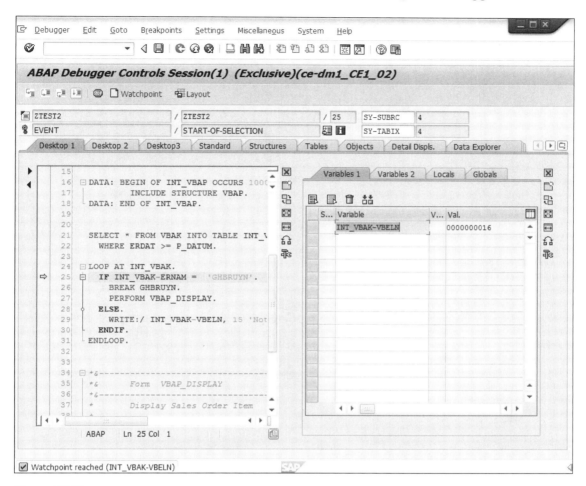

Figure 19.22
When a watchpoint is triggered the program stops at the line where the variable has changed.

Internal Tables

One of the most important tabs is the Table tab. The contents of internal tables can display in this view. To display database table values, you must use the General Table Display. Run your test program once again. This time, set a breakpoint just after the SELECT statement from the database table VBAK. See Figure 19.23.

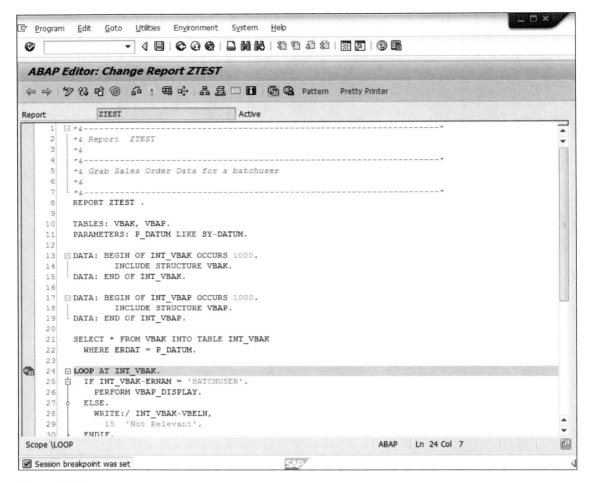

Figure 19.23
A breakpoint has been set just after the SELECT statement in your program.

With the marker right after the SQL statement, you hope that an internal table is populated. If SY-SUBRC displays below the four rows with a value other than zero, there will be no records in your internal table. Try using a different date until you retrieve data. Now that you have data in your internal table, it is time to look at its contents. Click on the Table tab and type INT_VBAK for the name of the internal table and press Return to display its contents.

For large tables you can use the scrollbar to move through the rows of the table and reach the end. You will see the last records in the internal table, as well as the total number of entries in the internal table.

For tables with many fields, you can use the Columns button to choose which columns to add or hide to the display. This allows you to pick the columns that are of interest to you and keep them displayed with additional scrolling left or right. See Figures 19.24 and 19.25.

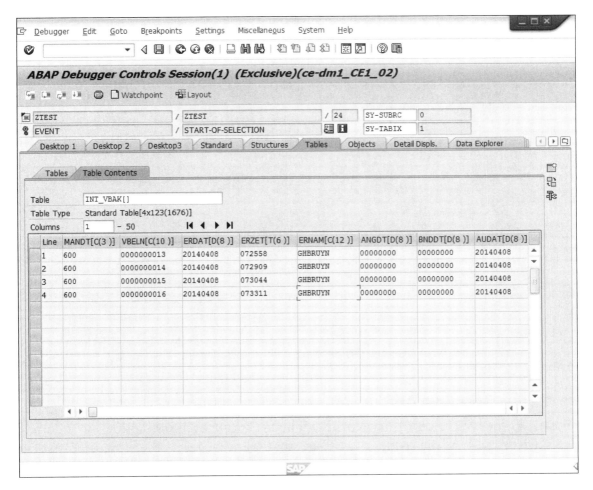

Figure 19.24
The internal table view of the internal table INT_VBAK showing what data it contains.

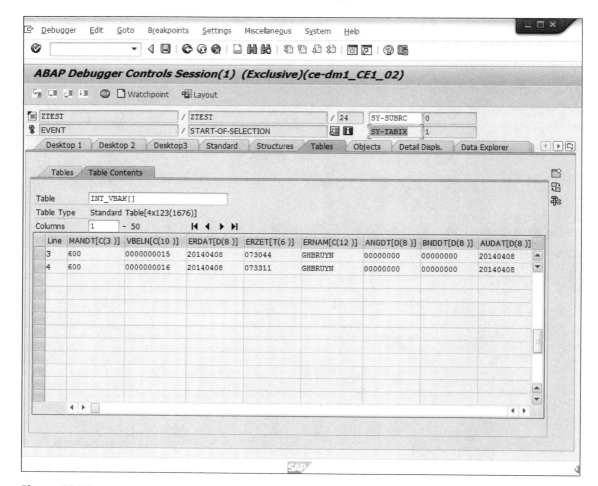

Figure 19.25
By scrolling up and down, you can navigate through the data stored in the internal table.

More About Breakpoints

You already know how to set breakpoints by double-clicking on lines, setting watchpoints, and coding breaks in the code. However, there are a few other methods worth mentioning.

The types of breakpoints that are very useful to you are shown in the expanded drop-down menu in Figure 19.26. A breakpoint is set at the beginning of each of these entities. If the program reaches one of these breakpoints, the program stops at that line. The choices for different types of breakpoints are shown in Figure 19.27.

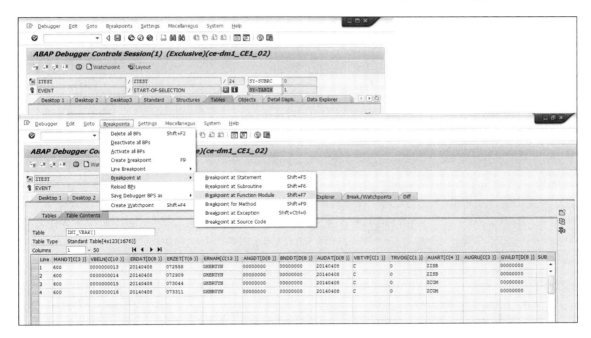

Figure 19.26
Drop-down menu of breakpoints.

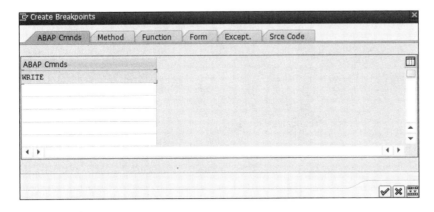

Figure 19.27
Breakpoint pop-up screen.

Here are the key ones:

- Form—Pick a form, a function module, or a method that is inside the program and stop automatically when a call to that subroutine is encountered. See Figure 19.28.

- Function—Pick a function call that is inside the program and stop automatically when a call to that subroutine is encountered.

- Method—Pick a method that is inside the program and stop automatically when a call to that subroutine is encountered.

- ABAP Cmnds—Set a breakpoint at an ABAP keyword. A keyword is any ABAP command. See Figure 19.29. If you enter any ABAP command, a breakpoint is set at every instance of that command inside your program or in any subsequent programs your program calls. When the program encounters the breakpoint, it stops in debug mode at that line.

In addition, you can also use a watchpoint on system fields like SY-SUBRC. This allows you to stop when a non-zero return code is generated or when a table index exceeds a certain amount.

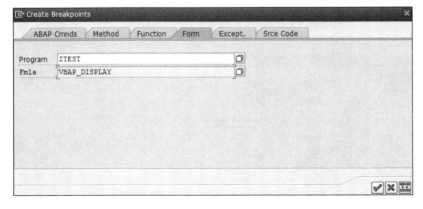

Figure 19.28
Pop-up box to enter form name.

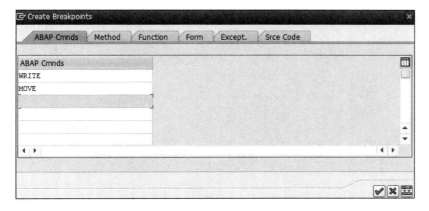

Figure 19.29
Pop-up box to enter ABAP keywords.

TIPS AND TECHNIQUES FOR DEBUGGING

Just as with anything you do in life, learning the parts does not always make you an expert on the whole. You must learn how to easily navigate through programs and quickly find the source of errors. There is no secret in this section to tell you how to do this except the old adage, "Practice makes perfect." Keep debugging and you will get more and more efficient at the process. This section contains some helpful tips.

Do not debug inside an open SELECT statement because you may get an ABAP short dump with some types of databases. While the database cursor is open (a SELECT statement has not retrieved all of its records from the database), debugging may not be permitted. Instead, set a breakpoint after the ENDSELECT statement and let the program run its course until it arrives at the breakpoint.

Set breakpoints at certain safety points: for example, in case you happen to click the Continue button instead of the Single Step button, and you don't want your program to finish. Try to set breakpoints at strategic points in your code where they will stop you just before crucial steps in your code. Use this technique especially when you are updating the database in any way.

If you have worked with SAP for a while, you probably noticed that certain programs run differently in background mode than in foreground mode. Foreground is typically defined as executing the program from the ABAP editor. Background mode can also be triggered from the editor, or it can be started from the job monitoring screen. If you execute a program in background mode, you can still debug the program from the job monitoring screen (see Figure 19.30).

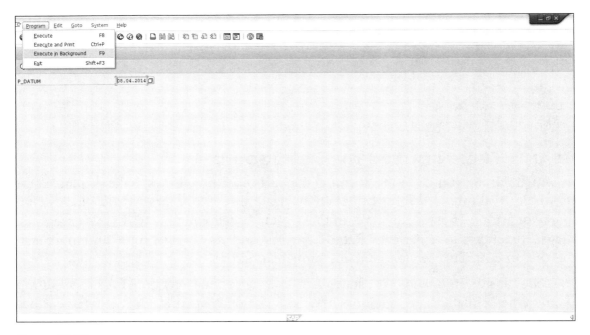

Figure 19.30
Path to execute in background mode.

Navigate to the job monitoring screen, which displays all background programs that are running. Follow the menu path from any SAP screen, System > Services > Jobs > Job Overview. You will reach the initial job overview screen. See Figure 19.31.

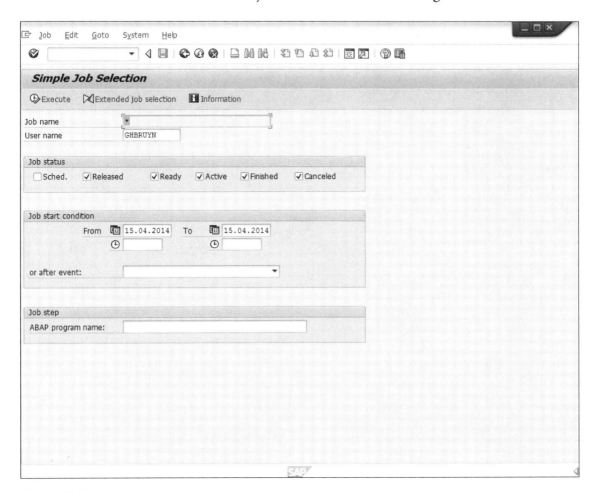

Figure 19.31
Initial job overview screen.

Enter the name of your program in the Job Name text box, replacing the *. Press Return. You reach a screen showing your program and its status. See Figure 19.32.

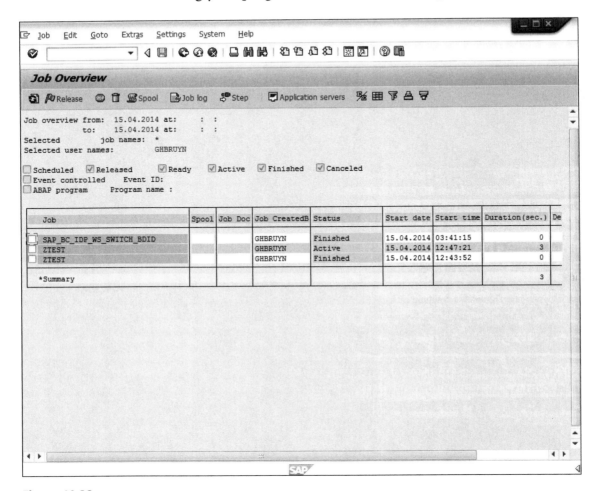

Figure 19.32
Screen showing the program as ACTIVE in background mode.

If the program is still active, click on it once, and then follow the menu path Job > Capture. See Figure 19.33.

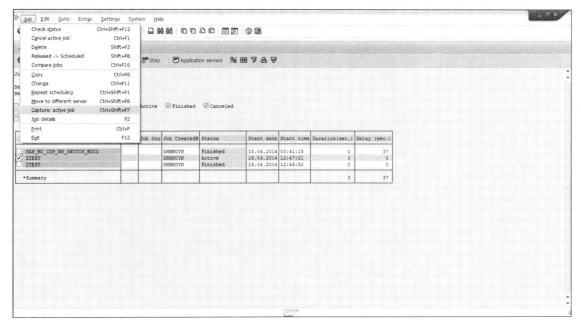

Figure 19.33
To debug a program running in background mode, follow the menu path and select Capture.

Be patient and wait a few seconds. A new screen will appear that looks exactly like the debugging screen you were working with. From then on, use all the techniques that were mentioned to debug the program as usual. To make the screen disappear and to get the program to continue, clear all breakpoints and click on Continue. You may not always be able to capture an active job. There are times—such as when a program is accessing the database or performing some internal SAP functions—when the capture will fail.

For fast and efficient debugging, you can use a combination of setting watchpoints on variables and setting breakpoints at keywords. Using these two features in conjunction proves to be very effective.

Caution

Be very careful about debugging in a production environment. If you debug a transaction and stop the debug halfway through, some records may be updated, and some may not.

Summary

The debugger is the second most important tool in the ABAP workbench. The first is, of course, the actual editor. This chapter covered how to navigate around the debugger tool, as well as the functionality of each of its parts. Knowing your way around the debugger and the functionality of each view and button is very important. The debugging tool in SAP is a very simple one, and if you work through it step by step, it will not be intimidating. Try to use each part, one at a time, before you tackle a complex debugging project.

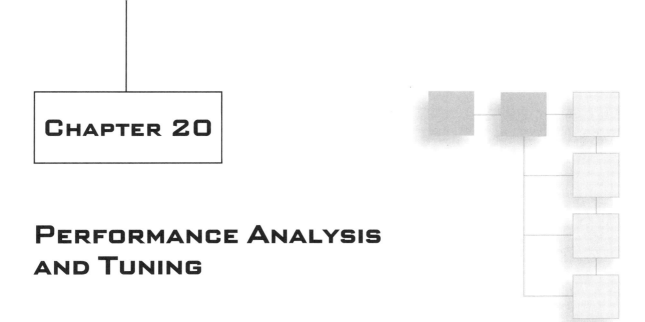

CHAPTER 20

PERFORMANCE ANALYSIS AND TUNING

IN THIS CHAPTER

- Using SELECT *
- Using the Primary Key
- Using CHECK Statements
- Using Tables
- Using the MOVE Statement
- Looping
- Choosing Internal Tables versus Field Groups
- Working with Logical Databases
- Using Batching versus Online Programs

Performance tuning is the task to which most of the senior ABAP programmers will be assigned. Essentially, this task is defined as making current code faster. This chapter highlights some methods by which you, as a new programmer, can accomplish this task in your own code. Whereas you might not be assigned performance-tuning tasks for some time, by following a few tips from this chapter you can gain a reputation for having clean, efficient code that doesn't need to be performance tuned.

SAP has graciously provided a list of performance tips for the programmer. Besides the tips listed in this chapter, it is an excellent resource from which to learn good programming skills. Follow the menu path System > Utilities > Runtime Analysis from any screen in SAP. A new screen will appear, which looks like Figure 20.1.

Click on any of the green hands and you will be hyperlinked to the supporting documentation that explains each tip.

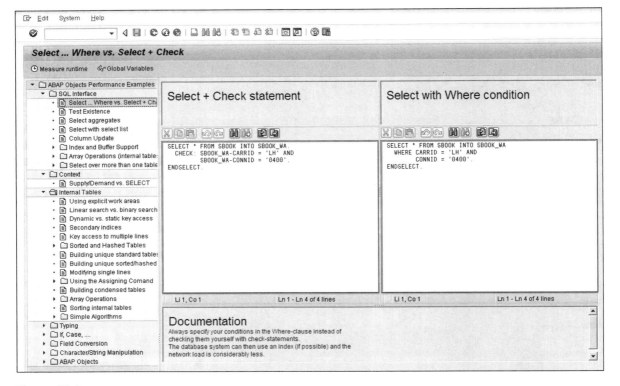

Figure 20.1
The "tips and tricks" screen in SAP contains helpful tips to make you a better programmer.

USING SELECT *

The most notorious problem in most ABAP/4 programs exists with the use of the SELECT * statement, which extracts data from database tables. If the search is done improperly, the program can take hours upon hours to finish; however, if the same program is written efficiently, it can take just minutes.

If you refer to Chapter 8, "Using SAP SQL to Access Database Tables," you will find new ABAP/4 functionality on how to write a JOIN statement in ABAP/4. If you are reading from multiple tables, make sure you learn how to use this statement effectively.

The first step is to choose the proper order by which you read the tables. Some tables exist in partnership with each other. There are header tables that contain the summary data for a particular part, while another table contains the line-item-level detail for that part.

Tip

Read the header table first and then the line-item table. If you need to read a certain table several times in a program, try to incorporate all those reads into one read so that you "hit" the database table only once, or at least a minimal number of times.

USING THE PRIMARY KEY

If you can fill in the primary key of the database table that you're searching, the read on the table will be faster. If you fill in the entire key, a SELECT SINGLE * statement is possible, which is a direct read on the database. The more of the primary key you use, the faster the read is on that table. If you use fields other than the keyed ones or very few of the keyed fields, the read is a sequential read, which is very slow. The primary key is described in Chapter 7, "Working with the Data Dictionary." You will want to go to the Data Dictionary and view the characteristics of the table. If the primary key cannot be used, there are multiple secondary keys that can. If your selection criteria does not fit within any of the keys, speak to your BASIS administrator about possibly creating a key for you!

Tip

Use as much of the primary key as possible when making your reads on database tables.

USING CHECK STATEMENTS

Try not to use CHECK statements unless they can't be incorporated into SELECT statements. By incorporating the restriction into the SELECT statement, fewer records are retrieved from the database, and fewer loops are processed through the SELECT and ENDSELECT statements.

Tip

Avoid using CHECK statements.

USING TABLES

If you receive specifications from your functional analyst detailing which tables you must read in order to obtain the appropriate data, don't take this information at face value. Check to see whether any of the tables referenced are long tables, cluster tables, or problematic tables that you prefer to avoid. Then use the information system in the Data Dictionary to try to find a table with the same data that doesn't present a performance problem to your program.

The following sections provide specific suggestions on when to use which kind of table.

Cluster Tables versus Transparent Tables

Reads on cluster tables, in our experience, must be done via the primary key. If any fields outside the primary key are used, the program will take forever to finish. A big culprit of many time-consuming programs in pre-3.1 SAP is the table VBFA (document flow), which is used primarily with the SD (sales and distribution) module of SAP. Access to this table using a SELECT * command requires the use of the primary key. Preferably, use as much of the primary key as possible to utilize the primary index for a faster read. Before 3.1, the document flow table was a cluster table. Now in 3.1 the table has been converted to a transparent one. The primary key must be used with cluster tables. This is a rule when dealing with cluster tables.

Transparent tables are relatively easy to access. The read can utilize any fields to extract the data from the database. The primary key is preferable, but other fields can be used as well. If the table is relatively large (many records), talk to your BASIS administrator about setting up an index for this table if you are using fields outside of the primary key.

A general rule of thumb with SAP is that data doesn't exist in one place only. If the table you want to read is a problematic—one that might tie up system resources—use the information system of the Data Dictionary to find other tables that are smaller or transparent and have the same data fields populated.

Avoid Tables with Many Records

Searching through tables with a great number of records is a burden to the system, both at the database and application server level. The one rule of the SAP R/3 environment is that data exists on multiple tables. This rule must be acknowledged, especially by seasoned mainframe programmers who are used to finding data in only one place.

The reason behind this emphatic tirade is that many programs that run slowly do so because they access the main tables with the greatest number of records. Typical tables include BSEG (accounting detail), MSEG (material master detail), text tables, and history logging tables. Most of the relevant data found in BSEG is also found in the BSIS table. Most of the data found in MSEG can be found in the MARC and MARD views. Ask your BASIS (system) consultant which tables are currently the largest or if any of the tables you plan to use are lengthy. Then use the information system to search for the same data elements from the lengthy table in other, smaller tables. As you gain more experience with SAP and your system, you'll learn which are the problem or large tables, just from dealing with them on a regular basis.

Selecting into Tables

The fastest possible read from a database table and copy procedure into an internal table is the version of SELECT * that reads the data it finds directly into the internal table:

```
SELECT * FROM dbtab INTO TABLE internal table
  WHERE condition clauses.
```

The database copies the records that match the WHERE clause into the internal table and adds them to the internal table directly. The entire process is one step, rather than the several steps required if you used the regular SELECT * statement along with some APPEND and CLEAR commands. If you compare the SELECT * ... INTO TABLE code with the following code, you'll see that the first set of code only takes one step, whereas the second set has five steps:

```
SELECT * FROM dbtab WHERE condition clauses.
MOVE dbtab TO internal table.
APPEND internal table.
CLEAR internal table.
ENDSELECT.
```

So the time you save in terms of steps is obvious.

USING THE MOVE STATEMENT

Every time you make the application server "think," you burn extra CPU time. The MOVE-CORRESPONDING command makes the application server think about where it needs to put the data that you're moving. MOVE-CORRESPONDING is a very convenient command, but a faster method of moving data to fields is using multiple MOVE statements. For example, if your program used the MOVE-CORRESPONDING statement in the following manner, it could be optimized by replacing it with individual MOVE statements:

```
TABLES:   BKPF,  MSEC,   KNA1.
PARAMETERS:  P_YEAR          LIKE BKPF-GJAHR,
P_MATNR       LIKE MSEG-MATNR, P_COMPANY    LIKE BKPF-BUKR.
DATA:    BEGIN OF DEMO_TABLE OCCURS 1000,
YEAR    LIKE BKPF-GJAHR,
MATNR   LIKE MSEG-MATNR,
```

```
COMPANY LIKE BKPF-BUKRS,
CITY    LIKE KNA1-ORT01. DATA:    END OF DEMO_TABLE.
SELECT * FROM BKPF WHERE GJAHR = P_YEAR AND
BUKRS = P_COMPANY.
MOVE-CORRESPONDING BKPF TO DEMO_TABLE.
SELECT * FROM MSEG UP TO 1 ROWS
WHERE MATNR = P_MATNR. MOVE-CORRESPONDING MSEG INTO DEMOJTABLE.
ENDSELECT.
SELECT * FROM KNA1 UP TO 1 ROWS
WHERE KUNNR = mseg-KUNNR. MOVE-CORRESPONDING KNA1 TO DEMOJTABLE.
ENDSELECT.
APPEND DEMO_TABLE.
CLEAR DEMO_TABLE.
ENDSELECT.
```

All of these MOVE-CORRESPONDING statements can be replaced by individual MOVE statements. The code change would be as follows:

```
PARAMETERS: P_YEAR LIKE BKPF-GJAHR, P_MATNR LIKE MSEG-MATNR,
       P COMPANY LIKE BKPF-BUKRS.
DATA:    BEGIN OF DEMOJTABLE OCCURS 1000,
YEAR    LIKE BKPF-GJAHR,
MATNR   LIKE MSEG-MATNR,
COMPANY LIKE BKPF-BUKRS,
CITY    LIKE KNA1-ORT1. DATA:    END OF DEMOJABLE.
SELECT * FROM BKPF WHERE GJAHR = P_YEAR ANDBUKRS = P_COMPANY.
  MOVE BKPF-GJAHR INTO DEMO_TABLE-YEAR.
  MOVE BKPF-BUKRS INTO DEMO_TABLE-COMPANY.
SELECT * FROM MSEG UP TO 1    ROWS

WHERE MATNR = P_MATNR. MOVE MSEG-MATNR   INTO DEMO_TABLE-MATNR.
ENDSELECT.
  SELECT * FROM KNA1 UP TO   1 ROWS
WHERE KUNNR = BKPF-KUNNR.
MOVE KNA1-ORT1   TO DEMO_TABLE-ORT1.
ENDSELECT.
APPEND DEMO_TABLE.
CLEAR DEMO_TABLE.
ENDSELECT.
```

The new code moves the data from the database table fields directly into the internal table fields, rather than comparing every field of the database table against every field of the internal table. Keep in mind that, despite the fact that typing the extra code is tedious, the performance enhancement to your program is important enough to do it.

Tip

Avoid using `MOVE-CORRESPONDING`.

LOOPING

In SAP, many records are read and processed, which implies that much data must be looped through in order to process the data. The commands to loop through this data must be used correctly; otherwise, valuable processor time can be wasted.

If your program is reading through only one or two tables, try to incorporate the processing inside the nested `SELECT *` commands. If three or more tables are accessed, move the data to an internal table that will be processed after all the data is read from the database tables.

If the internal table method is used, you must use the correct commands to loop through the internal table or process any other set of data that must be looped through. The `WHILE`, `DO`, and `LOOP` commands are used in this case. The following three sections review the positives and negatives of each. It's essential that you understand the subtle differences between these commands and when to use one rather than the other.

Using WHILE

The `WHILE` loop contains a logical expression along with the `WHILE` command. All commands included between `WHILE` and `ENDWHILE` are executed as long as that logical expression remains true. It's also possible to put an `EXIT` command inside a `WHILE` loop, but it's preferable to make the `EXIT` part of the logical expression.

If you can define a logical expression to process your data, use the `WHILE` command. The `WHILE` command exits at the first line of the loop, whereas a `DO` or `LOOP` command processes several lines further before "realizing" that it's time to end the loop.

Tip

If you can define a logical expression to process your data, use `WHILE` instead of `DO` or `LOOP`.

Using DO

The DO loop is used when the number of loop passes is known, or when an EXIT or STOP command is part of the commands in order to prevent an endless loop. DO loops are used most of all when reading flat files from the application server. Flat files contain an unknown number of records most of the time, so the DO loop continues endlessly. To exit at an appropriate time, an IF statement is incorporated after the READ DATASET statement to check the status of SY-SUBRC. If the value is not 0, the program exits the loop and assumes that the file has been completely read into the internal table.

Using LOOP

The LOOP command is used to loop through internal tables to read the data line by line automatically. The LOOP command can also be used in the context of LOOP AT internal table WHERE logical expression. By utilizing the LOOP command in this context, you can loop through only certain records of internal table—those in which your selection criteria are met.

For a review on looping, see Chapter 5, "Using the Looping Commands." As you code more and more programs, you'll learn by experience which is the best LOOP command to use in which situations.

CHOOSING INTERNAL TABLES VERSUS FIELD GROUPS

The number of records allocated to an internal table is a number that at minimum is zero and at maximum is a parameter set by your system administrators. A general rule is that in your entire program you shouldn't have more than 100,000 records allocated to internal tables. This number defines how much memory will be allocated from the system to your application. Don't just pick a random number out of the air and give that number to your internal table.

If the amount of memory you allocate is too large, the program will fail to initiate and won't run. If the number you pick is too small, each record appended to the table after that number is stored in the paging area of memory. This memory area is slower to respond than the allotted memory claimed by your program. So the consequences of underestimating the number of records is a performance issue with your program.

However, it's better to choose a number that's too small than a number that's too large. If the number is too small, the program runs a little slower. If the number is too large, the program won't run, and it impedes the performance of other applications running on the system.

Tip

Remember, it's better to pick a record number size that's too small than one that's too big. The program with the smaller number will run, but the program with too much memory allocated to it will fail. The extra records will be stored in the paging area, rather than in the memory allocated to the internal table.

A good way to estimate the number of records that will be stored in the internal table is to ask the functional analyst who is working with you in developing the specifications for the program. Remember, programming in SAP is a team effort. Utilize the resources you have at hand, which most importantly are composed of the human talent all around you.

Another way to estimate is to write the program and find out how many records are generally extracted from the database. Then go back into the code and adjust the number of records to reflect an accurate number. This last suggestion is tougher to do, as most development environments don't have a good data copy of the current production system. Talk to your system administrator to find out the current status of the system.

If you define an internal table as having no records, all of the records appended to it will be stored in the paging area of memory. As mentioned in Chapter 10, "Advanced Data Outputs," the field groups are all written to the paging area as well. The difference in access time between an internal table with an OCCURS statement of 0 and field groups should be zero. However, field groups are much more efficient in their storage handling. The data is compressed and can be stored much more efficiently than internal table records.

Tip

If the number of records you will extract from the database is large, try to use field groups instead of internal tables. By avoiding internal tables, you free memory for other applications running at the same time.

WORKING WITH LOGICAL DATABASES

Logical databases are a good idea if you utilize them to view which tables you should read and in what order. If you actually want to use a logical database and the GET command, make sure that the user knows to fill in as much data as possible in the selection screen provided with that database. If only one field is filled in (or only a few), the program takes a long time to retrieve the data the user wants to view or analyze. If all the fields are filled in (of course, this is very rare), the data return is very fast, and the hit on the system is very low.

Reading Specific Tables

At the logical database screen (review Chapter 13, "Working with Logical Databases"), click the option button for the structure of the logical database and display it. SAP has set up the database to read the data from the top level down. Rather than hitting all the tables that SAP will hit automatically if you use the logical database, you can type code directly into your ABAP Editor. Specify that you read from only the tables you want, and then read them in the same order as SAP suggests from the viewed structure.

Optimizing with Obligatory Fields

One way to make sure that the users fill in a required number of fields is to do a check at the beginning of the program to see whether any of the fields are still initial. If certain fields are initial, give the users an error message, saying that they must enter data in those fields before the program will execute.

Using Batching versus Online Programs

If your online program will run for more than 15 minutes, run it in background mode instead. It will have to be a scheduled program that your administrator sets up, but at least it won't time out after 15 minutes of run time. Fifteen minutes is the limit for an online program to run without the system automatically canceling it.

If you feel that one of your programs will hinder the system if it's run in online mode, do a check at the beginning of the program to make sure that batch mode is turned on (the program is being run in the background). Otherwise, send an error message saying that this program can be run only in background mode:

```
REPORT ZABAP.
IF SY-BATCH <>    '    '.
MESSAGE E999 WITH 'PROGRAM ONLY TO BE RUN IN BACKGROUND MODE'.
ENDIF.
```

Summary

This chapter highlighted some useful tricks of the trade for speeding up your code. After reviewing this chapter, you should have a pretty good idea of how to improve the performance of your current code and how to write better code in the future. In Chapter 21, we move on to covering web services.

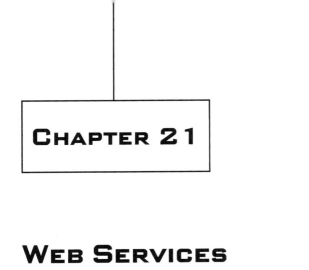

CHAPTER 21

WEB SERVICES

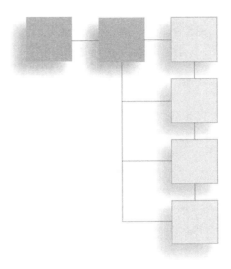

IN THIS CHAPTER

- Creating and Publishing a Web Service in SAP
- Creating a SOAP Web Service
- Creating a REST Web Service

CREATING AND PUBLISHING A WEB SERVICE IN SAP

One topic we wanted to cover was creating web services out of SAP. SAP allows RFCs (remote function calls) and BAPIs to be published as web services. They can be published as SOAP web services and REST web services.

The creation of SOAP web services is a bit simpler of a process. SOAP is typically used in A2A (application to application) and B2B (business to business) scenarios. SOAP messages are formatted in XML and sent via HTTP. The data sent are messages. Creation of SOAP web services is supported by the standard ABAP Workbench in SAP. Publishing them requires configuring and setting up the service library in SOAMANAGER.

The creation of REST web services is of medium complexity and also can be done in SAP. However, to create REST web services in SAP, you need to install an ABAP add-on called SAP NetWeaver Gateway. REST web services created in SAP support the JSON and ODATA formats. The rule of thumb is that for mobility and any user facing solution, REST web services are the right way to go. REST web services are less rigid and more lightweight than SOAP. They are easier to use by a third party who has no knowledge of the internal SAP system. These web services are created via the Service Builder transaction, SEGW, in SAP.

Creating a SOAP Web Service

Creating a SOAP web service could not be easier in SAP. There is a wizard that is set up that converts any remote function module or BAPI into a web service. We assume that you can create a remote function call on your own. Simply put, a remote function call is a function module that has the RFC flag checked in its settings. There is a little more than that—as you have to set up security and a user to access that RFC—but it is not necessary for web service creation. A BAPI can be created in the same process as an RFC, or it can be created from the BAPI Explorer (transaction BAPI). For the BAPI transaction, the first menu path you would use would be Tools > Create Web Service. Then you click the Start Wizard button, as shown in Figure 21.1.

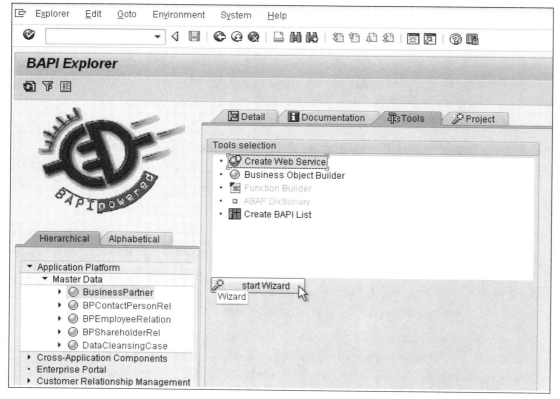

Figure 21.1
Creating a web service from a BAPI transaction.

Here, you'll see how to build a web service from the Function Builder screen:

1. Enter the transaction se37 to navigate to the Function Builder screen, as shown in Figure 21.2.

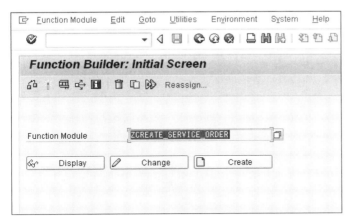

Figure 21.2
Creating a web service from se37.

2. Choose a function module and display or change it.

3. Navigate via the top menu to Utilities > More Utilities > Create Web Service > From the Function Module or From the Function Group (see Figure 21.3).

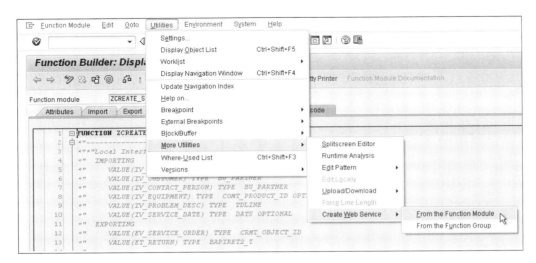

Figure 21.3
Starting the Web Service wizard.

4. Now just perform the steps in the wizard. First, enter the web service name and description and click Continue (see Figure 21.4).

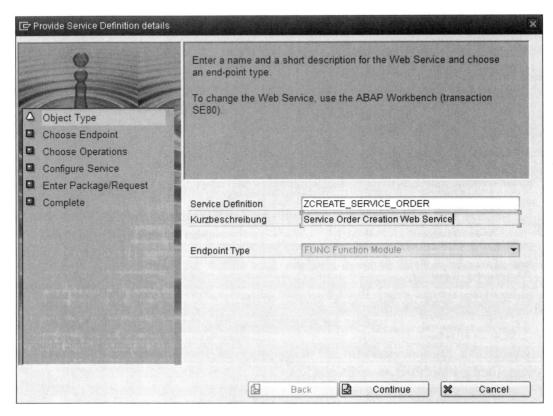

Figure 21.4
Providing a service definition.

The function module name should already be populated, as you can see in Figure 21.5. Click on Continue.

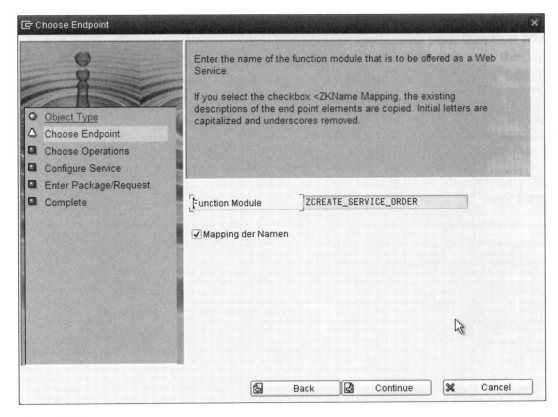

Figure 21.5
Function module to convert.

Next, you determine which profile to use. See Figure 21.6. For now, just use the default, which is the LOW security (user/password). Click on Continue.

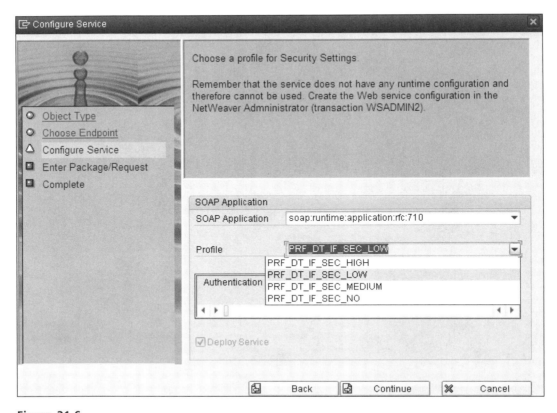

Figure 21.6
Authentication and security.

Next, as shown in Figure 21.7, you enter a development class and a correction. Do not set it as local object if you want to use the web service. Click on Continue and then Complete.

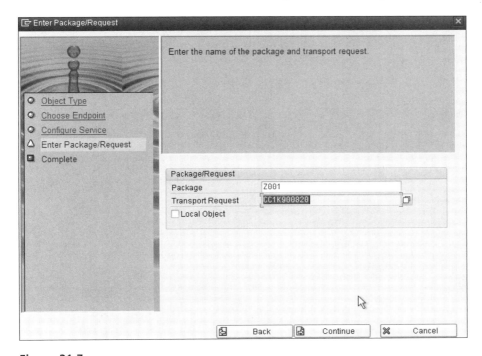

Figure 21.7
Function module to convert.

The last step, but most the important, is to save and activate it.

5. Now you need to call the transaction SOAMANAGER to access the WSDL. Type in the transaction, and a web page will open with SOAMANAGER. See Figure 21.8.

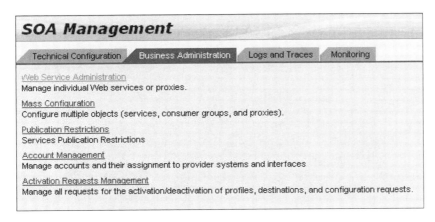

Figure 21.8
The SOAMANAGER screen.

6. Choose Web Service Administration. On the following screen, search for your service name (it's named the same as the function module). When you find it, click on Apply Selection. On the Overview tab of the service definition screen, you'll see links to open the WSDL document, as shown in Figure 21.9.

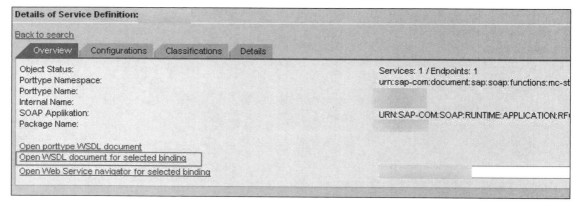

Figure 21.9
Overview tab of the service definition screen.

CREATING A REST WEB SERVICE

As mentioned, NetWeaver Gateway must be installed on your system to create a REST web service. It is possible to create the web service manually via se80; however, SAP provides some nice tools to make creation much easier. The first step is to call transaction SEGW, the Service Builder. If NetWeaver Gateway has not been installed, this transaction will not be available to you.

SAP provides a nice walkthrough of the Service Builder in the following link: http://help. sap.com/saphelp_gateway20sp05/helpdata/en/cb/5dc700314e4e27be92de2d7065ce8e/ content.htm.

SUMMARY

Web services are commonplace in the app and web world. In the enterprise world, they are relatively new to SAP, but they are an important part of how developers integrate with external applications. That's why it's important that you know how to create and publish a web service in SAP.

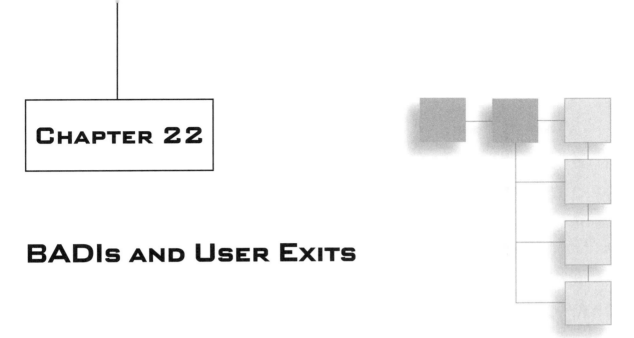

CHAPTER 22

BADIs and User Exits

IN THIS CHAPTER

- Understanding BADIs
- Finding BADIs
- Learning About Useful BADIs
- Understanding User Exits

This chapter defines the concept of using business add-ins (called BADIs) as enhancements. It further explores the use of BADIs, including how can they be implemented and some useful examples. It also discusses how to find relevant BADIs for use and how they differ from User Exits.

UNDERSTANDING BADIs

BADIs are a SAP technique of implementing standard enhancements. These are basically used to accommodate user enhancements that are too specific to be included in the general functionality. SAP does this by inserting them at predefined points in the software. These enhancements can include changing existing data of an object, adding new fields to an order, and raising error messages and exceptions. BADI objects are based on the concept of object oriented planning. A BADI is comprised of the following:

■ Business add-in definition

■ Business add-in interface

■ Business add-in class that implements the interface

Basically each implementation is a class and has methods that can be executed to execute specific functionality. In order to search for different business add-ins, open transaction code se18 (see Figure 22.1).

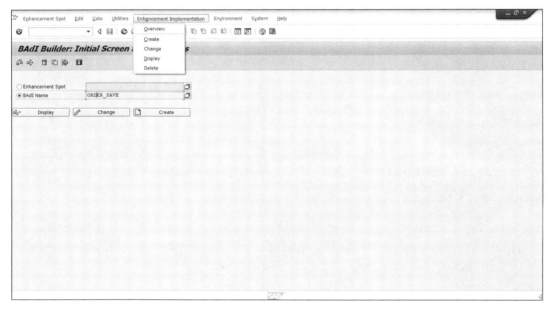

Figure 22.1
se18 transaction code.

From this screen, once you have entered the BADI name, you can click on the Enhancement Implementation menu option. These are different options for existing implementations, to create a new implementation, and to change existing ones. You can also display or delete an existing implementation. To search for an existing implementation, just click on Overview, and you will be directed to existing implementations for a BADI. From there, you can see that there are multiple implementations for an existing object. This is particularly useful, since you might need to implement different functionality, depending upon various conditions.

Using Filters

An important attribute of a BADI is whether to use a filter in the BADI definition. This is useful in making the implementation filter dependent. Instead of having multiple implementations of a single BADI, you can have a single implementation and define various filters. For example, this could be based on country code, postal code of the customer, or status of an order. Figure 22.2 shows an example of BADI that's used for actions and is of importance to developers.

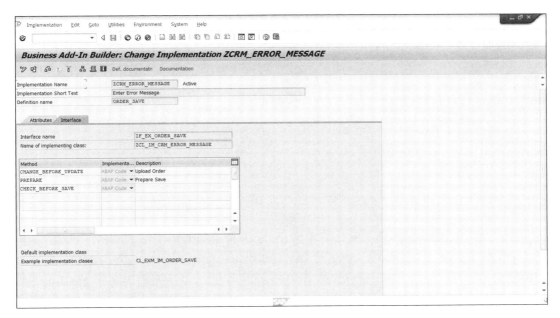

Figure 22.2
BADI definition.

You can see a check box for multiple implementations. Certain BADIs have this checked, and there is an option not to select this check box. It simply means a BADI can have more than one implementation if the Multiple check box is marked.

Creating a BADI Implementation

To create a new implementation, click on the Create option. A new dialog box will open in which you are required to enter the name. Once you enter an implementation name, you will also be required to enter a short description and then save it to a package. This consists of the BADI definition. Once you create the implementation, the interface name and implementation class are automatically created. The various methods included in the BADI interface can be seen in Figure 22.3.

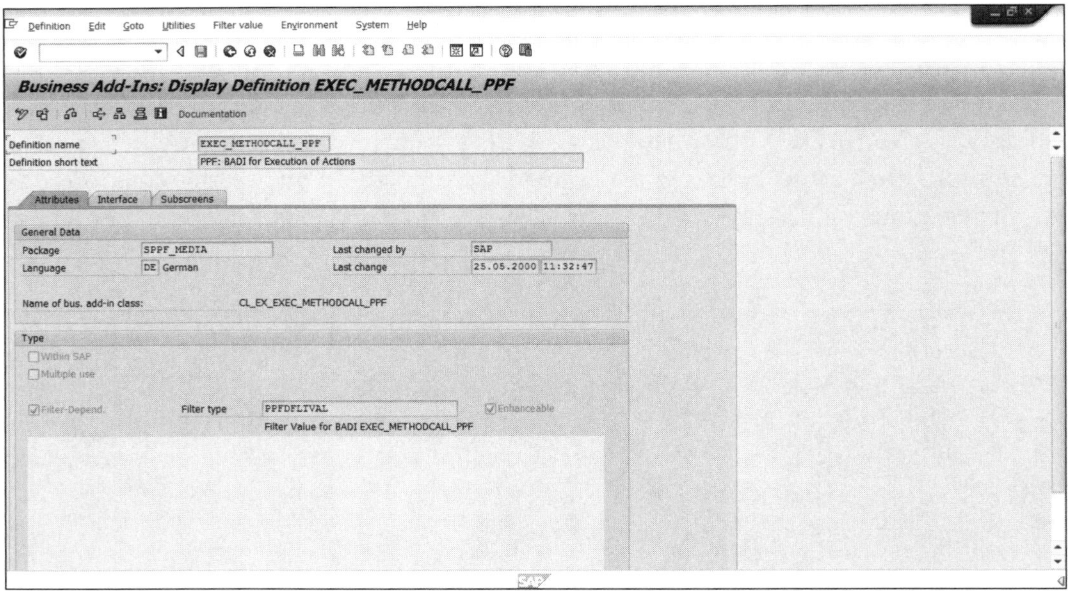

Figure 22.3
A BADI interface.

These methods vary, depending on the BADI name entered. When you're using class variables and static methods, you must declare the corresponding class in the method. You can open the implementation class and edit the various methods according to your specification, or you can directly edit them from this screen. The following sample code throws an exception message if an order does not have an external reference number.

```
method IF_EX_ORDER_SAVE~CHECK_BEFORE_SAVE.
    data:   lt_header_guid TYPE CRMT_OBJECT_GUID_TAB,
            lt_sales   TYPE CRMT_SALES_WRKT,
            ls_sales TYPE CRMT_SALES_WRK,
            lv_process_type type crmt_process_type_db,
            lt_requested_objects type CRMT_OBJECT_NAME_TAB,
            ls_requested_objects type CRMT_OBJECT_NAME,
            lv_item TYPE STRING,
            lv_message TYPE STRING.

    select single process_type from crmd_orderadm_h
      into lv_process_type
      where guid = iv_guid.

    check lv_process_type eq 'ZSVO'.
```

```
    insert iv_guid into table lt_HEADER_GUID.
    ls_requested_objects = 'SALES'.
    insert ls_requested_objects into table lt_requested_objects.

  CALL FUNCTION 'CRM_ORDER_READ'
    EXPORTING
      IT_HEADER_GUID        = lt_header_guid
      IT_REQUESTED_OBJECTS  = lt_requested_objects
    IMPORTING
      ET_SALES              = lt_sales
    EXCEPTIONS
      DOCUMENT_NOT_FOUND    = 1
      ERROR_OCCURRED        = 2
      DOCUMENT_LOCKED       = 3
      NO_CHANGE_AUTHORITY   = 4
      NO_DISPLAY_AUTHORITY  = 5
      NO_CHANGE_ALLOWED     = 6
      OTHERS                = 7.

  check sy-subrc eq 0.

  READ TABLE LT_SALES INTO LS_SALES INDEX 1 .

  CHECK LS_Sales-PO_NUMBER_UC is INITIAL.

  MESSAGE ID 'Z_ERROR_QUANTITY' TYPE 'E' NUMBER 000
          WITH lv_item
          INTO lv_message.

  CALL FUNCTION 'CRM_MESSAGE_COLLECT'
    EXPORTING
      IV_CALLER_NAME        = 'external_reference_no'(001)
      IV_REF_OBJECT         = IV_GUID
      IV_REF_KIND           = 'A'
    EXCEPTIONS
      NOT_FOUND             = 1
      APPL_LOG_ERROR        = 2
      OTHERS                = 3
                .
  IF SY-SUBRC <> 0.
    MESSAGE ID 'Z_ERROR_QUANTITY' TYPE 'E' NUMBER 000
            WITH LV_MESSAGE.
  ENDIF.

  RAISE DO_NOT_SAVE.

endmethod.
```

This implementation gets called for a particular process type when an order is getting saved and checks for the attribute external number. If the reference number field is not INITIAL, then it exits the code; otherwise, it will raise an error message, and the document will not be saved. This is one of the functionalities for which a BADI can be used.

FINDING A BADI

Sometimes it becomes difficult to find the relevant business add-in required for your use. It is not possible to have knowledge of all User Exits for a particular process. To find the appropriate BADI, use the following steps:

1. Open transaction se24 and enter the CL_EXITHANDLER class.

2. Put a breakpoint in the GET_INSTANCE method.

3. Run the required business process. For example, change the business partner details, add details to a business transaction, or maintain information for a particular material.

When you go through the process step-by-step, you will notice that the breakpoint gets triggered at various places. Check the variable EXIT_NAME and look at the corresponding BADI name. See Figure 22.4 for more details.

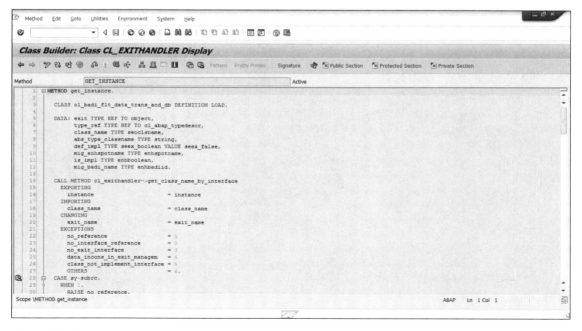

Figure 22.4
Class interface.

Another possible way of finding a relevant BADI is by putting a breakpoint in the SXV_GET_CLIF_BY_NAME function module. When you execute the business process, the breakpoint will be triggered multiple times. Now if you have a scenario in which you want to see which BADI get triggered while saving a document, you can see the corresponding names in the variable NAME after you click the Save button. See Figure 22.5 for more details.

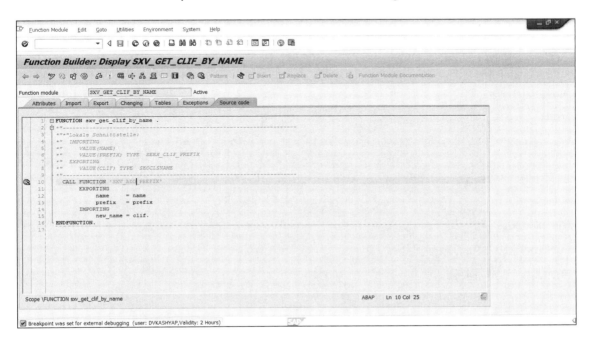

Figure 22.5
Function module interface.

USEFUL BADIS

Here are some examples of useful BADIs in ECC and CRM with their respective uses:

ORDER_SAVE	Used at the time of saving the order
COM_PARTNER_BADI	To check for business partners
CRM_DATAEXCHG_BADI	To exchange data between ECC and CRM system
CRM_ORDER_STATUS	To control events when a specific status is set
BUPA_GENERAL_UPDATE	To update a business partner

EXEC_METHODCALL_PPF	To execute actions
BADI_SD_SALES	Enhancements for sales order processing
BADI_SD_BILLING	Billing enhancements
MB_DOCUMENT_UPDATE	To update materials
CUSTOMER_ADD_DATA	To process enhancements for a customer master record

UNDERSTANDING USER EXITS

User Exits are points in a SAP application program that are planned by developers to insert additional pieces of code. Unlike BADIs, they can be used only once. A User Exit is a three-character code. System exits are represented by S followed by two digits, whereas customer exits start with U followed by two digits. Different types of exits that can be created are

- Menu Exits
- Screen Exits
- Function Module Exits
- Field Exits

Menu exits add items to standard SAP applications. You can either trigger an entire application or call up a screen. Screen exits are used to add fields to the standard screen. The function module exit calls a separate function module when triggered. It controls the flow of data between the standard program and User Exits. It follows the syntax CALL CUSTOMER-FUNCTION '001'. Next are field exits, which allow you to create your programming logic for a particular data element. You can use this to perform checks, convert values, or perform a business-related process. Transaction RSMODPRF is used to create exits.

Finding User Exits

Previously we discussed different methods of finding relevant BADIs. This section explains the various ways to find User Exits. Enter the transaction code for the relevant business process in se93 and click Display. Copy the program name, open transaction se37, and input the following as displayed in Figure 22.6. The naming convention for function module exits is `EXIT_<program name><3 digit suffix>`. Figure 22.6 shows an example list of User Exits for tcode `XK01`.

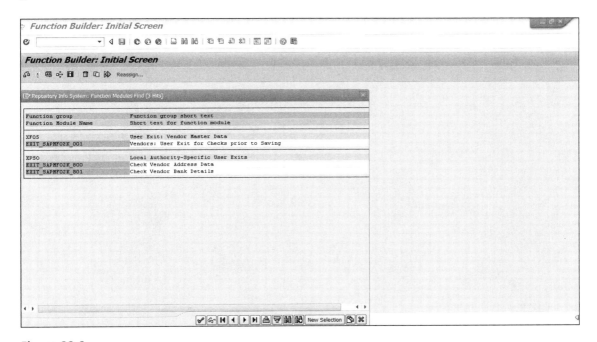

Figure 22.6
User Exit function module list.

If the first method does not work, there is another way of finding User Exits for a particular transaction. Copy the package name from the display screen of the business transaction. After this, enter transaction `SMOD` and press F4. This will open a dialog box where you need to press the Information System button. After you click the button, fill in the package name with the one that you copied and press Execute. These will give you a list of User Exits with descriptions, as shown in Figure 22.7.

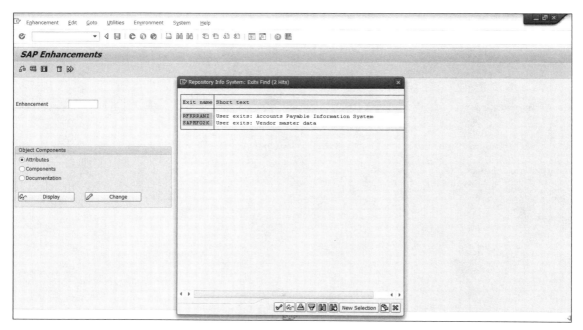

Figure 22.7
User Exit list from SMOD transaction.

SUMMARY

This chapter discussed various ways of enhancing standard SAP objects. The reason you might need to enhance standards objects is due to the fact you need to introduce specific functionality in the program. The two methods discussed were business add-ins (BADIs) and User Exits. You explored the use of BADIs, what they are comprised of, and how to implement them. Further, you looked into different ways of finding the appropriate business add-ins. User Exits are a useful means of enhancing standard objects. The chapter briefly introduced them and described different methods of finding User Exits for a particular transaction.

CHAPTER 23

OBJECT ORIENTED ABAP

IN THIS CHAPTER

- Understanding Object Oriented ABAP Classes
- Understanding Object Oriented ABAP Basics
- Understanding Visibility Concepts
- Handling ABAP Objects

This chapter introduces object oriented ABAP and the background information required to be able to develop programs utilizing this concept. Although this concept has been around for a long time, SAP recently utilized this concept in the newest version of SAP ECC. Learning these concepts and setting a foundation for how to utilize them will make the transition from the old ABAP to the newer object oriented ABAP easier.

Object oriented programming (OOP) is a programming paradigm that represents concepts as "objects" that have data fields (attributes that describe the object) and associated procedures known as methods. Objects, which are usually instances of classes, are used to interact with one another to design applications and computer programs. —Wikipedia

Object oriented ABAP programming emphasizes objects that represent abstract or concrete objects. These objects form a container that connects the character to its respective behavior. These objects' character and their properties are classified by their internal structure and their attributes (data). ABAP objects signify an extension of ABAP that provides the language with the tools to support the object oriented programming model.

Key features of the ABAP object oriented approach are as follows:

- Emphàsis on things that do those tasks.

- Programs are organized into classes, and objects and the functionalities are embedded into methods of a class.

- Data can be hidden and cannot be accessed by external sources.

- New data and functions can be easily added whenever necessary.

- **Object:** A section of source code that contains data and provides services. The data forms the attributes of the object. The services are known as *methods* (also known as *operations* or *functions*). They form a capsule that combines the character to the respective behaviors. Objects should enable programmers to map a real problem and its proposed software solution on a one-to-one basis.

- **Class:** Describes an object. From a technical point of view, objects are runtime instances of a class. In theory, you can create any number of objects based on a single class. Each instance (object) of a class has a unique identity and its own set of values for its attributes.

OBJECT ORIENTED ABAP BASICS

This section begins by covering the ABAP object oriented basics. It covers aspects of what makes up a class and the object oriented approaches related to how to use the associated class concepts within the SAP environments.

Classes

Classes are considered models for objects and are an abstract template of an object. A class makes up a set of instructions for developing an object. ABAP objects classes can be globally or locally declared. Global classes and interfaces are defined in the Class Builder (Transaction se24) in the ABAP Workbench and are stored in class pools in the repository class library. There are no specific differences between a global class and a local class.

The attributes of an SAP object are typically defined by the components of the class, which describe the state and behavior of the object. Global and local class are defined by SAP as follows:

- **Global class:** Global classes and interfaces are defined in the Class Builder (Transaction se24) in the ABAP Workbench. They are stored centrally in class pools in the class library in the R/3 Repository. All of the ABAP programs in an R/3 system can access the global classes.

■ **Local class:** Local classes are defined in an ABAP program (Transaction se38) and can only be used in the corresponding ABAP program in which they are defined. Within the ABAP program, the local class will be used; if not found, the global class is used.

ABAP Class Structure

A structure of a class is made up of the following:

■ Class components

■ Attributes

■ Implementation of methods

Class Components

Class components are declared in the declaration part of the class and are defined by the attributes of the objects in the class. Each component is assigned the visibility section of public, private, or protected, which defines the external interface of the class. All of the components of a class are visible within the class, and all the components of the class must have a unique name within the class.

The two kinds of components in a class are those that exist separately for each object and those that exist only once for the whole class, regardless of the number of instances.

■ Instance-specific components are known as *instance components*. Instance components exist separately in each instance (object) of the class and are referred to using the instance component selector, ->.

■ Components that are not instance specific are called *static components*. Static components exist only once per class and are valid for all instances of the class. They are declared with the CLASS keyword. Static components can be used without even creating an instance of the class and are referred to using the static component selector, =>.

Attributes

Class attributes are data fields within a class that can have any ABAP data type defined. The status of an object is determined by the contents of its attributes. The attribute of a class is any data, constants, and types declared.

There are two types of attributes:

- **Instance attributes**—The contents of instance attributes define the instance-specific state of an object. You declare them using the `DATA` statement.

- **Static attributes**—The contents of static attributes define the state of the class that is valid for all instances of the class. Static attributes exist once for each class. You declare them using the `CLASS-DATA` statement. They are accessible for the entire runtime of the class.

All of the objects in a class can access its static attributes. If you change a static attribute in an object, the change is visible in all other objects in the class.

Methods

Methods within a class are logical procedures that define the actions of an object. Methods have the ability to access all of the attributes of a class, which allows them to change the data content of an object. All methods contain a parameter interface, which gives users the ability to supply the methods with values when they are called and in return can receive values. Private attributes of a class can be changed only by methods in the same class.

The definition and parameter interface of a method is similar to that of function modules.

Highlights of methods:

- These methods are similar to ABAP function modules.

- A method can access all attributes of its own class.

- Methods are defined in the definition part and implemented in the implementation part.

- You can call methods using the `CALL METHOD` statement.

There are two method types:

- **Instance methods**—You declare instance methods using the `METHODS` statement. They can access all of the attributes of a class and can trigger all of the events of the class. They require an object instance to be created before they can be called.

- **Static methods**—You declare static methods using the `CLASS-METHODS` statement. They can only access static attributes and trigger static events. They are called directly without requiring an instance to be created.

Visibility Concepts

All class components need to have a visibility identified. The visibility concept of a class definition is categorized into three visibility sections: PUBLIC, PROTECTED, and PRIVATE.

Public Section

Data declared in the public section can be accessed by the class itself and by its subclasses, as well as by other users outside the class. All of the components declared in the public section are accessible to all users of the class, and to the methods of the class and any classes that inherit from it.

Protected Section

Data declared in the protected section can be accessed by the class itself and by its subclasses, but not by external users outside the class. All of the components declared in the protected section are accessible to all methods of the class and of classes that inherit from it.

Private Section

Components that you declare in the private section can only be used in the methods of the same class.

Handling ABAP Objects

Within an ABAP program, object references are used as pointers to objects and are used to access those objects. The references are contained as object reference variables in the ABAP program. Objects are instances of a given class, and each object has a unique identity with its own attributes. A class can have any number of object instances.

Object Reference Variables

The two types of variables that can contain references in an ABAP program are object reference variables and data reference variables. Object reference variables consist of references to a given object and either are initial or contain a reference to an existing object. An object reference variable can contain references to objects with the identity of an object, depending on its object reference. When a reference variable points to an object, that variable will recognize the identity of that given object. On the other hand, the instance-dependent components of a given object can only be referred to by using a reference variable that points to that object. Lastly, object attributes can also be defined as reference variables.

Data Types for References

Data types for references are typically predefined in your ABAP program. However, the full data type is not defined until it is explicitly declared in the ABAP program. The object reference variable data type defines how the ABAP program handles its value, which is the object reference. The two types of object references are class references and interface references.

Class references are defined using the TYPE REF TO class addition in the TYPES or DATA statement. A class reference (referred to as cref in ABAP) permits a user to create an object instance of a corresponding class. Using the cref->comp syntax allows the user to access all visible components comp of the object that are also contained in the class class.

Creating Objects

When creating an object instance, define a class reference variable cref with reference to a class class. Using this syntax creates that class instance in your ABAP program:

```
CREATE OBJECT cref [TYPE class].
```

Example:

```
DATA: pmc_get_matnr TYPE REF TO zcl_pmc_tool_get,
CREATE OBJECT pmc_get_matnr.
```

In order to give your program the ability to call the methods defined in the class as well as other components defined in the class, you need to create an instance of the class class and the reference variable cref, which will allow the program to use objects within the class. The next sections outline this concept further and provide more detail.

Addressing the Components of Objects

ABAP programs can only access the instance components of a class object using references in object reference variables. This is done using the object component selector -> (ref is a reference variable):

- To access an attribute attr: ref->attr
- To call a method meth: CALL METHOD ref->meth

Static components can be accessed using the class name or the class component selector => and the reference variable. You can also address the static components of a class before an object has been created.

■ Accessing a static attribute attr: class=>attr

■ Calling a static method meth: CALL METHOD class=>meth

Example:

```
CALL METHOD grid3->set_table_for_first_display
  EXPORTING
    i_structure_name    = structure
    is_layout           = l_layout
    it_toolbar_excluding = t_tlexcl
  CHANGING
    it_outtab           = table.
```

Note

The properties of instance attributes behave like static components, therefore it is possible to refer in a LIKE addition to the visible attributes of a class.

Each class implicitly contains the reference variable me, known as self-reference. In ABAP objects, the reference variable me always contains a reference to the respective object itself. Within a class, the self-reference me can be used to access the individual class components:

■ To access an attribute attr of your class: me->attr

■ To call a method meth of your class: CALL METHOD me->meth

Example:

```
me->load_message_table(  im_werks = 'XXXX' im_matnr = space
                         im_type = c_message_type_error
                         im_id = c_message_class
                         im_number = '293'
                         im_message_v1 = l_messv1 ).
```

When working with attributes of your own class in methods, specifying a reference variable is not required. The self-reference me is implicitly set by the system and allows an object to give other objects a reference to it. Access to attributes in methods from within an object even if they are obscured by local attributes is also possible

Declaring Methods

Once the object class instance has been created with a CREATE object statement, a method can be called directly from a corresponding class. A method can also be defined within a public section of an ABAP program and later called in the implementation section. The example later in the chapter shows how to call a method within a class.

This is the syntax to declare instance methods; use the following statement:

```
METHODS meth IMPORTING [VALUE(import1  import2 ...importN [)] TYPE type [OPTIONAL]...
             EXPORTING [VALUE(export1  export2 ...exportN[)] TYPE type ...
             CHANGING  [VALUE(change1  change2 ...changeN[)] TYPE type [OPTIONAL]...
             RETURNING VALUE(r)
             EXCEPTIONS exc1  exc2 ... .
```

To declare static methods, use the following statement:

```
CLASS-METHODS meth...
```

Example:

```
*------------------------------------------------------------*
*        CLASS lcl_process_data DEFINITION
*------------------------------------------------------------*
*
*------------------------------------------------------------*
CLASS lcl_process_data DEFINITION.

  PUBLIC SECTION.
    CLASS-METHODS: print_grid2_report IMPORTING title TYPE lvc_title
                                         structure TYPE dd021-tabname
                              CHANGING table TYPE STANDARD TABLE.
ENDCLASS.                     "lcl_process_data DEFINITION
```

As you declare a method, its parameter interface needs to be defined using the syntax additions IMPORTING, EXPORTING, CHANGING, and RETURNING. The parameter additions specify the input, output, and input/output parameters, as well as the return code. In addition, attributes of the interface parameters are defined, whether a parameter is to be passed by reference or value (VALUE), along with its type (TYPE) and optional parameters (OPTIONAL, DEFAULT). In order to pass a parameter by value, the syntax has to be explicitly passed using the VALUE addition. The return value (RETURNING) parameter must always be passed explicitly as a value, which covers the situation for methods that return a single output value. The exception parameters (EXCEPTIONS) enable users to react to error situations when the method is executed.

Example:

```
* Get material data
    CALL METHOD pmc_get_matnr->get_materialdata
      EXPORTING
        im_pmc_tab              = g_t_prodmenu_marc
      IMPORTING
        ex_matnrdata_tab        = g_t_matnrdata
        ex_matnrdata_error_tab = g_t_error_tab
        ex_marm_tab             = g_t_marm.
```

Implementing Methods

As you declare a method, you must implement all of the methods in a class as part of the implementation section of the corresponding class using this syntax:

```
METHOD meth.

 ...
ENDMETHOD.
```

Example:

```
*-------------------------------------------------------------*
*        CLASS lcl_process_data IMPLEMENTATION
*-------------------------------------------------------------*
*
*-------------------------------------------------------------*
CLASS lcl_process_data IMPLEMENTATION.

  METHOD print_grid2_report.

*getting the reference for the splited container (row 1 & col 2 container)
    IF container_2 IS NOT BOUND. " OR g_backbutton2 = c_set.
      CALL METHOD splitter_1->get_container
        EXPORTING
          row       = 2
          column    = 1
        RECEIVING
          container = container_2.

    CREATE OBJECT container
      EXPORTING
        container_name = c_container.
```

```
      CREATE OBJECT grid2
        EXPORTING
          i_parent = container_2.
    ENDIF.

    REFRESH: g_t_fcat.
    PERFORM build_field_catalog USING structure.

    l_layout-grid_title = title.
    CLEAR: g_toolbar, g_toolbar_zpmc3.
    g_toolbar_zpmc2 = c_set.
    l_var_save = 'A'.
    l_variant-report = g_repid.
    CALL METHOD grid2->set_table_for_first_display
      EXPORTING
        i_structure_name = structure
        is_layout        = l_layout
        is_variant       = l_variant
        i_save           = l_var_save
        i_default        = c_set
      CHANGING
        it_outtab        = table
        it_fieldcatalog  = g_t_fcat[].


*Handlers for the events
    CREATE OBJECT event_receiver_2.
    SET HANDLER event_receiver_2->handle_user_command
                event_receiver_2->handle_menu_button_2
                event_receiver_2->handle_hotspot_click_3
                event_receiver_2->handle_toolbar_2 FOR ALL INSTANCES.


**calling the interactive toolbar method of alv
    CALL METHOD grid2->set_toolbar_interactive.

    g_structure = structure.
    CREATE DATA g_tabdata TYPE STANDARD TABLE OF (structure).
    ASSIGN g_tabdata->* TO <tabdata>.

    CREATE DATA g_tabline LIKE LINE OF <tabdata>.
    ASSIGN g_tabline->* TO <tabline>.
    <tabdata> = table[].


  ENDMETHOD.                         "print_grid2_report
```

When implementing the method, there is no requirement to specify any interface parameters, as these are defined in the METHOD declaration. The interface parameters of a class method interact like local variables within the method implementation. Additional local variables can be defined within a method using the DATA statement. When implementing a static method, the method only works with the static attributes of your class. On the other hand, instance methods can work with both static and instance attributes.

Static Method Call

Static methods can be called directly without the need for an object instance to be created. They are called with this syntax:

```
CALL METHOD meth EXPORTING   import1 = field1   import2 =field2   ...
                 IMPORTING   export1 = g1   export2 =g2   ...
                 CHANGING    change1 = f1   change2 =f2   ...
                 RECEIVING           r = h
                 EXCEPTIONS  excep1 = rc1 excep2 =rc2   ...
```

Within the implementation part of a class, you can call the methods of the same class directly using their name meth.

```
CALL METHOD meth...
```

Outside of the class, the visibility of the method depends on whether you can call it at all. Visible instance methods can be called from outside the class using

```
CALL METHOD ref->meth...
```

where ref is a reference variable whose value points to an instance of the class.

Example:

```
  CALL METHOD zcl_pmc_tool_get=>get_pmc_struc_fields
    CHANGING
      ch_pmc_tab = g_t_prodmenu_1.
```

Visible instance methods can be called from outside the class using

```
CALL METHOD =>meth...
```

where class is the name of the relevant class.

Example:

```
CALL METHOD lcl_process_data=>print_grid2_report
  EXPORTING
    title     = text-t03
    structure = 'ZPMC_STATS_STRUC'
  CHANGING
    table     = g_t_pmc_stats.
```

As you call a method in your ABAP program, you must pass all non-optional input parameters using the addition EXPORTING or CHANGING within the CALL METHOD syntax. Importing the output parameters into your ABAP program using the additions IMPORTING or RECEIVING is allowed, but not required. In addition, you can handle any exceptions triggered by the exceptions using the EXCEPTIONS addition.

This is the syntax to pass and receive parameter values to and from a class method:

```
... Formal parameter = Actual parameter
```

As part of the corresponding addition, interface parameters are always on the left side of the equals sign, and actual parameters are always on the right. The equals sign serves to assign program variables to the interface parameters of the method and is not an assignment operator. When the interface of a method has only a single IMPORTING parameter, you have the ability to use the following shortened syntax of the method call:

```
CALL METHOD method( value ).
```

The actual parameter value is passed to the input parameters of the method.

If the interface of a method consists only of IMPORTING parameters, you can use the following shortened form of the method call:

```
CALL METHOD method( import1 = field1   import2 = field2 ...).
```

Each actual parameter field1 is passed to the corresponding formal parameter i1.

Example:

```
rpt_alv->set_screen_status(
      pfstatus     =  'FILEUPLOAD_UTIL'
      report       =  'ZPMC_FILEUPLOAD_UTIL'
      set_functions = rpt_alv->c_functions_all ).
```

Constructors

Constructors are executed automatically by the class to set the initial state of a new object and related components of the corresponding class. The constructor methods are special methods that are defined within the class and have predefined names. The two types of constructors are instance constructors and static constructors. The example in the following pages shows how to create a constructor within a custom class. A CONSTRUCTOR can also be defined in a public section of your program using this syntax:

```
METHODS CONSTRUCTOR
        IMPORTING [VALUE(]import1  import2 ..importN.[)] TYPE type [OPTIONAL]...
        EXCEPTIONS exc1  exc2 .... .
```

Constructors are typically implemented in the implementation section of the corresponding class and are similar to any other method. Instance constructors are called once for each instance of the class and directly after the object has been created in the CREATE OBJECT statement. Input parameters of the instance constructor can be passed and can handle the exceptions using the EXPORTING and EXCEPTIONS additions in the CREATE OBJECT statement.

SAP TOOLS EXAMPLE: CREATING A SAMPLE CLASS AND METHOD

This sample class will be used to read the Purchasing Document Header table EKKO with selection parameters sent through the class method. This class will consist of a constructor method and a regular method to be used in a simple ABAP program later in the chapter. The constructor is used to first clear out the data in a global internal table that is defined as a type within the class. The class method will be used to select data from the internal table with parameters that will be sent in through the method call in the ABAP program. Follow these steps:

1. Go to Transaction se24.

2. Enter the name ZCL_SAMPLE_CLASS and click the Create button, as shown in Figure 23.1.

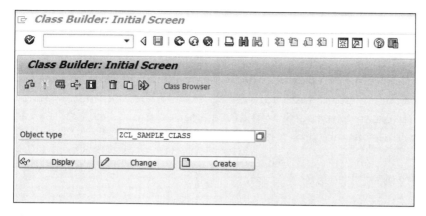

Figure 23.1
Initial screen of the Class Builder.

Note

The typical naming convention of a custom class has a prefix of ZCL_.

3. Enter the description for your class and click Save. Save the class as a local object. See Figure 23.2.

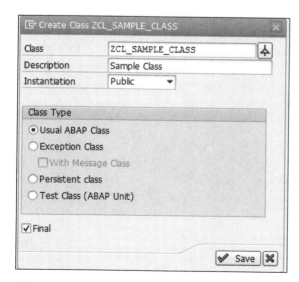

Figure 23.2
Class attributes pop-up box.

4. Click on the Attributes tab and enter the values defined in Figure 23.3.

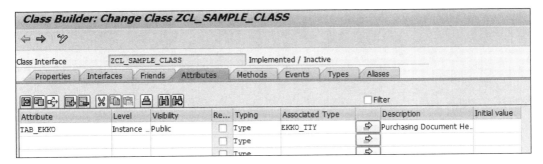

Figure 23.3
The Attributes tab shows all the corresponding required columns.

Note

Associate type `EKKO_TTY` is a table type that has a structure like `EKKO`. Using a definition of a table type defines the attribute as an internal table.

5. Create a constructor method by clicking the Class Constructor button. See Figures 23.4 and 23.5.

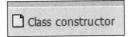

Figure 23.4
The Class Constructor button.

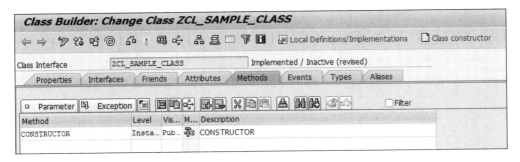

Figure 23.5
The constructor method is automatically created under the Methods tab.

6. Double-click the constructor and add the logic shown in Figure 23.6.

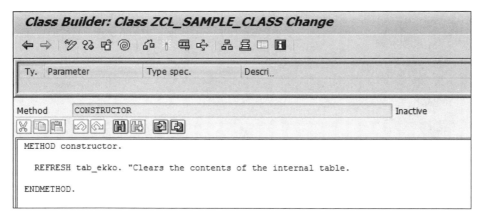

Figure 23.6
The method editor in change mode is ready for code.

7. Save and activate the code.

8. Create a new method with the name GET_EKKO_DATA. Use the details shown in Figure 23.7.

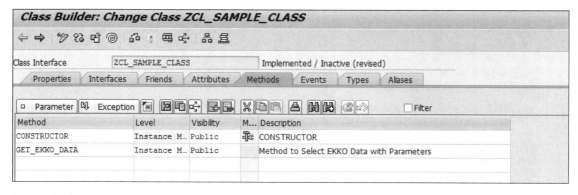

Figure 23.7
Under the Methods tab, you can see the list of methods within your class.

9. Highlight the new method and click on the Parameter button, as shown in Figure 23.8.

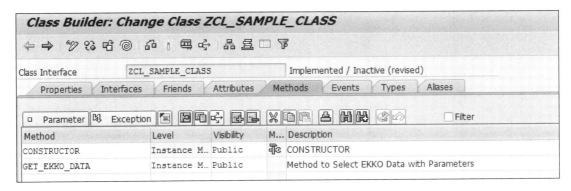

Figure 23.8
The Parameter button at the upper-left side of the Method tab.

10. Here you define parameter values that will be sent into the method and parameter values to return back to the calling program. In this step, you will define two import parameters and one export parameter, as shown in Figure 23.9.

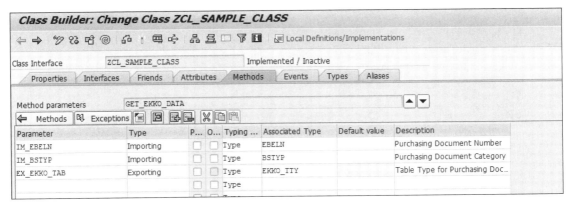

Figure 23.9
The parameters of your method are displayed here.

Note

The import parameters will be sent from the calling program, and the method will return an internal table with the selected data. A typical naming convention is as follows: all importing parameters should have a prefix of IM_, and all exporting parameters should have a prefix of EX_.

11. Double-click on the GET_EKKO_DATA method. Add the ABAP code to your method as shown in Figure 23.10.

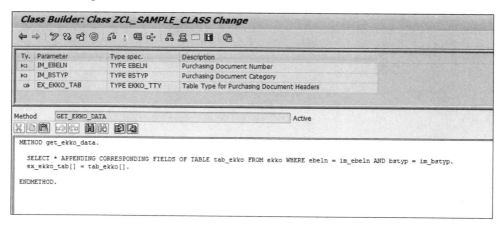

Figure 23.10
Add your code to your method using the ABAP editor.

12. Save, check, and activate your new method.

13. Save and activate your class. See Figures 23.11 and 23.12.

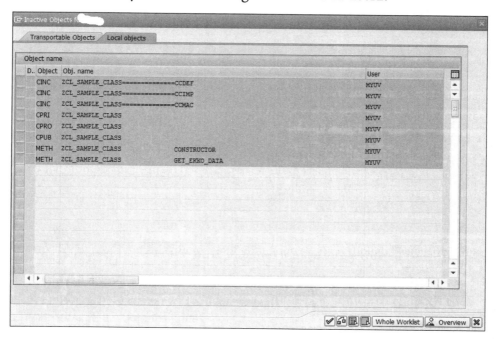

Figure 23.11
The new GET_EKKO_DATA method is listed.

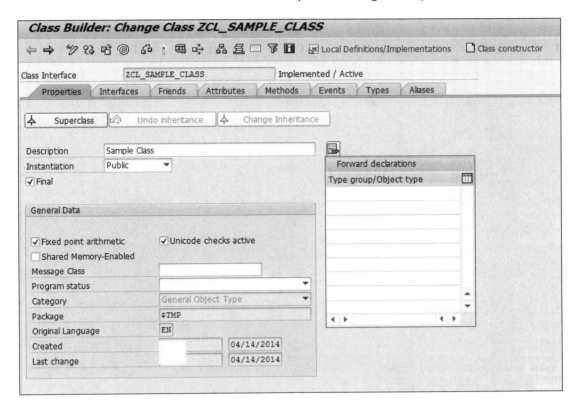

Figure 23.12
Properties tab of your class.

You have just created your class, and you are ready to create an ABAP program to call your new class. Great job!

To call the new class ZCL_SAMPLE_CLASS in an ABAP program, follow these steps:

1. Go to Transaction se38.

2. Create a program with the name ZTEST_CLASS_METHOD_CALL, as shown in Figures 23.13 and 23.14.

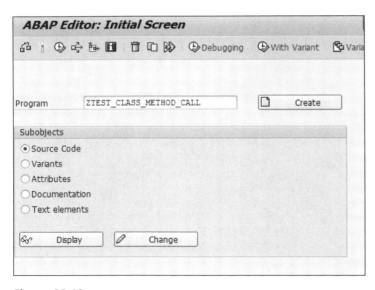

Figure 23.13
The ABAP program editor initial screen.

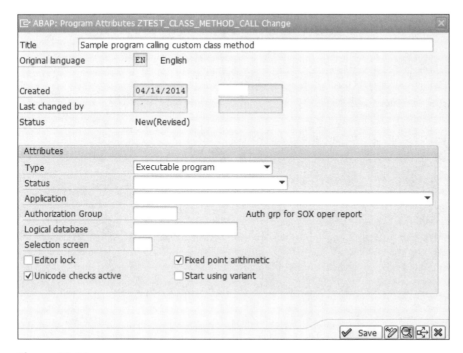

Figure 23.14
The ABAP program attributes pop-up box, showing the program description and other relevant program details.

3. Save as a local object.

4. Copy the ABAP code shown in Figure 23.15.

Figure 23.15
ABAP program editor in change mode, which should be displaying your code.

5. Save, check, and activate your ABAP program.

Note

The ABAP code utilizes the object oriented concept defined in the prior pages. The code uses the CREATE object statement and the CALL METHOD statement that calls the method in the associated CLASS. You will be able to navigate to the method logic by double-clicking the method itself, in this case ekko_get->get_ekko data.

6. Execute your program. Enter your selection parameters as shown in Figures 23.16 and 23.17.

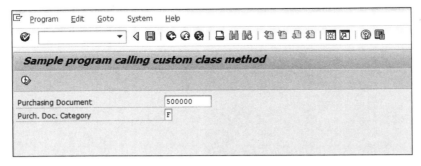

Figure 23.16
ABAP program selection screen displayed here. Enter your associated input values.

Note

Your document number and document type may be different than what's shown here, based on the data you have in your given SAP environment.

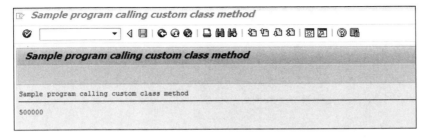

Figure 23.17
Final report out of your ABAP program, which is displaying the data that was retrieved.

This simple report will display the document number that was retrieved from EKKO table with the given selection parameters. To able to see the method in action, try running this program in DEBUG mode.

Extra Help

When you're adding the statement CALL METHOD in your ABAP program, use the Pattern button, shown in Figure 23.18, to help you with the proper syntax.

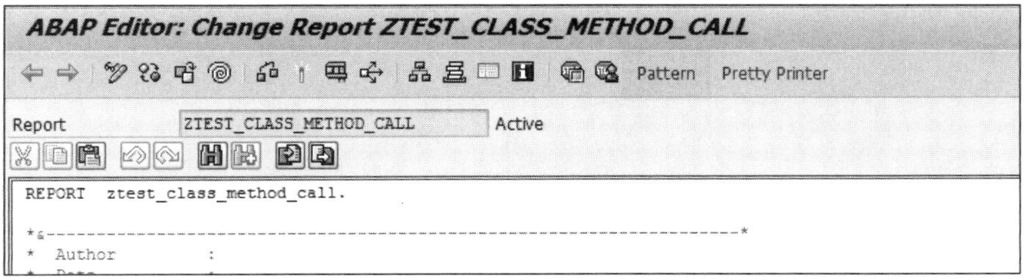

Figure 23.18
This is the Pattern button within the ABAP editor.
Source: SAP AG or an SAP affiliate company. All rights reserved.

Select the ABAP objects pattern shown in Figure 23.19.

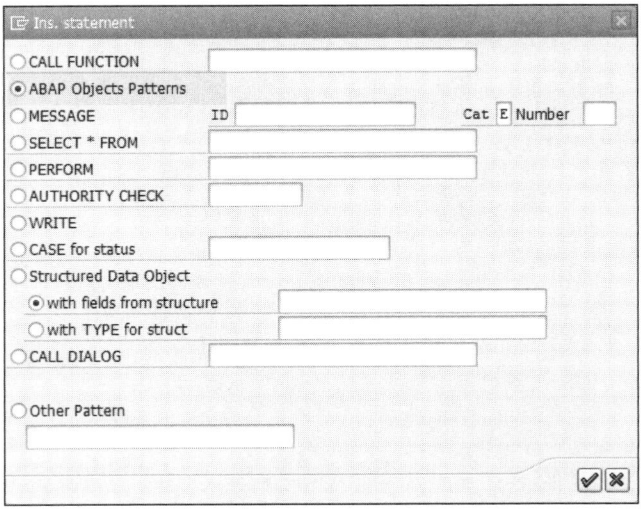

Figure 23.19
The ABAP Objects Patterns selection box.
Source: SAP AG or an SAP affiliate company. All rights reserved.

Enter the values for your instance (defined in your ABAP program), class, and method, as shown in Figure 23.20.

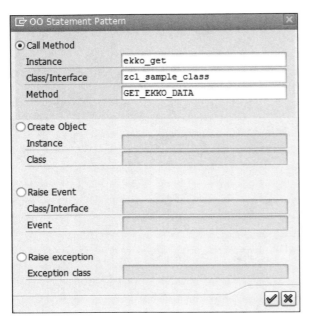

Figure 23.20
A pop-up box for the OO ABAP pattern is displayed. You enter the instance, class, and method that you plan to use.
Source: SAP AG or an SAP affiliate company. All rights reserved.

The method call statement will appear. Update the corresponding parameter values with the variables that you defined in your ABAP program.

```
CALL METHOD ekko_get->get_ekko_data
    EXPORTING
      im_ebeln   =
      im_bstyp   =
*   IMPORTING
*     ex_ekko_tab =
```

Note

The Pattern button can also be used for other pattern help, such as with function methods, messages, and even authority checks.

SAMPLE ABAP PROGRAM USING OBJECT ORIENTED CONCEPTS

Follow these steps to try this sample ABAP program:

1. Go to se38.

2. Create a program with name ZTEST_CLASS_METHOD_LOCAL.

3. Apply this code:

```
* & ----------------------------------------------------------------*
* & Report   ZTEST_CLASS_METHOD_LOCAL
* &
* & ----------------------------------------------------------------*
* &
* &
* & ----------------------------------------------------------------*
REPORT  ztest_class_method_local.
*----------------------------------------------------------------*
*Class Methods
*----------------------------------------------------------------*
*----------------------------------------------------------------*
*       CLASS lcl_event_receiver DEFINITION
*----------------------------------------------------------------*
CLASS lcl_display DEFINITION.
  PUBLIC SECTION.
    METHODS: write_text IMPORTING text TYPE char25.

ENDCLASS.                    "lcl_event_receiver DEFINITION
```

```
*----------------------------------------------------------------*
*        CLASS lcl_event_receiver IMPLEMENTATION
*----------------------------------------------------------------*
CLASS lcl_display IMPLEMENTATION.
  METHOD write_text.
    WRITE: text.
  ENDMETHOD.                       "lcl_display
ENDCLASS.                          "lcl_display IMPLEMENTATION

DATA: zcl_display TYPE REF TO lcl_display.
PARAMETERS: p_text(25).

START-OF-SELECTION.
  CREATE OBJECT zcl_display.
  zcl_display->write_text( text = p_text ).

END-OF-SELECTION.
```

4. Save, check, and activate the code.

5. Execute the program. See Figure 23.21.

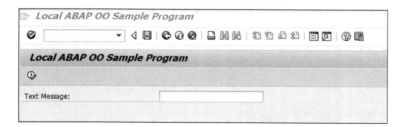

Figure 23.21
The selection screen of the ABAP program.

6. Enter a value in the selection screen. See Figure 23.22.

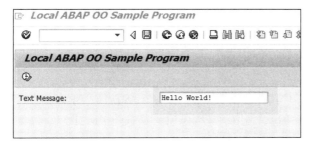

Figure 23.22
The text value specified in the selection screen field.

7. Execute the program. See Figure 23.23.

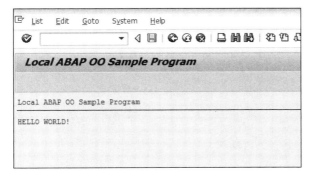

Figure 23.23
The final report out of the program based on the selection screen text value from Figure 23.22.

Congratulations! You've just created an ABAP program using object oriented programming concepts! Use this program and modify it to add more methods to your local class. Try to apply the different concepts that you've learned in this chapter. Continue to develop and use your newly acquired skills.

SUMMARY

In summary, with the latest version of SAP ECC utilizing the object oriented concepts for programming, it would be a great advantage for you to understand these concepts and the corresponding tools to stay on track with the current technology. Gaining the foundation and knowledge through the basic concepts and examples in this chapter will give you the ability to use these development tools for your future programming projects as well as grow your programming skills to another level. With the combination of your current knowledge of ABAP and integrating these new concepts and tools, your skills will increase by "leaps and bounds," and the potential for further opportunities career-wise will grow with it. As with any new skills, it takes a considerable amount of effort and practice to be able to master these concepts, so keep practicing and always try your best to use these tools as often as you possibly can.

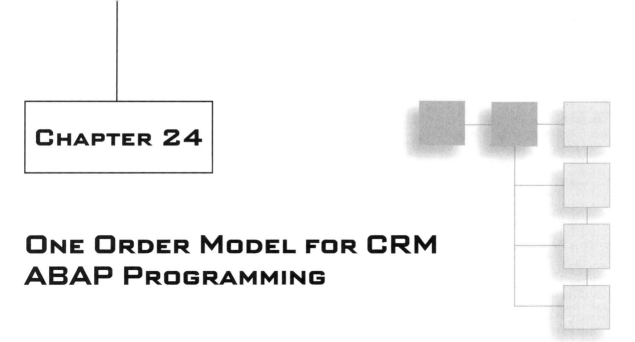

ONE ORDER MODEL FOR CRM ABAP PROGRAMMING

IN THIS CHAPTER

- Understanding Table Structure in CRM
- Understanding the One Order Framework
- Understanding the Concept of GUID
- Seeing Examples of Transactions
- Understanding Function Modules in CRM
- Debugging and Finding the Data You Need
- Using BADIs in CRM

So far we have focused on one of the modules in SAP, namely ECC. This chapter introduces one more module, called CRM (Customer Relation Management). This further can be divided into Marketing, Sales, and Service. The way data is handled in CRM is different from ECC. That is why it is important to introduce the concepts of GUID, the one order framework, and basic function modules that can help you with basic CRUD (Create, Read, Update, and Delete) operations. Most business transactions follow the one order framework architecture, which means all data is stored under the same tables and follow the same nomenclature.

For example, in a sales order, there are header details for order ID, description, create date, transaction type, and so on. For each sales order, there can be multiple line items. These items can have their own business partners status, which can be different from the ones at header level. We'll discuss this in more detail in this chapter.

INTRODUCTION TO TABLE STRUCTURE IN CRM

The database tables in ECC are based on the order types. For example, sales order has the corresponding table VBAK and sales item has the corresponding table VBAP. For billing, a VBRK document is used. So each transaction has a corresponding database table.

This is handled differently in CRM. Most business transaction types have a primary header table called CRMD_ORDERADM_H and a different item table called CRMD_ORDERADM_I, which is common to all transactions. Each record has a different GUID (global unique identifier), which will be explained later in more detail. For now, in a particular transaction there are different segments—the main ones are partner, organization, product, sales, status, pricing, dates, and texts. Each has a corresponding table to store data. The segment header and item data are stored in different tables, and the reference key is a GUID. There is a table CRMD_LINK that is further used to link different segments to header details.

In CRM data is more commonly retrieved using function modules instead of tables. The concept of function modules was introduced in Chapter 12, "Using Function Modules and BAPIs"; if you are still unclear on some topics, we advise you revisit that chapter. For example, to read header details, you will use function module CRM_ORDERADM_H_READ_OW instead of using table CRMD_ORDERADM_H. Similarly, to get partner details, you will use function module CRM_PARTNER_READ_OW. Figure 24.1 shows the function call for the function module.

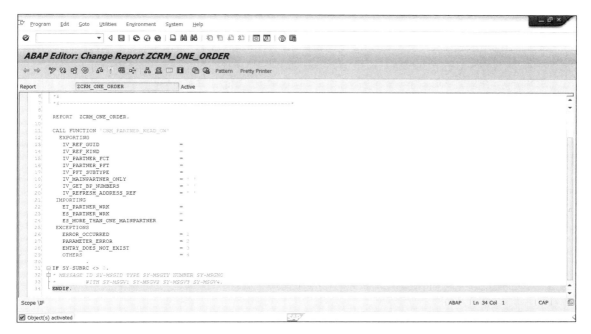

Figure 24.1
The function module call.

As you can see, the import parameters IV_REF_GUID and IV_REF_KIND are mandatory. For the reference GUID, you can input either the header or item GUID. For the reference kind, you should input A for header and B for item. You can get details of a single partner by inputting the partner function number, or you can list of partners for the header or item.

UNDERSTANDING THE ONE ORDER FRAMEWORK

The one order framework follows the concept of using common database tables to store different parts of a transaction, whether it is a sales order, activity, opportunity, complaint, or service order. This allows for an easier copy control for follow-up transactions, since they all will use the same structure. This model is further extended to BAPIs and BADIs as well. There are common function modules that can be used to read, maintain, and create data for these transactions, for example, CRM_ORDER_READ, CRM_ORDER_MAINTAIN, and CRM_ORDER_SAVE. All this is possible through the use of GUIDs.

UNDERSTANDING GUID

GUID is a computer-generated global unique key that's used to uniquely identify CRM objects such as sales documents, business partners, campaigns, leads, opportunities, and so on. Different table relationships are tied together using GUIDs. It is of type RAW (uninterpreted sequence of bytes) represented by 32 characters, generally. It can be found as a table key in most of the tables. It is a hexadecimal value that's generated automatically and is therefore different every time. It is used to represent single records and allows easy access of CRM tables. See Figure 24.2.

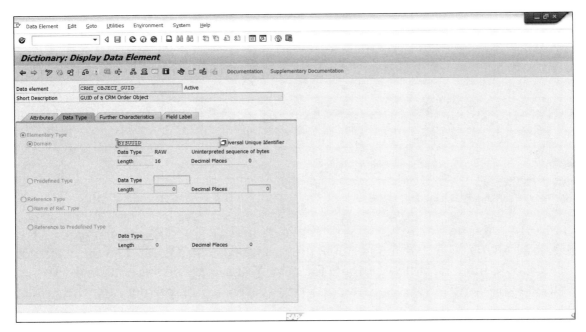

Figure 24.2
Representation of GUID.

The header GUID for a business transaction is stored in the CRMD_ORDERADM_H table, whereas the item GUID for the transaction is stored in the CRMD_ORDERADM_I table. Each corresponding segment is referenced to either the header or item table. This means the relationship between each segment and its corresponding header or item can be retrieved by passing the GUID as reference.

Each transaction type has a unique business object and process type. Business objects are just like templates and contain particular functionalities encapsulated within them that are unique to them. Runtime objects are created by passing key fields at the time of selection. For example, BUS2000115 is used for CRM sales transactions, and SW02 and SW01 are transaction codes (*tcodes*) that can be used to browse and display different business objects. Multiple process types are assigned to a single business object. There are standard process types. Custom process types can also be created and assigned the same business object. This is useful if you want to add new functionality to an existing transaction type, depending on client requirements.

LOOKING AT SOME EXAMPLE TRANSACTIONS

To view different business transactions, use tcode CRMD_ORDER. There are different inputs on the start screen for different select options. Figure 24.3 shows the options to find sales transaction by transaction type, by sold to party, by business partner, or by status and date intervals. Similarly, different business objects will use different selection parameters. On pressing Execute, you'll get a list of orders. By double-clicking on a single row, you can open a business transaction. You can also open a transaction directly by inputting the transaction ID (see Figure 24.4).

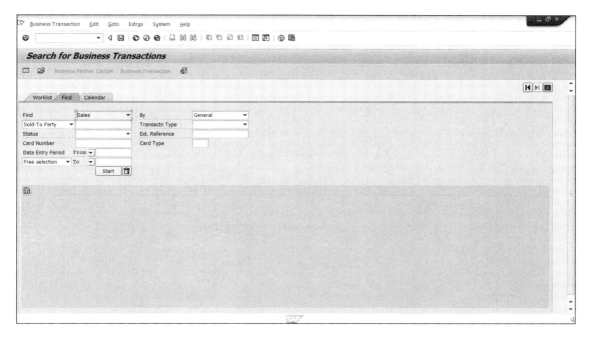

Figure 24.3
View business transaction.

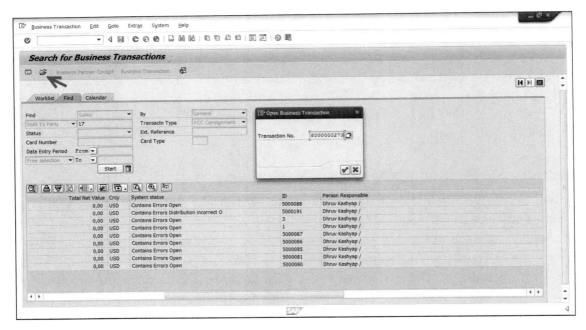

Figure 24.4
Open single business transaction.

There are multiple business objects in CRM. Figure 24.5 shows an example Sales Order transaction. Currently the header node is expanded. You can see there are different tabs or segments for header details, partner details, products, prices, texts, status, and so on. If you look at the bottom of Figure 24.5, you can see that the FANDECK node is expandable. On expanding this node, you can get the corresponding item details, which are similar to header details. There is no separate transaction for editing a business transaction; you do this simply by clicking the Pencil tool to get the transaction in edit mode. On the same toolbar you can see options for creating new transactions, copying the currently open transaction, creating a follow-up transaction, viewing related transactions, and viewing error and warning logs.

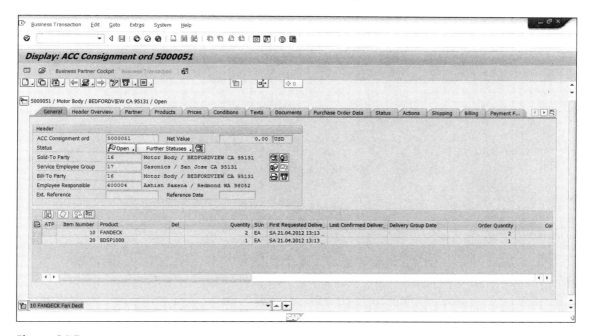

Figure 24.5
Sales order business transaction.

Figure 24.6 illustrates an example of a service order. Though the underlying objects are the same, the layout is completely different. This is because different business objects have different key fields and attributes. The different segments on header details and item details can be seen under the Transaction Data and Item Details tabs, respectively.

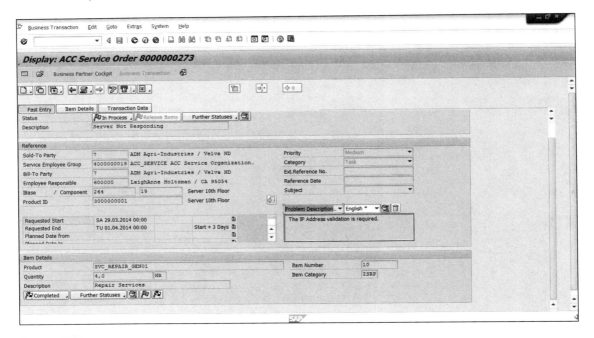

Figure 24.6
Service order business transaction.

To view different transaction types from a program, you can use the program CRM_ORDER_READ. Figures 24.7 and 24.8 show the selection screen parameters for the program. You can obtain the details of a transaction by adding either the transaction number or the GUID. This can be done on the header level and on the item level. Further, you can obtain details about multiple transactions by entering more than one transaction number or GUID. You can choose which segments you want to display the details of by using the Objects to Be Read option.

In the output screen, each of the output tables corresponds to a different segment of a transaction. You can view the details of the segment by clicking on the table and viewing the required fields. For example, to view the order description, click on the ET_ORDERADM_H export parameter and search for field description.

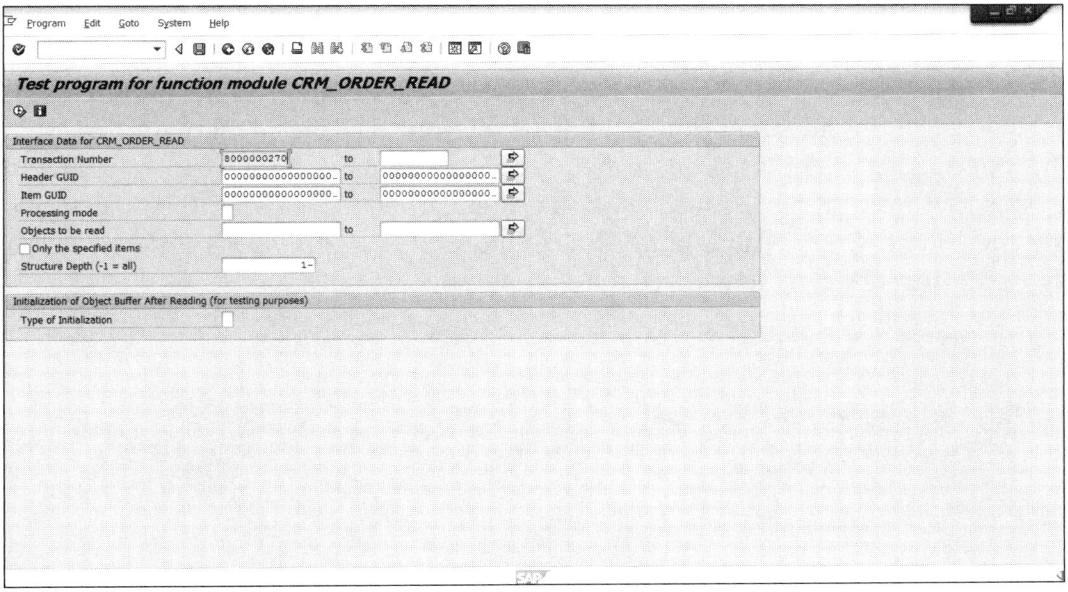

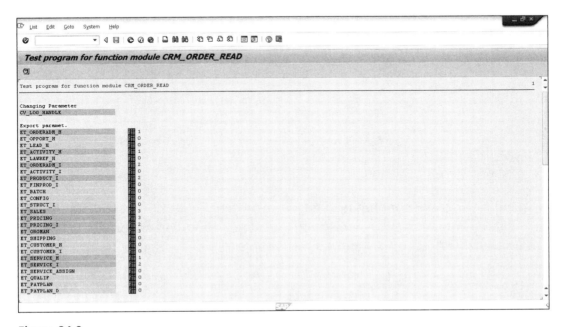

Figure 24.7
Input screen for CRM_ORDER_READ.

Figure 24.8
Output screen for CRM_ORDER_READ.

The program for maintaining business transactions is CRM_ORDER_MAINTAIN. The input selection screen follows the same convention as the read program. Enter the required transaction number that needs to be maintained. Along with this, fill in the required segments that need to be maintained by clicking on the button labeled Partial Objects to Maint. This opens a list of child segments that can be maintained, from which you should select the ones that need to be changed. The values for different fields can be maintained by clicking the Maint. Entry Value button (see Figure 24.9). This opens a list of tables where different attributes can be changed.

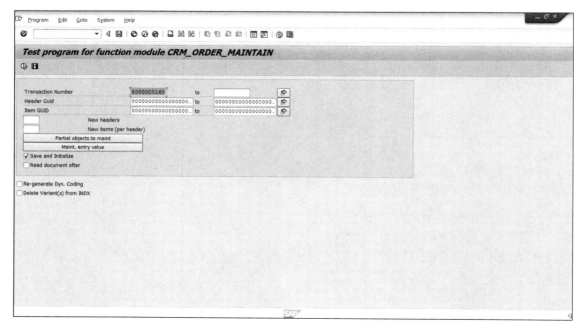

Figure 24.9
Input screen for CRM_ORDER_MAINTAIN.

Make sure to enter the corresponding field name under table CT_INPUT_FIELDS and the relevant object name. For example, to maintain the description for an order, you enter DESCRIPTION under table FIELD_NAMES and object name ORDERADM_H. Figure 24.10 illustrates this concept.

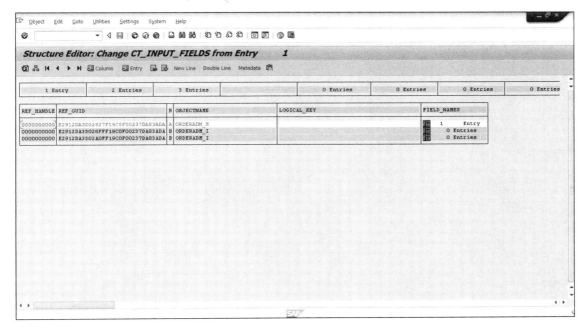

Figure 24.10
Maintain screen for `CRM_ORDER_MAINTAIN`.

If the business transaction is maintained successfully, you will see an entry beside the `ET_SAVED_OBJECTS` table (see Figure 24.11). Inside the table, there will be GUID and transaction number of the transaction you maintained.

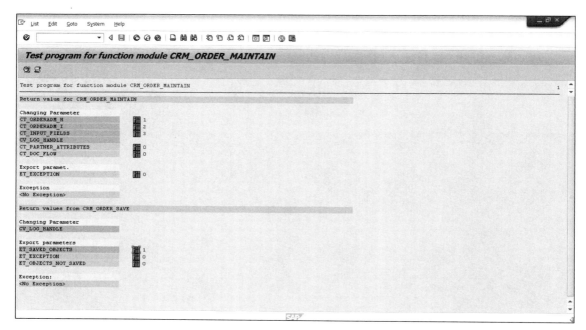

Figure 24.11
Output screen for CRM_ORDER_MAINTAIN.

FUNCTION MODULES USED

Earlier in the chapter, we briefly touched on the concept of using function modules for retrieving and maintaining data. The CRM one order framework provides a wide variety of function modules to perform such operations. The main ones are CRM_ORDER_READ, CRM_ORDER_MAINTAIN, and CRM_ORDER_SAVE. These three function modules can read and maintain multiple segments at once, so if you want to read more than one segment, it is always a good idea to use these function modules. However, if you are reading just a single segment like header details, there are specific function modules for each relation as well. The read function module has the naming convention CRM_[segment_name]*READ_OW for each individual relation. Some examples of the different relations are ORDERADM_H, ORDERADM_I, PARTNER, PRICING, SERVICE_I, and ACTIVITY_H. Similarly, the maintain function modules have the naming convention CRM_[segment_name]*MAINTAIN_OW. For a list of different segments, refer to the export parameters in the function module CRM_ORDER_READ or the import parameters in function module CRM_ORDER_MAINTAIN.

The following programs illustrate examples for these function modules:

```
REPORT  ZCRM_ONE_ORDER.

include CRM_OBJECT_NAMES_CON.

PARAMETERS: p_trans type crmt_object_id.
data: lt_requested_objects type CRMT_OBJECT_NAME_TAB,
      ls_requested_objects type CRMT_OBJECT_NAME,
      lt_orderadm_h type crmt_orderadm_h_wrkt,
      ls_orderadm_h type crmt_orderadm_h_wrk,
      lt_status type crmt_status_wrkt,
      ls_status type crmt_status_wrk,
      lv_guid type crmt_object_guid,
      lt_guid type crmt_object_guid_tab.

select single guid from crmd_orderadm_h into lv_guid
  where object_id = p_trans.

insert lv_guid into table lt_guid.
ls_requested_objects = gc_object_name-orderadm_h.
insert ls_requested_objects into table lt_requested_objects.
ls_requested_objects = gc_object_name-status.
insert ls_requested_objects into table lt_requested_objects.

CALL FUNCTION 'CRM_ORDER_READ'
   EXPORTING
     IT_HEADER_GUID                 = lt_guid
     IT_REQUESTED_OBJECTS           = lt_requested_objects
   IMPORTING
     ET_ORDERADM_H                  = lt_orderadm_h
     ET_STATUS                      = lt_status
   EXCEPTIONS
     DOCUMENT_NOT_FOUND             = 1
     ERROR_OCCURRED                 = 2
     DOCUMENT_LOCKED                = 3
     NO_CHANGE_AUTHORITY            = 4
     NO_DISPLAY_AUTHORITY           = 5
     NO_CHANGE_ALLOWED              = 6
     OTHERS                         = 7
     .
IF SY-SUBRC = 0.
  read table lt_orderadm_h into ls_orderadm_h index 1.
  read table lt_status into ls_status index 1.

  write: 'Description:', ls_orderadm_h-description, / 'Status:' , ls_status-txt30.
ENDIF.
```

This example makes use of the read function module. The input parameter is the transaction ID, and based on the value passed in the parameter, we will read the details of that order. The header GUID is retrieved from the transaction ID and passed to the function module. In this case, you are required to read the description and status of the order. You can use input parameter requested objects, in which you will only pass the required relationships that you need to retrieve data for:

```
REPORT  ZCRM_ONE_ORDER.

include CRM_OBJECT_NAMES_CON.

PARAMETERS:  p_trans type crmt_object_id,
             p_desc type char40,
             p_status type J_ESTAT.

data:  lt_requested_objects type CRMT_OBJECT_NAME_TAB,
       ls_requested_objects type CRMT_OBJECT_NAME,
       ls_orderadm_h_read type crmd_orderadm_h,
       lt_orderadm_h type crmt_orderadm_h_comt,
       ls_orderadm_h type crmt_orderadm_h_com,
       lt_status type crmt_status_comt,
       ls_status type crmt_status_com,
       lt_field_names type crmt_input_field_names_tab,
       ls_field_names type crmt_input_field_names,
       lt_input_field type CRMT_INPUT_FIELD_TAB,
       ls_input_field type CRMT_INPUT_FIELD,
       lt_objects_to_save type crmt_object_guid_tab,
       lt_saved_objects type crmt_return_objects,
       ls_saved_objects type CRMT_RETURN_OBJECTS_STRUC.

select single * from crmd_orderadm_h into
  CORRESPONDING FIELDS OF ls_orderadm_h_read
  where object_id = p_trans.

clear: ls_status.
refresh: lt_status.
* Set the new status
ls_status-ref_guid = ls_orderadm_h_read-guid.
ls_status-ref_kind = 'A'.
ls_status-status = p_status.
ls_status-user_stat_proc = 'ZSRV_HDR'.
ls_status-activate = 'X'.
insert ls_status into table lt_status.
```

```
clear: ls_input_field.
refresh: lt_input_field.

ls_field_names-fieldname = 'ACTIVATE'.
insert ls_field_names into table lt_field_names.

ls_input_field-ref_guid = ls_orderadm_h_read-guid.
ls_input_field-ref_kind = 'A'.
ls_input_field-objectname = gc_object_name-status.
concatenate p_status 'ZSRV_HDR' into ls_input_field-logical_key RESPECTING BLANKS.
ls_input_field-field_names = lt_field_names.
insert ls_input_field into table lt_input_field.

CLEAR: ls_input_field.
refresh lt_field_names.

* Set new description
MOVE-CORRESPONDING ls_orderadm_h_read to ls_orderadm_h.
ls_orderadm_h-guid = ls_orderadm_h_read-guid.
ls_orderadm_h-description = p_desc.
insert ls_orderadm_h into table lt_orderadm_h.

ls_field_names-fieldname = 'DESCRIPTION'.
insert ls_field_names into table lt_field_names.

ls_input_field-ref_guid = ls_orderadm_h_read-guid.
ls_input_field-objectname = gc_object_name-orderadm_h.
ls_input_field-field_names = lt_field_names.
insert ls_input_field into table lt_input_field.

CLEAR: ls_input_field.
refresh lt_field_names.

CALL FUNCTION 'CRM_ORDER_MAINTAIN'
  EXPORTING
    IT_STATUS          = lt_status
  CHANGING
    CT_ORDERADM_H      = lt_orderadm_h
    CT_INPUT_FIELDS    = lt_input_field
  EXCEPTIONS
    ERROR_OCCURRED    = 1
    DOCUMENT_LOCKED   = 2
    NO_CHANGE_ALLOWED = 3
    NO_AUTHORITY      = 4
    OTHERS            = 5.
```

```
IF SY-SUBRC = 0.
  insert ls_orderadm_h_read-guid into table lt_objects_to_save.

  CALL FUNCTION 'CRM_ORDER_SAVE'
    EXPORTING
      IT_OBJECTS_TO_SAVE = lt_objects_to_save
    IMPORTING
      ET_SAVED_OBJECTS   = lt_saved_objects
    EXCEPTIONS
      DOCUMENT_NOT_SAVED = 1
      OTHERS             = 2.
  IF lt_saved_objects is not initial.
    read table lt_saved_objects into ls_saved_objects index 1.
    IF sy-subrc = 0.
      commit work and wait.
      write: 'Transaction Changed Successfully.'.
    ENDIF.
  ENDIF.

ENDIF.
```

This report makes use of three input parameters—transaction ID, description, and status. On the basis of the input parameters, the report performs changes to the description and status of the business transaction. It is mandatory to call the save function in order for the changes to get reflected. One more important point to note is that the entries that need to be passed to maintain the function module should exactly match the entries in the order. This will be discussed in detail in the next section.

DEBUGGING AND FINDING THE DATA YOU NEED

Now that you know more about relationships and one order framework, you can look more deeply into real-time scenarios. So far, we have been using simple examples to illustrate various concepts used in CRM. In order to read data for a transaction, you can refer to the different tabs in Figure 24.6 and read the corresponding attributes that are required. This can be done easily by running the report CRM_ORDER_READ in tcode se38 and finding the corresponding data in the output tables. However, sometimes it is not as straightforward as it looks.

In Figure 24.6, the Priority and Product ID fields are tricky because you cannot be sure where to read them from. An easy technique for this is to press F1 on the field, which will open a dialog box. Click on the Technical Information button, which will open a screen similar to Figure 24.12. From that screen, you can see the field name and table name. In the table name, the corresponding object `REFOBJ` is mentioned, so you can quickly map it to the corresponding table.

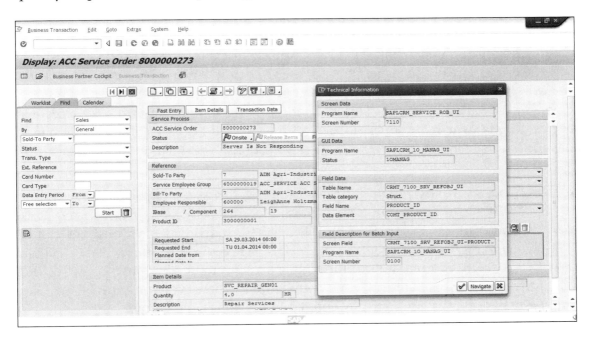

Figure 24.12
Technical information field.

Sometimes this technique is not helpful, and you'll need to determine where the data is coming from. For this kind of problem, simply put a breakpoint in the `CRM_ORDER_MAINTAIN` function module. After this, open the corresponding transaction in `CRMD_ORDER`. Change the required field for which you need details. This will trigger the breakpoint; check the internal table `CT_INPUT_FIELDS`. In this table, check the object name and corresponding table name. Since function modules for read and maintain follow the same structures, this is a good way of knowing where data is stored.

As discussed earlier, when you pass data to change the order, you need to do it in a specific way. This can be achieved by matching the data in debugging mode to the data that will be entered in the `CRM_ORDER_MAINTAIN` function module. This concept is really useful with the one order framework and is used time and again.

USING BADIS

Just as with function modules, one order framework BADIs are also available and enable you to achieve different functionality. One of the most important BADIs is ORDER_SAVE. It has three methods—PREPARE, CHECK_BEFORE_SAVE, and CHANGE_BEFORE_UPDATE. The first method is used to manipulate data. The data can be changed and filled automatically at the time of saving the document. There is no need to call the CRM_ORDER_SAVE function module since it is already incorporated in the BADI implementation class. The Check Before Save method, as its name suggests, can be used to code conditions when a document does not need to be saved. This method is useful for raising error messages and exceptions. The last method (CHANGE_BEFORE_UPDATE) is used to perform additional operations like executing actions or sending email notifications. This method cannot be used to change data.

Apart from these, CRM also provides BADIs for individual segments like STATUS, PRICING, REFOBJ, and ORDERADM_I. The naming conventions for these are CRM_<segment_name>_BADI. Only PARTNER and PAYPLAN start with COM*. Using these individual functionalities can be achieved by creating implementations of BADIs. There is one more BADI, named CRM_COPY_BADI, which is used for performing copy control operations. Using it, you can copy different attributes to follow-up transactions. This saves you time by avoiding entering redundant information already entered in previous transactions.

SUMMARY

In this chapter, you learned about the basics of CRM one order framework. This chapter explained how tables are structured in CRM and discussed the concept of GUID, which is used to uniquely identify transactions. You also looked at different business transactions and how data is retrieved and maintained. The different options to do this are using tcode CRMD_ORDER, using function modules, and using BADIs. You looked at sample programs that perform different functionalities and form the base for most CRM enhancements. You can explore different business transactions, function modules, and BADIs to learn more about the one order framework.

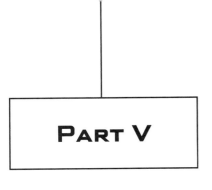

Part V

ABAP Appendixes

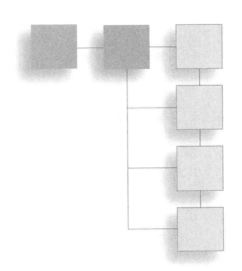

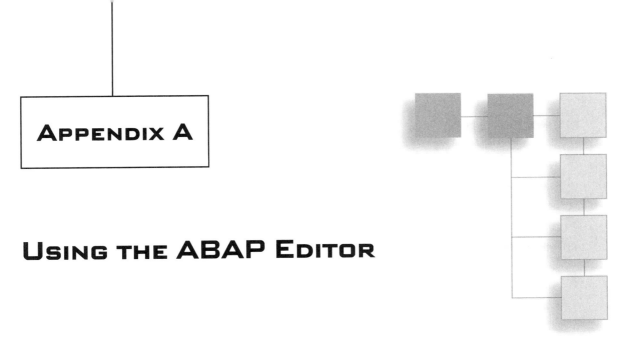

APPENDIX A

USING THE ABAP EDITOR

SAP includes the ABAP Editor, which you can use to write and manage ABAP programs. This appendix reviews the basic features and commands of the ABAP Editor, discussing creating, copying, renaming, deleting, and executing programs. It also covers the most useful commands.

GETTING TO KNOW THE EDITOR

To reach the ABAP Editor, you must either type the transaction se38 or navigate to the menu path of Tools > Development Workbench > ABAP Editor. Figure A.1 shows the main screen of the editor.

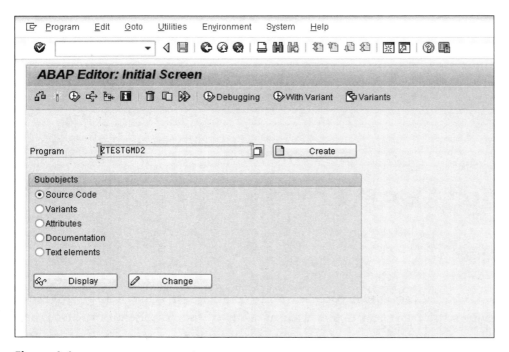

Figure A.1
The ABAP Editor.

The main screen includes several useful features:

■ To create a new program, you can type the name of the program in the Program box and then click on the Create button.

Note

In general, all user-created ABAP programs must start with the letter Z or Y. If you register for a special customer prefix, you can start with another prefix, but you must be a special partner with SAP. As a developer for a client or end customer of SAP, just use Z or Y.

■ The Check button checks the specified program for any syntax errors. Any errors will be called to the user's attention.

■ The Activate button first checks the program for any syntax errors. Then it generates the program so that it can run. A program must be active before it can run.

- The Execute button runs the program. If there is a selection screen, that is displayed first. The user enters the specified information and then lets the program proceed.

- The Where-Used button is a powerful button that is enabled in many screens in SAP. In the Data Dictionary, you can search for where data elements are used. On this screen, you can search for where this particular program or set of code (specified by the program name) is used.

- The Delete button is very simply the button you must press to delete the program named on this screen. SAP will ask for confirmation before deleting the program, but once it's done, it cannot be undone.

- The Copy button copies the program listed and creates a new program that's identical to the program on this screen. The user is asked what the new program should be named.

- The Rename button allows the user to rename the program listed on this screen to something else.

- The Debugging button executes the program in debug mode. The program only goes into debug mode after the selection screen is done.

- The Execute with Variant button executes the program but prompts the user for a saved variant before proceeding. A *variant* is a set of data that makes up entries in a selection screen that a user has saved for future use.

- The Display button displays the source code (assuming the Source Code radio button is chosen) on the screen. If the radio button is pointing to something else (variants, attributes, documentation, or text elements), those items are displayed.

- The Change button is exactly like the Display button, except that the user can change the attributes displayed in the next screen.

Figure A.2 shows the buttons defined here.

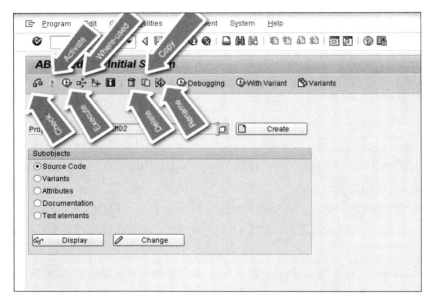

Figure A.2
The main buttons on the ABAP Editor.

To search for a particular program, navigate to Utilities > Find Program, as shown in Figure A.3.

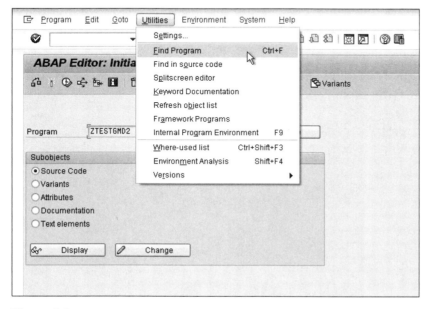

Figure A.3
Searching for a program.

To search the code of a particular program, navigate to Utilities > Find in Source Code, as shown in Figure A.4.

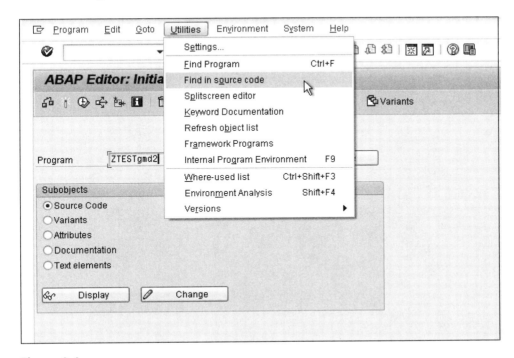

Figure A.4
Finding a particular element in the source code.

Find in Source Code is a very useful feature because it searches for something not only in the referenced program, but in the hierarchy of the program as well. For example, if a parent program uses this code, or if this code references other code (INCLUDE statements), then the search parameter will be referenced there as well.

Figure A.5 shows an example hit list for a search item.

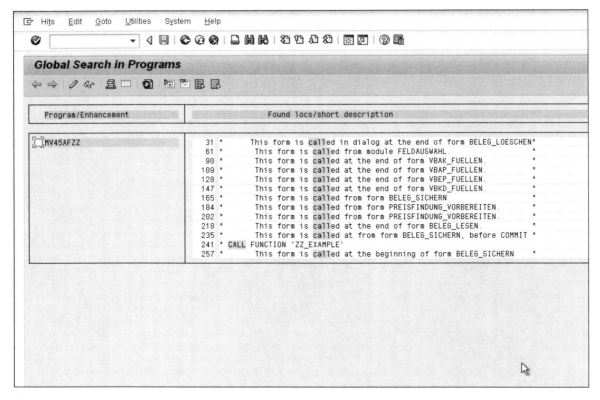

Figure A.5
Hit list for a particular search term.

EDITING PROGRAMS

If you choose a program and click Change or Create New Program, you'll see the source code for that program. See Figure A.6.

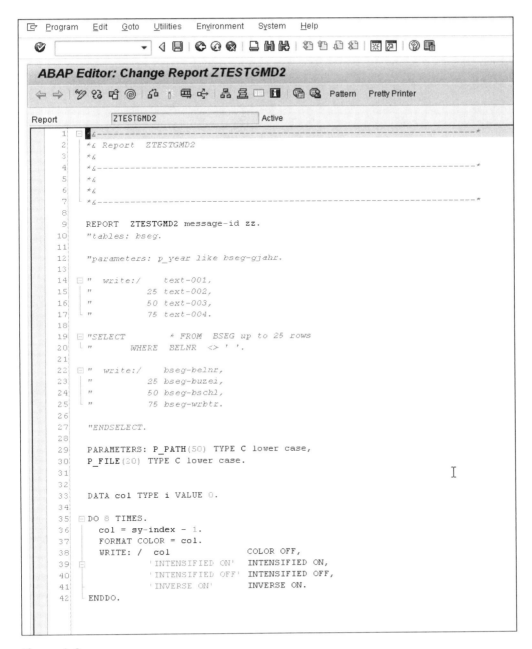

Figure A.6
Example source code for a program.

On this screen, there are a few buttons that you'll want to pay particular attention to. Refer to Figure A.7.

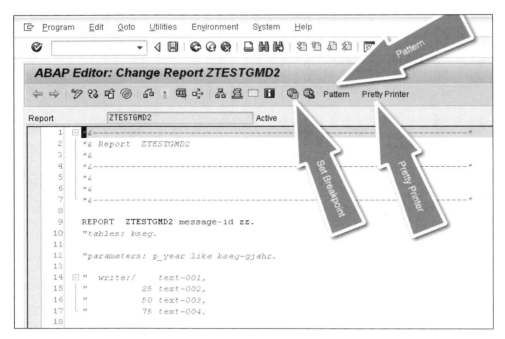

Figure A.7
ABAP Editor source code buttons.

■ The Set/Delete Session Breakpoint button sets or deletes a breakpoint in the program. When the program runs, the code will stop at the line where the breakpoint exists, and the user will be put into debug mode.

■ The Pattern button allows the user to insert a certain set of code by referencing the object. A user can enter a function module name, an object pattern, a message, a SQL statement, a subroutine call, an authority check, a WRITE statement, a CASE statement, and other custom patterns. The nice thing is that you do not have to refer back to the object you are calling. The program will bring up the parameters so you can choose what is pertinent and what is not. See Figure A.8.

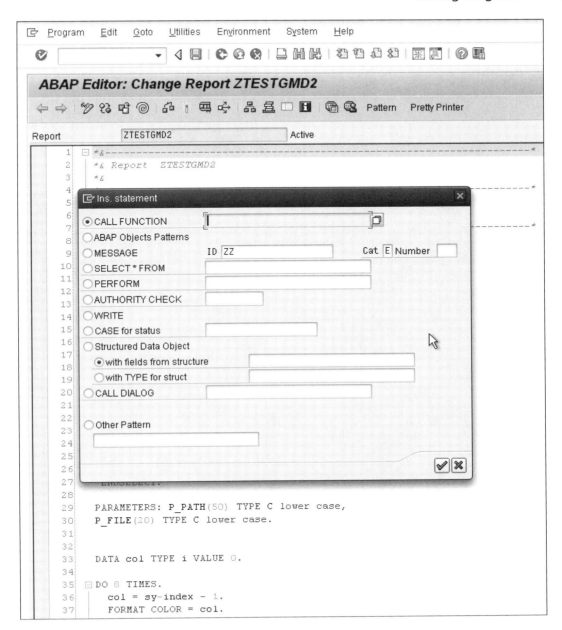

Figure A.8
The Pattern button's choices.

- ■ The Pretty Printer button formats the code with the right indents so that it is easier to read.

The last and possibly most helpful button in the editor is the Help On command. Refer to Figure A.9 to see where it is located. Navigate to Utilities > Help On to bring up the help screen.

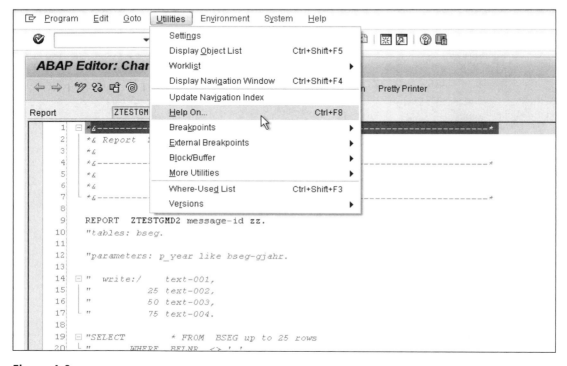

Figure A.9
Navigating to the Help On command.

A pop-up window is displayed, asking the users what ABAP keyword they want to search for.

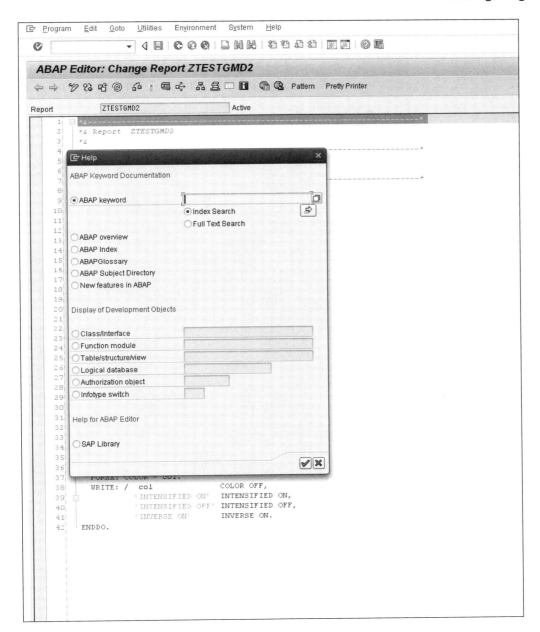

Figure A.10
The Help On pop-up.

You can search for any of the commands outlined in this book. The latest syntax and usage will pop up for your review.

APPENDIX B

SAP SYSTEM FIELDS

This appendix contains the full listing of the system fields utilized by the SAP software. Throughout this text, this table is referenced by the sample code. In the book's code, the fields are referenced by the prefix SY, a hyphen, and the field name listed in the table (for example, SY-SUBRC).

Field Name	Data Element	Data Type	Description
INDEX	SYINDEX	INT4	Loop index
PAGNO	SYPAGNO	INT4	Current list page
TABIX	SYTABIX	INT4	Index of internal tables
TFILL	SYTFILL	INT4	Row number of internal tables
TLOPC	SYTLOPC	INT4	Internal ABAP system field
TMAXL	SYTMAXL	INT4	Obsolete ABAP system field
TOCCU	SYTOCCU	INT4	Obsolete ABAP system field
TTABC	SYTTABC	INT4	Obsolete ABAP system field
TSTIS	SYTSTIS	INT4	Internal ABAP system field
TTABI	SYTTABI	INT4	Obsolete ABAP system field
DBCNT	SYDBCNT	INT4	Processed database table rows

(Continued)

Field Name	Data Element	Data Type	Description
FDPOS	SYFDPOS	INT4	Found location in byte or character string
COLNO	SYCOLNO	INT4	Current list column
LINCT	SYLINCT	INT4	Page length of list
LINNO	SYLINNO	INT4	Current line in list
LINSZ	SYLINSZ	INT4	Line width of list
PAGCT	SYPAGCT	INT4	Obsolete ABAP system field
MACOL	SYMACOL	INT4	Number of columns on left margin of print list
MAROW	SYMAROW	INT4	Number of columns in top margin of a print list
TLENG	SYTLENG	INT4	Row length of internal table
SFOFF	SYSFOFF	INT4	Internal ABAP system field
WILLI	SYWILLI	INT4	Obsolete ABAP system field
LILLI	SYLILLI	INT4	Selected list line
SUBRC	SYSUBRC	INT4	Return value of ABAP statements
FLENG	SYFLENG	INT4	Internal ABAP system field
CUCOL	SYCUCOL	INT4	Horizontal cursor position at PAI
CUROW	SYCUROW	INT4	Vertical cursor position at PAI
LSIND	SYLSIND	INT4	Index of details list
LISTI	SYLISTI	INT4	Index of displayed list
STEPL	SYSTEPL	INT4	Index of current step loop line
TPAGI	SYTPAGI	INT4	Obsolete ABAP system field
WINX1	SYWINX1	INT4	Obsolete ABAP system field
WINY1	SYWINY1	INT4	Obsolete ABAP system field
WINX2	SYWINX2	INT4	Obsolete ABAP system field
WINY2	SYWINY2	INT4	Obsolete ABAP system field
WINCO	SYWINCO	INT4	Obsolete ABAP system field
WINRO	SYWINRO	INT4	Obsolete ABAP system field
WINDI	SYWINDI	INT4	Obsolete ABAP system field
SROWS	SYSROWS	INT4	Screens, number of lines

Field Name	Data Element	Data Type	Description
SCOLS	SYSCOLS	INT4	Screens, number of columns
LOOPC	SYLOOPC	INT4	Visible lines of a step loop
FOLEN	SYFOLEN	INT4	Internal ABAP system field
FODEC	SYFODEC	INT4	Internal ABAP system field
TZONE	SYTZONE	INT4	Date and time, time difference to UTC reference time
DAYST	SYDAYST	CHAR	Daylight savings time selection
FTYPE	SYFTYPE	CHAR	Internal ABAP system field
APPLI	SYAPPLI	RAW	Obsolete ABAP system field
FDAYW	SYFDAYW	INT1	Factory calendar weekday
CCURS	SYCCURS	DEC	Obsolete ABAP system field
CCURT	SYCCURT	DEC	Obsolete ABAP system field
DEBUG	SYDEBUG	CHAR	Internal ABAP system field
CTYPE	SYCTYPE	CHAR	Obsolete ABAP system field
INPUT	SYINPUT	CHAR	Internal ABAP system field
LANGU	SYLANGU	LANG	Language key of current text environment
MODNO	SYMODNO	INT4	Index of external session
BATCH	SYBATCH	CHAR	Program is running in the background
BINPT	SYBINPT	CHAR	Program is running under batch input
CALLD	SYCALLD	CHAR	ABAP program, ABAP program call mode
DYNNR	SYDYNNR	CHAR	Current screen number
DYNGR	SYDYNGR	CHAR	Screen group of current screen
NEWPA	SYNEWPA	CHAR	Internal ABAP system field
PRI40	SYPRI40	CHAR	Internal ABAP system field
RSTRT	SYRSTRT	CHAR	Internal ABAP system field
WTITL	SYWTITL	CHAR	Selection for standard page header
CPAGE	SYCPAGE	INT4	Current page number of a list

(Continued)

Field Name	Data Element	Data Type	Description
DBNAM	SYDBNAM	CHAR	Logical database of an executable program
MANDT	SYMANDT	CLNT	Client ID of current user
PREFX	SYPREFX	CHAR	Obsolete ABAP system field
FMKEY	SYFMKEY	CHAR	Obsolete ABAP system field
PEXPI	SYPEXPI	NUMC	Spool retention period (print parameters)
PRINI	SYPRINI	NUMC	Internal ABAP system field
PRIMM	SYPRIMM	CHAR	Print immediately (print parameters)
PRREL	SYPRREL	CHAR	Delete after printing (print parameters)
PLAYO	SYPLAYO	CHAR	Internal ABAP system field
PRBIG	SYPRBIG	CHAR	Selection cover page (print parameters)
PLAYP	SYPLAYP	CHAR	Internal ABAP system field
PRNEW	SYPRNEW	CHAR	New spool request (print parameters)
PRLOG	SYPRLOG	CHAR	Internal ABAP system field
PDEST	SYPDEST	CHAR	Output device (print parameters)
PLIST	SYPLIST	CHAR	Name of spool request (print parameters)
PAUTH	SYPAUTH	NUMC	Internal ABAP system field
PRDSN	SYPRDSN	CHAR	Name of spool file
PNWPA	SYPNWPA	CHAR	Internal ABAP system field
CALLR	SYCALLR	CHAR	Start location of list print
REPI2	SYREPI2	CHAR	Internal ABAP system field
RTITL	SYRTITL	CHAR	Name of print program (print parameters)
PRREC	SYPRREC	CHAR	Recipient (print parameters)
PRTXT	SYPRTXT	CHAR	Text for cover page (print parameters)
PRABT	SYPRABT	CHAR	Department on cover page (print parameters)
LPASS	SYLPASS	CHAR	Internal ABAP system field

Field Name	Data Element	Data Type	Description
NRPAG	SYNRPAG	CHAR	Internal ABAP system field
PAART	SYPAART	CHAR	Print format (print parameters)
PRCOP	SYPRCOP	NUMC	Number of copies (print parameters)
BATZS	SYBATZS	CHAR	Obsolete ABAP system field
BSPLD	SYBSPLD	CHAR	Obsolete ABAP system field
BREP4	SYBREP4	CHAR	Obsolete ABAP system field
BATZO	SYBATZO	CHAR	Obsolete ABAP system field
BATZD	SYBATZD	CHAR	Obsolete ABAP system field
BATZW	SYBATZW	CHAR	Obsolete ABAP system field
BATZM	SYBATZM	CHAR	Obsolete ABAP system field
CTABL	SYCTABL	CHAR	Obsolete ABAP system field
DBSYS	SYDBSYS	CHAR	Central database system
DCSYS	SYDCSYS	CHAR	Obsolete ABAP system field
MACDB	SYMACDB	CHAR	Obsolete ABAP system field
SYSID	SYSYSID	CHAR	Name of the SAP system
OPSYS	SYOPSYS	CHAR	Operating system of application server
PFKEY	SYPFKEY	CHAR	Current GUI status
SAPRL	SYSAPRL	CHAR	Release status of SAP system
TCODE	SYTCODE	CHAR	Current transaction code
UCOMM	SYUCOMM	CHAR	Function code that PAI triggered
CFWAE	SYCFWAE	CUKY	Internal ABAP system field
CHWAE	SYCHWAE	CUKY	Internal ABAP system field
SPONO	SYSPONO	NUMC	Spool number of list print
SPONR	SYSPONR	NUMC	Obsolete ABAP system field
WAERS	SYWAERS	CUKY	Obsolete ABAP system field
CDATE	SYCDATE	DATS	Obsolete ABAP system field
DATUM	SYDATUM	DATS	Current date of application server
SLSET	SYSLSET	CHAR	Used selection screen variant

(Continued)

Field Name	Data Element	Data Type	Description
SUBTY	SYSUBTY	RAW	Internal ABAP system field
SUBCS	SYSUBCS	CHAR	Internal ABAP system field
GROUP	SYGROUP	CHAR	Internal ABAP system field
FFILE	SYFFILE	CHAR	Internal ABAP system field
UZEIT	SYUZEIT	TIMS	Current time of application server
DSNAM	SYDSNAM	CHAR	Internal ABAP system field
TABID	SYTABID	CHAR	Internal ABAP system field
TFDSN	SYTFDSN	CHAR	Obsolete ABAP system field
UNAME	SYUNAME	CHAR	Username
LSTAT	SYLSTAT	CHAR	Obsolete ABAP system field
ABCDE	SYABCDE	CHAR	Latin alphabet
MARKY	SYMARKY	CHAR	Obsolete ABAP system field
SFNAM	SYSFNAM	CHAR	Obsolete ABAP system field
TNAME	SYTNAME	CHAR	Obsolete ABAP system field
MSGLI	SYMSGLI	CHAR	Obsolete ABAP system field
TITLE	SYTITLE	CHAR	Contents of title line
ENTRY	SYENTRY	CHAR	Internal ABAP system field
LISEL	SYLISEL	CHAR	Contents of a selected list line
ULINE	SYULINE	CHAR	Horizontal Line
XCODE	SYXCODE	CHAR	Internal ABAP system field
CPROG	SYCPROG	CHAR	Calling program
XPROG	SYXPROG	CHAR	Internal ABAP system field
XFORM	SYXFORM	CHAR	Internal ABAP system field
LDBPG	SYLDBPG	CHAR	Database program of a logical database
TVAR0	SYTVAR	CHAR	Text variable for placeholders in list headers
TVAR1	SYTVAR	CHAR	Text variable for placeholders in list headers
TVAR2	SYTVAR	CHAR	Text variable for placeholders in list headers

Field Name	Data Element	Data Type	Description
TVAR3	SYTVAR	CHAR	Text variable for placeholders in list headers
TVAR4	SYTVAR	CHAR	Text variable for placeholders in list headers
TVAR5	SYTVAR	CHAR	Text variable for placeholders in list headers
TVAR6	SYTVAR	CHAR	Text variable for placeholders in list headers
TVAR7	SYTVAR	CHAR	Text variable for placeholders in list headers
TVAR8	SYTVAR	CHAR	Text variable for placeholders in list headers
TVAR9	SYTVAR	CHAR	Text variable for placeholders in list headers
MSGID	SYMSGID	CHAR	Message class
MSGTY	SYMSGTY	CHAR	Message type
MSGNO	SYMSGNO	NUMC	Message number
MSGV1	SYMSGV	CHAR	Message variable
MSGV2	SYMSGV	CHAR	Message variable
MSGV3	SYMSGV	CHAR	Message variable
MSGV4	SYMSGV	CHAR	Message variable
ONCOM	SYONCOM	CHAR	Internal ABAP system field
VLINE	SYVLINE	CHAR	Vertical line
WINSL	SYWINSL	CHAR	Obsolete ABAP system field
STACO	SYSTACO	INT4	First list column displayed
STARO	SYSTARO	INT4	Top displayed line
DATAR	SYDATAR	CHAR	Selection for screen field input
HOST	SYHOST	CHAR	Name of current application server
LOCDB	SYSTLOCDB	CHAR	Obsolete ABAP system field
LOCOP	SYSTLOCOP	CHAR	Obsolete ABAP system field

(Continued)

Field Name	Data Element	Data Type	Description
DATLO	SYSTDATLO	DATS	Local date for current user
TIMLO	SYSTTIMLO	TIMS	Local time of current user
ZONLO	SYSTZONLO	CHAR	Time zone of current user

Source: SAP America, 2014. © 2014 Cengage Learning.

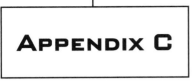

APPENDIX C

ABAP ERP and CRM Tables

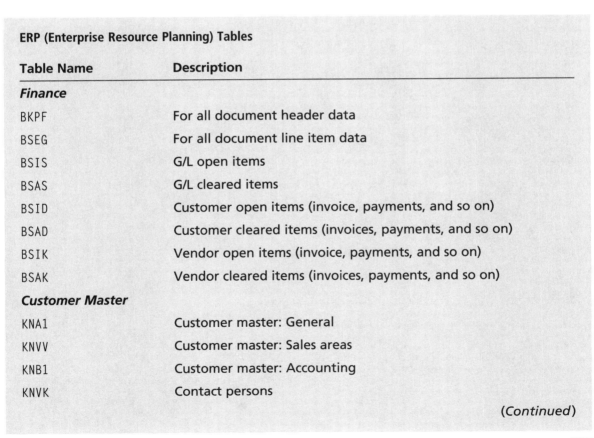

ERP (Enterprise Resource Planning) Tables

Table Name	Description
Finance	
BKPF	For all document header data
BSEG	For all document line item data
BSIS	G/L open items
BSAS	G/L cleared items
BSID	Customer open items (invoice, payments, and so on)
BSAD	Customer cleared items (invoices, payments, and so on)
BSIK	Vendor open items (invoice, payments, and so on)
BSAK	Vendor cleared items (invoices, payments, and so on)
Customer Master	
KNA1	Customer master: General
KNVV	Customer master: Sales areas
KNB1	Customer master: Accounting
KNVK	Contact persons

(Continued)

ERP (Enterprise Resource Planning) Tables (*Continued*)

Table Name	Description
KNVA	Unloading point
KNVI	Tax indicators
KNVP	Partner functions
KNVD	Documents
KNVL	Licenses
KNVS	Customer master: Shipping
KNVH	Customer master: Hierarchies
Material Master	
MARA	Material master: General
MARC	Material master: Plant <plants>
MAKT	Material master: Short description
MARM	Material master: Conversion factors
MVKE	Material master: Sales <sales org/distr ch>
MLAN	Material master: Sales <country>
MAEX	Material master: Export licenses
MBEW	Material master: Valuation
Sales Documents	
VBAK	Sales document: Header
VBAP	Sales document: Items
VBEP	Sales document: Schedule lines
VBUK	Header status/admin data
VBUP	Item status
VBUV	Incompletion log
VBPA	Partner functions
VBBE	Individual requirement
VEBA	Contract
VBLB	Forecast

VBFA	Document flow
VBKD	Sales document: Business data
VAKPA	Partner index
VEDA	Contract
VBKA	Sales activity document
SADR	Address
NAST	Output
JSTO	PP status
STXH	Text: Header
STXL	Text: Lines
KONV	Conditions
LIKP	Delivery: HEADER
LIPS	Delivery: ITEM
VBRK	Billing: HEADER
VBRP	Billing: ITEM

Source: SAP America, 2014.

CRM (Customer Relationship Management) Tables

Table Name	Description
BUT000	BP: General data
BUT020	BP: Addresses
BUT050	BP relationships/role definitions: General data
BUT051	BP relationship: Contact person relationship
BUT0BK	Business partner: Bank data and details
BNKA	Bank master data
BUT100	BP: Roles

(Continued)

CRM (Customer Relationship Management) Tables (*Continued*)

Table Name	Description
ADR2	Telephone numbers (business address services)
ADR6	SMTP numbers (business address services); contains email and ID of the BP
ADRC	Addresses (business address services)
COMM_PRODUCT	Master table for product
CRMD_ORDERADM_H	Business transaction details
CRMD_ORDERADM_I	Business transaction item details
CRMD_CUSTOMER_H	Transaction: Customer extension
CRMD_CUSTOMER_I	Transaction Item: Customer extension
CRMC_PROC_TYPE	Master table business transaction type
CRMC_ITEM_TYPE	Business transaction item type
CRMC_PARTNER_FCT	Definition of partner functions
TJ30T	All the status code and text
IBIB	Installed base/Ibase
IBIN	Installed base components
HRP1000	Infotype 1000 DB table
HRP1001	Infotype 1001 DB table
CRMM_BUT_FRG0041	Sales classification
CRMM_BUT_FRG0081	Sales area: Partner function
CRMM_BUT_CUSTNO	Map business partner customer
CRMM_BUT_CONTNO	Mapping table business partner relationship: Contact person
CRMD_MKTTG_PF_H	CRM marketing: Profile
CRMD_MKTTG_PF_S	CRM marketing: Filter
CRMD_MKTTG_SAL	CRM marketing: Selection attribute list
CRMD_MKTTG_SA	CRM marketing: Selection attribute

Source: SAP America, 2014.

INDEX